MORE

It's the way your ma... you was a kid

COPYRIGHT NOTICES

Published by
Sally Cotton Publishing

Printed and bound by CPI Antony Rowe Ltd

ISBN 978-0-9561114-1-8

Dedicated to Mum

and for my precious grandchildren Tom, Althea, Joe, Jack and Sally

ACKNOWLEDGEMENTS

I must express here my sincere and grateful thanks to my family without whose help, encouragement and assistance with the complexities of publication, this book would not have got beyond the first draft and a special thanks to Paula for the artwork.

My grateful thanks also to all the friends with whom I have reminisced over the years, providing me with a collection of little anecdotes which hopefully have added the extra dimension to this book. Thanks guys. Your participation has been invaluable.

Sally Cotton

MORE COTTON REELS

It's the way your mam put your hat on when you was a kid

STREAM LANE
CHURCH
BALCOMBE GREEN
BREDE LANE
FIELDS
PUMP
BLACKSMITH
BRIDGE
OAKLANDS PARK
COTTAGE LANE
WESTFIELD PLACE
PETLEY WOOD
MARLEY LANE
THE TRICKY HOLLOW
SYLVIAN
HARTS GREEN
MARLEY HOUSE
BATTLE BIG WOOD
STREET
FARM
BRIDGE
TO THE RIDGE AND WAYSIDE

INTRODUCTION

'More Cotton Reels,' which carries on from an earlier book called 'The Cotton reels,' follows the continuing fortunes of the folk living in and around the village of Sedlescombe, through the ups and downs, the austerity of the immediate post war years.

The book begins with preparation for the Fete at Westfield Place, a large country estate owned by Lord and Lady Newton. There is much excitement surrounding the resumption of this event after the long years of war, when a large part of this considerable estate had been requisitioned by the Government to facilitate the billeting of Canadian troops.

Bangy Smith, the bow-legged villager with the sparkling eyes and keen sense of humour is still there and still singing a song or two, often accompanied by his old squeeze box. He is joined by three more rustics. Two of these, old Fred and George also live in the village and along with Bangy, they vie with one another to tell the tallest story or recall events of a bye gone era with the most elaborate verbal exchanges, always gesticulating wildly to emphasise some relevant point. The last of these rustics is old Tom who lives in Kent Street. Although unable to read and write, he is able to tell the difference between a crow and a rook from a distance of a couple of hundred paces - or so.

Deffy and Bill still continue to live a hermit lifestyle in their old shack at the edge of Battle Big Wood, merging with nature itself and into the ancient woodland that surrounds them. No trace of their urban upbringing remains.

The youngsters at Blackbrooks continue to explore the countryside at every opportunity, accepting with varying degrees of tolerance the obligatory chores that come their way and the shortage of sweets, which along with practically everything else, are still on ration. They are mostly oblivious to what is happening out there in the big wide world. Occasionally however, some significant news item appears, reminding them that much is happening beyond their own little world and temporarily facing them with life's stark realities.

To recap on some of the other people mentioned in the earlier book:

Dolly and Pop Cotton continue their challenging lifestyle at Sylvian, their smallholding at Blackbrooks with a great deal of help, often reluctantly given, from the younger members of the family. Betty is now living and working in London, but Freda, Hazel, Sally, Pat, Dorothy and Jacky are very much in the picture.

Hilary Elkins, Sally's best friend and regarded as 'one of the family,' is very much part of the story. She lives at Windy Ridge, near Paygate Corner with her parents, her elder sister Jean, and younger brother Ronald.

Amy Powell who lives with her family at Uplyme, a bungalow close to Paygate Corner, is in and out of the story. Her brother Tony, who in the earlier book got stuck in a milk churn while hiding from an attacking German plane, puts in an occasional appearance. Amy's mum, sister Vera with her daughter Janet and other members of this interesting and hard working family are also there.

The Winchester family with their quick wit and infectious sense of humour, weave their way in and out of the book with Molly, their mother and mainstay of this family, very much in the picture. Patty and Basil, two of the youngsters in this busy and uproarious family are always around and readily join the other local children for anything from a game of skipping to a romp through the fields and woods.

This family live in Crazy Lane, in a bungalow called Brookside. I must apologise here for relating tales in my first book, of their father Ron when in fact he was in the Army at the time. The incidents mentioned took place after the war, and most likely resulted from his experiences while in action.

Sorry guys.

Ron (or Willy) Monk and his friend Roy Chapman, who live in East View Terrace, are still very much around. It does not take much persuasion from Hilary and Sally, for them to be willing participants in a prank or two.

Albert Soan is now in the Middle East, playing his part in the post war attempt to attain some semblance of normality after the turmoil of war. This natural story teller with his unique ability to soak up, memorise and then relate with a bit of embellishment here and there, jokes and stories relating to the goings on within the village community, is legendary. His temporary absence from village life is acutely felt.

George Partridge (Porky), the young farmer, is still running Beanford, the family farm, along with his mother and his brother John. Luckily for him, the youngsters seem to have outgrown the desire to lock him in the shed with the old bull, or to roll his clean milk churns down the muddy slope near the milking sheds.

I have failed to differentiate between the two Mrs Moons, which may cause a bit of confusion. Mrs Moon who lives at Blackbrooks and is the mother of Daphne, was the unfortunate recipient of the soggy missile delivered from the deadly accurate hand of Basil Winchester, in The Cotton Reels. She is an indifferent cook – to put it mildly. The other Mrs Moon is a teacher at Sedlescombe School and sister to Mrs Vallor who teaches at the same school. Both of the Mrs Moons are taller than average and always immaculately dressed.

The members of another family put in a brief appearance in this book. The Reverend Smith along with his unique family is about to take up residence in the old Manse on Chapel Hill.

More about this kindly and quite extraordinary family in the next book.

Henry Maplesden, monosyllabic but with a rare talent for mimicry, be it birds, trains or just a passing car, is now the proud owner of a sturdy old bicycle. A clay pipe has also just come into his possession, which he sucks on thoughtfully while riding his beloved contraption. The consensus is that this pipe, stained and very ancient, must have lived at least part of its life buried somewhere beneath the ground.

The emphasis in this book is more on the activities and ongoing freedoms of the children than the hardships caused by the post-war shortages – a child's eye view of events. Now and then however, a kind of reality creeps in. The only sweets to be had without producing a ration book are called 'little imps'. Readers old enough to remember them would know that no child in its right mind, no matter how desperate, would willingly expose its taste buds to these horrid little things.

Sally is currently working on a third novel which follows this one chronologically and is set in the same area. If anyone has any information which might be of use to the book be it photos or anecdotes, please contact her on 01424 215477 or email sallycottonpub@talktalk.net or jonheasmansec@talktalk.net

CHAPTER 1
SUMMER 1945

"When cats run home and light is come.
And dew is cold upon the ground.
And the far off stream is dumb.
And the whirring sail goes round
And the whirring sail goes round.
Alone and warming his five wits.
The white owl in the belfry sits. . . . .."

Sally chanted softly to herself in the pearly stillness of a high summer dawn. Then a bit louder in a sing-song voice,

"D'yer ken John Peel at the break of day,
d' yer ken John Peel with his coat so gay.
D'yer ken John Peel when he's far, far away,
with his hounds and his horn in the morning."

She paused and waited, then watched silently as Patsy sat up, yawned and rubbed her eyes. Sally giggled, as her sister who now insisted on being called "Pat," as she thought it sounded more grown up, moaned, stretched and struggled to remove herself from horizontal dreams.

"It's the Fete today remember, Lady Newton's, Westfield Place," said Sally, in a loud whisper. "It's always fun, but this year it's going to be even better. The war's over don't forget, for us lot anyway. And Mr Collins told me and mum it's going to be really hot again today."

"Ssh," said Pat crossly, her voice still full of sleep. "You're making too much noise. You'll wake Dora up and then she'll be in here, climbing all over us and trying to poke our eyes out. You know what she's like."

"You mean the minimal don't you," said Sally giggling, determined to do her best to prevent Pat from sinking back into the land of nod.

"Why do you call her the minimal?" Said Pat, clearly not amused and still trying to get back to sleep. "I think it's really silly."

"Because she's a little animal - minimal - little animal, get it?" Sally replied brightly. "You can't argue with that can you?"

Pat groaned, then laid back down with her sister, and with arms folded upwards, open hands cradling heads full of contemplation, they stared at the plain, old ceiling. Its one concession to decoration was a narrow wooden beading, which criss-crossed its flat surface. This, along with just about every other thing around, had been fitted by their father with his usual dogged precision.

I wonder what Dad would say if we painted some daffodils up there," said Pat, her index finger following her train of thought as she pointed upwards and around the dull white space. She was wide awake now and more than willing to embark upon a discussion be it on flowers, ceilings or anything else for that matter.

"He'd probably make you paint them all out again and put vegetables, onions, carrots, that sort of thing up there instead. You know what he's like," replied Sally. "I can just hear him saying, 'You can't eat flowers'. But I don't fancy seeing vegetables up there, do you? Anyway, at least we can see the ceiling now he's taken that old air raid shelter down. Right monstrosity that thing, glad to see the back of it." She smiled and shook her head. "That's a bit unfair I know, it would have saved our bacon if a bomb or a doodlebug had landed right on top of the house but it made me feel really closed in, claustrophobic I think it's called. He's going to make a gate at the bottom of the field with part of it, you know."

She paused as she sought to analyse her reaction to the removal of this cage of iron and steel, her feeling of relief, deliverance almost. Its demise symbolised an end to this wretched war, that was it and the uneasiness she had felt when confined within its swaddling bonds had been a mere inconvenience, a mild discomfiture when compared with what it represented - well, mostly anyway.

"Come on then, let's get up and cadge some of dad's tea," said Pat, suddenly kicking off the blankets and exposing one pyjama clad knee. "He's up and about now, I can hear him. Leastways someone is." She paused for a few seconds, her open hand cradling the flap of her ear before continuing. "Of course it's dad, I heard him sniff. He gives himself away all the time he does. Talking about tea though, it's strange really that when you take a mouth full of your own it tastes disgusting but when it comes from your mum or dad's saucer, it tastes bloody delicious."

***

Pat and Sally were just finishing their breakfast when dad walked back into the kitchen having been on chicken patrol. He needed a hair cut Sally reckoned and it was just as well that his two brothers were due here for a visit shortly and that one or other of them would give him a short back and sides. They were like three peas in a pod, these men. Uncle Alf the eldest of the trio, was a fraction taller than dad and uncle Fred, but they were all slim to the point of being skinny.

"If the number of bees out there is anything to go by Doll, old Harry should be getting a goodly amount of honey this year," dad was saying as he stood just inside the scullery door. "Which reminds me, did I tell you what old

Bangy Smith told me the other day about using bees to cure his rheumatics?" As mum shook her head, he continued. "Well, he reckons that once a year, he gets a few or several of the creatures I believe he said, and puts 'em down his back. Then he agitates them around a bit till they sting him and once they've done their bit, he's off with his vest and shakes the creatures back out of it. Of course they're pretty well dead by that time. He reckons it's the only thing that works for him. When I said that sounded a bit painful and wouldn't he rather try something like wintergreen ointment or even the old Sloan's liniment, he just looked at me with that twinkle in his eye, shook his head and told me that his type of screws needed action not ointment."

"Well my old mum always reckons that stinging nettles do the trick for her and they're a darned sight easier to handle than bees. That's debatable I suppose, but they're a darned sight easier to catch I would say," replied mum smiling. "And there's always plenty around the field here if you ever feel need to try the cure."

Sally grinned, remembering ruefully the times these vicious weeds had caught her off guard and she had been on the receiving end of some of their painful stings. Still, if her Grandma's theory were correct, she would never, ever get this thing referred to as the 'screws.' She reckoned she had already received enough sap from this noxious weed to last her a lifetime.

After she had scraped the last bits of shredded wheat from around her dish and licked her lips, she looked quickly around the kitchen, elbows on table, from one familiar object to another. An old range had once occupied the place where the Rayburn now stood, and in her minds eye she could still picture her mum as she had bent over the thing, her face red and shiny as she vigorously burnished its black shiny surface with the help of a tin of Zebo and two well worn brushes. The pot bellied Primus stove, which occupied one side of the small table under the window, had stood there on its little legs for as far back as she could remember. It was always at the ready to boil a kettle or an egg or two, or even to singe the downy feathers off the chickens, an essential part of their beauty treatment. And the table at which she sat, with its substantial winding gear beneath on which they played their noisy acrobatics, had been around forever as far as she was concerned. Even the cloth beneath her elbows, used to protect this fine example of Victorian vernacular furniture, had been around for aeons and looked as though it had been washed to within an inch of its life.

"Well this won't do," she said almost to herself as she rose from the table followed closely by Pat. "We've got things to do, you know."

As the two girls set off across the field on the milk run, they talked about Lady Newton, whose generosity had brought about this fun day. The youth club, organised in days gone by, by this illustrious lady, had been a favourite with Freda and Betty and with a lot of other children from the area. The only thing her sisters had objected to was the obligatory curtsy for Lady Newton on their entry to and exit from the big house. They eventually compromised by shaking hands, then bent forward ever so slightly as they thanked her. As Freda said, this formality of bowing and scraping was a bit over the top. Surely saying thank you was the important thing. Sally thought secretly to herself that she would rather curtsy to someone like Deffy and Bill who lived a simple life in their little shack at the edge of the wood and had taught them so much about nature and things. Then she smiled to herself as she imagined their reaction to this overture. They would think she had gone soft in the head, have fifty fits and die laughing.

They continued to chat enthusiastically about the games they would take part in and who would partner who in the three legged race. Sally and Hilary had been practicing this particular race together and in spite of the height difference between them, were managing to co-ordinate reasonably well. As long as they remembered to take small steps and to lean slightly forward as they ran, and of course, did not get a fit of the giggles, they reckoned they stood a good chance of getting in the first three. Now Pat and Sally were trying to decide who would make a suitable partner for Pat - Pam Webb perhaps or Beryl Smith - Or maybe Diana Woollett, with those beautiful copper ringlets of hers. After a while they gave up this guessing game, not really sure who, apart from their own little group, would be about on this fun day, and concentrated instead on getting the milk safely home.

***

Later, with the sun high over their heads and not a cloud in the sky, Hilary, Amy, Pat, Patty and Sally strolled up Crazy Lane on their way to the fete. With arms linked they straddled the lane from side to side, chatting nineteen to the dozen as they made their way to Westfield Place and the excitement of the fete.

"Hey, look up there, it says duck eggs 2/- and farm eggs 1/6," said Amy suddenly, extricating one arm from the straggling column and pointing towards a notice on the trunk of a massive oak tree, which stood at the entrance to an old farm track. And she giggled. The lettering on the notice, torn and faded as it was and clearly the victim of a few seasons of variable weather, took the other girls a moment or two to decipher.

"Well what about it then. That notice is old as the hills and I don't expect they even sell eggs there now. What's funny about it anyway? Asked Sally.

"Well, it says farm eggs and I've never heard of a farm laying eggs have you?" Amy replied. "It would be a blooming miracle if you ask me. It's been there for donkey's years by the looks of it and do you know, I've never noticed it before. Perhaps, you never know, maybe farms did lay eggs in the olden days, what do you think?"

"That you're as daft as a brush," replied Sally. "You and your peculiar sense of humour, I worry about you sometimes. Do you know what, now that we've stopped I think I need to go behind the hedge here to have a wee. I forgot to go before we left home and we've still a way to go before we get to the fete. Yes, I know you reminded me Pat," she added hastily, anticipating her sister's intervention by the deep, self righteous intake of breath from the smallest member of the group. "But I still forgot see, and when you've got to go you've got to go." She chuckled and disentangled herself from the group. As she moved away from them, she called over her shoulder; "Don't go without me will you, and just keep an eye out along the lane, just in case someone comes along." With that, she squeezed through the hedge, wincing as a stinging nettle invaded the bare flesh between the top of her sock and the hem of her skirt. Then she disappeared. The only indication of her whereabouts was a light shuffling as she rearranged the undergrowth within the narrow strip of trees and shrubs encircling Oaklands Park.

***

The buzz of activity at the Fete assailed their ears long before they actually reached the huge wrought iron gates which, wide open now, invited them through, and into a scene of organised chaos. There were people milling around the stalls and side shows that had been hastily erected around the vast lawn that fronted the big house. And in the middle distance, they could see areas that had been cordoned off for the races and coconut shies. Even further a field, Sally could just make out the shape and unmistakable plod of a couple of donkeys but remembering her sister's penchant for most four legged creatures, decided to keep this information to herself.

"Look, there's old Micky Morris over there," said Amy, as they passed through the gateway. "He's sorting through all those sacks over there. I bet he's picking out the best one for himself in the sack race. He'd certainly need the roomiest one wouldn't he?" She giggled, as she contemplated this blubbery youth from the cottage at Blackbrooks who seemed oblivious to their scrutiny, now entirely focussed on him.

"Just look at the size of his legs, it's a wonder those khaki shorts still fit him. Well they don't really fit him, do they? Know what I mean? They fits where they touches, sort of. Never mind about him, let's see what's going on, and where. We don't want to miss anything, do we?"

Amy drew their attention towards a large display board where little groups of youngsters were all craning their necks to read what was on the notices pinned to it.

"It's the sack race first, I guessed it would be. That's why Micky's messing about with that sack," said Pat. "That's at half past one, we'd better find out what the time is now." And she looked around anxiously.

"Don't worry, dad's let me borrow his pocket watch." Said Hilary.

" He often lets me borrow it on special occasions like this," she added. "But you don't need to worry about time anyway. See that man over there with that trumpet thing in his hand? He'll be using it to broadcast the races and he'll do it well before they're due to start. But we might as well sort out a sack each before all the best ones go. Come on, they're getting chucked about all over the place. Look at all that dust!"

"I wonder what my sack's had in it?" Mused Sally, wrinkling her nose and examining at arms length the dusty bag she was about to climb into.

"Turnips, potatoes, wurzels maybe, or even sheep's treddles. You never know do you. Come to think of it, it does smell a bit like manure. Never mind some things just have to be put up with," she said as she placed herself in line with the twenty or so other enthusiastic competitors and waited for the signal to start.

She was not altogether surprised when she did not come first, or second, or even third, but it was good fun.

"What about that then?" Said Hilary, puffing away and pushing her hair back off her face as she joined the other girls at the end of the race. "Second, that's not bad. I was leading to start with and I really thought I'd got it, and then that Micky overtook me and came first. I reckon you were right Amy. He did sort himself out the best sack, but he did get to them before we did and we'd have done the same thing if we'd got there first I suppose. Anyway, it's the three legged race next, but we've got plenty of time before that starts."

Hilary decided that perhaps she and Sally should also get in a bit of practice and asked her friend to bring her leg over to be bound up with her own. "I've just got to make sure it's not too tight or else we're in trouble. I'm really pleased that we remembered to bring these crepe bandages with us though. The ones they dish out here are tough as old boots and don't give an inch," she added as, bent double now and red in the face, she bound the bandage carefully around their lower legs and ankles. "That'll do. Lets get a bit of practice in before the race starts then, shall we?" she added as she straightened up again.

Once the race started, Hilary and Sally got off to a good start and maintained this momentum and their rhythm throughout, not stumbling once in their progression along the fifty or so yards of roped off track. "First by a whisker!" Exclaimed Sally excitedly as, bent almost double and panting, they crossed the finishing line. They looked up as one of the boys called out from the sidelines. "Fancy old Hilary and Salary coming first, who'd have guessed that. The rest of you were all arms and legs and bums, you didn't half look a sight," he giggled. "You'll have to give us lot some lessons you two, when you've got time that is. Bags me first."

Sally didn't much like being called Salary, same as the expression 'Cotton reels' used to upset her at one time, but that was boys for you. The more notice you took of them, the more outrageous they became. As she bent down with Hilary to remove the now redundant bandages from around their ankles, she just smiled in their general direction.

"Look there's old Wig over there, looking like six penn'th of gawd elp us. And he's smoking a cigar," exclaimed Amy pointing in the direction of the little man. "It's a wonder he doesn't fall off the end of the thing. I expect he's celebrating the end of old Hitler and all that, don't you? Now, what's next I wonder," she said looking around for inspiration.

The hair competition now took her fancy, her only reservation being that she had forgotten to wash her hair in readiness for this event. The other girls followed her lead and they all wandered over to where a group of girls were standing, and after collecting some name tabs and filling them in, stood around waiting for further orders.

There were three haughty lady judges for this event. They were sitting on high backed chairs behind a wooden trestle table. All eyes were on them as they whispered amongst themselves, writing now and again on bits of paper that had been fixed to their clipboards. When the order came all the girls lined up in an orderly fashion, then filed slowly past the now upright judges, pausing for just long enough to allow these serious ladies to tweak and rub a lock of their hair between thumb and fore-finger. When the last girl had received her critical examination, they all stood grouped quietly together. They were watching the judges who, seated again now, were absorbed in the notes they were scribbling on their clipboards, pausing every so often to talk in low and earnest tones amongst themselves. After a few minutes, the names of three girls, one of them Patty, were called out and each one hesitated before stepping forward nervously.

When Patty was declared the winner, she grinned from ear to ear. Then having received her prize, she moved away from the judges and over to where the others were standing.

"One of those ladies said she'd seen a lot of shades of auburn in her lifetime, but none quite like what I've got," Patty whispered to them as they walked away from the scene. "I'm glad I remembered to wash it last night, that's all. It always shines more when its been washed. They've given me this bit of paper to take to some hair dressers in Battle to get it cut and styled or some such thing for free. How posh is that?" Looking at her now and really noticing the shade of her hair for the first time, Sally could well believe what that lady had said. If she had been the least bit poetic, she'd have said that in this bright afternoon sunshine, Patty's hair looked like molten gold.

Pat was the first to notice the donkeys, which were plodding slowly around a little roped off arena in the distance, and pointed in their direction, clearly excited with her discovery. The other girls turned with rather less enthusiasm, then followed her slowly across the grass as she insisted on moving over to take a closer look. They walked to the area where a gaggle of small children stood awaiting their turn for a close encounter with the Donkeys, eyes solemnly following the slow progression of these shaggy brown creatures. They were singularly uncoordinated were donkeys, Sally thought, with their slow, uneven gait and those oversized ears, which seemed to move independently of each other. As she watched Pat mount, she noted with reluctant interest the general demeanour of this particular animal. She studied the drooping, elongated face and noted the spasmodic blink of his sad, dark eyes with their extraordinarily long lashed lids. There was an overall impression of soulful acceptance here she thought, along with sadness and embarrassment.

Once they had watched Pat perform a slow circuit of the arena, they moved back to the area of side shows and bring and buy stalls. As they moved from one display to another, they pointed this way and that, towards any piece of frippery that took their fancy. Suddenly Sally spotted an iron on one of the stools, and pointed towards this most vernacular of items, which stood out from amongst the array of finery on show. She quickly passed the sixpence over to the lady in charge, then as she picked up her purchase, realised all at once just how heavy the thing was. The lady, seeing the consternation on her face, smiled then offered to keep the iron beneath her stall until home time. Having ensured that her purchase had been safely stowed away beneath the bench, she moved along to the next stall, where Pat was examining a metal grater, just like the one Mrs Collins possessed, she assured them. As the asking price was a penny, she decided to purchase the thing, gaining Sally's approval by explaining how useful it would be when mum made them a cheese and potato pie. She was surprised and a little perplexed when the lady, after passing the item over to her, gave her a wooden grater, which had been standing right next to the one she had purchased. She had no idea what its purpose in life could be but thanked the lady as she took it from her.

She was about to move on when her beady eyes spotted a bundle of see through papers printed with deep blue lines on one side, the patterns depicting various wild flower arrangements and she decided that she had to have these iron on transfers. She decided there and then, that Sally could try out the iron she had just bought for this very purpose. And that her sister would also have to give her a lesson or two on embroidery. As she handed over her pennies, chatting away half to herself all the while, the stall-holder bent down and produced as if by magic, a box of assorted silks, each with its individual, immaculate black girdle still intact. "Here you might as well have these to go with your transfers," she said, beaming at the bemused child. "They'll keep you out of mischief for a while." Pat beamed back, almost too surprised and pleased to say thank you.

While Pat stood there admiring her purchases and gifts, Sally was still thinking about the iron she had just purchased and for some reason a vision of Mrs Pope, who ironed everything from a shirt to a duster, popped up in front of her. She was very house proud was Anne's mum, and she always insisted on the removal of shoes at the front or back door no matter what the weather. Still, she was kind, that was the main consideration and always offered the youngsters a drink when they called at her house. Sally reckoned that some people were just like that, and that was all there was to it.

As they moved towards the next stall, Hilary spotted an item that she just could not do without, she decided. It was a hand trowel that was propped up against an old cardboard box, and she picked up the implement and began stroking its smooth wooden handle lovingly. She managed to buy the thing for just sixpence and stowed it carefully away, more than pleased with her purchase.

Happily, they continued wandering from stall to stall wondering what else they could spend their money on. Sally's attention was drawn suddenly towards something quite extraordinary. “Look at this,” she exclaimed excitedly pointing towards a long chain dressed up to the nines in silver ornamentation. “It's a shilling, and I've still got one and thruppence left from the half crown mum gave us all. I've got to have it, I've just got to!” She lifted the bundle of treasure lovingly from its rude surroundings and carefully examined each charm, from the naive to the most exquisitely embossed miniature boxes. “Look, there's scissors here, two pairs in fact, a penknife and even a thimble. And there's a nail file and I think that's a cuticle shaper there or something, looks like it. And look at this nail buffer, it's covered with chamois leather and wow, just look at this weeny salt and pepper set and this little silver slipper. Wouldn't Granpy just love this?” The chain with its miniature appendages jingled deliciously as she raised it from the stand with one hand while with the other she proffered her precious pennies to the stall-holder.

“That's what I call a frippery thing,” said Amy teasingly as she leant over Sally's shoulder and began to finger each dangling item critically. “These ‘ere boxes are not big enough to cage a flea and don't imagine for a moment that you'll be able to cut sticks out of the hedge for your bows and arrows with that puny knife. As for all this nail stuff, forget it, when have you ever needed to file your nails, I ask you. You wear yours down climbing trees and grubbing about in ditches, just like the rest of us do.”

She lifted her head disdainfully, and looked further afield, the chain and its fripperies forgotten in an instant. “Why does that woman keep dabbing that old bloke’s face with that big hankie? Look, over there. He's sitting in that chair with wheels on it. He doesn't look too happy about it does he?”

“Because he keeps dribbling, that's why,” offered Pat. “I reckon he's got some really dreadful disease. She's mopped him up several times already. I've been watching her. Now stop staring, all of you, it's rude,” she added bossily as they all strained to observe this interesting scene. “You wouldn't like it if a crowd of kids gawped at you like that, would you?”

“Well I go to Stoke, talk about don’t do as I do, do as I say,” replied Amy, as she walked off to where a line of boys were about to start their hundred yards sprint. “Let’s bring a bit of tension into their lives, like they do to us,” she added grinning wickedly around at her pals. She was beaten to it however, by more vociferous voices belting out dubious encouragements even before the race had started.

“Come on Wangy, can’t you do better than that?” shouted a boy as the race got under way. Ron Hudson was sprinting down the track, arms and legs flailing. “My old Granny’d move faster than you lot, with her knickers round her ankles, and blindfolded. It's a good job Pucker's not here, he'd knock you all into a cocked hat." Arthur Puxty, or 'Pucker' as he was commonly called, was the fastest runner for miles around.

In spite of, or maybe because of, the taunts however, Ron pipped the other contestants to the winning line.

"Whew, I made it," he said as he stood there, bent double, feet apart and with his hands clasped firmly around his knees, as he puffed his way back to normality. Then as he stood up, he grinned around at his audience. "It was the hair that did it, see?" And he nodded his head to emphasise the significance of that normally carefully cultivated 'cowlick' of his, which was now protruding from his forehead at an angle of forty-five degrees. "With hair like mine, who needs legs? Well, come on then. They're selling drinks over there. Who's gonna stand me a nice cold drink then?" He asked, breathing more normally now and obviously proud of his achievement and all the attention he was receiving. Several youngsters followed him, Pied Piper fashion across the grass towards the drinks stall, where he selected a tall glass, full to the brim with foaming liquid. Once he had got enough down him to quench his immediate thirst, he slapped his tuppence down onto the bench. Then he held the glass at arms length and examined the contents critically. "Is this supposed to be ginger beer or something?" he asked moving it around under their noses. "Tastes more like water with an infection to me. Still beggars can't be choosers I suppose."

As he began to move away from the girls, he hesitated, then added as an afterthought. "Why do you suppose a milking stool has only got three legs then?" The girls looked at him with puzzled expressions on their faces. "It's because the cow's got the udder one, see?" This was greeted with a chorus of groans. Ron chuckled, then he and his pals moved away from them, seeking other distractions and adventures. They very quickly disappeared from sight, merging into the general melee. That liquid has certainly had the desired effect on him, restoring him to his normal, garrulous self, Sally thought to herself.

"Look! There's Lady Newton - over there," said Hilary, having just spotted their benefactor in amongst the milling crowd, and she nudged Sally with her shoulder to draw her attention to this elegant lady. "She's talking to Wig, of all people and by the look on his face he's just telling her a joke. I hope it's a clean one, that's all. Look, if he doesn't watch out he'll disappear feet first into that grin on his face and never be seen again. *And all that was left of the Cheshire cat was the grin,*" she added, in a mock theatrical voice. "I like Alice in Wonderland, but it used to frighten me to death when I was little."

When late afternoon saw the gradual movement of bodies towards the big wrought iron gates become a steady flow, the thoughts of the girls turned reluctantly towards the long trek home. Creeping hunger pangs were now overriding their desire for more fun.

"I mustn't forget to pick up mum's iron," said Sally, pointing over to the stall where the two ladies who had stored this precious item for her, were busy packing away the residue of their stock of assorted nick-nacks into large wicker baskets, their silver hair shining in the late afternoon sun.

"There you go," said the taller of the two, as she passed the heavy iron to Sally. "We thought you'd forgotten to collect it, or you didn't fancy carrying it home, and had abandoned it. You're going to know you've got it by the time you get there."

"No, I wouldn't not bother collect it. Not when I've paid for it," replied Sally with a puzzled frown. What a waste of her precious pennies that would have been, she thought. No, she would carry it all the way home even if she had to drag it the last bit. Or better still maybe she would be able to persuade one or other of her pals to take a turn now and again. What a good idea, she thought, and smiled. Yes, they could all take a turn she decided.

"That's taken care of then," she said aloud and grinned as the others looked at her blankly, wondering what crafty plan she was hatching.

As they wandered home, past the tall conifers, which sheltered and fed the tufty eared squirrels, they were quiet. Sally was idly observing the lazy hedge hopping of the little birds and was only half conscious of the incessant hum of insects, their gossamer wings shimmering iridescently in the failing sunlight.

Her eyes began to follow the movements of a fat furry bumble-bee, as it dipped and fumbled along the hedgerow like a miniature barrage balloon, fussily investigating every pollen receptacle it came into contact with.

"It's difficult to think about the war on such a perfect day," reflected Sally aloud, her words a natural progression of her thoughts.

"Yes and it's not over yet, not in the Far East it isn't. There's awful things going on over there," said Hilary. "Mum's worried about her brother, your Uncle Fred. He's out there, isn't he? Did you hear what she was saying about him the other day? She was saying she hates to think about what he's been through and the awful sights he must have seen. Him, and lots of others. He's a lot younger than she is, isn't he, and she says he seems like not much more than a kid to her. He's in Burma or thereabouts as far as she knows, which is an important country because there's stuff like rubber and tin and oil and that sort of thing there, according to dad. They've been trying to keep it out of the hands of the Japanese. The Burma Road, now that's always had a kind of magical sound to it for me, but when I said that to him one day, he told me a bit about all the bloodshed and suffering around there, and that put me off good and proper. You don't always think about things like that, do you? By the way the grown ups are talking though I wonder if the Japanese will ever give in."

"After what they've got up to, I don't suppose they'd dare. They'd be frightened of getting a damned good hiding and serve then right," replied Amy.

"What they've done to some of our side, soldiers and airmen and such like, is beyond belief. And I don't suppose we've heard the worst of it yet. They seemed to think they were on to an easy win after they'd bombed the American ships out of the water at Pearl Harbour, and for some time after that they seemed to be winning most of the battles as well. I suppose they thought that gave them the right to treat their enemies with as much cruelty as they liked. We're lucky we've got so many countries on our side, fighting with us. Them winning just doesn't bear thinking about. But I don't know how it's all going to end. All I know is that millions of people have died already and others are still suffering awful cruelty and things, like." As she took a deep breath to elaborate, Sally intervened.

"Don't keep on, you're making me feel sick," she said. "I've heard enough about all this cruelty and things to last me a lifetime. I don't suppose they were all like that, cruel fanatics that is, I hope not anyway. A lot probably just got caught up in this war same as us lot did, but it seems like the Japs are particularly cruel. Man's inhumanity to man, dad calls it."

Then, in order to steer the conversation away from what she had started and what was in danger of becoming more than her squeamish stomach could cope with, she added. "What was it Churchill said recently, after the end of the war in Europe I think it was? It was something like, 'We may allow ourselves a brief period of rejoicing,' yes that was it. I think we should take him at his word, don't you?" she added, jingling her chain of pure magic around in her pocket.

As she finished speaking, Pat glanced over her shoulder and noticed Eileen Lawrence hurrying towards them, and they all turned and waited until this 'miniature replica of her mother,' caught up with them.

"Whew, I thought you'd have got past the corner and out of sight before I caught you up, and you would have done if Pat hadn't seen me," said Eileen breathlessly. "I did see you at the Fete but you just kept disappearing before I could get anywhere near you. Anyway, my mum said if I saw you, I was to tell you to let your mum know that my Aunty and my Cousin Peter are coming down to us tomorrow and they're going to stay with us for a few days. We'll all be coming up to your place on Tuesday and perhaps us lot can go and see Deffy and Bill up in the woods there. Peter's never seen them. Then we can have a go on your swing."

"Come up, early as you like, then you can give us a hand with the pumping," said Sally, and grinned.

As they were close to the junction by Ashdown Cottage by this time, they decided to walk to Eileen's house with her and then take the footpath home beside Stafford's Stream. Another reason for this slight detour, was Pat's need to use the Lawrence's lavvy. She said she did not fancy crouching down behind the bushes and risk getting her bottom scratched to pieces on the brambles, thank you and there was always a danger of being seen by passers by.

"I'd rather risk my bum behind any old bush, even the prickliest hawthorn and with any amount of people to-ing and fro-ing the Fete, than go near that old lavvy of theirs," whispered Sally behind her hand, into Hilary's ear. Hilary nodded in grave and silent agreement.

The Lawrences' old lavatory must have been there since Doomsday, Sally reckoned. The tree against which it stood was now in its death throes, metamorphosing into the luxuriant ivy, which was slowly insinuating itself through the tree, the wooden lavvy and far beyond. Every sense was assaulted by this Augean stable, from a feeling of fear and trepidation, which invaded every step along the narrow overgrown pathway leading to it, to the fuggy smell within, which assaulted the nostrils with a mixture of decaying leaves, rotting wood and overall, the odour of stale human excrement. And always, always, that mere hint of Jeyes fluid. Dark it was in there, and eerie, especially when the wind blew and the scraggy sticks of ivy, malformed over countless movements of the door, scraped menacingly above the doorway. The holes, once symmetrical, which had been drilled for ventilation along the top of the now decomposing door, drew the eye towards a cribbed, abstract, ever changing vision of the scrub oaks which edged the far section of their garden. Fearful eyes, half shaded by trembling eyelids, saw darkly through these age distorted holes, images of Witches' wart encrusted noses, weeping scabs and even, in a certain coincidence of light and branch movement, the broken wing feathers of small birds. When overcome by morbid imagination and claustrophobia, unwary fingers made careless by their indecent haste to escape, would be caught and painfully trapped by the door. This distorted rectangle, loosened from the body of the lavatory by its rusting hinges, flagged and caught on the uneven flooring beneath, then whipped back viciously unless expertly restrained.

Sally could never fathom how a door so ancient had so much power, so much life still in it. This domicile for ivy, woodworm, death watch beetles and God only knows what, should be left to these ancient colonisers and have done with it, she reckoned.

As they entered the Lawrence's small cottage, Sally was struck as always by the contrast between this haven of ordered domesticity and the smelly hutch lurking malevolently at the far end of the garden. No speck of dust was allowed to settle on any surface here. The whole cottage gleamed, from its polished wood floors up to the last piece of yellow brass ornamenting the stone fireplace. Even the scullery, with its dull red stone floor, was always spic and span.

The copper, built into the corner for the Monday washday ritual was dust free. The recess beneath for the wood fire was swept clean of any ash left over from this long and arduous chore. On top of the round heavy lid lay the long wooden copper stick and the wooden tongs, both bleached unnaturally white by countless insertions into hot soapy water.

Along the nearside wall stood a solid iron bathtub, perched precariously on four slender legs. The feet that supported the whole thing were surprisingly elegant, the ornate decoration on them more like carved wood than iron; Ebony or dark stained Mahogany, like the front room furniture at Sylvian, perhaps, thought Sally. A sheet of plywood topped the bath, covered by a large sheet of unbleached calico, painstakingly hemmed around its edges. The material fell into thick pleats around the four corners. It looked just like some strange mythological creature in a short skirt, thought Sally, but in reality, Mrs Lawrence's nimble fingers had been at work here as well.

Beyond the scullery window, in the back yard, the ornate iron winding gear for the old well stood to attention, bucket at the ready, awaiting the next trip down into its unfathomable depths. The less one said or even thought about deep dark wells the better, Sally reckoned. She would not dwell on an analysis of the virtues or otherwise of this particular specimen of vernacular craftsmanship.

"Mind your bum on that seat, its lethal," called Eileen to Pat's fast retreating back, now heading like greased lightning down the overgrown pathway towards the lavatory. "It's split in two places now, so sit sideways on your right cheek, or better still, put your hands under your bum."

By this time however, Pat had disappeared from view and her fate along with her bum, was very much in the lap of the Gods - or whatever.

***

"Here, take your blooming iron, will you," said Amy to Sally, as they cut across the fields in the last rays of mellow evening sunshine. "You bought the darn thing anyway." As she passed it gratefully over, she began to flex her arm to relieve the accumulated cramp, glancing sideways to examine with critical interest, her well-muscled biceps. "Look at that," she said proudly, offering her arm around for inspection. "A lot of blokes, including Trev and Ken would be proud of muscles like these, don't you think?"

"Don't kid yourself. They look more like sparrows' knee caps," retorted Sally dryly, offering up her own muscles for inspection. The two girls continued bantering for a while, skipping perilously close to the stream as they did so, while vying with one another to think up some or other witty riposte. Then Pat, having heard enough of all their incomprehensible conversation, sought to steer their thoughts away from such nonsense and on to something more worthwhile.

"Do you believe in God?" She asked and paused as she seriously examined each face in turn to gauge their reaction to this question that had been plaguing her since Micky had told her that God did not exist. Momentarily stumped by this sudden and profound question, she was met by a stony silence and the same blank expression on each and every face.

Patty was the first to regain her power of speech and with it, a chance to get back into a conversation that had been dominated by Amy and Sally for long enough. "Of course there's a God, and on a day like this surely nobody could be in any doubt about his existence," she said profoundly. "Who made all the flowers and trees and birds, all that sort of thing, if it wasn't God? And I bet he had something to do with me winning the hair competition as well," she added for good measure.

"Yes, there's a God alright," replied Amy, "but I wouldn't kid yourself that he's got time to concern himself with who wins or loses competitions of any kind Patty. No, what puzzles me is not the question of whether he exists or not, but why he allows awful things to happen, like wars and people killing one another. You'd think with all the power he's supposed to have, he'd be able to ban anything evil wouldn't you? Look at all this," she said raising her arms as if to encapsulate the whole world, or at least as far as her imagination would stretch. "Fancy creating something as marvellous, as beautiful as all this and then allowing blood to be spilt all over it. Doesn't make sense does it?"

"What you're doing is overlooking the role of the old Devil in all of this," said Sally. "He's powerful just like God, don't forget and devious. I suppose when he was kicked out of Heaven for being so wicked, he thought he'd get his own back by being even more wicked. I reckon God's got his hands full with that one. There's a picture of him, the Devil I mean, in one of dad's books in the front room. I couldn't tell you which one nor do I aim to find out because it frightens the life out of me. Anyway, this thing's got the most fiendish grin on its face, horns on top of its head and cloven hoofs at the end of thin, hairy, bandy legs. It's just sort of squatting there holding a stick with three sharp points at the top. The whole area behind it is filled with flames, all blazing fire and smoke with wraith like images hovering in the background with their mouths wide open. They're screaming I expect, well you would be wouldn't you if you were trapped in those conditions and with a monster like that." She paused and shuddered, "even God must be scared stiff of him."

"It puzzles me how people think they know what he looks like, nobody's seen him as far as I know," said Hilary. "Nor God either - well apart from Moses and a few old Prophets and Jesus I suppose when he was in the wilderness. But did they actually describe him though I would like to know, God I mean, I'm talking about God now. I remember something about Saul and the burning bush," continued Hilary, completely muddling up her bible stories. "But that was only a disembodied voice I think not an image. When it said, 'Saul, Saul why persecutes thou me,' it frightened the poor bloke half to death. Well it would do wouldn't it, so anyway he went blind for a few days after that so I expect that was through fear, don't you. He mended his ways though, did Saul and even changed his name to Paul and he became one of Jesus' disciples."

"What's this, Bible classes?" asked Patty, "It's not Sunday you know, and we only talk about God and things like that on Sundays, well mostly. Mind you since Mr and Mrs Smith started coming out from Hastings to take us for Sunday school, it's been much more interesting. I think someone said they were hoping to move into the Manse before long. You know, to live there. They don't just teach you about God himself, they make you see nature, trees, birds and things like that through his eyes. Mrs Brockway was a good old stick but she was pretty old wasn't she and we did play her up from time to time. I felt really guilty that last Sunday, before she went away for good, when she plonked that box of jewellery in front of us and invited us all to rummage through it. I've never seen such an assortment of jewellery before in all my life. It took me ages to chose just one item - well two actually. Look at this," she added feeling around her neck as her fingers sought and then withdrew from the top of her dress, the daintiest silver cross and chain Sally had ever seen.

"Wow!" They all echoed in unison.

Mrs Brockway, their old Sunday school teacher, had retired. She must have been all of ninety, Sally guessed. She was going to Africa for one last look around, she said, and to visit her Husband's grave. On her return to England, she planned to stay with friends somewhere in Kent, if Sally remembered rightly, but hopefully nowhere near that old farmer Watson, or whatever his name was.

Sally thought about the exquisitely embossed silver bracelet she had chosen from Mrs Brockway's collection of jewellery as a farewell gift. It was now carefully stored away in that little chest of drawers, given to her by the nurses in the Buchanan Hospital all those years ago. Silver, especially when embossed like this precious bracelet, must be the prettiest metal in the world she thought.

Mr Smith mostly conducted the services in the Chapel these days. 'A true Christian' along with the rest of his family, that was what their mum said. While their father referred to the family as enlightened, whatever that meant. But then he had said the same thing about the Farrows and also the Gosse family who farmed the few acres of land along Crazy lane. Also the Websters at the Waterfall, if it came to that.

There were five Smiths in all, Mr and Mrs Smith of course and their two children, Olive and Daniel and then there was a Miss Smith who, while not a blood relative, was very much an integral part of this extraordinary family.

When facing his congregation, Mr Smith looked every inch a preacher, a dignified man of God. However, as he had confessed to their father, in front of the girls, he was a farmer at heart, a frustrated man of the soil. While he passionately endorsed the teaching of Jesus Christ, whom he looked upon as being the ultimate example of good opposing evil, there was nothing he enjoyed more than messing about with tractors, tilling the soil and making things grow, and of course, caring for farm animals. He believed in reincarnation and said that he had already put his name down on God's register to be brought back as a farmer in his next life. He just hoped and prayed that his tally of rescued souls would be adequate when he died, enough anyway to enable him to be granted this simple request - a Scholarship - he called it. As he had stood looking around benevolently at them all, he had suddenly grinned then winked at their dad adding; 'and how about yours Mr Cotton, your soul? Is it to be saved or just left to the discretion of the Almighty?'

Amy broke into Sally's thoughts here with a sharp tap on her shoulder. "You're not listening to a word I'm saying are you," she said accusingly. "You're always day dreaming, that's your trouble."

"I was only thinking about Mr Smith and his tally of rescued souls. You know, when he was talking to us about wanting to save enough of them so's he could come back as a farmer next time around. He's such a decent old chap. I reckon he deserves to come back as whatever he chooses to come back as. I can't wait for them all to come and live up at the Chapel."

"Nor can I," replied Hilary. "But I reckon that when you die you don't get a choice, you just join a queue and take pot luck as to what's available when it's your turn. "Can you imagine anyone volunteering to come back as a grave digger or worse still, a hangman or any other rotten job like that, no fear. You'd all be jostling one another for a job as a gardener or for the lifestyle of a Lady Newton or something nice like that. I would volunteer to be a gardener myself, anytime," she added after a short, thoughtful pause, forgetting her 'no choice in the matter' observation.

"Do you think it all goes on for ever and ever, then?" asked Patty, clearly perplexed by the concept of this eternal circle, this endless transmigration of bodies and souls.

"Well, the sky or rather space does," replied Hilary. "Or so Jumbo James says, though I just can't get my head around imagining anything that doesn't start and finish somewhere, can you? I think even he finds it hard to comprehend, or at least he found it difficult to explain to us lot in simple words. We just sat there in silence, looking stupid when he pointed upwards and outwards, as he struggled to demonstrate physically as well as verbally, the feasibility of such a mind boggling idea. He was wasting his time with us lot I can tell you and in the end he just looked at us with that exasperated expression of his and said, 'well if space does come to an end, then what is beyond that?' And left it to us to work it out for ourselves, or not, which was more like it."

"Well, I'm blowed if I know," replied Sally thoughtfully. "I think I can understand what mum thinks about things going on forever though, the life everlasting bit. She says that to her it is simply the cycle of life as she calls it, the birth, the death and then the regeneration of plants and trees and things and also the generation after generation of humans and other animals that live, reproduce and die. That's a kind of forever thing I suppose in its own way. Mind you, who's to say whether that can go on forever? God I suppose."

After another thoughtful pause in which she sought to steer the conversation away from the sublime towards, if not the ridiculous, then on to a more mundane subject, she continued. "By the way Amy, why did you thump me on the shoulder like that just now? That didn't half hurt. I'll have a great big bruise there later on, you mark my words and then you'll be sorry. You don't know your own strength, that's your trouble" As if to emphasise her pain and discomfort, she began to massage the assaulted shoulder with her open palm and screwed her face up into what she assumed to be an appropriate expression of pain and effrontery.

"Well I go to Stoke! Talk about delayed reaction," exclaimed Amy, tossing back her thick shoulder length hair. "I only gave you a little tap to wake you up, cause you were day dreaming again. If you'd been listening to what I was saying to you in the first place, it wouldn't have happened, would it? I sometimes wonder if your brain leaks you know. Hang on a minute," she said after a short pause, "I'd better check you out. Come over here, now bend your head this way and let's take a good look. Yes, there's something here, some white stuff. Looks like sawdust to me, what do you lot think?" She asked as she turned around to face the other girls with an exaggerated, theatrical gesture.

"Scurf, that's what that is," replied Hilary. "It's only scurf and that's because she doesn't bother to dry her hair properly when she washes it. Always in too much of a rush that one," she said, as she ruffled Sally's hair lightly.

Then she turned away from the group, her expression solemn. Weariness was suddenly apparent in the droop of her shoulders and the set of her jaw. "I'm tired and I'm hungry and my feet are killing me," she said. Then she paused and added thoughtfully. "Useful things though feet, aren't they?"

"Yes they stop your legs from fraying," replied Sally dryly.

CHAPTER 2

Satisfaction tempered with caution was their father's reaction to the result of the recent General Election. Sally, as she sat around the table with Pat and Hilary and listened with interest to the debate between him and his two brothers Alf and Fred, who were on a visit to Sylvian the weekend after this momentous event.

Although Sally was not yet old enough to appreciate the finer points of her father's and uncles' lively discussions, it was clear that they very much welcomed the new Labour government. Sally was impressed with their references to the proposed National Health Service. She remembered how much it had cost their dad to have her and her older sisters immunised against the killer, diphtheria, after mum and dad's first-born, Sylvia, had died of this scourge.

The three brothers went on at length about the aftermath of the war, the money we (the country) owed the Yanks and how easily the working classes could be 'bought' by the establishment.

"Give 'em an extra shilling in their pockets, then they'll think they've gone up in the world and go and vote Tory," Pop was always saying.

After a while, mum interrupted the debate, as the men got more and more and carried away with the exciting new brand of politics, with its emphasis on a fairer deal for the working classes.

"Move your elbow, Pop," she said as she moved towards the table carrying a tray laden with cups of steaming tea in her arms. The liquid quivered and slopped gently around the cups as she moved, threatening but never quite succeeding in spilling over. Not one drop made its way from thin china cup into its matching saucer as she placed the tray with its contents gently onto the table in front of them. "There you go then," she said as she straightened up. "I thought is was about time for a bit of light relief and refreshment. Talk for England you could, you boys. Anyway, I thought you might enjoy a bit of fruitcake with your tea as well, the oven was just right. It's a bit crumbly as it was still warm when I cut it up, but I don't suppose for one minute that'll put you off. Lean as greyhounds the three of you, in spite of your appetites. It's just not fair. There's me only has to look at food to add a pound or two to me waistline."

She turned to the children, "I must say you girls have been remarkably quiet while the men have been talking. Couldn't get a word in edgeways, I suppose. Even your knitting has been laid aside, now that really is unusual," she added, as she looked around the table at them all. "There's enough cake here for all of you of course."

"You're too good to us, Dolly," said Uncle Alf, as she moved away from the table. "Best grub in all the world down here, in this house I mean, and always a smile to go with it. Beats me how you do it with all these mouths to feed, especially when I think of all the other work you get through, all the time you have to spend in that old copper house of yours. Your lines of washing are always a joy to behold especially when there's sun and breeze in equal parts, like today's weather for instance. Just standing there this afternoon watching it flapping gently too and fro and with the field and the woods in the background, was an uplifting experience. And the smell of your washing, Dolly, is something else. If you could bottle and sell that, you'd make a small fortune. But I suppose it's not fair really, to compare this place with London, especially the state it's in at the moment. Our poor old Smoke, like many cities across Europe, has taken a right old hammering in this war. There's dust and grime everywhere, but incredibly, in places willow herb and thistles and nettles have started growing already, pushing up between the rubble on the bombsites. Mother Nature is a resourceful old bird, she's always there, ready and waiting when any old nook and cranny, any old patch of ground needs a bit of redecorating. She must have a fair old army of Acolytes at her beck and call. God help us if she ever goes on strike. Or you Dolly, if it comes to that," he added, as he moistened his fingers and gathered up the residual cake crumbs from around his plate and licked them into his mouth.

"Sing us a song, Uncle Fred - please!" pleaded Pat, taking advantage of the lapse in conversation. "What about The Penny Steam boat, that's my favourite."

"Well, I don't see how I can refuse when you put it like that," replied Uncle Fred, clearly more than happy to air his lungs and considerable talents. "You girls join me in the chorus. You probably know it better than I do anyway," he said, as he stood up. Then he licked his lips, took a deep breath and began to sing:

"When I was young I thought I'd like to see some foreign lands
So I jumped onto a penny steamboat bound for Hindustan
And after I'd been there a while, it seemed a pleasant shore, shore
The natives when they saw me, set up this terrible roar
The natives when they saw me, set up this terrible roar.

Karabidyrango ju jo jiggero, up up Sam the Negro
Talikatalorum talang talugo
Talikatalorum, all together please.

An Indian chief came up to me, and this is what he said
If you don't take Jojo for your bride you're bound to lose your head
Now fancy me a going to church with Jojo for a bride, bride

Now Indian maids of ninety are not yet in my line
Now Indian maids of ninety are not yet in my line.

Karabidyrango ju jo jiggero, up up Sam the Negro
Talikatalorum talang talugo
Talikatalorum all together please.

Now in an Indian kitchen I had no desire to cook
So one dark night to sea I went on a chance to sling my hook
I saw a pill box floating by and jumped in rather cool, cool
And after floating around for forty years, I landed in Liverpool.

Karibidyrango ju jo jiggero, up up Sam the Negro
Talikatalorum talang talugo
Talikatalorum all together please.

Once more with the chorus then," he said, as grownups and youngsters alike clapped him appreciatively.

"Right, it's your turn now Alf," said Uncle Fred, adjusting his trouser legs as he sat back down again. "It's no good looking to that old table cloth for inspiration either," he said, as Uncle Alf sat there in silence, elbows on table and with his hands pressed together as though in prayer. "And if you don't watch it, you'll stick those fingers of yours right up your nose. What'll it be then you girls, what's your favourite song, after The Penny Steam Boat, that is?" he asked, as he looked at each one in turn.

"Frisky old Herbert," said Hilary and Sally in chorus and giggled as once again, they had given voice to the same words at the same time.

Uncle Alf stood up. He was wide awake now and his eyes twinkled merrily as he grinned from ear to ear. He backed away slightly from the table and with legs apart and his tummy, if he had had one, thrust slightly forward, began to sing:

"Frisky old Herbert's me name, I'm known throughout the village.
A hundred years or more, since I went to school for knowledge.

When I was born what a time we all had ... ..."

By the time he reached this part of the song, he was rocking from one foot to the other in time to the rhythm of the tune. And then, as he got to

"We rang all the bells and the firemen came out, to see such a beautiful sight,"

he began to move stiff legged from one foot to the other, still grinning from ear to ear. As he finished the song and made as if to sit down, Sally said, "Sing from *'but I'm getting old, getting quite old, older and older each day,'* again please uncle. I know all the words up to that bit. But I've just got to learn the whole thing."

"Will that do then?" said Uncle Alf, as having satisfied all members of the group, he was allowed to take his seat once again. "I wonder what old Billy Whitlock would have made of that. More than likely he'd have shut me up after the first couple of lines, tutt-tutted and given you all a proper rendering of it. And who could blame him. Anyway, I reckon it's your turn now Pop. What'll it be then, a song or a dance I wonder."

"A dance, a tap dance," shouted Pat, before anyone else had time to draw breath. "Your mouth organ's in the cupboard under the stairs, dad. I know it is. I saw it there the other day. Go on, you've been sitting down for ages, it's about time you did something." She paused for a few seconds, gauging dad's reaction to her bit of cheek. Then, as he did not respond, she jumped out of her seat, opened the cupboard door and withdrew an oblong box from on top of one of its shelves. "There you go then," she said as she handed it over. "If you do a bit of Alexander's Rag Time Band, we can all sing along with you." And she went over and opened the scullery door, purposefully.

"Can't argue with that one, can you Pop?" said uncle Alf, as he walked around his brother's chair and made as if to lever him out of his seat. "She's made a good choice too, as far as I'm concerned. Brings back a good few memories that old song. What say you?"

Pop sighed good-naturedly and began tap dancing and playing his harmonica. When he had finished his turn, he came back through the scullery door breathing heavily and sat down again, laying the precious instrument down in front of him. As he brushed the hair from his forehead, Uncle Alf said, "looks like I'll have to give you a bit of a hair cut before I go home. That's one chore Dolly shies away from now, I understand."

He winked knowingly at mum, reminding her of the time when in her haste to get that disagreeable task done, she had clipped dad's ear, creating an inordinate amount of blood which ran down and soaked into his vest.

"Clipped your dad's ear she did, that mother of yours," he said and he grinned around the table at everyone. "As if clipping his wings wasn't bad enough, she has to blood him, I ask you. Just thank your lucky stars you girls that it's your dad who cuts your hair. You moan and groan and squirm when he puts those clippers up the backs of your necks, but I've never seen him draw blood, not yet, anyway."

"Trust you to remind everybody of that," replied mum. "I don't suppose I'll ever live that down. I expect I'd been up half the night with one of these girls, and just lost my concentration."

She grinned ruefully at the memory. "I didn't half get a ticking off though, I do remember that. Anyway, guess what we've got for dinner tomorrow," she said brightly, changing the subject completely.

"A nice piece of beef. Pop's going to dig some nice fresh carrots and potatoes to go with it, aren't you Pop? And the girls can pick and shell the peas. I'll cut the cabbage and clean it up a bit. I'll have to make sure there's no caterpillars in it or I'll be in trouble, won't I?" and she grinned at the girls as they visibly shuddered at the thought. She paused here for a few seconds then added as an afterthought, "leastways I hope it'll be alright, this beef. It's well marbled with fat and a decent size so it should be all nice and juicy and tender."

"Well, as long as you wipe its bum and cut off its horns, it'll be alright by me," said dad. Mum studiously ignored his remark.

CHAPTER 3

Dad sat and stared at the newspaper, spread out in front of him on the kitchen table, with a puzzled frown on his face. "I can't for the life of me imagine how just one bomb could have caused so much damage, but that's what it says here. Listen, I'll read some of it out to you, Dolly," he said, as he shuffled the pages and lifted the newspaper up at an angle the better to view its contents.

"It says, 'In the late evening of 6 August the following dramatic announcement was made by President Truman: Sixteen hours ago an American aeroplane dropped one bomb on Hiroshima, Japan. The bomb had more power than 20,000 tons of T.N.T, and more than 2,000 times the blast power of the British 'grand slam,' which is the largest bomb (22,000lb) yet used in the history of warfare.' Blowed if I can get my head round that. All that power in one bomb," he said incredulously.

After a long pause, he continued.

"According to the chap on the wireless this morning, there's still massive fires burning all over the place, but then you listened to the news same as I did so you heard what the man said. I don't know about you but it scares the living daylights out of me. These weapons of war are just getting more and more powerful and destructive all the time. And how did they manage to get it into the air in the first place, this bomb, I wonder? There can't be many planes powerful enough to lift a thing like that off the ground.

We can thank our lucky stars neither the Germans nor the Japs got their hands on something like that first. God help us if they had. That would have been our lot. Of course, Hiroshima is, or was, I should say, a great Japanese naval and army base, so it was an obvious target. The old Americans certainly know what they're doing. Well if that doesn't bring the war to an end, if this doesn't persuade them to surrender, then I don't know what will." He sighed heavily, overwhelmed by it all.

"The thing is, the Yanks will be remembering Pearl Harbour," he continued, "and I don't think they'll accept anything less than unconditional surrender with no quarter given, and who can blame them? Especially when you also consider what a particularly nasty and bitter war this one in the Far East has been. There has been a whole lot of suffering and loss of life, an unimaginable amount. Poor buggers though, the people in Hiroshima, you can't help feeling sorry for them can you. I know the old Japs have got up to some nasty things in this war, and I mean really nasty, but not all those thousands of civilians who've been killed and maimed by this thing were to blame. But then that's war for you. The innocent suffer along with the guilty. You've only to look at some of our cities that were bombed to blazes during this war. A hell of a lot of people were killed and injured during the course of those raids, though not with quite that degree of destruction, I grant you."

He paused here, shaking his head as he scanned the surface of the newspaper as though an answer to the whole mess lay hidden within the neat and dispassionate printed words.

"I don't know what to think," replied mum. "I just couldn't imagine a nastier weapon than those V2 rockets that old Hitler bombarded us with, but this is a whole lot worse. Where's it all going to end? There's one thing for sure, wars like this one and also the Great War of course just can't be allowed to happen again. Organisations like the League of Nations will have to be given a real voice, a whole lot more power and the people who wield that power must be carefully chosen."

"Well, the League of Nations didn't stop this lot!" Retorted dad.

"I know", replied mum. "Let's just hope the Americans agree to take part now, do their bit to try to prevent this sort of thing happening again. And of course you've just got to forget about this vengeance thing, difficult though that will be. The people on our side who've suffered in this war, who have lost loved ones and such like, will be looking for revenge. It's only natural. And we don't know the whole story yet, the full extent of the horrors of this war, all the atrocities that have taken place. Trouble is this vengeance thing has never worked. It only makes those you've got the better of, bitter and determined to have another go. You've only got to think about that awful Treaty of Versailles and its repercussions to realise that penalising your enemy in such a way, is not the way to ensure a peaceful future. Make the old Generals and such like stand up and take their punishment, they've got a lot to answer for, but don't punish the ordinary folk who have suffered enough anyway.

A few days after the Hiroshima bomb, another great city in Japan, Nagasaki, was hit by a second huge bomb. As the announcement came over the radio, dad called through to mum who was standing at the sink in the scullery rinsing out a couple of tea towels, which until a few moments ago had been simmering away on top of the kitchen range.

"Hey Doll, come in here quick, and listen to this. I can't believe it, they've dropped another of those bloody bombs on Japan!"

Sally looked across the table at Pat, whose hand, carrying a spoonful of egg white was poised halfway to her open mouth, and then at her eyes, which carried an expression of fearful incomprehension, and she took a deep breath. It seemed as though this dreadful war she had decided was dead and buried, had resurfaced to haunt them once more. Apart from the click of the scullery door as mum shut it behind her, there was complete silence as they listened to the drone of the newsreader, as he outlined the action that had wrecked another of Japan's great cities. 'Another very important strategic strike, and even more successful than the first one,' they heard him say.

"There'll be nothing left of Japan if this carries on," said mum at last, her voice full of concern. "Japan's not that big a country really, it's not going to take that many more bombs of that size and destructive power to destroy the whole country. They must be in a terrible state over there, wondering if it's going to be their turn next. They, the Japanese high command, must realise it's all over now, surely. They have got to surrender, to save what's left of their country."

"I reckon they and old Hirohito, or whatever his name is, will have their heads very close together right this moment. It can't be long now before they give in," replied dad. "I don't trust or even much like the Japs, but I don't like what's happening out there."

Sure enough, shortly after the Nagasaki bomb blast, the Japanese High Command agreed to an unconditional surrender, albeit with one proviso, that their Emperor's position should be preserved.

There was silence in the room as they listened to the King's speech, delivered in his usual hesitant voice. "A syllable away from a stutter," as dad would say. *"We now have our part to play in restoring the shattered fabric of civilisation. It is to this great task that I call you now,"* stated the King, with as much solemnity as he could muster. They all looked solemnly at one another. Sally was not absolutely sure what her part would have to be in all this, but for the moment it was enough to know that this dreadful war was at an end, really at an end this time. At the back of her mind however, was the feeling that the repercussions would be reverberating around their own little world for some time to come. But she would not think about that just yet. It was her dad's voice she was listening to now.

"Well that's it then, looks like its all over and done with, bar the paper work and thank the Lord for that," said dad. "It's not quite an unconditional surrender but as near as damn it I would say. Seems to have satisfied the Americans and that's what counts at this stage." He paused here for a few seconds as though finding it difficult to take in the full implications of this momentous event. Then, "thank God, thank God," he said as though those few seconds of contemplation had brought the full realisation that this brutal war was finally at an end. He sat back in his chair, an audible sigh escaping his lips. "Make us a cup of tea please Doll, will you?" he said.

Sally peered over her dad's shoulder as he sat with the day's newspaper spread out on the table in front of him. She pointed to the words that seemed to leap out from the page. "The unendurable must be endured, it says there," said Sally, a puzzled frown on her face. "That's a funny thing to say. If something's unendurable then it can't be endured surely," she said. "Who would say something like that?"

"They're the words of the Japanese Emperor, Hirohito and I know exactly what he means," replied dad. "If you think about it, that's what a lot of folk have been doing throughout this war and throughout the centuries if it comes to that. Let's just cut it down to size a bit and think how frightened we all were when we were bombarded by those doodlebugs. You could say that was unendurable, if you think about it, but we had to put up with it didn't we? It was out of our control. And what about the poor devils who've been maimed and goodness knows what else in this war and also those who've lost loved ones. They're having to endure the unendurable if you really think about it, and that's just simplifying things."

"Well I don't know," said Sally, as she moved away from the table and looked through the window. Then she spotted her friend hurrying across the field.

"Here comes Hilary!" She shouted, her thoughts turning eagerly away from the complications of trying to fathom something she barely understood.

"I expect you're right, dad," she called, as she ran thankfully towards the door to meet her pal. "I won't be long. Me and Hilary have got to get our stuff sorted out for hop-picking. We'll do the pumping later," she added as her father shook his head, unable to keep up with this sudden change of mood and tempo. If they had stayed around a bit longer they would have heard him mutter, "These scatterbrained youngsters, they're in a world of their own. Blowed if I know what goes on inside their heads."

***

"Anyone about?" called Mr Linch, as he knocked on the scullery door and peered short-sightedly into the kitchen.

"Yes I'm in here," replied mum, rising hurriedly from her seat beside the kitchen table, wiping her hands automatically down her overalls as she did so. "I'm just peeling the potatoes for dinner and, as it happens, I've just made a pot of tea. I don't suppose you'd say no to one, would you?"

"Right first time, how could I refuse a cup of your tea, Dolly," he replied.

"Now Mrs Moon down yonder, well her tea that's a different kettle of fish altogether. Talk about water bewitched, tea begrudged, that stuff's weak as dishwater. Last time I called in to see her she offered me a cup and although I should have known better, I accepted. As soon as I'd finished she poured me another which I held my breath and drank straight down. 'My,' she said, 'you really like your tea don't you,' to which I replied before I could stop myself, 'yes I do, it's taken me six cups to get a taste of the stuff," and his eyes twinkled merrily. Mild mannered as he was, Sally wondered if he'd actually spoken those words or if, as she suspected, they'd stayed on the very tip of that humorous tongue of his. She grinned as she remembered their encounter with Mrs Moon and Daphne, ages ago now, while on their way home from Sunday school. She could still picture the concentration on Basil's face as he stood up and fired his soggy missile with deadly accuracy onto Daphne's cheek and his satisfied grin as he dived for cover. The memory of her startled yelp and Mrs Moon's reaction to it, almost made her laugh out loud. She was also remembering Betty's encounter with Mrs Moon's rock cakes. This lady, having sampled their mum's tasty buns, had decided to try her hand at these semi-sweet culinary delights, and had used the Cotton girls as guinea pigs. Sally could still remember the taste and sensation of these conical lumps of baked sawdust that had stuck stubbornly at the back of her throat. She had run to the lavvy and emptied the whole desiccated mess into her large old hankie, to be disposed of along the lane on their way home. However, as she returned to the room, a satisfied grin on her face, she was just in time to hear, with astonishment, Betty actually praising these incredible objects. Where upon she was set upon by a very persuasive Mrs Moon, and forced to eat another one. Sally could still remember the horrified look on Betty's face as she took hold of another of these dangerous missiles and, with a trembling hand, forced it towards her reluctant mouth. She also remembered that her first reaction had been a smug, 'serve her right for being such a hypocrite,' followed by a more sympathetic, albeit with an element of self interest, 'poor old Betty, thank God it's not me.' These so called rock cakes were enough to choke the life out of you and could have been used as their secret weapon in this ere war that had just ended.

As Sally dragged her thoughts away from these humorous reminiscences, she heard Mr Linch ask if he could borrow dad's long arm pruner.

"I only need it for a couple of days. Some of my bushes and trees have really got out of hand this year, what with one thing and another, and I can't reach with those loppers of mine," he said.

"I don't see why not," mum replied. "Pop won't need them now until he's ready to prune the fruit trees, and that won't be for a week or two at the earliest. They're in one of the sheds, round the back there somewhere. I'll look them out and then I can call Pop in for his tea at the same time." Sally recalled the time when she had tried to use the wretched thing. Dad had warned her that it was not nearly as easy to use as it looked and, having insisted on having a go, she soon discovered that he was not joking. The thing definitely had a will of its own, and bucked and swung around until within minutes it seemed as if her arms were ready to fall off.

"I did warn you," he had said mildly, surprisingly with no hint of reprimand in his voice. "You need strong, well developed stomach muscles as well as strong arms to control pruners. Next year maybe you'll be strong enough to do the whole orchard for me, how about that?" And he had grinned as she hastily passed the weapon over to him and without more ado, had raced down towards the house to cadge a cup of cocoa from her mum. "You'll be lucky," she'd said under her breath. "That bloody thing's lethal."

***

"Damn and blast this bloody hair," said Pat. "I'll never get this dolly ready for the flower show this after noon at this rate." And she frowned with impatient concentration as she struggled to control the tufts of bright yellow wool that, no matter how hard she tried, stuck stubbornly up and outwards at all angles as she tried to stitch it onto the bald head of the rag doll she was making.

She stubbornly refused help, insisting crossly that this had to be her work and hers alone. Luckily, she was too engrossed in her task to notice the look of amusement that passed between Hilary and Sally, or the grin that stretched across their mouths from corner to corner as they observed her futile attempts to control the improbable material. No matter what she did, or how hard she tried, the little rag doll still looked for all the world as though it had been struck by lightening.

"That'll do, it'll have to," announced Sally after a while. "We've got to get our things up to the show an hour before it actually starts. That means leaving home in about half an hour and we're going to need something to eat before we go. We can always get a drink up there if we want. Now where did I put that cross-stitch? Ah there it is, all wrapped up in its tissue paper so it won't get dirty. Mum's idea that was. And here's your teddies Hilary, in this bag over here. I love the way you've dressed the pair of them."

As they approached the big Manor House, the first sight that met their eyes was a huge marquee standing majestically in the centre of an enormous lawn, the Union Jack fluttering on its topmost pinnacle. This enormous tent was a hive of activity, a blur of colour and movement as industrious ladies moved their flower arrangements and other produce into its vast interior. There were men too, carrying boxes of all shapes and sizes, and with goodness knows what inside. Others were struggling with armfuls of greenery, and yet others were wheeling wheelbarrows stuffed to the gunnels with huge marrows and other miscellaneous vegetables.

The buzz of activity was accompanied by a low hum of abstract voices in a sort of minor key. The major or higher notes would come later when almost the whole population of the village would be sure to be assembled there

"Look there's old Lottie Shambrook!" Shouted Sally. "You can tell her a mile off with that bright red coat of hers. On a day like this, too. She must be boiling.

I wonder why she's here this early? She doesn't normally show anything. Ah, now I can see what she's up to, she's on the earole. Look at her following Mrs Bishop around. I bet she's seeing what cakes she can cadge from her once the judging's over. She's a wonderful cook is Mrs Bishop, but not quite as good as our mum, though. I'm ever so pleased she cooks our school dinners, and not Mrs Moon. Much as I like Mrs Moon," she added hastily.

"No, we'd all starve, laughed Hilary "Come on. We'd better get our stuff into the tent or else we'll be out of time and disqualified. We've got to find out what's supposed to go where. Its usually somewhere at the back if I remember rightly. Look there's old Mr Saville and his sister," she added, pointing in the direction of the flower borders. They're doing a tour of inspection before the show begins I expect and hoping that there's not too much damage to their precious flowers. They're right keen gardeners according to my dad and do their fair share of the work around here. They've got gardeners of course. They couldn't do all this lot themselves, now could they?"

As they entered the tent, all muggy and full of odours, Sally sniffed the air appreciatively, trying to distinguish the various smells, one from the other. The earthy smell of vegetables mingled with the heady scent of freshly picked flowers, and in there somewhere was the delicious and mouth watering aroma of newly baked cakes. The admixture of smells, though different here, reminded her of the grocers down the street, with its characteristic smell which she'd worked out was a mixture of candle wax, cheese, bacon rind, earthy vegetables, mice and snuff.

"Right, that's our stall over there," said Hilary, in a very businesslike manner. She pointed to the notice with the word 'HANDICRAFTS' printed on it.

"Look, over there" she said pointing to the far end of the tent. "There's a few bits and pieces there already, looks like we've got a bit of competition this year. Toys here it says. If you put your dolly there Pat, I'll put my teddies next to it, and they'll keep each other company. Your cross stitch goes over there Sally," Hilary added, as she removed the tissue covered embroidery from her friend's hand, walked a few paces and then placed it carefully on the bench. "Right let's get out of here. It's a bit too stuffy for me."

As they emerged into the bright sunlight slightly disorientated, they blinked and looked with astonishment as a steady stream of people were already making their way across the freshly mown lawn towards the side stalls. The fete was well and truly open and by the look of things, the stall holders and side show performers were more than ready to do business. Pat had already spotted the gingerbread stall with customers beginning to line up for their yearly fix, and she scampered off across the grass to get her piece.

"Hey, wait for us then. We like Mrs Bishop's gingerbread same as you do, called Hilary." If you get there before we do, get me and Sally a bit, will you?" But by the time she had finished the sentence, Pat had disappeared amongst the crowd and all they could hope for was that she would have the sense, and more importantly, the money to pay for three pieces of this culinary delight.

A few minutes later, Pat returned with the goodies. As Sally munched her way through her sweet sticky morsel, she looked around and noticed with some surprise, Miss Dengate's distinctive figure amongst the crowd. It seemed such an unlikely venue for this very private lady that she looked again just to make sure. It was indeed this venerable lady, decked out as usual in a long dark skirt and jacket of a similar hue. She was not however, wearing that long khaki coloured apron that was very much a part of her workaday attire nor had she any rabbits on her person. Sally grinned as she recalled this lady's words to her Father when he had remarked on the popularity of the rabbits she sold locally or took all the way to Battle Market on her bike. Her answer had been that she always snared the creatures. Sally even remembered her exact words. 'I keeps me gun fer them thar burgulers, not fer them nice plump rarebits, which I snares. Darnt want to be pickin and pokin around me marth hunting out bits of lead all the time, nor do me carstomers.' Sally had thought at the time that they had better not let her catch them trespassing across her fields or they might just get a bullet up their backsides. No, that was not true. That would never happen, they all knew that. She was a good old stick, a real character who, if they happened to come face to face with her while walking out in the countryside, would always have a fresh snippet of information on the whereabouts of any particular fruits, berries or nuts and even the location of early or rare wild flowers. And she was always smiling, revealing teeth solid and serviceable, and only slightly discoloured with age. Behind the smile however, Sally knew was a keen, intuitive mind. Dad, who had a lot of time for this wise old lady, said that she tolerated most folk, genuinely liked just a few, but that she definitely did not suffer fools gladly. That somehow seemed to sum up this lady with her close association with wild nature.

After a short while, Hilary drew her attention away from the ancient to the modern, as she pointed across the grass to where Amy stood chatting to Ivy and Dorothy Simmons. As they walked towards them, they could see that they were all dressed up to the nines, hair immaculate and powder and lipstick expertly applied. The thought passed through Sally's mind that this elegant trio had not had to fetch milk from the farm or to pump water from underground tank to top one before they came here. So obviously they had had the time to titivate. Then she felt a bit ashamed of herself. They had probably had chores to do same as she had. She supposed she was just a wee bit jealous really. And if she were being perfectly honest, she had neither the time nor the inclination to dress up, and thankfully neither had Hilary.

"I've been looking for you," said Amy walking towards them followed by the other two. Then she lifted a round box with the words, 'Ponds Powder' on its lid and then a bottle of 'Drene' shampoo carefully from her handbag. "I found these on that stall over there. They're not full of course, it's a secondhand stall, but they'll keep me going for a while. There's a bottle of 'Evening in Paris' scent there as well if you want it. There's not much left in it though and I thought sixpence was a lot to ask for it. Anyway, you'll see it there. It's in a blue bottle that's got a lovely shape to it. It's up to you."

"I don't think so, we haven't got money to waste on things like that," replied Sally. "And dad wouldn't let us use it anyway. He can't stand scent and make up and that sort of thing. I reckon he'd go along with that silly poem I heard the other day. It goes, 'little pots of powder, little pots of paint, make a girls complexion look what like it aint." And she grinned wickedly at her old friend. "Best be on our way then. We don't want to miss all the bargains do we? If we see anything we think you'd like, we'll come and find you." With that the two groups moved off in different directions, with different aspirations and very different ideas of entertainment in mind.

Pat's comments on donkeys or rather the absence of them anywhere on or within reach of these immaculate lawns, fell on deaf ears. Hilary and Sally were more interested in the here and now than a discussion on 'absent friends'. After a while she resigned herself reluctantly to this oversight on the part of the organisers of this event and lack of interest in her observations from Hilary and Sally, and followed the two girls around silently as they moved around the arena.

"I wonder what the time is," said Hilary after they had done the rounds of stalls with their offerings of fruit, vegetables and all sorts of miscellaneous items. "Look the flap of the tents open now, that must mean the judging's over and so forth. Let's go and have a look, shall we?"

As they re-entered the fuggy tent, they were surprised to see so many heaving bodies all bunched up around the various displays. A sensation of keen anticipation emanated from these disparate groups and, once tuned in to the individual voices, their exclamations of surprise or disappointment, their whoops of success were clearly audible. Sally, the first of the three to manage to claw her way through the throng of bodies to the handicrafts table, exclaimed loudly and in surprise, "look I've won first prize." Then she fell silent as she read the accompanying message. "It says here, 'a very neat piece of needlework, but why the teddies?' That's exactly what you said when I was making it Hilary," she said crossly. "If they ask me face to face I'll tell them same as I told you. What's wrong with putting teddies in Noah's Ark?" She lapsed into silence for a few moments as she digested this unwanted comment, and then her natural enthusiasm resurfaced. "Look we've all got prizes. Pat's doll's got a highly commended ticket on it, and yours says, 'Very neat. An imaginative use of materials and good colour combinations.' I like that, Hilary." Pat was grinning like a Cheshire cat by this time, clearly very proud that her 'raggy old dolly' as she had called it, had won this accolade from no less a person than a Judge. He clearly had a sense of humour after all, Sally thought to herself, and she decided there and then to forgive him for the comment he had made on her teddies.

Sally turned as Mrs Carter, who was standing close by, interrupted their eager chit-chat. "I haven't won a thing. I did this bit of embroidery in the winter of '42 when my rheumatics was pretty bad, that's why it looks a bit shaky," she was saying regretfully. "I've got another bit on the go though, I'll just have to see what I can do with that before the next show." They spent a few minutes commiserating with this deaf old lady, having to articulate every word to an embarrassingly loud degree of sound. It was only as they walked away, that Hilary remembered that Mrs Carter could lip-read, and for some reason they found this very amusing.

They moved around until they came to the vegetable produce stall and edged their way through to the front of the benches until they were able to examine the exhibits in detail. They were pleased to see that Mr Charlie Soan had won first prize for his cabbages, which he grew on his allotment. Sally remembered him telling them once, when they had stopped to watch him working, that when you started work on an allotment, the first thing you did was to mark out the boundaries of the plot and neaten up the edges. Once you've done that, you start digging or clearing from one end, planting or sowing your crops as you go. You can see what you're doing then. Sounds like common sense, he had said but you would be surprised at how many folk go at it like a bull in a china shop and then wonder why the hell it all goes pear shaped. She thought she knew what he meant. It was the same with needlework really.

The prizes were handed out by Mr Saville, a very grave looking man, but whose kindly eyes put Sally somewhat at her ease. She still felt a bit awkward and embarrassed however, as she received her half a crown prize money from his warm, weather-beaten hand. 'Well done,' was all he said and unable to formulate a reply, she walked away from him in silence.

Once the prize giving ceremony was over, they collected their exhibits and began to wend their way along with the rest of the crowd, towards the drive, which would lead them back on to the main road. They paused at the end of the driveway to admire the neatly clipped out shrubs and trees in the front gardens of the old Manor cottages. Each one had been carefully shaped to resemble in magnified proportions, the images of birds as well as various items of kitchenware. The girls had often watched fascinated, as Mr Blundell perching perilously on a pair of rickety steps, had clipped out with the utmost precision, these intricate shapes. Their favourite had to be the tea pot, with its spout curved at just the right angle, and it's ample body almost a replica of their old brown one at Sylvian.

The crowd had thinned out somewhat by the time Hilary, Pat and Sally made their way down the main street, their aim now to cover the distance between them and the promise of food, as quickly as they could. The chunk of gingerbread they had consumed earlier in the afternoon was now just a distant, tasty memory and they were starving. As they approached the old village pump, the thought of a draught of cold refreshing liquid, drew them towards this well of deliverance. They moved swiftly across the grass towards the pump itself, where they deposited their belongings onto one of its large, high backed wooden seats. Hilary was the first to reach the large iron handle and began to pump it up and down vigorously, then as the water began to gush out, Pat and Sally took it in turns to dip their cupped hands beneath the flow and slurped the reviving liquid gratefully into gasping mouths. Then Sally, after hastily wiping the back of her hand across her mouth, moved from forward to aft to take control of the pump, neatly side stepping Hilary who was more than ready for her turn at the receiving end.

Hilary bent forward, and Sally had a sudden vision of the black depths from which this water had been released and she shivered. The fear of deep dark wells was always there, but was mostly fixed firmly down into her subconscious mind. She must force herself to think of other things and get this fear back where it belonged.

As they walked wearily up the field on the last stage of their journey, mum came to the door. By the time they reached the top gate, Sally could tell by her body language that another chore awaited them.

"Tea's not ready yet, so I wondered if you'd pop up to Mrs Floyd's shop to get some soap flakes," said Mum. "She'll still be open, and I've got some blankets I want to get washed and dried while this weather holds. I thought I had some, but they're stuck hard to the bottom of the box and I just can't get them out.

I've cut you up a slice of fruit cake each to keep you going till teatime. Don't let your dad see, that's all."

A hint of a scowl appeared on Pat and Sally's faces, but Hilary intervened. "That's not far. It's only just the other side of Whydown Hill. It won't take us a minute. We don't mind, do we?" She smiled at the other two girls. The look that accompanied the smile however, left them in no doubt they had been well and truly compromised. Hilary would do anything for Mum.

"See if Mrs Floyd had got some prunes while you're up there," said Mum as they sat at the kitchen table eating their cake. " Then I can soak them overnight and stew them up tomorrow. You all like them, and they'll go nicely with a rice pudding."

Mrs Floyd's shop in Kent Street was small and cluttered, full to the brim with this and that, some things going back to the time of the ark, Sally reckoned. It also looked as though the roof was ready to cave in at any moment. It had looked that way for as far back as she could remember, but still it continued to weather the winter storms.

There was always a strong smell of paraffin and methylated spirits. This was in spite of the fact these pungent substances were stored in a lean-to shed outside the back door, in a vain attempt to avoid tainting the cheese and bacon.

For some reason the shop was often referred to as 'Dickie Bushes', and if she remembered rightly, it was something to do with The Great War. Whether this Dickie Bush had been a relative of Mrs Floyd, and had fought in this war or whether it was the name of some battle that had taken place at that time, she could not remember now. She would have to ask her dad. He was bound to know.

Mrs Floyd was able to supply them with a bag of prunes as well as the packet of soap flakes. She told them that their mother was welcome to anything that she stocked in her old shop. She also said their mum was one of a rare breed of ladies, whatever that meant, and added that they probably did not appreciate all that she did for them. Then she told them to run along home as fast as they could so that their mother could get her woollies washed and on to the line while the weather was fine. She reminded them how long woollen things took to dry, even at this time of the year, she said.

After this mild lecture, they left the shop and were approaching the entrance to Norton's Farm when they spied Dolly Pilbeam pottering around in her garden. She was short and plump and even from this distance, they could see the smile that always hovered around her mouth. The house in which she and her family lived, was the middle one of three clapboard cottages, which lay back several yards from the road and was reached by a narrow pathway.

"I hope she doesn't spot us," said Pat in a whisper, ducking her head instinctively, hoping the vegetation between them and this lady would conceal their whereabouts. "I like her, she's really nice but we can never get away from her, and I'm starving hungry. I don't want to stand around chatting, I just want to get home now and get some tea."

"You know she's got a boyfriend don't you?" said Sally, also in a whisper and with a furtive glance over her left shoulder, ready to take evasive action if necessary. "It's old Mr Weller, up the top of Whydown hill. I know boys exaggerate but several of them reckon they've seen the pair of them up in Jaybez's wood, kissing and cuddling. The first time they said was way back, last autumn when they were looking for chestnuts. They've followed them a few times since then but they've never been caught. I think it's a bit silly myself," she whispered, quite forgetting her own part in the pursuit of old Dicky Hayward and his girl friend.

"No I don't believe it. He's got to be ninety if he's a day, by the look of him. He's much to old for her, or anyone else for that matter, said Hilary standing upright now and quite forgetting to keep her voice down. "I've just got to ask her. No I won't ask her outright of course, but you know what she's like. It's so easy to coax things out of her. We won't stop now, we've got get home but I'd love to find out if it's true or not. We'll be seeing her again before long, we're bound to."

"Talking about the Pilbeam's, did you hear about that cat of theirs that fell down the old well in their back garden?" said Sally. They were out of sight and sound of Dolly by this time, with the need for stealth now unnecessary. "No, I didn't think you had," she added, as she saw their startled expressions. "I can't for the life of me remember who told me now. But anyway, they saw it go in when it missed its footing as it tried to jump across the top, but they couldn't do anything about it. They tried for ages to get it out. They kept lowering the bucket down into the well but the poor thing was too scared to climb into it. So in the end they just had to leave it there and it drowned of course. It was down there for ages until it fell to bits but they still kept drinking the water. Makes you feel sick, doesn't it? But then if there's no other water around, they wouldn't have had much choice, would they? All the people in those cottages share that well as far as I know. Anyway, eventually it came up in their old bucket bit by bit, but no one got sick or anything, which is surprising when you come to think of it. They must have strong stomachs, the people in those cottages."

"Thank goodness we've never needed to get a drink there and I never will now, neither," replied Pat wrinkling up her nose. "At least our cat can't fall into our tank and get drowned, because dad's put a top on it. That old well we used to have got filled in because Betty nearly fell down it, didn't it? Thank goodness for that."

"And our water goes through a filter, well through those pebbles anyway," replied Sally. "Nothing could get through that, I wouldn't think, except perhaps a worm or two, and we'd see them coming out of the tap. But that would be bad enough. Let's not think about things like that though, let's get home and have our tea. I'm starved." With that she stooped and picked two large clover heads and began sucking noisily on their nectar. "That's better," she said. "Now don't forget, Hazel's going to teach us another card game this evening."

***

Sally stretched, and with arms above her head, yawned widely. "It's been a long day and I'm tired," she said sleepily. "I'm full to the brim with jacket potatoes, cake and cocoa and my brain is aching with concentrating on this 'beat your neighbours out of doors card game. Much as I enjoyed playing it," she added hastily, looking towards Hazel as she spoke. She looked longingly across the room to where, at the back of the sideboard, lay her latest and possibly scariest Rupert book, all yellow bound and immaculate. She was very lucky. 'Jumbo' James the schoolteacher had allowed her to be the first to borrow the book from the school library and she was determined to keep it away from her little sisters' probing, indiscriminate and grubby little fingers. She adored Rupert and pictured him now as, dressed in his yellow check trousers with matching scarf and red jumper, he represented excitement, adventure but above all, good overcoming evil. This new story contained all her favourites. Bill the badger, Algy the pug, even Edward the elephant and Ozzie the kangaroo and of course, Tiger Lily. It would take the whole crew, she reckoned to overcome and oust that evil ruthless dragon from their kingdom. There were no mischievous elves in this one though, and she was thankful for that. They most certainly would have sided with the evil old dragon, and she dreaded to think what the outcome might have been then. She thought back to when she'd been in hospital, all those years ago and how Rupert had sustained her when that awful, painful feeling of homesickness had threatened to overwhelm her.

"Penny for your thoughts," said Hilary, leaning across the table and tapping her on the shoulder. "Daydreaming again you were. Anyone would think you'd had a busy day." And she grinned as her friend jumped and sat up with a guilty look on her face.

"I was only thinking about Rupert," was all she could think of saying by way of an explanation, and it was true anyway. "And I have had a busy day," she added indignantly.

CHAPTER 4

It was a grey, misty morning but this did nothing to diminish the feeling of excitement or quell the buzz of activity that accompanied the start of the hop-picking season.

Groups of women and children stood around chatting and watching as large, open backed lorries disgorged their cargoes of canvas and wooden bins. As these were stacked against thick poles, which had been hammered into the soil, a group of young men stood nearby waiting to position them at the end of the long rows of bines. As the women watched this operation, they were also assessing the quality of the cone shaped hops which, generously interspersed with lush green leaves, hung down on thick stems from the mother plant.

"This one's for me!" Shouted Mrs Maplesden, pushing rudely past a group of eager women. "There's some good 'uns in this row. I know, I've had a good old butchers at 'em. They're all hanging down regular like, nice and easy to pick." And she grinned around wickedly at the group of women, now watching her mostly in stony silence, though one or two were tutt-tutting to themselves. By the time she had finished the sentence, she had moved her considerable bulk to the bin of her choice, the disapproving sounds going on around her not worrying her in the least.

"It doesn't matter to me where we go," whispered Hilary moving towards the back of the crowd. "One row of hops looks the same as the next one to me, darned if I can see any difference. They're all hops after all and even if some of them are manky, they've all got to be picked."

In a surprisingly short time, order suddenly came out of mild chaos and all the bins stood like cross legged sentinels at the edge of the field, soon to begin their slow, snail like progress down between the straight and orderly rows of bines.

"Right, stand well back while I pull this, or you'll get covered in wet pollen and goodness knows what else," said Hilary as she prepared to pull down the first thick bine. She reached up and gripped the long length of thick, sinuous creeper firmly between both hands and, with one jerk, brought the whole lot down and across the bin. "Right that's it then. Lets see how far up the row we can get before dinner time."

Later, as Sally took time to look around, she noticed several small children picking hops into upturned umbrellas and old wicker baskets. She smiled as she studied their facial expressions and the way they sat. She was particularly taken by the way they picked the hops, carefully one by one from the leafy branches, and dropping them down into the various containers. She wondered how long this task would hold their interest and when they would weary of the task and scamper off across the fields, seeking more interesting forms of entertainment.

"Right, its time we picked out some of the leaves," said Hilary breaking into her thoughts. "The measurer's coming and we don't want to get a reputation for having a dirty bin, do we?" With that she stooped and began the unenviable task of bin cleaning.

As Sally followed suit, busily swishing the contents of the bin around to extract the larger leaves, she felt her legs being firmly grasped and suddenly she was propelled head first into the bin. As she scrabbled up, covered in hops and pollen, she saw Denis Crow's face grinning down at her. "Got yer," he said with the utmost satisfaction. "I've bin waitin' to get me own back on you ever since you threw that sand in me face, down Crazy Lane that time." With that he turned around, squared his shoulders, and made his way back over to where his mother, head down, carried on picking hops into the bin they were sharing, as though nothing had happened.

Hilary's face was a mixture of concern and mirth as she gazed down at her friend. "You don't half look a sight," were her first words as she leaned over the bin and began to pull at Sally's arms, clothing and anything else she could get a grip on. "Mind the hops," she said worriedly as Sally scrabbled around trying to regain her balance. "They're already squashed to bits. We've probably lost a couple of bushels now and all because of that bully over there. It's no wonder he's got no friends, the way he behaves."

Every time Sally glanced in Denis' direction, he was looking at her and grinning like a Cheshire cat. "I'll knock that grin right off his face one of these days," Sally hissed through clenched teeth, when it had happened for the umpteenth time. "I've a good mind to stick one of those land measurers down his neck when I get one. That'll make him squirm. On second thoughts, I couldn't be that cruel – to a caterpillar, that is. I'll just have to think of something else, and I will. Don't you worry about that."

"I wouldn't dream of worrying about it." Replied Hilary, grinning. "I know you will! Anyway, it'll soon be dinner time, and if I'm not mistaken, someone's already lit the fire." She lifted her head up and began to sniff the fragrant wood smoke drifting on the air.

"I can taste the tea already," she said, as she pointed over to where a pile of faggots were just beginning to crackle and spit, sending up jets of bright sparks, which died as quickly as they were born. "I hardly touch tea at home but here in the hop fields, it's always bloody delicious. It's the smoke and fresh air, I suppose, and it's always lovely and sweet. There's always enough sugar in it to make it tasty, not like at home. Every time I put my spoon into the sugar bowl, mum calls out, 'now go easy with that sugar. It's still on ration you know.' Makes me really nervous she does. Anyway, we've brought enough milk with us to have two cups if we want. I'm starving, aren't you?"

"You bet," replied Sally with feeling. "I can't wait to get my teeth into mum's apple pie. No one makes apple pies like my mum, do they? And we've got spam sandwiches and fish paste as well. Come on with that tea," she added, more to herself than to anyone in particular, glancing impatiently towards the young man who was busy controlling the fire and waiting for the steam to rise up from the billycan.

Later that afternoon, as Hilary moved the stripped bines from around her feet, she spotted a 'hop dog'. The furry yellow caterpillar was motionless, its back arched in an unnatural way. "Look at it, poor little thing," she said cradling it in the palm of her hand. "I hope we didn't kill it. I can't see a thing wrong with it, can you?" And she passed the little creature into Sally's wary hand.

"I expect it's got internal injuries or something like that," replied Sally seriously having heard that expression at some time or other. She was wondering as she gazed at this little grub, why she felt a sort of compassion for it. Something as small as this wouldn't have feelings surely, she thought to herself. Out loud she said. "Lets just take it back down the row and cover it with a few old bines. That'll stop the birds and things eating it. And she hurried off a few paces back down the row to perform the last rites on this little creature.

Later, as they piled into the back of the lorry that was to take them home again, Sally noticed that Denis Crow had an angry red weal on his face that went across his left cheek and right down his neck. As he saw her looking at him, he mumbled, "me mam pulled one of them scratchy bines right down on top of me and it caught me good and proper. She could have warned me in time. She never even said sorry. She said I should've been paying attention to what she was doin' and not gawping around. It's really sore, it'll probably go septic," he said sulkily. "She's right murdy these days me mam. Cept wiv me bruvver and e's a bloody goody-goody."

"I expect you were too busy thinking how clever you were to have tipped me into the bin," said Sally. "As your mam said, you should have been paying attention." Secretly though she felt rather uneasy. Could she possibly have had something to do with his accident? After all she had spent a good half hour angrily and secretly plotting revenge on him. She would have to curb her anger in future and try to keep her thoughts of revenge at a lower key. It would not be easy she feared. People like Denis made her so cross at times. He did look pathetic though sitting there with that woe-begotten look on his face. And just like that last time in Crazy lane, she began to feel sorry for him.

To the disappointment of most of the youngsters in the back of the lorry, the driver took his vehicle sedately over the hump back bridge that spanned the river at the bottom of Bodiam hill. On the outward journey, Sally had been caught totally unaware by the lorry's sudden spurt towards the bridge, taking off like a bat out of hell. Her stomach had left its normal position and elevated itself to some higher plane, as all four tyres left the road at the same time and the lorry bumped its unsteady way down to the bottom of the bridge. She'd had to swallow hard to force it down again and the discomfort had lasted for a few minutes. She didn't fancy a repeat performance, no fear. Those youngster's who were bemoaning the drivers' lack of bravado, were crazy, she reckoned. Who in their right mind would clamour to be frightened out of their skins by a maniacal driver, bent on giving his passengers the jitters, mental and physical, she wondered. It just did not make sense. Butterflies in the stomach one of them called it. To her it was more like having a blooming hedge-hog down there.

At last they were home, or very nearly anyway. As soon as the lorry came to a halt at Paygate corner, the women and children spilled out with all their accompanying goods and chattels, to make their weary way home to their cottages. For the women anyway, the toil was not yet over. There would still be a meal to prepare and sandwiches to be cut and packaged ready for the next day's picking. The very first chore for them on reaching home however, would be to scrub their hands free from the thick yellow hop resin, which stuck stubbornly to the skin and always took a minute or two to remove.

Hilary was going home to have some dinner and a quick wash, and she would soon be back up to Sylvian to call for Sally. They had already planned an evening adventure, and would probably stay out until it was almost dark.

Later that evening, as Hilary and Sally sat dangling their legs from the thick, low branch of their tree seat in Crazy lane, their chatter was mostly about trying to calculate the final tally of their earnings from all the hops they would have stripped into their bin by the time the season came to an end. According to their calculations, they should have enough to buy a coat, shoes, socks and knickers and things, and even enough to buy a couple of dress lengths of material if they were lucky, and worked really hard.

Hilary's mum had already shown them a dress pattern that she had been using since before the war. It had a round neck and was tight fitting down to the waist. Then it flared out from there into a really full skirt, the material cut on the cross for this section of the dress. What made the dress just a little bit special however, was an oval piece of material that was stitched at the front centre, to hold in place the narrow lengths of material used to circle the waist and that were then fastened at the back with a bow. They were quite excited at the challenge of this project and only hoped that they would have, not just the money, but also enough clothing coupons for all these things. They would also be able to use the sewing machine at school. Sally could not wait. She had watched her dad working away on his old machine enough times and apart from the fact that he worked his with a treadle, leaving his hands free to guide the material through with both hands, they were much the same really. As Hilary said, it was just a question of hand coordination and more importantly, making sure you kept your fingers well away from the needle as it bobbed up and down over the material. It had to be worth that risk however, even though stitching your fingers would be a bloody and painful experience. Not only would the stitching be neater done on one of these machine, but think how much sooner the dress would be finished and ready to wear.

Thinking about dad, machines and making things, reminded Sally of something Uncle Alf had told her while he was fixing a puncture on her bike recently, and she grinned as she reiterated this tale to her friend. He had told her how her dad had put a bicycle together from bits and pieces he had found on scrap heaps and such places when he was a boy. To start with, he had shaped a piece of wood for the saddle and covered it with one of gran's old Tammy hats, but he did improve on the design as time went on because it made his bum sore. Uncle Alf said that he could never afford or find tyres for the thing so he rode it around on its metal rims. ' Rattled like hell it did, but it got your dad where he wanted to go a whole lot quicker than shankses pony,' were his exact words. Followed by, 'make do and mend, that's what us lot were all about in those days, and still are if the truth be known.' And then he had chuckled as he elaborated on the story, telling her how the racket had scared all the old stray cats and dogs in the neighbourhood half to death. 'They ran a mile when they heard him coming,' he said. 'They must have thought old Beelzebub himself was out to get them.'

Hilary grinned while she was telling her this story, and Sally was half regretful that she had mentioned Beelzebub at all. The mention of the word had fired up her friend's imagination, and she began to invent all sorts of elaborate stories in connection with this nemesis of theirs until Sally expected to see the apparition himself appear round the corner on his drop handle bicycle. She was quite relieved when her friend suddenly changed the subject.

"Look, there's red ants down there, thousands of them, and they're the ones that bite you," Said Hilary, peering more closely. With that, she pulled up her legs smartly until her knees were almost under her chin, continuing to observe the little creatures from a sideways position. "Better get your legs up as well, just in case. I know they don't quite reach the ground like mine do but I expect they can jump, those ants. You'll soon know it if they do, they can't half sting," she warned, as she continued to observe them from a safe distance.

Having given Sally time to tuck her legs up safely, she continued.

"They're busy little things, aren't they? Always rushing around, and it makes you wonder what they're up to most of the time. Your dad reckons they're well organised in their own way. They work together for the common good of each and every ant. Wasn't it Communists of the insect world or something, he called them? He reckons that they work together in a way that human beings would never do. A bit like bees and things, I suppose really, and he did mention them as well. He does say some strange things at times your dad, doesn't he? But he does say a lot of things that make sense really when you think about them, and he does make you laugh at times. When he's in a good mood, that is." Hilary's grin widened as she recalled something else.

"Remember the other day when he was telling us about old Mrs Evans, down the lane?" she continued. "She'd asked him if he'd upholster a couple of chairs for her, hadn't she, and when he went down there to have a look at them, she was eating her breakfast. When she came to the door to let him in, one of her cats jumped up onto the kitchen table and started to chew up the bit of bacon on her plate. Your Dad said she just took it out of the cat's mouth, put it back on the plate without even washing it and then she ate it herself. He's not fussy, as you well know. Well he couldn't be, with all those stinky things he uses on his vegetables, could he? But he said it made him feel really sick. He turned down the cup of tea she offered him and I can't say I blame him. She lets them crawl all over the place, those cats. They're in and out of any cupboard she leaves open, and they're always all over the table sniffing around and licking any food that she leaves out."

Sally grinned and then she started giggling. "Sorry, I was thinking about what you said about dad not being fussy. Obviously, you've never seen him pick up the cod liver oil spoon by mistake and stir his tea with it, have you? He spits and splutters and carries on as though mum had tried to poison him. I wouldn't mind so much if he didn't make us take the stuff. He says it'll give us strong bones or something. He didn't take it when he was a kid, I know that for a fact but his bones seem to be tough enough without.

Still I'm a bit fussy, I suppose, but only about the fat on meat," she concluded. Except crispy bacon fat of course, that's bloody delicious. But I hate all other fat. It makes me heave. I'd rather eat six plates of stringy cabbage – well I think I would. I've never exactly tried it. But as you were saying, dad has got a strong stomach for most things. He doesn't bat an eyelid when he empties the lavvy bucket, or makes up that smelly feed for his vegetables but a snifter of cod liver oil sends him into some kind of frenzy."

They sat quietly for a while but soon they felt a damp coolness on the air that made them shiver. They jumped off the bough, completely forgetting the red ants and began to make their way home. As they were passing the hedgerow that formed the north boundary of Amy's garden, Sally peered into the thick undergrowth hoping for a glimpse of the iridescent glow-worms that she'd spotted there many times before. They were magical little creatures and not worms at all, but little beetles. When she had first seen them, she had shone her torch on them, and their lights had been immediately extinguished. If she had not known just where they were, she would not have been able to spot them. They were so well camouflaged.

"It's not dark enough yet," said Hilary, knowing exactly what Sally was looking for. "Once you can count a hundred stars in the sky, then you just might spot what you're looking for. They're there, those glow worms but they'll not be showing off until it's a lot darker than this and then only if they're trying to attract a mate. Tell you what, we'll have a look along here on Saturday evening when you're staying at my house. Another thing we'll do on Saturday is to pop up to Beanford farm to find out if those pears of Mrs Partridges' are ripe enough yet. She always lets us pick up the windfalls, and as far as I'm concerned they're the sweetest of the lot. They might be small and some are a bit scabby on the outside but they're bloody delicious. I often swallow them down core an all."

"We'll take a couple of dad's buckets over with us, that's what we usually do, and if Len's around, he'll give us a hand with them, he's good like that. And even Porky, who's always busy, has popped a few in our buckets when he's been around," replied Sally. "He's a good bloke is Porky, and I sometimes feel a bit guilty about him. It's because the older girls gave him a hard time with all the mischief they used to get up to on his farm, I suppose. No wonder he got angry with them."

She paused suddenly as Hilary grabbed her arm with one hand and pointed along the road with the other. "Look there's old Mrs Stapleton coming along the road," she whispered. "There look, just this side of Paygate corner. I wonder what she's doing so far from home and so late in the evening. I expect it's got something to do with hop picking." And they both leaned as far as they could into the shelter of the thick hedge and watched as she passed by. They stood watching silently until she had reached the bend in the road, leading towards Farrows steps, then they both started talking at once, which made them giggle nervously.

"Tell you what, I wouldn't trust her any further than I could see her," said Sally having got the upper hand conversation wise. "Micky Marsden who lives next door to her reckons she poisoned his cat. All it did was to scratch up her garden to do its business a couple of times that's all. And they've got to go somewhere, haven't they? He said she always keeps a bucket of water and a few bits of brick just inside her back door and she's pretty accurate with both. It's not always cats she chucks things at either. He said him and some of the other boys have had to duck and run when she's caught them looking over her hedge. They're trying to catch her out doing something bad they said. His mum reckons she gets out in her garden at about midnight, when there's a full moon. She mutters to herself and she, his mum I mean, is frightened to death that she might be casting some sort of evil spell on them. She's an old cow I reckon," she concluded, moving a little closer to her friend for comfort.

"Don't say that," replied Hilary at once. "I like cows and I love beef. Except the fat of course, that's foul. You'll just have to think of some way else to describe her, like an old besom or something. Yes that'll do, an old besom. I don't know what it means but it sounds right. I wonder what those boys round East View Terrace call her? It's bound to be rude. Anyway, she's gone now, and look how dark it's getting. Best get a move on or Mum'll start worrying. I'll see you up to your house, don't worry," she added hastily. "I wish I were staying up with you so we could go off together in the morning but there you go. You can't have everything, can you?"

They climbed through the gap in the hedge, avoiding as far as possible, the tangle of stinging nettles that grew in profusion here, and made their way towards Paygate corner. By the time they had climbed the field and reached the top gate, it was quite dark. Although they had been chatting away all evening, they still spent a few more minutes standing and talking on the underground water tank. They were reluctant to part company, and unwilling to leave such a special day behind them.

As Hilary left, Sally stood on the underground tank and watched as her figure began to fade into the darkness. Then she waited, lips pursed ready to return the whistle, which would signal Hilary's arrival at her gate. It puzzled her that Hilary showed no fear of the dark whereas she, a consummate coward, regarded every shadow with the utmost suspicion. She had never really understood why she was like this, so different from Hilary. She was what she was and that was that and all about it. Perhaps, who knew, one day she would learn to be brave.

***

It was late Saturday afternoon, and Hilary and Sally had arranged to meet Willie and Roy on the pump seat in the village. They were just waiting for Mr and Mrs Elkins to go out then they would escort Hilary's little brother, Ronald, over to the Winchesters' house as had already been arranged, and then they would be on their way. They had given the boys an approximate time rather than an exact one for the meeting, so they would not get moaned at for being late. Hilary's parents knew where they were going and their only stipulation was that the girls be home before dark.

Once they had seen Ronald safely settled, they walked briskly up through Crazy Lane, down Chapel Hill and into the village. From the top of the hill they could make out figures on the pump seat but it was only as they approached the bridge that they could make out who they were. As they made their way across the grass, Willy and Roy jumped up from the seat and came trotting down towards them.

"Well here you are then at last, you're late. But better late than never," said Willie and then he grinned. "Alright, alright you're not late then," he added swiftly, as he noted Sally's disapproving glance. "Our bums are pretty sore though, with all this sitting about and waiting. We were just trying to decide which way you'd be walking and then we were going to come and meet you."

"Well we're here now." Said Sally, " but we've got time for a bit of a sit down before we go back down the road," she added as she walked up to the seat. As she sank down for a brief rest, she whispered, "Don't look now, but I think old Mr Cooper's on his way over here, tin hat and all. I expect he's been on his own all day and needs someone to talk to."

"Hello Mr Cooper," She said looking up at the old man, feigning surprise at his sudden appearance. "Here, sit down with us."

She ignored the barely suppressed groans of the two boys, and continued to talk to him. "There's no need to wear your tin hat now, the war's over," she told him. Then as she complemented him on his singing in the Chapel choir, the boys began to fall about with laughter. Hilary and Sally joined in, trying all the while to disguise their mirth. The old man was deaf as a post and sang enthusiastically, but right out of tune and pace with the rest of the Chapel choir. The youngsters always snickered and giggled, as the rest of the congregation tried with varying degrees of success to drown him out. Mr Smith, who often took the service, had been asked many a time to speak to him about it but his reply had always been the same. 'We are all God's creatures and should be allowed to communicate with him in our own individual way,' he always replied. And that was that.

"Right beezled I am," said Mr Cooper, ignoring their giggling. "I've been out all day with old Percy Ferret, not 'is real name, of course, but that's what us always calls him, suits him it do. One of the best gamekeepers 'e was in 'is day. We've got ourselves a few rabbits and accidentally on purpose 'e up and went and shot a pheasant. It's diddy but there be enough on it for me. I ain't fussy. We got a fair number of squoggers too."

"What's a squogger?" asked Sally.

"Grey squirrel, destructive things they be. Come from America. Not like our little red uns, they don't do no harm. Course we wont eat them, though I've eaten 'em in the past and very tasty they be too. A bit more gamey in flavour 'en a rabbit, I'd say they were. As far as I'm concerned all wildlife is either eatable or vermin."

"That's a bit of a horrid thing to say, " Hilary called over to him, raising her voice and accentuating every syllable so that he was able to hear her from that distance. "What about birds then, they're not food or vermin, well mostly not anyway."

"Depends how you looks at things, don't it," he replied. "Now when I was a young un, we netted any old bird we could get hold of. We took 'em home and our mams never complained, no fear they didn't. They just plucked or skinned even the diddiest of 'em and served 'em up all ways. Mostly roasted or stewed they were. They knew what to do with 'em. Trouble is, with you youngsters these days, in spite of this war, you be too well fed. You don't know what it feels like to be really hungry. You think that getting a bit of an appetite is what hunger is all about, well it bloody isn't. What I'm talking about is real hunger. That gnawing away at your guts kind of feeling. Ask your dad, he and me have done a bit of talking from time to time and he weren't always what you'd call well nourished. He's known the time when he's got home from school, hungry as a rat and all there was to eat, if anything, was a bowl of watery rice. It weren't his mam's fault. She took in washing and all sorts. It were just the way things were in them days. Lots of kids got rickets and T.B. especially up in them big cities and towns. Well, there ain't no rabbits and wildlife much up there to shoot or ferret, is there now? And not much room to grow fruit and veg and things. Just count yer blessings, you young uns. As for you, young lassie," he said, fixing Sally with his beady eyes. "I mind the time your dad wheeled you into the village with that arm of yours. White as a ghost you were and all over frightened. Fracture was it? You look a mite less timorous now, if I might say so."

Sally shuddered, remembering all too well the painful incident.

Roy stifled a yawn. "Come on you lot. It's getting late, I want to see what's in that cellar, and it'll soon be too dark. Basil's been down there, and he says that you can stand up without banging your head. He's often been down there since the people moved out of the place and he says it's been made into sort of rooms with open doorways." He was smiling enthusiastically now, tiredness forgotten. "And there's a big rocking horse down there as well."

"Yes, we'd best be on our way. We'll leave you to it, Mr Cooper," said Hilary rising to her feet and smiling at the old man. "We'll remember what you told us. Come on then, Sal," she said, putting her hands under Sally's armpits and pulling her onto her feet. "Chop-chop girl, look lively," she said, as she and the boys began to make their way from the pump seat and down across the Green. "If we go back up Chapel Hill and down Crazy Lane, we'll be able to get to the Lavender Bowl cellar through Basil's garden."

"Hang on a minute, didn't Jean and Amy say they wanted to come with us?" Sally suddenly said, frowning. "They're just as curious about the cellar as we are. As we're this far we might as well carry on up, then we can pop down the twitten to call for them. It won't take long."

As they walked briskly up Chapel Hill, Sally looked at the clump of coltsfoot, which was growing on the bank opposite the Chapel. It had been there forever, she reckoned, never changing its position. It neither expanded nor shrank, but just stood in its little bit of ground apparently doing nothing. Plants were living creatures, she knew that, but unlike chickens and other animals, they survived by ways unfathomable to her. She could never imagine any human being having the patience and fortitude of all these other creatures and life forms. If God made everything then his ways were certainly difficult to understand.

After they had called for Jean and Amy, they hurried along eager to get down into the cellar and investigate its treasures. Basil was nowhere to be seen as they crossed the bottom of his garden and made there way towards the boundary between the Winchesters bungalow and the garden of Lavender Bowl Cottage. He had told them he and Ronald might be waiting, but no doubt they had become impatient and had decided to go off somewhere with Basil's old terrier instead. As they crawled through the hedge they fell silent, each preoccupied with the task of crossing the garden unseen. Crouching low, they crept along the hedgerow, Crazy Lane side, until they drew level with the cellar entrance, then in one movement they leapt across the short distance between the hedge and cellar door, and disappeared. Although the place was empty, they were anxious not to be caught trespassing. Not only would it spoil their fun, but they knew they would get a good ticking off from anyone who recognised them.

"I don't think anyone saw us, do you," said Willie. It's a bit dark in here though. Didn't anyone think to bring a torch?" The silence that followed gave him the answer.

"Never mind, I think we can see far enough without one, for now anyway," he said after a short pause. "A bit spooky, isn't it, like going down into the bowels of the earth, if you know what that's like," he whispered, as they crept further into the cellar.

"Where's Roy?" he whispered fearfully after a few minutes of groping his way through the gloomy dank interior. "He was here a minute ago." As he paused to listen, there was a sudden movement and he jumped sky high as Roy's head popped up over an upturned bedstead. "You silly bugger, you frightened the life out of me," he said as he recognised his old mate. "I thought old Beelzebub had got you. Who does he remind you of?" he asked looking back through the gloom towards the girls. I'll give you a clue then," he added as they stood there shuffling their feet. "What no bloody torch!"

In a split second the word 'Chad' echoed through the chamber and they all giggled nervously. Then he changed his mind. "No, come to think of it you look more like old Tintin, that's who. Where's your dog then?" He added giggling with relief.

"Shush, not so much noise, you boys, this is a serious business," whispered Jean. "I only came down here because Hilary and Sally kept on about it. And I did remember to bring a torch so there. I just didn't think we needed it back there." With that she took the reassuring beacon of light out of her pocket and directed its beam around the gloomy space.

"Look, there's the old rocking horse Basil was telling us about!" Hilary exclaimed, butting in on her sister's half-hearted reprimand. "Bags first go!"

She broke away from the group and made her way over to the carved wooden shape standing majestically at the far end of the room.

Even in this light, the signs of wear and tear were clear to see. As Hilary rocked it to and fro, it was clear from the squeaks and creaks that it needed a good oiling as well as a lick of paint. "Your go now, Sal," said Hilary, cocking her leg over the saddle and sliding gracefully back onto the ground. "I reckon Jean and Amy think they're too grown up for such things. They don't know what they're missing."

After a while they moved further into the cellar, and noticed piles of old hessian sacks full of goodness knows what, and tied up securely with bits of string.

"It don't feel like bodies or anything like that," said Roy, poking the sacks with his forefinger and laughing nervously at the same time. "But I don't intend looking inside to find out, no thank you. But look at this old pub sign. This is really interesting. Blowed if I can make out where it's come from. There's not enough light coming through that dirty old window to see what it says. Here, Jean, bring your torch over and see if that makes any difference."

He grabbed the torch and after trying unsuccessfully to read the writing on its peeling surface, he directed its beam further afield. Sally gasped as the light revealed a wall covered by rusty old chains, hanging on massive hooks and nails driven into the rough brick wall. They were thick and heavy. In the dim light, they exuded a kind of undefined malevolence.

"I wonder what these were used for," said Roy, clearly surprised and affected by the sight of so much hardware in a place like this. "Perhaps it was used to shackle prisoners down in those dungeons in the old days. Or it might even have been used in those slave ships that I've seen pictures of in the history books at School. They really had a tough time of it, those slaves," he added, now letting his imagination run away with him.

"How the hell they got here I've no idea. But they give me the bloody creeps," and he shivered involuntarily.

Then Amy took the torch and moved forward purposefully. The others followed, examining objects as the beam exposed their hiding places. Several trunks stood on the floor, some covered in material with a kind of thick decorative ribbon around their lids. And right up against one wall stood an old clothes wringer, with a huge intricately decorated cast iron handle. They were in the process of examining it, and discussing how on earth anyone had managed to get such a thing down into a place like this, when Hilary shushed them.

"There's somebody moving about upstairs," she whispered, grabbing Sally's shoulder. "Listen, you can hear them talking now. Who the hell can it be? There's nobody living here. Perhaps it's someone who wants to move in and if it is, they'll be down here sooner or later to have a look round. We'd better make ourselves scarce. Come on you lot, don't just stand there," she said, pushing the two boys forward and falling in behind them with Sally, leaving the other girls to follow in their wake.

As they crept towards the cellar entrance, Roy, who was in the lead, caught his sleeve on one of the rough logs stacked just inside the doorway. The stack came tumbling down with an almighty clatter. Then, as they stood there in stunned silence, someone let Polly out of prison, and they all started giggling uncontrollably. At the same time they heard a man's raised voice shouting, "what the hell was that? Must be rats or something down in the cellar. We'd better take a look."

They all gasped, then instinctively rushed forward and scrabbled through the doorway falling into the garden. As they picked themselves up, they heard the same voice calling out, "It's not rats it's kids, bloody kids! Look they're running off down the garden right now!"

The bloody kids rushed headlong across the grass, and shot through the gap in Basil's hedge, across his garden, through a gap in the next hedge, and fell and scrabbled down the bank and into Crazy Lane.

"Quick, across the road before they see us. Get into Gosse's field!" Ordered Hilary. "They'll never catch us then. We'll have to go through Stafford's wood, up to Cottage Lane and then back down Crazy Lane and through the twitten there," she puffed as she scrabbled up the opposite bank. As she burst through into Gosse's field, she looked around her. "Where's Jean and Amy then?" she asked anxiously. "I thought they were behind us. I hope they haven't got caught, that's all. No they wouldn't be that silly. They had plenty of time to get out in time. Perhaps they got through the side gate without being seen. I can just imagine them walking down the lane in that ladylike way of theirs, as though butter wouldn't melt in their mouths. That's something we'd never get away with, Sal," she added, with a breathless giggle.

As they made their roundabout way homeward, they chatted nineteen to the dozen but always with watchful eyes and ears, keened to pick up any untoward sound that might threaten their freedom. By the time they reached the twitten, with its close proximity to Lavender Bowl Cottage, they had instinctively lowered their voices to a whisper. It had suddenly occurred to them that they did not have the faintest idea what the visitors at the cottage looked like. They would simply have taken off like a streak of lightning if any strange face had appeared anywhere near them, no matter who they might be.

When they thought they were safe, and were feeling a little less guilty, Sally broke the silence. "Do you remember Dickie Sutton who lived here with his family at one time?" she asked. "I wonder why they moved out? They weren't there for long, were they? They were related to Griff and Ron Griffin you know, that's probably why they moved here in the first place. We never seemed to get on with old Dickie, did we? Nor did Basil and his lot. He had a withered arm and a little leg, but none of us as far as I know ever teased him about it, not like we were always teasing Ellen Brown. Now we did give her a hard time. That is until mum told us off, and didn't she have a go at us! Mind you, we were unkind to Ellen when you think about it, walking just behind her and pretending to hold our knickers up like she does. She used to go mad at us, didn't she?"

As they sauntered through the twitten, relaxed and at ease now, they saw Mr Geering pottering about in his garden. They stopped for a while to admire his immaculate lawns, surrounded on three sides by deep borders, still ablaze with an assortment of flowers and shrubs. Partially hidden by a slatted wooden fence was his substantial vegetable plot. He grew asparagus, just like Mr Rudge, whose garden abutted this one, but on the main road. Sally could see the frondy foliage moving gently in the soft breeze and was reminded of her mum's fondness for this delicacy. She herself couldn't stand the slimy stuff. In fact it made her retch. But for a month or two in the spring, her mum would eat it until it almost came out of her ears. These two avid and successful gardeners knew this and almost on a daily basis, would trudge up the field with a neat bundle for her to steam and devour. It was her one and only luxury, as far as Sally could tell.

As her eyes travelled back to Mr Geering, she was struck as always by his curious appearance. He had been involved in an accident years ago while out on his police duties. Dad had told her this when curiosity got the better of her and she had asked him. He had tried to stop a car, reported stolen, by walking out in front of it, and holding his hand up. This sounded quite foolish to Sally, and not something she could imagine this staid and sensible old man to have done. Anyway, this once tall and well-proportioned man was almost dwarf like now with the bandiest legs Sally had ever seen. He was lucky to be alive, let alone walk again, dad had told her, and the fact that he had lost at least six inches from his height was a small price to have paid for this, he reckoned. 'He's a tough old blighter. In his hey-day he was a power to be reckoned with. That old motor was the only thing that ever got the better of him,' dad had said with a chuckle.

The sun was now well down as they continued on their way, through the twitten and towards Hilary's house. In the fading light, as Sally glanced sideways, she could just make out her own house, nestling in the side of the field, with the last of the evening sun lighting up its attic windows with an orange glow. Sylvian was the friendliest house in the whole wide world, thought Sally.

"Let's take a short cut through here," said Hilary pointing towards the piece of ground to their left, which was covered in rough grass and thistles. No mans land as they called it. As the boys ran on ahead, she suddenly remembered the old well that was situated right in line with them and the entrance to Hilary's garden. "Mind the old well over there, it's been mostly filled in now but there's still a big hole there. Look, it's right ahead of you now, slow down!" Hilary shouted. But she was too late. Before he had had time to reply, Roy just disappeared as though into thin air. Sally shrieked in horror, then grabbed Hilary's arm and they just stood rooted to the ground for a few seconds. Willie, who had been just behind his friend, was now looking into the hole and scratching his head in puzzlement. Then he turned and grinned at the girls and they, partially reassured, began to move forward gingerly for a closer inspection. Roy was just sitting there, the top of his head a few inches below the level of the ground and he was covered in dust and bits of straw and bracken, and by his body language, feeling rather sorry for himself. What had once been a working well was now reduced to a receptacle for any old building rubble and garden waste and it was lucky for Roy that Hilary and Sally had recently put that thick layer of straw and bracken in the bottom while they were making up the thing to use as a den. The cover to the well, suffering from the ravages of time, had been set aside and lost in all the long grass. It probably wouldn't even have fitted the hole, which by this time, had been enlarged by many interfering hands.

"Don't just stand there gawping, give us a hand up will you," pleaded Roy, still very much in a sitting position but with his arms stretched upwards and indeed looking very sorry for himself. "I don't know why you wanted to come across here anyway, it's not much of a short cut. I just hope I haven't broken any bones, that's all. You could at least have given us a bit more warning."

"You didn't give us a chance. You went across that grass like a long dog and disappeared before we could say Jack Robinson," said Sally, trying not to snigger. "You look a bit like Basil's old dog when it comes up out of a hole. I hope you're not going to twist round and round on your backside like she normally does, that's all. We'll throw you back in again if you do."

With that they all bent down, and as Willie grasped him by the scruff of his neck, the girls took hold of an arm each and hoisted him, with his back to the side of the well, out into the open again. "You don't half look a sight," giggled Sally, as she and Hilary began dusting him down. "And you weigh a ton, too. Though nobody would guess that by the look of you. Never mind, there don't seem to be any broken bones, and your trousers will live to see another day. In fact by the time we've finished with you no one, least of all your mum, will guess that you've been wallowing about in dust holes. Looking for buried treasure, were you?" she asked, sounding unsympathetic, though secretly feeling very relieved that he had surfaced safe and sound, mostly for his sake, but also from a feeling of guilt. She and Hilary had been unaware that this den of theirs represented danger of any kind to anyone. It just had not entered their heads.

"It's not funny, I could have really hurt myself," Roy replied sulkily and sounding a bit sorry for himself. "I wondered where the hell I was going. I really thought I was a goner, do you know that? That's bloody dangerous that hole. It's about time someone sorted out a decent cover for it. That's something we could see to, Willie," he added, looking round at his friend. "We could make one easily with a few planks of wood and a bit of roofing felt. I can't see these two doing anything about it."

As they made their way slowly towards the boundary between 'no man's land' and Hilary's garden, Sally began to hum the tune to, 'Ding dong bell, pussy's in the well,' looking sideways at Roy as she did so. He however, looked straight ahead, totally ignoring her jibe and then after a short silence began to chant, "There was a little girl and she had a little curl, right in the middle of her forehead. When she was good she was very, very good but when she was bad she was horrid." He did not as much as glance in Sally's direction but she knew, without a shadow of doubt that he was trying to get his own back on her. Serves me right, she thought to herself.

"Let's have some cocoa, I think there's enough milk if we have it half and half," said Hilary, once they had reached the house. "Looks like Jean and Amy got away from the Lavender Bowl safe and sound," she said, as she picked up a note left on the table for her. " Its from Jean. She says that they ran through the side gate and then just walked away down the road as though nothing had happened. She did glance back just the once she says, and saw three people looking up and down the road, but for some reason they didn't seem to think that she and Amy had had anything to do with it. I told you they could turn on the old adult bit, didn't I?" Hilary paused to read on.

"Amy's gone home by the way, and Jean is staying with friends overnight. But I knew that anyway. I mustn't forget to pick Ronald up from over the way. He's supposed to be indoors by nine-thirty. Anyway that still gives us time for a game of cards and our cocoa. What about 'Beat your neighbour out of doors.' Pass us the cups, please Sal," she said, as the milk and water began to bubble up in the saucepan.

CHAPTER 5

It seemed as though this war would never go away. It was late autumn now and the talk was all about the problems that faced a devastated world. The initial euphoria of allied victory had been replaced by all this talk about physical and mental rebuilding. And of course there seemed to be no end to this rationing business. Sally thought back to the celebrations in the summer, with the victory parade that had been organised in the village along with every other town and village in the country. How all the children had dressed in fancy dress costume and, beaming proudly, had marched from one end of the village to the other, all thoughts of Hiroshima, Nagasaki and other wartime tragedies temporarily forgotten. Then at the end of it all, the party to end all parties, with the grown ups giggling and dancing around in preposterous hats, and behaving as though they had entered into a second childhood. She also vividly recalled the pictures that had dominated the newspapers at the time. Of the King and Queen driving slowly through London in an elaborate carriage, acknowledging the crowds with that curious wave of theirs.

Sitting around the kitchen table with her family now and listening to the chatter, Sally recalled the King's words after the Japanese surrender.

'We now have our part to play in restoring the shattered fabric of civilisation. It is to this great task that I call you now.'

This statement alone, she told herself, should have made her realise that there was a lot more to war than just the winning. The word 'Gestapo,' was enough to send a shiver up and down her spine these days, and as for the horrific revelations surfacing with the liberating of the German concentration camps, well they just defied comprehension. 'Man's inhumanity to man,' her dad called it. Some of the leaders of Nazi Germany, the men responsible for these and other atrocities, were to go on trial soon it seemed. As far as she could make out from reports in the News Chronicle, they were to be tried by something called an Allied Military Tribunal in a place called Nuremburg. The grainy images of these monsters that had accompanied these reports had made her blood run cold.

As for some of the Japanese atrocities that her other Uncle Fred, her mum's youngest brother, had just been referring to, these horrific revelations had made her cover her ears and close her eyes to try to stop the nightmare images penetrating her mind.

He had just returned from the Far East, where he had spent much time in Burma towards the end of the war. He talked about the Burma Road where there had been enormous loss of life on both sides. He wondered, along with many others, if all the bloodshed had been justified. Then he brought things down to a more mundane level.

"You wouldn't believe what that bloody jungle's like, Doll," said Uncle Fred, looking across the table at mum. "And I mean jungle, not puny woods like we've got in this country. You can't make out who, what or where your enemy is. You're on tenterhooks the whole time, wondering whether the strange animal sounds you hear all the time are just that, or some bloody mimicking Jap patrol trying to lull you into a false sense of security. It was creepy, I can tell you that and I've never sweated so much in all my life."

Uncle Fred continued. "Those Chindits we came into contact with now and then, they're something else. They must have felt fear, same as we did, and they lost a lot of men, but I never once heard them bellyache, not like our lot. Mind you, I suppose I did my share of complaining, but at least most of us managed to keep out of the clutches of the bloody Japs. I shudder to think what would have happened if they'd caught us."

"You'd have joked your way out of danger knowing you!" Interrupted mum, looking around the table and noting the expressions of the youngsters, who were sitting there all goggle eyed and anxious. "That's if they'd had an interpreter with them of course, preferably one that spoke Oxfordshire. You certainly haven't lost your accent, have you? Anyway, don't forget you're the joker of the family and if you're in danger, you're allowed to use any means to defend yourself. I reckon your Oozlam bird joke would have gone down a treat with them, even if they haven't got much sense of humour. I don't suppose you got close enough to them to find out, did you? I think you aught to tell us that one again, that's Sally's favourite and mine too if it comes to that. And what about telling us the one about the frog in the waistcoat, and his adventure on that old rocking horse as well? Then when you've finished, I'll make us all a nice cup of tea."

As they sat with their hands around their mugs of warm milky tea, elbows on table, the voices of the youngsters fell to a low mumble. They were relaxed now, the discussion on war statistics taking place were incomprehensible to them. The war deaths it seemed were being estimated in millions, country by country and whether Russia or some other luckless country came top of that list seemed irrelevant, an accident of birth or some such thing. Death was death, just that, and they just could not get their heads round the enormity of it all. As for accounts of the gratuitous slaughter of all those people who did not conform to the Nazi racial or political doctrine, well that was something that even the grown ups shook their heads over in disbelief. No, this so-called victory was just the beginning, just the first big step on this long and painful road.

"Hilary and I are going out now, mum," said Sally rising from the table, taking them all and especially her friend by surprise. "It won't be dark for ages yet. You can come with us as well if you want to," she added magnanimously, tapping Pat on the shoulder as she walked towards the Scullery door. She was suddenly up to her eyeballs with this retrospective war business and needed a breath of fresh air.

"Aren't you going to finish your drink?" asked mum. "I made it especially milky for you, just the way you like it. And don't forget to say goodbye to your Uncle Fred before you go, he'll be gone by the time you get back. And don't get up to any mischief!" She called out after them, as they said their farewells and rushed out of the door.

They hurried down the field and were just passing Micky's garden, when his face suddenly appeared over the hedge by the old pear tree, startling them all to a standstill. "Where are you lot off to, then?" He asked, walking towards his gate and coming out into the lane to meet them. "I promised to call for Basil this afternoon, I'll tag along with you if that's okay." Taking their noncommittal grunts as agreement, he fell into step beside them and together they crossed the road into Crazy Lane and headed for Basil's.

"He's been eating raw onions, that Micky. His breath is hot enough to scorch your whiskers off," whispered Hilary as she, Pat and Sally followed the boys down through the twitten towards Amy's house. The two boys were talking nineteen to the dozen, Basil seemingly unaffected by the fumes contaminating the air anywhere near Micky. "Don't forget to turn right at the bottom here, will you? We're going to call for Amy to see if she wants to come with us," she shouted to their fast retreating backs. "Might just as well talk to a tin of Spam," she muttered as the boys hurried ahead without once glancing back to acknowledge her message.

Amy's dad came to the door in answer to their knocking, then without uttering a word he turned, called her name then walked slowly back indoors again. He did not look at all well, Sally thought to herself. "I'm surprised to see you lot, especially at this time of day," said Amy, shutting the door behind her. "If you give me a couple of minutes to get changed, I'll come with you, but I've got to get back in time to get ready for the dance tonight. I'm meeting up with Jean, Ivy, Joan and all that lot. We're going to have some fun, I can tell you."

"We'll wait back out on the road for you then, don't be too long," said Basil turning and moving away from the doorway. "We've only got a couple of hours or so before it gets dark and we want to get there and back again before it does, don't we?" he said, smiling conspiratorially at Micky. They're up to something those two, Sally thought to herself a few minutes later as she stood on the grass verge opposite Amy's house, waiting for their friend to appear.

As they waited, Sally looked towards the brooks, past little groups of dung smeared cows to where the faded browns and greens of late autumn were being transformed into a soft grey haze as the wintry sun shone through. "I love this time of year," she said out loud, forgetting as she always did, that she said the same thing day in day out, or as often at least as the mood took her. "You can see for miles and miles now the leaves are dropping off. That's if it's not all grey and misty and such like." She turned her head and looked up as Amy trotted down the garden path and crossed the road towards them. Then the girls turned their faces towards the village, the main road way, and began moving in that direction.

"We thought we'd go a different way today, along New Road to Marley Lane and across the brooks to the village that way," said Basil hastily.

Before they had time to protest, he and Micky began moving decisively towards Paygate Corner. As he looked back over his shoulder to check that they were following, he added, "It's more interesting this way and us two have got things to do, haven't we Micky?" And he winked knowingly at his friend. They're up to something those two, Sally thought to herself for the umpteenth time.

They trudged up the road, their footsteps muffled by the thick, coarse grass that covered the narrow footpath on this side of the roadway. On the other side, the bank rose steeply and in the early summer would offer up a harvest of wild strawberries. For a week or two they would visit the area frequently to pick hasty handfuls of these miniature delights and cram them into their mouths, revelling in the sweet yet slightly acidic flavour of this delicacy, which nature always provided in abundance. If their cousin Anne Saul happened to be with them, they would watch her carefully to see if she would dare to defy the wishes of her mother and eat more than the small handful she was allowed. According to her mum, more than that would give her the collywobbles. Anne's mum also provided special toilet paper for her daughter, forbidding her to use the cut up newspapers that hung on a string on the doors of their lavatories. Now and again, the strawberry harvest would provide more than enough to satisfy their immediate needs and they would fill a jar or two with enough fruit for mum to make a filling for a sponge or trifle. Or even, on one occasion, a bit of jam. But that season was a long way off and not even a leaf could be seen amongst the grass to indicate where this simple fruit would suddenly spring to life.

Micky was the first to reach the stile leading on to the brooks and as he scrambled over, he looked so comical that Sally could not resist commenting on the spectacle taking place before their eyes. "Look at old mouth and trousers there, no wonder he won the sack race," she said. "I reckon he's practicing for next year's show. Look at his arms, all up and under his chest with his elbows sticking out and he didn't once use his arms while he was climbing over that stile, did you notice?"

"What are you lot gawping at?" asked Micky, as once on the other side, he looked back to check their whereabouts. "Well I'm off, can't wait around for you lot to make your minds up," he muttered, huffing as he moved off in the direction of the village. "Some of us have got things to do."

Once they had reached the bridge spanning the river, the boys stopped and instead of crossing, began to make their way down to the water level. When they began to gather handfuls of the soft mud that lined the edge of the river then walked back up the bank with it, it suddenly dawned on the girls just what they were up to. "I'm having nothing to do with this," said Pat indignantly and she, Hilary and Amy turned determinedly away, crossed the bridge and began to make their way towards the village. Sally hesitated then turned back and watched fascinated, as the boys began to coat the stile with a liberal dressing of mud, then she followed them down the bank to add her contribution to theirs. This is better than making mud pies any day, she thought to herself. After a while, Micky decided to add a bit of fresh cow dung to the mixture and chuckled as the colour and texture began to change.

"Poo, it stinks a bit this stuff but it's worth it I reckon," he said, totally oblivious to the state of his clothing. "A bit more on this top bar and I think we're done," he said. As they stood back to admire their handywork, they heard voices. It took them a moment or two to make out where they were coming from.

"It's three old ladies and they're just along by the Blacksmiths, heading this way. Come on you lot, under the bridge. God help us if they catch us here."

They listened in silence as the voices and footsteps came closer and closer. They froze as the footsteps stopped right over their heads. The next sound was a loud intake of breath followed by an indignant exclamation.

"What on earth's been going on here?" Followed by a short pause. Then, "I wonder if it was something to do with those girls we saw walking up through the village just now. They came from this direction. It's disgusting and it smells vile." They watched through a crack in the planks as the women, gingerly and with a lot of clucking and tutting, tried to avoid the worst of the mud as they clambered over the stile. By this time Sally was beside herself with laughter, stuffing her hankie into her mouth to muffle the sound, but not quite succeeding. Even a vicious dig in the ribs from Micky could not stem the bubbles of mirth that threatened to expose them all to these irate women. Luckily they were too absorbed in the task of avoiding this muddy confrontation, as they lifted up and held each others skirts with fastidious fingertips, each one having to run the gauntlet of this boobytrap. At the same time, they kept up a running commentary on the state of mind of the culprits and what should be done to them.

Basil was the first to emerge from the sanctuary of the bridge, poking his head out and giving the all clear. "You bloody idiot," he said, rounding on Sally who was still flushed from the effects of subdued laughter. "You nearly gave the game away, you did and then what would have happened. They'd have reported us to the school and Micky and me would have got the cane, that's for sure. You girls are all the same." Then he grinned the biggest grin she'd ever seen and as he looked across to the far side of the Brooks and the slowly retreating backs of the women, mere dots by this time he added. "By eck, that was a bit of fun though that was. Did you hear that last one shout out? I reckon she caught her legs on that big bit of cow shit that was right on the top there. It's disappeared anyway." With that, he and Micky fell on the floor convulsed with laughter.

"Don't forget that either we've got to get over there to look for the others or they'll have to climb over the blooming thing to reach us and they won't like that," said Sally. Tell you what, let's walk along to the main road and climb up the bank beside the river bridge. We can get through there somehow. If we get a move on we'll probably find them before they get a chance to see what we've done and tell us off for it. I won't tell them if you don't. Come on now you two, stop laughing and get your backsides off the ground."

As they walked towards the main road, Micky looked down and for the first time noticed what a state he was in. "Blimey, look at me trousers now, all covered in cow shit. Mother, she won't half sus me," he said.

"Serve you right, I reckon this was your idea in the first place," replied Sally sternly. "Now up this bank the pair of you and let's go and look for the others."

They found the girls, sitting on the pump seat talking to Bangy Smith. His face was, as usual, wreathed in smiles and he was talking away to them nineteen to the dozen. Pat was so absorbed in what he was saying that she did not notice the arrival of the three miscreants and jumped in fright when Sally tapped her lightly on the shoulder.

" Don't do that, you moan enough when anyone does it to you," said Pat testily. "You really give me the jitters you do." Then when she had recovered her equilibrium, she added. "You should have come with us you should, Mr Smith has been telling us all about what he did when he was a kid. He watched this pump being built, you know. He reckons there's a secret compartment right up in the top here but you have to know exactly where the catch is to let yourself in there. He used to get up there by putting one foot on the bottom of the pumping handle, another on the bit where the water comes out and then swinging up from there. He's too old to do that now though of course," she added seriously. Then she continued, "he told us about beating the bounds, where everyone walked right round the boundary of the village. Can you imagine that? It used to take them ages. They were really thirsty by the time they got back and all the men used to go straight to the pub for a drink. Well they would wouldn't they? And he told us how to cut a hedge properly. Well it's called layering really. You have to cut some of the branches half way through and then bend them down across the hedge without breaking them. It's a bit tricky but it keeps the hedge nice and thick and if dad did that round our field it would stop those sheep from always getting out. There used to be fairs here on the Green too, with Maypole dancing and all that sort of thing, and he often used to play his Banjo. I wish I had lived in the olden days, don't you?"

All the while Pat was talking, Bangy watched her indulgently. Then, when she paused for breath he said. "I reckon you youngsters should be getting along home now. It'll soon be pitch moonlight." Then he grinned around at them all revealing his pink gums.

CHAPTER 6

It was January now, the season of coughs, colds and sore noses. Christmas had come and gone. The silver thrupenny pieces, hidden within the puddings and then held aloft one by one, as the finder of these treasures held them up excitedly for inspection, had been carefully put away for next year's puddings. For the first time, Sally had worked out that the person in the red and white outfit was not Father Christmas at all, but their dad. His shoes or rather his old boots, scuffed and liberally coated with dubbin had given him away. Added to that were the twinkling eyes, the only feature visible through the thick mass of white whiskers that surrounded his face and neck. She'd have recognised those eyes anywhere she reckoned, forgetting that for goodness knows how long, she had failed to notice that they had indeed belonged to her dad. When she had whispered as much to Hazel, her sister had just smiled knowingly but without comment. Mentioning her discovery to Pat, Dorothy or Jacky was out of the question. They were far too young to know about such things. It was still just as exciting though to be handed a present that had been carefully removed from the tree, and to open it with trembling hands while all the family looked on. Mostly, she and her sisters had received items of clothing, mittens, multi-coloured scarves, socks and even some new hankies, which had been carefully hemmed around their pure white edges. From Sally downwards however, there was one special present that had made their eyes sparkle and in the case of Dorothy and Jacky, rush around the room excitedly. They were dolls, with beautiful china faces and soft, malleable bodies, all dressed from top to toe in different coloured cotton and white lace. Sally's was dressed mostly in green, which she decided from now on would be her favourite colour. She learned later that Aunty Mabel, the daughter of Great Aunt Sarah and Granpy, had made each and every one.

***

Hilary and Sally were now on their way to see Margery Freeman. They were taking the usual short cut, up the lane, past the farms and through bits of woodland. They looked for Deffy and Bill as they passed by their little shack, but they were nowhere to be seen. There was no wisp of smoke escaping from the bent tin chimney at the side of their house so the two old men must have been absent for some time. Margy did not know that they were coming but hopefully, would be somewhere round and about. She was always pleased to see them and such good company. Sally was never quite so sure about Mrs Freeman, who could be a bit abrasive at times and who was also rather rude to her own husband. Sally thought her attitude to him might be something to do with that nasty accident with the swap. She could not for the life of her, think what else could possibly have caused this discord. It hadn't really been Mr Freeman's fault. He had been swapping the grass just outside the back door when Margy had rushed out and had caught the full and powerful swipe of his newly sharpened blade, mid way up her right leg. The impact had cut clean through the flesh and muscle and into the bone and it had seemed for a while that she would be lame. However, after a few months she was able to walk almost normally and before long was cycling to and from school again. From that day on though, she had walked with a slight limp and of course would always bear the scar. She accepted the accident and its aftermath in her usual philosophical way, blaming herself not her Father for what had happened.

It was a bright day but not brilliant, and as Sally scanned the countryside, she noticed clumps of sheep's wool captured on barbed wire fences, flapping about and looking for all the world like the wind flayed skeleton of an ancient hanged highwayman. And she shivered as though someone were walking over her grave. "Are you cold?" asked Hilary, as ever tuned in to the varying moods of her friend. "Here, take my mittens and put them over yours, my hands are warm as toast."

Margery answered their tap-tapping at the door, wiping her hands down her dress as she moved aside to let them in. Before they walked through to the kitchen, they removed their wellies, divesting themselves automatically and thankfully of these necessary but cumbersome bits of kit. "You only just caught me in, I was just about to go up through the woods to call for Sylv," she said. "I'm really glad you've come though, it'll be more fun with the four of us." And then she smiled at them.

As Sally looked at Margery, she thought, not for the first time, what a thoroughly decent, down to earth girl she was. No matter when they called and how inconvenient it might be, somehow she always managed to adjust her own schedule to fit in around them. And she always made it sound as though it were the simplest thing in the world and just what she would have chosen to do anyway. She also possessed a keen sense of humour with a quick wit to go with it. Like her mum's, but without the bite.

Sylvia Glyde was the only child of Norah Partridge, Porky, John and Len's sister, and lived with her parents up in Battle Big Wood. Mr Glyde was the 'Keeper' in the big wood and he also worked making palings and stakes. He kept a pig in the back garden, just as Granny Sansom used to, when she'd lived at Ambrosden, in Oxfordshire. He also kept ferrets, and took Sylvia on regular forays to trap and kill the rabbits that proliferated on the outer edges of the wood. Sylvia was made responsible for keeping the nets her dad used to cover all the escape holes, tangle free. These trapped the unfortunate creatures as the mean looking ferrets bolted them from their holes. The rabbits would then get a quick and expert chop on the back of the head with the heavy stick that Mr Glyde always carried around with him.

He was lean, just like Pop Cotton, and you knew just by looking at him that his work was hard and physically demanding. He was tough as old boots and his hands were enormous.

As they approached the little clap-board cottage, they saw Mrs Glyde moving around in her garden. She was picking sprouts and was quite oblivious to their approach. Her woolly hat was pulled well down over her ears to fend off the winter air, and as she bent to snap the miniature cabbages off their thick stems, her fingers, protruding from her cut off mittens, looked red and swollen. She was the image of her mother, Mrs Partridge, small and wiry, and always on the go. And like her mother, she wore a wrap around cotton apron that peeped out from beneath her dark grey overcoat and hid the tops of her muddy black Wellingtons. She was kind too, and would always rustle up a few buns or a piece of cake for the girls and she never, ever told them to remove their shoes or wellies when they entered her kitchen. The large garden, in which the cottage stood, had been hacked out from dense woodland. Here and there, remained the sturdy stump of a felled tree that had so far defied the efforts of the forester to remove it from its ancient soil.

Mrs Glyde, totally absorbed in her chilly task, visibly jumped as the girls suddenly appeared in front of her. "Bless my soul, where on earth did you spring from?" She cried. "Not many people are able to creep up on me like that! Sylvia did mention that you might be popping in sometime Margery, but it had completely slipped my mind. Go on in will you, Sylvia will be pleased to see you, and I'll be in as soon as I've finished here." She stooped and continued picking her sprouts while the girls ambled towards the latched door of the little cottage.

Before they had even entered the kitchen, the aroma of hot scones hit their noses and taste buds and Sally found her mouth beginning to water in just the same way as it did when she walked into her own home and mum had been baking. The same thing happened when she was on milk collecting duty, and Mrs Collins had just taken a batch of scones or buns out of the oven. The smell of food mixed with fresh air had to be one of the best things in life, she reckoned.

The Glyde's cottage had a well just outside the back door, a replica of the one at the Lawrence's house. Sally however, did not examine the thing too closely. She always stood well back when the handle at the side, with its characteristic squeak and creak was turned, and the tightly secured bucket was lowered into its stygian depths. Give her the safe and solid underground tank at Sylvian any day. Although she moaned and would no doubt continue to moan when it was her turn to pump up the water into the header tank, it was a small price to pay for not having to peer down into that diabolical hole.

Fortified by hot scones and homemade jam, the four girls set off towards the marshy area between the cottage and battle Big Wood. Here, in the spring, kingcups would turn the grey bog into a carpet of green and bright yellow. On the way, they followed the little stream at the edge of the wood, as it tinkled and frothed between the thin branches and roots of the weeping willows dotted along its banks. Here and there a stunted hawthorn bush caused the path to deviate from the straight and narrow, and they had to duck to avoid the savage prickles of this inanimate porcupine. Now and then they stopped to investigate the footprint of some animal hoping to identify one that had used this path recently, a fox perhaps or a deer, or even a badger.

There were certainly badgers in the area. They knew that for sure. They had looked closely at the deep holes, some half filled with droppings, that had been dug into various parts of Sylvia's garden by these nocturnal creatures. These holes were very different from the surface scrapes made by rabbits.

As they moved on, the terrain began to change. Scrubby little bushes now predominated. Hilary was the first to spot the little Jenny Wren, tail cocked and hopping in and out of dead ivy-covered branches. "Look, there's a Jenny Wren down there," she said quietly, pointing to where the tiny brown bird was scuffling around in the shrivelled brown leaves. "And look there's another one over there. They must be mates, otherwise they'd be fighting," she added, pointing a few yards away to where another little bird was gently investigating a clump of leaves that had become trapped in a mass of twiggy undergrowth, since the winds had blown them there back in the autumn.

"They're looking for seeds and grubs and things," said Hilary. "My dad reckons they spend all their time and energy this time of the year just searching for food, imagine that. Poor little devils, I expect they're hungry right this minute, that's why they've let us get this close to them." After a few minutes silently contemplating these fascinating little creatures, she added. "Better leave them to it, I suppose," and they began to tiptoe reluctantly away.

After a while, they began absentmindedly to rustle the dead leaves around with their feet, moving on through the wood and chatting about this and that.

"When I said to my dad what untidy useless things these dead leaves were, he almost told me off," Sylvia was telling them. "He said to me, 'ah that's where you're wrong. They have their uses, along with lots of other so-called rubbish. Same applies really to my old compost heap, which is made up of waste from the kitchen, peelings and that sort of thing. Takes a while for it all to rot down but when it does it's the best thing for the garden. Why do you think our vegetables and things grow so well in our garden?' he asked me. Well of course I didn't have an answer to that one. The other girls just nodded their heads, not really knowing enough of the subject to say yay or nay.

When Hilary began talking about Jumbo James's, the headmaster, and his experiment with a test tube and a jar of blue-black ink, Sally found it difficult to suppress her giggles, her vivid imagination recalling this hilarious incident in minute detail. Hilary was relating the incident for the benefit of Sylvia, who for some reason, attended school in Battle and had thus missed this bit of fun.

"It was the science lesson, wasn't it, when Jumbo James was doing one of his experiments," she was saying. "He was supposed to suck this ink up to a certain line and hold it there, while he did some kind of experiment and so forth with it. Well, it didn't work out quite as he'd intended, did it" she said and she grinned from ear to ear. "He must have sucked too hard because the next thing we saw was him spitting and spluttering into his nice white hankie and the thing got soaked with the stuff. When he took his hankie away, his mouth and lips had turned bright blue. Then as he opened his mouth to say that he would have to pop home to clean up a bit, we saw that even his tongue was stained with the stuff. Well that was the last straw, I can tell you and we all fell about laughing. He didn't tick us off though, did he? That would have been pointless. He could have threatened us with anything, the stick even, but it wouldn't have made any difference and he knew it."

They had seen their Headmaster later that day, heavily stained and trying unsuccessfully to appear nonchalant about the incident, and still giggled at the memory. Any one of them or their class mates had only to whisper the word 'ink' at any silent time, prayers even, to set those within range to giggle uncontrollably. Sally had learned this to her cost and now kept her fingers if not in her ears, then close enough to cover them as soon as the person next to her as much as took a deep breath.

He wasn't a bad bloke, old Jumbo James, and she liked him even more now that she knew he didn't think much of fox hunting. Or at least that was the impression she got from a poem he had read to her class one afternoon recently. She could remember some of the words even now, and began to recite them silently to herself.

'And here as he ran to the huntsmen's yelling, the fox first felt that the pace was telling. His body and lungs seemed all grown old, his legs less certain, his heart less bold. His pride in his speed, his joy in the race were withered away for what use was pace. He had run his best but the hounds ran better, then the going worsened'..........

That was all she could remember, but the whole poem had made quite an impression on her. It seemed to illustrate how her mum and dad thought about the whole fox hunting issue.

Soon they reached the marshy area and they stooped to examine the watery surface with its growth of weed more closely. "I reckon there's going to be even more Kingcups than usual this year," said Hilary. "Look, just under the surface, there's masses of roots and things and if you look on the top, you can see the leaves beginning to grow as well." She looked up to make sure they were looking in the right direction, when something else caught her attention.

"Look over there," she whispered pointing to the far side of the bog, where a fox was standing, its forepaws in the water. It stood stock still, with its head up, gazing at them as though trying to fathom out what they were doing in its territory. "I didn't expect to see a fox at this time of day, he must be hungry or thirsty or both," whispered Hilary, glancing round at the others.

"I wish Pat had come with us. She'd love to have seen him. Bags tell her about it when we get home. Keep still. Let's see how long he stays there, I don't want to move until he does anyway." The fox stayed around for several minutes, watching them the whole time without moving. Then suddenly it turned, shook its head and ambled off into the more wooded area.

"Well I go to Stoke!" Exclaimed Sylvia loudly, the need for silence having been removed with the departure of the fox. "I've seen them in the garden at night, lots of times, but they always scoot when my dad goes out there with his hurricane lamp. I've never seen one just stand there, staring back without batting an eye-lid. I can't wait to tell my dad about it. Mind you he'll probably tell me he's seen it all before. He works around these woods a lot you know. He takes me out ferreting with him as well, but I expect I've told you all about that."

"In that case, can you ask him if he's any idea where that old village might have been," said Sally. "You know, the one that disappeared from the woods here years ago because of the Black Death. You never know, there's just a chance that he might have noticed something interesting. I would love to know where it used to be. Well I don't know about you Hilary, but I think it's about time we got cracking," she said after a short pause. And she moved over to stand a bit closer to her special friend. "I expect you two will wander back the way you came," she added looking towards Margery and Sylvia. "Hilary and I can cut up through the wood here and down the lane by your gran's place, Sylvia. It's not just the quickest way but it's also the best - well I think so - and we came that way anyhow."

Once they had left the wood and were wandering down the lane past Partridges farm, Sally looked closely into the hedgerows for any sign of life. All she could see however, was a tangle of brown sticks with a few desiccated catkins hanging disconsolately down.

"You won't see any primroses yet if that's what you're looking for," said Hilary stopping to look over Sally's shoulder anyway, just to make sure. "Tell you what though, there's some decent sticks and things in there. Let's come back another day and cut a few to make bows and arrows. Dad had a go at my penknife for me the other day so it's sharp enough to cut through these little branches. He'll burn off the ends of the arrows for us as well so we can get a good point on them." She paused suddenly and sniffed the air.

"I can smell creosote around here somewhere," she continued. "I bet Porky's doing one of his sheds over. I've never seen anyone work as hard as he does. Well, mum does of course and so does dad if it comes to that, but you know what I mean. Mind you it could be something to do with John or Len. I'm pretty sure I saw them in the field over there when we walked up here earlier on. Well someone was anyway. It's supposed to be good for colds, this creosote stuff, or so I've been told. The smell of it of course, you wouldn't want to drink it, would you. It's a pity really that we haven't got a cold, us two. It could have done us the world of good if we had."

Don't be daft, you wouldn't want to have a cold just so you could make it better by smelling the stuff," replied Sally seriously. Then she grinned as she saw the mischievous expression on her friends face. "You're pulling my leg again, aren't you?" She said. Then, "it smells bloody good though, doesn't it. Mind you, it doesn't smell half as good as streaky pork and split peas. That's what we've got for dinner today, with sprout tops. That's my favourite and I'm starved. Let's get a move on."

Later on, in the early evening, they walked down the field on their way to Hilary's house, flashing their torches around illuminating narrow ribbons of lank grass in split second bursts. When they reached the lane, and were negotiating the ruts and bumps throughout its length and breadth, they focused the beam of their torches very much towards their feet and just a small area in front of them.

"It's about time dad put a few more cinders in this lane," said Sally. "The ruts are getting worse and worse. The tractors use it all the time and they really churn it up. On second thoughts, its not cinders it needs but something a bit more chunky, like stones and bits of brick, that sort of thing," she added as her foot slid into one of the holes. "Sorry, I didn't mean to pinch you like that," she said apologetically as she grabbed Hilary's arm to steady herself.

As they walked passed Lavender Bowl Cottage, they stepped carefully over the little channels cut into the grassy pathway by Arthur Dawson the lengths man, to drain off the surplus water from the side of the road. "It's hard to imagine how different this is all going to look in two or three months time," she added. "We'll be sprinting along here like long dogs and playing on that bit of grass down there," and she flashed her torch in the direction of Pay Gate corner. "I can't wait."

They entered Hilary's house through the back door and walked straight into the warm kitchen. Hilary ignored the note on the table, her hand moving instinctively towards the pile of sandwiches close by. As she lifted the top layer of thick white bread on one of them, she lowered her head and sniffed the contents appreciatively. "Mmm, stinky fish paste sandwiches for supper," she said." I was hoping it would be. Mum knows we love them. Better read this then I suppose," she added picking up the note, which was actually written on the back of an old envelope. "She's reminded me that Ronald's staying at Peter's place tonight, but I'd remembered anyway. She also says that we're not to go out anywhere and that there's plenty of milk for a hot drink. And that's about all really. Well if Willie and Roy turn up, and they always do if they say they will, then I reckon we'll be going out somewhere or other. It's not that cold, is it?" she said as she removed her coat and wellies.

A brief tap on the back door announced the arrival of Willie and Roy and as they stepped inside they rubbed their hands together, " It's nice and warm in here," said Roy. "We forgot our gloves and our hands are a bit cold, that's all. It's not too cold to go out though," he added hastily. "Not if you remember your gloves, it isn't," and he grinned.

"Best make it soon then," said Hilary. "My mum doesn't want us to go out this evening really but I'm sure she wouldn't mind if she knew you two were going to be with us. She won't know anyway and what you don't know doesn't hurt you, as they say. The village and back, then a nice mug of cocoa when we get back," she added, picking her coat up from the back of the chair where she had left it and buttoning it snugly around herself. "Here let me give you a hand with yours," she said to Sally who was struggling to get her arms through the narrow armholes. "It would help if you put your coat on before those thick gloves of yours, not afterwards," she said, smiling as she tut-tutted.

As they walked along the main road, they flashed their torches around from time to time to check the state of the path, which had been somewhat neglected by the lengths man during the cold winter months. Perhaps he did a bit of hedge cutting or something like that in the winter, Sally thought to herself. When they reached the village, they made straight for the Coach and Horses pub and the window at the side of the building where under age customers were served.

"We're in luck this evening, they've just had some crisps delivered," said Willie. "Dad told me about it earlier on. He even gave me the money for them." He rang the little bell and they waited for a few minutes until the Landlord appeared and opened up the window. "Four bags of Smiths crisps please," said Willie grandly, feeling around in his pocket for the precious shilling, which he proffered to the Landlord.

"Are there any other kind," the Landlord muttered grumpily as he took the coin from Willie and turned away from them. When the fat, crinkly bags were placed in front of them, they all made a grab, crushing some of the contents in their desire to get away from there. "Mind the step," said Willie as, a few feet in front of the others, he almost lost his footing. "Blast that step," he muttered. "I forgot it was there. Don't open them until we get to the pump, we'll eat them there," he added.

When they reached the pump they sat on the north side, sheltered from the prevailing winds. There was hardly any wind tonight, but despite this, the seat was still cold and damp. Then they opened their bags, feeling carefully for the twist of blue paper, which contained a goodly measure of salt. Careful sprinkling was a must here or all the salt would accumulate in one place causing them to spit and splutter with the acrid taste of the stuff.

As they sat there, Willie pointed towards a small oak tree which they could just see by the light coming from the windows of the Queen's Head pub. It stood bang in the middle of the bit of green, just below the Brick Wall Hotel. "That there tree was planted by Horace Shambrook. He was killed quite early on in the war, you know." Said Willie, knowledgably. "Dad says we've got to look after it because it's a kind of memorial to him. Lots of men from around here were killed in the war you know."

"Yes, Jimmy Franklin, John Noble, Henry Read and others," replied Hilary. There were a few minutes of silence from the group as they sat in the dark with their individual thoughts and feelings about the death, the loss to old village families, brought about by this war. At last and with a sigh, Hilary broke the silence. "Well I think we'd better move from here before my backside goes numb," she said wincing as she raised herself from the seat. "And don't forget, my mum works in the Queen's Head. I know it's dark and all, but someone who works with her might just wander over here and then I'm in trouble. Let's walk up the road to get warmed up a bit."

They half walked and half ran down the slope, onto the main road and then began to walk briskly towards the top end of the village. At the driveway leading into the old Manor House gardens, Roy paused. "Fancy a look round the back here?" he asked. "If we're quiet, no one's going to know we're here. They've got an old dog but he's deaf as a post, and anyway we needn't go as far as the house."

They crept forward, Sally holding onto Hilary's arm for all she was worth, both for physical support and because, for some reason she was scared out of her wits. As they drew level with the back gardens of the Manor cottages however, Roy spread wide both his arms to halt their progress. "Look over there, can you see those lines? They're full to overflowing with washing." And he pointed to where, in the dull glow from the windows, they could just make out lines of limp washing, hanging straight down, the longer bits almost touching the muddy ground.

"We can have a bit of fun here," chuckled Roy. As there was no immediate response from the puzzled trio, he said. "Well, it's obvious isn't it? We just get in there and change the whole lot over. Mrs Blundell has got no sense of humour at all and I'd give anything to see her expression when she looks out there in the morning and sees her knickers on someone else's line." And he snickered. "Ssh," he admonished himself. If we're going to do this, it's got to be in silence."

With Roy leading the way and taking charge, they climbed over the hedge and into the first garden. "You two girls can start to take the washing off this line, and Willie and me can see to next door," he whispered, clearly in his element. "When you've got yours off, just rustle that old crisp bag you've got in your pocket, but not too loudly mind and we'll swap over. If anyone does come out here, just leg it. It's each man for himself from now on," he added dramatically.

"Bags you start up the top end, by the house," whispered Sally. "You're taller than me and the line looks a bit higher at that end," she muttered as a feeble excuse for wanting to be as far away from the back door as possible. Apart from the muffled rustle of wet washing, all was quiet as they methodically removed the clothes. Then Sally began to giggle, "yuk, I've got an old pair of bloomers here and they've dripped all over me," she whispered through her mirth. "They're more like the ones old Mrs Brooman wears. I've seen hers when she sits on the pump seat with her legs wide apart. You listen when we pass these over to the boys. I bet they'll fall about laughing when they get to these."

"Ssh," whispered Hilary, as Sally's voice began to rise with the humour of it all. "Someone will hear you. Come on, quickly now, let's see if the boys have got theirs ready for us," and she rustled the crisp bag deep within her pocket. After an almost silent exchange of booty, they set to pegging the exchanged washing onto the respective lines. "Right last one coming up. Now let's wait in the driveway for the boys," said Hilary. "You can tell they're not as used to pegging out washing as we are."

Grabbing Sally by the arm, they giggled their way back to and over the hedge. They stood there for a few moments listening to the soft rustle of wet washing accompanied by the occasional stifled giggle as the two boys struggled nervously with the limp, uncooperative garments. Suddenly there was a crash, followed immediately by the two boys leaping over the hedge and landing in a heap at their feet.

"Get down," hissed Willie. "How was I to know someone had left a bloody pail of peelings and things outside the back door. I'll have a bloody great bruise on my shin now." Before he had time to enlarge on his experience however, the back door opened and a shadowy figure peered through the gloom. It looked carefully around and then they heard a voice say, "bloody cats." That was all, then the person moved back through the doorway and disappeared. "Whew, we were lucky there," said Willie. "Better get away from here pretty darned quick. Keep your heads down, all of you until we get back on to the road again."

Once they were clear of the cottages, Sally remarked light heartedly. "If that was old Mrs Blundell who came through that doorway then she should be ashamed of herself. Did you hear what she said? She said 'bloody,' when she goes to church and all. She's always so pious, preaching to us lot about following in the footsteps of Jesus. I remember one of the boys saying to her once that he was sure Jesus wasn't above the occasional swear word, especially that time he got into a temper with those money lenders or whatever they were in that Temple. She was shocked and just walked away from him in disgust. She's a funny old girl."

"I bet she swears sometimes. She certainly shakes her fists about anyhow, when she goes to the cricket matches, in the village and down Hastings as well," said Roy. "She's always there in one of the best seats at Priory Meadow, come rain, hail or shine during cricket week. I know 'cause I've seen her, both places. But anyway, I've got a bone to pick with you girls. Why didn't you warn us that there was a bloody great sheet amongst the washing you gave over to us? Willie and me nearly got strangled by the thing. It had us both by the neck once, and the more we struggled, the more it grabbed hold of us. And worst still, we were up the top end of the garden where old Bangy empties his bucket and we could smell the bloody stuff. Frightened to death we were that we'd fall in. You know what bloody great holes he digs when he's emptying the stuff. Anyway, in the end we just draped the rotten sheet across the line, stuck a few pegs in it and hoped for the best. And what about those bloomers, eh Willie? Leastways that's what we reckoned it was, a pair of enormous bloomers. I suppose, if you come to think of it, it could have been a secret weapon left over from the war. If the old Jerries had seen something like that coming towards them, they'd have run for their lives. You could fit all our class at school into one leg I reckon, with room to spare. You know, I wouldn't mind betting she lends the thing to Mrs Baker to make our suet puddings in at school, your favourite, eh Sally? I bet every time you go up for seconds from now on, you'll think about that." And he chuckled as she huffed and gave him a half-hearted shove.

"It'd take more than an old pair of bloomers to put me off my suet puds," she replied. "Even Harry Haddock never managed to do that. Or even old Denis, picking his nose and eating it, though that did come pretty close I must admit. He picks his ears as well, have you seen him? He's really got some disgusting habits, that kid."

"Talking of disgusting habits reminds me of Barbara Swift and the time she picked a big bogy and smeared it onto the top of your desk at school Sally, hoping you wouldn't notice," said Hilary. "Some hopes she had. You've got eyes like a hawk, you have. Anyway, I remember you telling me about it at playtime and you kept retching when you described having to wipe it off with your hankie. How I managed to keep a straight face I don't know." And she giggled hoping that with the passage of time, Sally would appreciate the humour of that particular occurrence. An intake of breath followed by silence, showed that for the time being anyway, the subject was taboo.

For a while they shuffled along in companionable silence then, one by one, they began to snicker and very soon they came to a breathless halt and, bent double with hands clasped around crooked and shaking knees, were consumed by the humour of their actions. Once the full scale laughter had subsided, they stood up and, as Roy looked around at their dark shadowed faces, he stuttered: "I'd give anything to see old Bangy's face when he looks out of his window in the morning. He'll take one look at those old bloomers, scratch his head and search the place to see if old Phillie Brooman has moved in during the night. Either that or he'll think the fairies have decided to give him something to hang his onions up in for the winter. He grows pounds and pounds of the things. Well he's got good fertile soil, hasn't he with all the stuff he digs into it. I'll hear something about it sooner or later I reckon and when I do I just hope that Sally's nowhere near me. She's bound to give the game away with her giggling. Anyway you lot, it's about time we got along that road, times getting on you know," he added, his voice almost normal now. "There's some rain dogs up there and they're coming this way. Willie and me don't want to get caught out in that lot. It'll be bloody cold that old rain when it gets here."

"Right then, best foot forward," said Hilary. "I reckon we'll all be more than ready for our cocoa by the time we get home. There's plenty of milk, I checked on that before we came out. We'll even share our smelly fish sandwiches with you boys, now how's that for magnanimity? What a lovely word and I can spell it an all. We've just learned it at school and I've been waiting for an opportunity to use it," and she grinned to herself. As they stepped through the back door and into the kitchen, she sniffed appreciatively. "Smells good in here. I'm hungry enough to eat a scabby donkey."

A couple of days later, Hilary's mum was to say, over breakfast, "you'll never guess what. Looks like someone swapped Bangy Smith's and old Mrs Blundell's washing over on their lines the other evening. Thought they'd gone mad they did. It took them ages to work out what had happened."

"Really?" Replied Hilary, innocently, and without looking up, praying silently that her mum would not notice the flush that was creeping up across her face due to suppressed mirth. She could not wait to tell Sally.

The day after the washing prank, being Sunday, Hilary, Pat and Sally called for Patty Winchester and they hurried up Crazy Lane together on their way to Bible class at the Manse. They were more enthusiastic then usual, as the Rev Smith and his family were making one of their visits to the Chapel. He would be taking the boys to Luff's Farm, where Mr Farrow had volunteered to show them around. That suited the Reverend who considered himself a frustrated farmer, and felt that he and Mr Farrow were blood brothers. Miss Smith, who was a close friend but no relation of the other members of the family, had promised to give the girls their first lesson in the gentle art of smocking. This had fired Hilary and Sally's imagination and they were already planning smocked bodice frock's for Dorothy and Jacky. Patty was less enthusiastic about the lesson. As she pointed out to them, she only had brothers and she could not imagine any one of them in a smocked frock or romper suit. She offered to have a word with Basil to see what he thought, but after a short frivolous discussion on the subject they all decided it would be a waste of time. There was a distinct possibility that the whole Smith family would be moving into the Manse in the not too distant future to take over the services at the Chapel, and all the other commitments that went with this exacting job. The local children had met the Smith's two children, Olive and Daniel, a few times now and found that they approached everything with the same kind of enthusiasm as their parents.

As the girls entered the little room, adjacent to the main sanctum, Miss Smith and Olive were busily arranging small pieces of material, skeins of thread, needles, thimbles and scissors on to separate tables. On the material were rows of evenly spaced little dots, which Miss Smith explained had been transferred on to it with a hot iron. On one table was a piece of finished work. As Sally looked at it she tried without success to fathom out the process, which had transformed a piece of material with spots on, into this intricate work of art. As they took their seats along with the other girls, she guided them through the first stage of smocking.

They applied themselves industriously, finding the process of joining up the dots with the thread, quite absorbing. So engrossed were they in their work and the easy interaction with their teacher in fact that they could not believe how quickly the time went by and before they knew it, it was very nearly time to go home. As there would not be time to complete these pieces of work this afternoon, they would be allowed to take the materials home with them where, with carefully explained instructions from Miss Smith, they would be able to complete these test pieces without too much difficulty. Mrs Smith who had quietly entered the room some time ago, while they were busy with their sewing, now lead them in the singing of a few hymns with Olive, an accomplished pianist, providing the melody. Then they listened quietly, as she said a short prayer, which showed that she was already involved with the village and its people.

"First, we'll say a special prayer for little Geoffrey, and ask that he be made well again. That he will in time, be able to run and play like all other children. We also ask God to look upon our friend Mr Cooper and ease his pain. Then we call upon Him, our maker to help all those in need, to bring solace to those who have lost loved ones and to all those who are suffering the many trials and tribulations of this world. Last of all but not least, we ask that we may follow in His footsteps and those of His dear Son, our Saviour, Jesus Christ. Amen."

Then as she looked up and smiled around at them all again, Sally was struck by the expression in the eyes of this lady. There was kindness and compassion there, and she suddenly realised that this expression was replicated in every member of this unique family. She felt instinctively, that these people were what her dad would describe as true Christians and she could not wait for them to become part of their lives and those of other villagers.

As they walked homeward, they talked about the work they had done and discussed the suggestions that Mrs and Miss Smith had made to them about putting together their own little shows, like Harvest and Spring Festivals. Another one could be based on the four seasons where individuals or small groups of children would describe in verse, the changing seasons with the activities and the flora and fauna peculiar to each one. It was not as easy at it sounded and would need a lot of thought. They decided not to include the boys in any discussion on the subject, for as Patty said they would only come up with silly suggestions like the re-enactment of Sweeny Todd the demon barber or some such thing.

When they reached Patty's gate, they suddenly switched from a discussion on concerts, needlework and boys and began to discuss instead, what they should do for the rest of the afternoon.

"I know, let's go over to The Bowlings, over the Brook's way and have a look round that old house," Patty suggested. "It's been empty for ages now and Micky Morris says he's been inside it. I don't think we should go inside, though, just a look through the windows and explore the garden a bit. It's huge, that garden and a bit overgrown but if we've got our wellies on, and we'll need them anyway because it's bound to be muddy over there, a few old brambles and things won't hurt us, will they?"

Once they had deposited their needlework at home and changed their clothes and footwear, they set off along the New Road at a brisk pace. As they passed Paygate corner, they could hear the sound of gushing water where an ancient watercourse had been diverted through a large clay pipe way down beneath their feet, when this road had been laid many years ago. Many times in the summer they had walked through this pipe from one end to the other when the flow of water had been reduced to a trickle. It was fun to enter the dark tunnel at one end and scrabble, bent double and crablike towards the circle of light at the other end. No doubt they would continue to participate in this exciting pastime for many years to come.

The windows of the old house looked blankly back at them as they approached, and Sally felt a twinge of sadness as she contemplated its dilapidated condition. As far as she could make out, it had changed from a bustling, utilitarian household soon after the death in the war of the young man who had lived here with his family. Maybe it was just her imagination, but there did seem to be an aura of suffering here. It seemed like the link with the past was apparent not only in the state of physical neglect of the place, but in something less tangible and difficult to define. Later, as she mooched around the garden, she saw with astonishment, the soft pearly white of snowdrops hiding beneath a tangle of old vegetation with here and there, blobs of mauve and yellow where the crocuses were fulfilling their yearly cycle. The dark cloak of winter was lifting slowly, moving aside to allow an embryonic spring to emerge fresh, reborn. She began to feel a strange kind of empathy with her surroundings. It seemed to her that inextricably linked with the needless and futile loss of young life, was the promise of a new beginning. There was a symbolic circle of life and death mixed up in all this somehow.

And overall, there was this tangible feeling of optimism that always seemed to accompany this special time of year.

CHAPTER 7

There was a sparrow in the garden. Sally watched it from the scullery window as it searched out bits of dried grass, jerking its head this way and that as it searched for the right size pieces with which to build its nest. Fussy little devils these sparrows, she thought. Hedge, house or tree variety, all seemed to share the same habits. Whether they were after seeds or grains or bits of dead grass as this one was right now, it had to be the just the right size and shape. Perhaps this one was building its nest in the tangle of ivy, which surrounded and was gradually choking the big old holly tree at the edge of the field. She hoped so. She would get Pat to check it out with her later on and if it was there, they would spot it. They'd just sit quietly in the field until it popped into the ivy and disappeared into and amongst its tough green leaves. Sparrows, like robins, often chose this safe site to brood and rear their young. Although apparently engrossed in its work, she could see its beady, watchful little eyes and knew that at the first sign of danger, which usually came in the shape of their old cat, it would be up and away in a split second. Thankfully, Nuggly was nowhere to be seen at the moment.

It must surely be spring now, she reckoned, even though the dawn had brought with it a keen, finger biting frost. In fact on her way to the lavvy first thing, she had stood for a few moments taking in the still whiteness of the scene around her, holding her breath as she looked even further afield to where the mist hung suspended over the hollow where the village slumbered. She sighed as she turned away from the window. Yes, spring was very definitely the best time of the year.

As she walked back into the kitchen, she paused. A shaft of sunlight angling through the window was distorting the shadow of the tassels on the old tablecloth and elongating them until they resembled the hairs on Rumplestiltskin's beard.

Sally shook herself quickly out of her reflective mood, moved swiftly over to the table and leaned over Pat, who was spooning the last scrapings of porridge into her mouth. She remembered suddenly that she had forgotten to tell her sister that she had arranged to meet up with Hope Gosse and Hilary to exercise the horses. Hope or Pops as she was known as by friends and family, lived on a small farm in Crazy Lane with her parents and younger siblings, a sister and two brothers. Mr and Mrs Gosse ran their farm almost single handedly, working very hard tending livestock and tilling the ground for the many and varied vegetables they grew. As far as Sally knew, the only help they had was seasonal, with the lifting of potatoes etc. Mr Gosse suffered from asthma, which though distressing to witness, did not seem to faze him or to stop him getting on with his work. 'Take no notice of my wheeze,' he would say to the girls when they watched him fearfully as he struggled for breath. 'I'll get the old oil can out when I've finished what I'm doing here.' Mrs Collins who also suffered from the same complaint, seemed to be far more seriously affected by the illness than this tall, muscular man.

At the word 'horses', Pat was on her feet. "Why didn't you tell me sooner," she scolded. "You know we've still got the pumping to do before we can go out. Come on, you prime it and I'll start pumping. The sooner we get it done, the sooner we can get away. And don't let dad know we're going out or he'll make us sow some seeds or something before we go. You know what he's like."

As they hurried up Crazy Lane, talking nineteen to the dozen, Sally came to a sudden halt. "Bloody hell," she said, gripping Pat's shoulder. "Here comes Denis and he's seen us, worse luck. Now don't say a word, let me do all the talking. He's got a face on him like thunder, so someone's upset him. Just be ready to run up the bank there if he turns nasty, that's all. We'll have to get through the hedge and into Gosse's field that way."

As Denis Crow brought his bike to a halt beside them with a screech of brakes, the girls instinctively backed away from him, almost losing their balance on the uneven, grassy bank. Anger dripped from him like balls of invisible mercury. "Hello Denis, where're you off to?" asked Sally in a shaky voice. "We're off to give Pops a hand with her horses. Hilary's up there already, or she should be by now."

There was silence as Denis eyed them up and down, and then he looked directly at Sally making her painfully aware of their last confrontational encounter in the hop fields. Then as though deciding that the need to confide in someone, anyone, was more important than settling old scores, he shook his head, sniffed loudly and began his tale of woe, still staring at Sally with his ferrety eyes.

"It's me mum see, I'm right beezled off with her. So I've jest told her to jump in the sewer. She keeps nagging me about the state of me bedroom, as though that's got anything to do with 'er and I tells 'er that till I'm blue in the face. Swop me bloody Bob, I said, give us a chance. I just gonna do it ain't I? Aint got Fifty pairs of bloody 'ands, I ain't and then she bloody cuffs me for swearin'. Can't do nuffin right fer her and that's a fact. So I whizzed off on me bike quicker'n a bat out of hell and told her she'd be bloody sorry if I got meself killed. Me dad's as bad and as bloody useless. Couldn't even cook a cuppa water 'e couldn't." Then he paused, straightened up his bike and looked from one to the other. "Ere, you are going up to Gosse's ain't you? You ain't just off to Chapel like what that Dolly Pilbeam always is. She's got religion good and proper she 'as. I swear I seed God sittin' between her eyebrows the other day, cross legged 'e was see. And cross-eyed too I reckon though I didn't get that close. Well you wouldn't would yer? Not to 'er anyways. You'd soon 'ave old Weller sortin' yer out, yer would. Ere, maybe it's cos of 'im she's got religion all of a sudden. It's summat to do with what the two of 'em get up to , that's what it is," and he chuckled.

Relaxed now, the altercation with his Mother forgotten for the time being, he threw one leg over his cross bar and with legs akimbo, he bent his backside into the saddle. Then, resting his folded arms on top of his handlebars as though he now had all the time in the world, he continued. "That reminds me, ave yer seen old Dickie 'Ayward lately? Finks 'e's the cats whiskers, 'e does, but 'e still looks like a moff eaten toad. E's still wiv that lanky fing yer know. I sees 'em together up along Cottage Lane, couple of nights ago. Best fing 'e could do, I reckon, ud be to put a bucket over 'er 'ead and swing on the bloody 'andle. Do 'em both a favour, see? 'She don't see 'is ugly mug and 'e gets a free ride." And then he chuckled wickedly before continuing. "Free ride's right an all. "Finks no one sees 'em as they creeps in alongside old Mr Dennis's 'ouse and into wood there but I were'nt fer beind 'em. Talk 'bout two rats tryin' to git out of a blanket, cept there weren't no blanket and fer as I could make out, they weren't tryin' to 'scape nuthin,' no ow. Right old carry on it were, I can tell yer." And he chuckled again, as he lifted his backside off the cross bar and moved his bicycle to and fro between his straddled legs.

"Ere, what you gawping at," he said to Pat as she stood rigidly at Sally's side and right up against her, her eyes fixed unblinking and fearfully on his face. "Want a ride on me crossbar do yer? Well jump on then an' we're be orf to Pop in 'ole Lane before yer can say Jack what's 'is name. That aw teach that hoity toity sister of yorn a lesson. Bitch, that's what she be."

"Bugger off, Denis," said Sally, suddenly very angry. "If you lay one hand on Pat, I'll bloody kill you," she added as she moved forward, clenched fists at the ready and now very red in the face. "You're wrong in the head you are."

He eyed her up and down and even through her anger she felt a shivering discomfort. Then without another word, he turned himself and his bicycle around and pedalled off up Crazy Lane, not once looking back in their direction.

Sally was shaking now, a combination of fear and waning anger.

"He gives me the bloody creeps, he does. I wish he'd keep away from us. He's made us late too. Hilary and Pops will think we're not coming."

As she reached for Pat's hand in a rare show of affection, she added. "I meant it when I said I'd kill him if he touched you, you know. God knows how I'd have done it though," and she giggled nervously.

"Well, if looks could kill, he'd have died on the spot. The way you looked at him just now was enough to turn him to stone, and that would have made him dead I think. He's scared stiff of you though, you do you know that, don't you?"

"Then he's got a funny way of showing it. Pity his fear doesn't keep him in his own garden where he belongs, that's all I can say. Anyway, best get a move on now. We've wasted enough time because of him. I just hope Hilary and Pops haven't got tired of waiting for us and gone off for a ride with the horses somewhere."

All was well however, and the two girls were in the process of saddling and harnessing the horses when Pat and Sally arrived.

Later that morning, tired and hungry, they sat around the table in the large kitchen of the Gosse's farmhouse, supping cocoa and munching delicious hot cheese scones that tasted strongly of the mustard, added to the mixture to supplement the meagre cheese allowance.

"You alright now, Sally?" enquired Pops. And Sally nodded, her mouth too full of cheese scone to reply immediately. " You're lucky then, you took a tidy tumble down there, you know" she continued. " You could have broken your neck and the horses too if we'd been riding on hard ground. You must learn to relax more around horses, move with them like Pat and Hilary do, rather than against them."

The girls had taken the horses down to the track that ran alongside Stafford's stream, for exercise and also for Pat and Sally to learn the art of 'rising to the trot.' Pat soon got the hang of it but Sally, nervous and edgy, had urged the horse forward before she had taken firm control of the reins and with just the very tips of her toes in the stirrups. As the creature moved forward at a brisk pace, instead of tucking her knees into its flank and holding firmly on the reins, she had lunged forward, reins aloft and with her legs sloping backwards, had bumped up and down on the horses back, completely out of control. As the horse reached and jumped the first obstacle, which came in the shape of a narrow drainage ditch, Sally had shot onto the poor animals neck and had hung suspended there for a few seconds before somersaulting over and on to the rough grass. Luckily her feet were well clear of the stirrups before she tumbled and as she and the horse parted company, she had just lain there for a few moments, afraid to move for fear of another greenstick fracture. Then as the other girls came running along, she had sat up and moved first her arms and then her legs before getting slowly back on to her feet again.

"Yes, I'm okay now," Sally replied quietly, the memory still very fresh in her mind and accompanied by a fair degree of shame. "I know what I should do and it's in my mind to do it, but it doesn't seem to register properly in my brain. In fact my brain just freezes over completely, and I'm sort of not in control if you know what I mean."

As she was talking, the tall and stately Mrs Gosse walked into the kitchen carrying an enormous basket of wet washing and asked in that rather posh voice of hers for volunteers to peg the stuff onto the washing lines. Mr Gosse having taken the younger children, Robert, Debbie and Tim to the Farrows farm for the morning had given her, she told them, a chance to catch up with a few chores. Hilary rose from her seat immediately and was followed by Pat and Sally, all eager to please this kindly lady. Hope was still in the process of fingering up the last meagre crumbs from around her plate and would no doubt follow them in her own good time.

As Sally lifted, shook and then pegged the clothes on to the line, she thought, not for the first time, how pleasant Mrs Gosse was. She was on a par with Mrs Farrow, Gran Powell and Mrs and Miss Smith, she reckoned. They all, like her own mum, always spared the time to listen to what the youngsters had to say, It was never, 'another time dear, when I'm not so busy,' or, 'not now, not now,' like a lot of grown ups said. And she did not grumble about inconsequential things, like not wiping their shoes carefully before entering her kitchen. She also had reason to believe, from comments made by her dad, that this intellectual, highly intelligent lady was a Socialist.

Once the last garment had been securely pegged on to the line, they returned the basket to the kitchen and prepared to take their leave. Pat had reminded Sally that Aunty Lilie was bringing Granny Cotton back down to Sylvian today, which brought her suddenly from an analysis of character to thoughts on the immediate future. Uncle Alf and Uncle Fred would also be down for the weekend, leaving their Aunties at home once again. Sally wondered secretly and not for the first time whether one of the reasons for their Aunties' infrequent visits, could be to do with the sanitary arrangements at Sylvian. She found the thought amusing for some peculiar reason.

Dad's older sister Elizabeth, or Lilie as she was always called, and Uncle Will, her husband, lived in Croydon's old town. Granny Cotton had moved in with them when she first left London, but she now moved around between various family members, spending most of her time at Sylvian.

As the three girls made their way back down Crazy Lane. Patsy was telling Hilary about their encounter with Denis, looking up and down the lane as she did so to make sure he was not lurking in the bushes somewhere. "He was in a right state he was and he frightened us to death," she said. "His mum had upset him or something and I really thought he was going to thump us. You know what he's like. He called Sally a bitch again but she stood up to him and just after that, he rode off up the lane, thank God. But it was touch and go I can tell you."

"That's funny," replied Hilary, "he was up by the stile near the tree seat when I came up here. I was in a bit of a hurry as I was rather late. He was looking at something he'd got wrapped up in a dirty old hankie, so he didn't spot me thank goodness. I ran down the farm track and then when I was out of sight, I lobbed a stone into the hedge the other side of the lane from where he was standing. It must have scared him because he shouted something, but I didn't hang around. I just went and found Pops. I did wonder what on earth he'd got in that filthy hankie. A great big bogey, I expect." Then she burst out laughing as Sally and Pat spluttered in disgust.

"I don't know why you're so scared of him. He's all arse and trousers, he is. Oh, and bogeys of course. Come on, race you to the bottom of the lane," she called as she ran homewards.

"They're here already!" Puffed Pat, referring to their expected visitors, as they ran along the lane towards the bottom of the field. "Look, mum and dad are just coming through the scullery door. And Uncle Alf and Uncle Fred are here as well, I can see them on the underground tank," she added excitedly.

They puffed up the field in time to see Uncle Will and granny being helped from the seats of the little old black car. Then Aunty Lilie rolled from the driving seat, her red hair with it's peppering of grey, standing out like a halo around her smiling face. Their cousin Cissie, who would normally have been with them, was staying with her older sister, Hettie. Though several years their senior, Cissie was rather childish in her ways, rather like Pauline Wilson and seemed to prefer the company of children.

The girls followed the grownups through the gate and as Granny Cotton walked up the path towards the scullery door, she passed wind, not just once but with every step she took. "Here she comes playing God save the King," dad remarked, and the girls giggled behind their hands. She however, took not the slightest notice.

The girls then focused their attention on Uncle Will, or old Willum as they called him amongst themselves. Hand in hand with Aunty Lilie, he was now shuffling along behind the others. He was tall and stick-thin, with a stoop that rivalled 'Old Death' whose picture lurked somewhere amongst the pages of an old book in the front room. All that was needed to complete the picture was a scythe and a black cloak from which, if she remembered rightly, peeped an exaggeratedly elongated toed shoe.

Sally nudged Pat mouthing the word 'eggs' silently to her sister and they both grinned as they recalled an incident that had occurred when Auntie and Uncle had last visited Sylvian. Dad had placed a tray of eggs on a chair just inside the scullery door when their arrival had caught him off guard and had hurried out to meet them. Before anyone could stop him, Old Willum had pushed through the door and as Aunty Lilie turned to speak to mum, had plonked himself down on the fragile harvest. Then even though his bum had been covered with the contents and shell of more than a dozen eggs, he had just looked around vaguely wondering what all the fuss was about. The only person who had not seen the funny side of it was dad. 'What a bloody waste,' he kept on saying. Even their Aunty had laughed and she was the one who had to wash his trousers off before they set on him like concrete. Sally was sorry that he was deaf and very short sighted, but she found him incredibly funny. More so because most of the time he just did not seem to know what was going on.

Aunty Lilie on the other hand, whose sharp and sparkling eyes did not miss a thing, was full of bustling energy. Her little black Morris 8 with its snub nose, was her pride and joy and was always polished to within an inch of its life.

Sally knew that as soon as her Aunty had finished her cup of tea, she would be out there cleaning the mud from the field off the wheels before it had time to dry.

Her little shop in Croydon, packed solidly from top to bottom, with this and that, came a close second to her motorcar in her list of priorities. From these premises she sold anything from a washer to the weekly groceries and anything you could think of in between. The oddest item as far as Sally was concerned was a pair of false teeth that grinned out from a stand just inside the right hand side of the front window and had been there, according to dad, since kingdom come, and rightly so. Who in their right mind would insult their mouths with second hand gnashers.

An hour or so later as they sat around the kitchen table, full of rabbit stew and apple pie, the girls listened to the grownups chatting, exchanging news and talking about 'old times.' Gran had disappeared into the garden after she had sucked the last vestiges of rice pudding from around her gums. Contemplation of the garden was a daily ritual, performed by her no matter what the weather. The rice pudding was also a daily requirement of hers or more precisely, an addiction. As dad said, she would go into a decline if the milky dish, with its thick crust of light brown skin, did not appear on the table in front of her immediately she had finished her first course. He also pointed out that gardens and gardening were a passion with her, a luxury she had never been able to afford in her younger days. The nearest she had ever got to it had been the tending of the lone aspidistra that had decorated their various window ledges, when the sighting of a new leaf had always given her the utmost satisfaction.

Dad clearly thought the world of Aunty Lilie who, while she was working as a cook at St. James' Palace, had sneaked left over food out to him and his brothers and sister as they waited at the back entrance of that grand and imposing building. They were talking about it now and Aunty Lilie was smiling as she recalled those far off days.

"I remember it as though it were only yesterday," she said. "I wasn't supposed to do it of course but it would only have gone to waste and I wasn't the only one sneaking bits of food out of that kitchen I can assure you. You were such scrawny little devils in those days that it was worth risking a good telling off just to try and put a bit of flesh on your bones. I can see your faces now as you stood waiting by the back door. Scared stiff you were and looking for all the world as though you were expecting the hangman or Old Nick himself even to pounce out on you. When mum started working there later on of course, things got a bit better for you all."

"I don't know how we'd have survived without it," said dad. "Sometimes we'd come home from school hungry enough to eat a scabby donkey and all there'd be was a spoonful of rice boiled in water. We couldn't wait to get round to the old Palace to get a bit of grub. It wasn't mum's fault. She just couldn't stretch the money she got from the old man far enough and she always tried to pay the rent before she did anything else. Mind you we were sold up a couple of times, had the old bums in for non payment of rent I've been told, but I can't remember that. Our George remembered it though, especially the time some lady put a sovereign in mum's hand as she walked the streets with us kids. There's always been some pretty decent caring folks around, but even so, the old girl would have hated the thought of having to rely on charity. He wasn't really nasty or anything like that, the old man, and he always had a job as far as I can make out but he was irresponsible, he always took the easy way out. He couldn't understand why he couldn't do what he wanted with the money he earned and if that meant spending a tidy bit of it in the pub on his way home from work on paydays, then that's what he did - often. Trouble was, he couldn't hold his drink, could he? That got him into more trouble than anything. Drunk and incapable was it they charged him with, a few times there? Anyway he could never pay the fine and got put away for six or seven days each time. Mum only had the bit of money coming in then that she got for doing the washing and ironing for the folks in those posh houses up Queens Road, which wasn't much. It didn't matter how hard up she was though, she never charged a penny for laying out the old bodies, did she? You wouldn't exactly call it a labour of love but I suppose she reckoned that their folks were as hard up as she was. And there were often other kids around that she fed when she could, weren't there? I suppose you could say that she had nothing but shared everything. You take that sort of thing for granted when you're a kid I suppose.

Anyway, going back to the old man. In his early days of course, he worked on the Queens Park Estate, Paddington. I think it was King Edward V11, when he was Prince of Wales, who helped to sponsor a scheme to house working people there. I know that after dad had worked there, he considered himself to be an Artisan, and very proud of the title he was. But thinking about the nature of the beast and him always taking the easy way out, he couldn't even be bothered to get his share of his father's property or properties when granddad died, could he? Not that it would have done him that much good I suppose with the way he was. They were chalk and cheese, dad and grandad. Our dad was happy go lucky to the point of stupidity almost. Then there was grandad, conscientious and a butcher in the true sense of the word. What did he call himself, a slaughterman, scalesman, salesman and manager? He had a shop in the Edgware Road – the old Roman Road as we used to call it. They poleaxed the old animals in those days of course, which was a tricky and dangerous business. The Old Boy had a few close calls according to dad. He owned that shop and his own house, I do know that and there was talk of him owning another property in the area but no one seems to be sure about that. And he didn't drink."

"No he didn't drink that's for sure and nor did anyone else in the family as far as I can make out," replied Uncle Alf. "The old man was what you would call the black sheep of the family. I never really knew how old he was, did you?

He remembered Regents Park Lake freezing over and then cracking when all those people were skating and sliding on the ice there though. And that was in about in 1863 I think, so he must have been getting on a bit when he died." He paused here and removed his elbows from the table, and after rubbing them absentmindedly, replaced them before continuing with his reminiscences. "As we were saying though, the old lady had a pretty tough time one way or the other because of him. Not that he knocked her about or anything, it was just that he did his own thing regardless and left her to cope with the consequences. But she's a tough old girl I'll say that for her. Do you remember the time her varicose veins broke as she was walking back from Notting Dale, and she lost all that blood? She just bandaged herself up with a bit of clean rag and carried on as usual, didn't she? Then when you think about it, she must have had to forge a few rent books in her time to get housed and she'd have hated doing that. You ask her about it though and she just gives you a dirty look, and you know what they're like! I remember some of the old landlords, do you? Old Soloman was one of them. Remember him? Public enemy number one we used to call him.

Then there was another one called Crooke who, in spite of his name was a good bloke really. We used to call him Mr Rent Book, didn't we? Going back to her being tough though, she did come down hard on us kids at times, didn't she? We had to duck and dive a bit to keep out of her way when we'd upset her. But she always stuck up for us when we were in trouble and I remember one time in particular when I wouldn't have wanted to be in the bloke's shoes when she was having a go at him.

Then there was that teacher of yours Pop, the one who always picked on you when you got to school a bit late or nodded off to sleep during the day because you were so tired. He used to cuff you round the ears and rap you on the knuckles or even drag you out in front of the class and ridicule you. Vicious bugger he was. And you were only late because, like me, you worked at a couple of those posh houses up Bayswater before school, getting up coal and that sort of thing. Anyway when the Old Lady got to know about it, she stormed up there and gave him a piece of her mind and frightened the old devil to death. Serve him right. He didn't give you such a hard time after that, did he?" He paused here to wipe his nose on a clean white hankie. Then as he stuffed it back into his trouser pocket, he chuckled. "Hey, do you remember when we used to raid the fruit and veg stalls down the market when we were kids? The old stall holders got to know us only too well. They never managed to catch us though did they? We might have been scrawny kids with little legs but we couldn't half run. I remember one bloke though with a battered old trilby, who came after us and very nearly got us, and he couldn't half run. I reckon he'd have caught you Fred, you being that much littler than us older ones, if he hadn't lost his hat. Came off the top of his head like a bloody spinning top, didn't it Fred? And he didn't half swear at us as he stooped to pick it up. We were a bit more careful after that."

"Do I remember? Could I ever forget?" replied Uncle Fred. "Mind you I soon learned to keep up with you after that. You and Pop between you certainly toughened me up, you with the boxing lessons and him with football. You did a bit of professional boxing at one time, didn't you Alf? Wasn't it at some time towards the end of the Great War that you took on the chap who said he was the Lightweight Champion of Calais, and beat him? He was nigh on a stone heavier than you as well. If I remember rightly, you got a watch out of that match and brought it home with you, which was really something in those days.

Mind you that wasn't all you brought back with you was it? You were lousy with fleas and lice. Mum soon got to work on them with her carbolic and paraffin though and ironed the old seams where they used to try and hide. The 'Big Game Hunter,' we used to call her.

You were no slouch yourself either Pop, were you? You were one of only a handful of lads who were chosen to represent your Battalion in their football matches at the end of the war and that was out of about a thousand men I believe. After the war of course you still played a bloody good game. Until you got your knee injury, that is. That put you out of first class football once and for all but you still couldn't resist knocking a ball about from time to time. It didn't put you off cycling though did it, that knee of yours? Nor did those boils you used to get on your backside and they didn't half give you jip. You just made yourself a cushion for that hard old saddle and it fitted the thing as though it'd been made for it, it did. Always good with the needle you were, and still are of course. Anyway once you'd done that you were able to sit down while you peddled the thing around, a bit gingerly though mind you. Necessity is the Mother of invention as they say."

"Sorry to interrupt but I've made the tea and I wanted you to drink it whilst it's still fresh and hot," said mum. As they moved aside for her to place the tray with its contents onto the table, she said. "Go and find your gran will you Sally. She won't be far away. Just tell her that she'd better get here quickly or the fruit cake will disappear. That'll bring her in, on the trot. She loves her food, especially cake and rice puddings. Heaven only knows why she doesn't put on weight. Well you boys are just the same aren't you? You're all fidgety britches, that's probably got something to do with it, and it's a rare treat to see Pop sitting around for a change. The only thing you're slow at is eating. I remember you getting here late afternoon once and sitting down to a couple of boiled eggs with bread and butter, Alf, and it took you two hours to clear the plate. Mind you, you and Pop were chatting nineteen to the dozen at the time if I remember rightly."

As Sally and Hilary walked out through the scullery doors, Aunty Lilie rose to her feet and tapped Uncle Will on the shoulder. "Come on old chap, best get you round to the lavvy before you take on any more liquid. Come to think of it, I need the use the thing myself."

Once the teacups were empty and every last crumb of cake had been fingered from the plates, the men rose from the table. "What's to be done then, Pop?" asked Uncle Fred. "I've been sitting down for far too long. I need to work off some of this grub. And we owe you a bit of labour for all the food you've sent up to us over the years. Even during this old war you managed to get the stuff to us when you could, didn't you, you and Dolly? When we saw Jack Griffin pull up in the road with that big old van of his, we knew we were in for a treat. There would always be a tea chest full of fresh vegetables, eggs, cake and almost best of all, those little old roasting chickens done up neatly in bits of hessian, all ready for the oven." He paused here for a moment and then he smiled and put his hands, palms downward on to the table and looked at dad. "I don't suppose we could have a bonfire could we? No I thought not, it's the wrong time of the year isn't it," he said as dad shook his head. "I promise to be more careful next time and not stand upwind of the thing. Last time it singed all my eyebrows and lashes off, if you remember. Would have done the same thing to my hair if I'd had any. Tell you what, me and Alf'll take a walk round the field and collect the eggs. If there's any of those bad tempered broody hens sitting in the coops, I'll get Alf to put his hands underneath. Those big old Light Sussex hens are right devils. They seem to know I'm nervous and they peck the living daylights out of me if they get the chance. Anyway, after that we'll chop up a bit of firewood. Baskets still in the copperhouse, Dolly?" he asked, as he made for the scullery door.

Hilary and Sally were in two minds as to whether to stay listening to the chatter around the kitchen table after tea that evening, or to go straight down to Windy Ridge where they would be spending the night. At the moment, the balance was definitely in favour of lingering awhile, the conversation centring on the experiences of the grownups during the Great War. Mum had just lit the oil lamp and as she placed it in the centre of the table, the flame spluttered and a curl of smoke rose through the glass funnel to be swiftly consumed by the rising heat level. The continuing flickering of the flame, fed by the currents of air coming through the air bricks, distorted into weird caricatures of themselves, the faces of the folk who sat with steaming cups of tea around the table. As they nestled themselves back comfortably into their seats after the slight disruption, all eyes turned towards Uncle Fred who was talking about one of his older brothers, killed in that other war.

"Poor old Bill. I reckon he didn't have much choice as to whether he joined up or not in 1914. He'd been sacked from his job because of the war and was told to join the army. He'd have been skint anyway. You didn't have much in the way of savings in those days. He was either very brave or foolhardy though to have volunteered for the hand grenade bombing section in 1915. But there again I suppose he had his reasons. Fancy being in the front line trenches with the old Jerries within spitting distance. It doesn't bear thinking about, does it? No wonder he got killed. At the Somme wasn't it? He was blown to pieces as far as I can make out, leastways his body was never identified. Poor devil he must have been absolutely terrified. Well you know something about it, don't you Alf? You being if not on the front line then still where all the fighting was going on."

"Yes, being in the Artillery was bad enough, we came under a lot of heavy shelling at times. We got moved all over the place. Mostly Belgium. Paschendaele, Ypres and all around there. But we also got sent to the Vimy Ridge and to the Somme as well. I never met up with our Bill but then I wouldn't have, would I? He was killed early part of 1916. We never did get the whole story about it. All we know is that a few fellers he was with said that they thought he went over the top and didn't come back. As you say Fred, seems like his body was never recovered, or not in one piece anyway. He'll just be a name amongst thousands on some monument somewhere near one of those battlegrounds. The only thing his wife got was a communication that he'd been killed in action, the usual thing. Makes you think doesn't it? Makes you wonder how on earth after that lot, we could have got ourselves involved in another lot of bloodshed. I don't think we'll ever learn from experience, from past history. Leastways that's how it seems to me.

Anyway, I got caught up in that last big German offensive in the spring of 1918 but then I got my foot run over, didn't I, by one of the gun trailers. I didn't notice it at the time but one of the sergeants saw the blood oozing out of my boot and I got sent to casualty. It took ages to heal and I didn't see much more of the war after that, luckily. The war made a big impression on you too, didn't it Pop? Though you were in the Far East, India most of the time of course. Where was it you were stationed? Rawalpindi was it? Sounds more like a disease than a place. Anyway, old Gandhi's been your hero ever since, hasn't he?"

"Hero's not the word I'd use." Replied dad. "That word suggests a one off kind of heroic action," replied dad. "Gandhi's been struggling with injustice for years and he's faced up to ridicule as well as brutality. The man's got guts and the staying power to go with it, scrawny as he is. I was a silent witness to the Amritsar riots, a British soldier with a rifle on my shoulder and I'm not proud of that. Those so called riots were termed another of 'Ghandi's acts of Civil Disobedience', but there was no excuse for all that bloodshed. Nor was there any need to make the Hindu students grovel in the dust at the end of a bayonet as I saw them do. Mind you the fact that they were high class Hindu's probably contributed to old General Dyer and Governor O'Dwyer being called home afterwards and I think, sacked. I suppose my experience of war was a bit different from yours Alf, in that we weren't facing the continual bombardments that you were. The climate out there is a killer though and the forced marches we went on brought a lot of the men literally to their knees. I counted my blessing then that I was a tough old bugger and got through it somehow. But by God it didn't half take it out of you. As for the Afghan tribesmen, well they'd put the fear of God into the devil himself. We encountered them more often than we'd have chosen to when we were trying to keep the Khyber Pass Heights open and safe for the merchants and such like to get through with their goods. Those hooded demons though had other ideas about control of the area. They were totally fearless and came at you from all directions. What made the biggest impression on me out there though was the poverty. A nation of beggars I think it's been called. We've seen a bit of deprivation over here, but this was different. The poverty we've experienced was nothing compared to this. The worse thing was the kids, all covered in flies, with their big bellies and stick thin arms and legs. It's probably always been like that even before the British went out there, I don't know. It's got a lot to do with their caste system of course, which is even worse than our class system, and that's saying something. It's more in your face if you know what I mean."

As the men continued to talk, Hilary and Sally sat there, elbows on table, totally enthralled. Never before had they heard the experiences of their uncles and their father being discussed in such detail and with so much frankness. It was only when mum reminded them how dark it was outside that they rose reluctantly to their feet and began to look around for a torch to light them on their short but hazardous journey to Hilary's house. As they shrugged themselves into their thick coats then rummaged around in the cupboard for their shoes, Uncle Alf told them that on their next visit to Sylvian, he would make sure that their Aunties came too. He and Aunty Lil owned a shoe repairing business in Neasden, and trade was very brisk. In fact they were so busy that he and aunty often worked late into the night to ensure that the folk in the area were kept well shod, their footware given a new lease of life and made ready for collection with a minimum of delay. This time aunty had stayed behind, responsible for the collection of the cleaned and mended boots and shoes, all neatly labelled and arrayed in tidy rows on shelves at the back of the shop, awaiting collection.

Uncle Alf knew there would be another batch in need of rejuvenation by the time he got home.

As the girls walked briskly down the field, Hilary swung the torch to and fro in front in front of them. "Do you know, I've never, not even once, trodden in sheep's treddles and they're everywhere if you think about it," she said.

"Touch wood," replied Sally, as she raised her left arm and touched her friend on the forehead.

CHAPTER 8

Summer was hovering. It seemed to be teetering on the very edge of spring as though psyching itself up for the daunting tasks that lay ahead. The thick, sticky buds of the horse chestnut had metamorphosed into an abundance of big green floppy leaves, and each branch and twig was showing off its candle like decoration. The pollarded willows across the Brooks had shed their Medusa disguise, their thin, elongated leaves and immature catkins, were now hanging down in supplication to the rippling stream at their feet. The Rowan with its ancient witch-craft connections, was now covered in a fine tracery of delicate leaves with here and there, clusters of tiny white flowers on fragile stems. Even the old sycamores at the back of the house had lost their skeletal aspect, their branches now covered with thick green leaves, which rustled characteristically in the lightest of breezes.

The war with all its horror, cruelty and hatred that had seemed to dominate the world for aeons, was mostly a distant memory. Now and again however, it resurfaced in all its horror, with yet more harrowing accounts of the mass killing in one or other of Hitler's monstrous concentration camps, accompanied by haunting images of unspeakable suffering. The trial of the Nazi war criminals was still on going and Sally wondered how on earth the witnesses and judges alike could bear to sit through accounts of the cruelty perpetrated or sanctioned by these monsters. It was enough for her to read the headlines and just a small part of the small print. She was then free to abandon the Newspaper and escape its horrors.

Also, other reports were still coming in from those who had been held as prisoners of war by the Japanese.

The photos that accompanied these stories brought tears to the eyes of the grownups and uncomprehending silence from the children. Side by side with these experiences however, were amazing stories of heroism and bravery that sent shivers of fear and admiration down their spines. There also seemed to be a lot of bargaining going on, not just within Europe, but in Africa and all over the Far East as well. There seemed to be a confusion of differing opinions with a feeling that the whole world was in a state of flux. It must be something to do with the Allied Powers wanting to do the right thing this time. They would do all they could to prevent another set of circumstances occurring that would set in motion more conflict, Sally reckoned. They would not repeat the mistakes that had been made after the end of that other war, the ones that mum and dad had often talked about. She had heard the expression, 'A European Carve Up,' mentioned from time to time but that was over her head and would have to be left to the 'Powers That Be' to sort out. What she did understand and more to the point was that sweets were still on ration.

***

The girls were on their way to Wayside this morning. Hilary was in front with the pram, with Dorothy trotting along beside her, chatting away nineteen to the dozen and holding on tightly to the handle. Inside the pram and tucked up fast asleep, was Jacky. Pat and Sally were walking just behind, and with Whydown Hill now negotiated, they could see all the way to Kent Street. As they passed Gotways Farm, Pat looked instinctively through the large double gates where, between the barn and the farmhouse, could be seen a small part of the field where the horses spent many hours grazing and exercising. If she had had her way, she would have run down the little track now a hundred or so yards behind them, that separated the field from the road, to gaze at her beloved horses. This was the track used by little Mrs Edwards and her family on their way to and from their little cottage.

As they walked towards the lane leading to Norton's Farm, Sally looked across the road to where Farthing Cottage with its hooded eyed windows, snuggled inside a thickly hedged garden, entwined with periwinkle and honeysuckle. She had seen an elderly lady in the garden from time to time and had passed the time of day with her, but did not know her name. Just as Sally was looking towards the house nearby, where the Forrest family lived, Hilary stopped suddenly in her tracks and Pat and Sally bumped right into her. "Sorry," she said, "but I can't resist this," and proceeded to pluck the thickest piece of grass she could find. Then she lined up the grass between her thumbs, cupped her hands around them and blew the most amazing whistle through the tiny gap.

"Let me have a go," said Pat excitedly, letting go of Sally's hand as she bent down to choose a likely piece of grass. No matter how hard she tried though, all she succeeded in raising was a hiss accompanied by plenty of spittle. As her face became redder and redder, the bursts of air more sporadic and spittle laden, Hilary prised Pat's hands gently apart.

"Let's try another bit of grass, shall we? You've gone and done this bit to death by the look of it."

As Pat stooped to select a fresh specimen, she paused for a second then drew her hand back swiftly and shot up, as though she'd been bitten. "There's a spider on that bit of grass and it's huge. I nearly put my hand on it," she said in a squeaky voice. And then she shuddered.

"It's only a money spider with muscles," said Hilary, "that's all and it's a darned sight more scared of us than we are of it, or it should be. Anyway, we'd best be on our way before this baby wakes up and starts crying. We'll look for another bit of grass later on." With that she turned and, picking Dorothy up, sat her on the bottom of the pram. "You can have a ride from here until we get to the bottom of Ebdens Hill," she told the little one. "We've not had a peek from you, no complaints, no nothing. You're a good little soul." As Dorothy beamed at her she added, "If I get tired then that Sally can take over for a bit, she's got some tidy old muscles on her."

As they came to the little shop, they paused without actually stopping, to peer inside. The door was open and Mrs Floyd was standing on a chair behind the cluttered counter, rearranging the goods on one of the shelves. Trying to make a bit of room for what was on the counter, Sally reckoned. How she found what her customers wanted in that chaos she had no idea. What had her mum called the place? An organised muddle, that's what she'd called it. It was not that good, surely! It was interesting though, even she had to admit that and when she and her sisters did odd bits of shopping there from time to time for mum, they always tarried awhile. They lingered as much for the earthy smell of the root vegetables and tallow, with the place overhung, even on the hottest summers day, by the pungent smell of paraffin and methylated spirits.

There was no sign of Lucy Hart or even Dollie Pilbeam, which was unusual. So the girls continued through the little hamlet of Kent Street and on to the expanse of road between Carpenters Barn Farm and the bottom of Ebdens Hill. They chatted from time to time, but mostly their minds and imaginations were elsewhere. Sally looked at the hedges on either side that had been layered in the autumn. She could see the uniformity of the posts with their chamfered tops still clearly visible through the lush new growth. Then she looked across the field on her right hand side, to where a majestic beech reigned supreme in a small copse of deciduous trees. The size of its leaves, oval and small, always surprised her. For a tree of its size and magnificence, its leaves should have equalled those of the horse chestnut - at the very least.

She came to with a start as Pat grabbed her by the arm. "Look in the field over there, no not there, over the other side, in Peggy Cain's place, Irelands farm," she said excitedly now pulling her sister around to face in the right direction. "There's lots of swallows over there and they're swooping all over those cows. I hope they're eating up all the flies and especially horse flies if there's any there. I hate those things. Their stings are even more itchy than chilblains, I reckon.

Hilary and Sally paused and, looking across the field in the direction of Pat's now pointing finger, watched the quicksilver movements and unmistakable flight patterns of the swallows.

"You know what they're supposed to be, don't you?" Said Hilary seriously, as she balanced the handle of the pram on her hip to prevent Dorothy's extra weight on the chassis upending the thing. "They're the souls of old men, on their flight of freedom before they go to Heaven. Mrs Wintergreen Edwards told me that." This Mrs Edwards also lived near Paygate Corner and was very similar in size and appearance to her neighbour of the same name. Summer or winter, she wore a long brown coat with button up boots to match, and she always smelled of Wintergreen ointment. She suffered with something called the screws, according to Basil.

"What happens to our souls then?" asked Pat. It's not fair that old men should get the best birds to fly around in.

"I don't know, do I? She never told me that and I never asked," replied Hilary. "Perhaps us lot are so good that our souls go straight to Heaven. Yes, I reckon that's it." She paused here for a few seconds as though trying to fathom out the vagaries of God's workings, then continued. "On second thoughts though, perhaps we get the barn owls. They're always gliding around the field at home aren't they? Hazel's seen them lots of times and if they're the ones we get, then I reckon they're already keeping an eye on us. They look a bit like Angels really if you think about it and I think God saved them specially for us kids. You'd like that wouldn't you Sally? Owls are your favourite birds, well one of them anyway. Still let's not think about things like that at the moment, 'cause our souls ain't going nowhere. Not for ages and ages they ain't. Come on then you two, we can't stay here all day. The swallows will probably still be here when we come back and if one gets close enough, I'll ask him if he's a bird or an old man. You'll have to get off and walk soon I'm afraid, little Dotty, she said," smiling down at Dorothy as she sat there with her legs crossed at the ankle and with her chubby little hands resting comfortably, either side of the pram handle. "It's a long pull up that old Ebdens Hill."

"How on earth did dad used to ride all the way up this hill without getting off his bike when he worked at that place on the Ridge during the war? It goes on forever," puffed Sally, now in charge of the pram and holding it at arm's length, body leaning forward to get more push. "We're only half way up it and I'm worn out."

"We'll stop over here then," said Hilary, pointing to a gap in the hedge.

As they manoeuvred the pram into the small opening, Hilary moved a few paces into the wood. "I've never been into this wood, you know," she said.

"I don't know why, it's not far from home, is it? Basil told me there's lots of old iron workings and so forth in here and he thinks people actually lived in here like they did in Battle Big Wood ages ago. And there's even some badger setts, he reckons. Mind you I don't think he's actually seen a badger, he'd have told me if he had. I don't know what it's called, this wood. Beauport Park's not far away so it's probably got the same name. Got you breath back yet?" she asked, looking at Sally. "Here, we'll both push the pram the rest of the way. We'd better keep well in, it's a bit narrow just here and there's no pathway at all."

They continued up the long drag of Ebden's Hill, Hilary and Sally in front with the pram and Pat and Dorothy, hand in hand, following closely behind.

"We're nearly there now," said Sally her voice echoing strangely around as, having turned right at the junction where the road divided, they walked beneath the old red brick bridge. As they emerged at the other side, she pointed westward, and down over the fields. "Look there's Harrow Farm over there," she said. Then she sniffed appreciatively. "You can smell pigs can't you? Just like old Porky's place when he's got the swill on the go."

The farmhouse itself, an odd combination of tin and timber, nestled with vernacular dignity, into the folds of the undulating countryside around it. The huge greenhouses, which would soon be awash with tomatoes and geraniums nearly, but not quite, dominated this settlement. The massive boilers housed within these glass cultivars, were powerful enough to protect with their regulated heat, the most delicate of plants, in the coldest of winters. This place with its combination of produce and livestock was a mixed farm in the truest sense of the word. As she paused here to observe the pigs that were snuffling around in an enclosure adjacent to one of the outhouses, she eased her hands from the handle of the pram, relinquishing the precious cargo to her friend. Then she moved towards the hedge and looked further a field to where a herd of black and white cows were scattered higgledy-piggledy in one of the lower fields. Some were cropping the lush green grass while others sat, legs partially tucked beneath their huge stomachs, chewing the cud.

As her gaze moved back towards the buildings, she spotted a man pushing a wheelbarrow down towards the pigsties. He was whistling, she knew he was. Not that she could hear him from this distance. She just knew he was by the way his head moved ever so slightly to and fro and side to side, just like Mr Freeman's did when he was performing similar chores. Mr Freeman always whistled when he worked around his beloved pigs. She could also make out the blurred image of another figure moving around in one of the greenhouses and reckoned that it was probably the old farmer Mr Down, or Old Alf, as Granpy called him. She had seen two younger men, Alfred and Henry, working there when she had visited the farm with her mum. Alfred was the son of old Mr Down and Henry worked with them. Old Mr Down also had two daughters, one of whom had worked on the farm before her marriage. The other, who had always been rather delicate, lived elsewhere.

Mum had regularly visited this farm right from the time she had arrived at Wayside as a young girl. She always spoke of old Mr Down with affection and as far as Sally could make out, he and his family had lived around here for a very long time.

Her attention was suddenly drawn away from contemplation of farming folk, this engrossing interaction between man and beast, to the sound of giggling. As she turned round, she saw Dorothy bending into the pram playing games with Jacky who, sitting bolt upright and very much awake now, was giggling at her favourite game. *"Clap hands daddy comes, with a pocket full of plums. Up Eyes!"*

As Dorothy recited the little rhyme for the umpteenth time, Hilary picked her up and sat her on the bottom of the pram once again.

"I reckon we've been here long enough, don't you?" Said Hilary, as she moved away from the hedge and on to the grass verge. "I'm parched and I need a long drink of water. We'll have to get it from the old well down there." And she pointed towards Wayside, which was just coming into view.

As they opened the gate leading into the bungalow, they paused to admire the riot of colour in the large front garden. Since Granny Sansom had moved here to look after her sister, their Great Aunty Sarah, and help with the chores, she had transformed the place. The whole area in front and to the side of the bungalow was divided up into small plots, each one filled to overflowing with flowers that were, or soon would be, every colour of the rainbow. The hollyhocks, lupins and delphiniums standing tall and majestic, had yet to reach their full glory. But the promise was there in the buds that were straining to burst through their protective layer of skin. The wallflowers were fading now but the clumps of sweet williams with their multi blossomed flower heads facing ever upward, were at their most colourful. The dappled pink, blue and white of the Canterbury bells, was interspersed with poppies, their astonishing crimson colour tempting the bees to partake of their overt beauty. Here and there, large clumps of campanula squatted in bright blue intensity, their bell-like flowers attracting their own fair share of attention from the bees and butterflies. The nasturtiums had begun to insinuate their stems and bright green leaves through the undergrowth and were already sporting the occasional bright orange flower.

Here and there however, a few clumps of dull, greyish green foliage was all that remained of the bright blue sea of forget-me-nots that had decorated the early spring garden.

Over the pathway leading towards the side door, was Granny's piece de resistance: her ornate rose covered archway. Pink fragrant flowers reached from one side of the path to the other. Evidence of its close encounter with Granny's secateurs in the autumn, the sloping cuts on the old wood, were still just visible through the new growth. And in there somewhere, were neat bits of green twine that had been carefully used to secure any long, trailing branch to the main structure. Trained up against the west wall of the bungalow and just coming into their line of vision, were the sweet peas, with their roots and lower stems, luxuriating in a thick layer of granny's special compost.

"There's Aunty Sarah," whispered Pat pointing towards the large wooden bench positioned beneath the front window, where their aunty sat drowsing in the sunshine of this warm spring morning. Her walking sticks were criss-crossed over her lap and her hands with the fingers all bent and misshapen, were folded above them. She suffered from some kind of progressive rheumatism, which had started way back. A direct the result of losing her two sons in that other war, mum reckoned.

As they tiptoed along the pathway towards the side entrance, Pat hushed the little ones prattling voices. "Ssh, Aunty Sarah's not well, we mustn't wake her up with a start or it'll frighten her to death," she said, her finger to her lips. "Let's go and look for gran, she won't be far away."

As they opened the side gate, and walked through to the back garden, they saw Granny Sansom. She was crouching down in her herb garden, picking something green and aromatic. Mint and parsley and a bit of rosemary, Sally reckoned, sniffing appreciatively. Then she took another loud sniff just to make sure. "We're here then gran," she called and they all moved forward as the old lady rose slowly to her feet, holding her precious herbs in one hand while she absentmindedly pushed her wispy grey hair back from her forehead with the other.

"Yes, I heard you, in fact I could hear you chattering all the way down the road. If I'd hung about doing nothing until you actually got here, I wouldn't have got anything done. Anyway, I expect you're hungry. You always are by the time you get here. I've got a nice bit of dripping on the go and a bit of fresh bread to go with it. Sally, go and call your uncle up from the piggeries. It's time for his cuppa. Old Fred's there with him. I don't suppose he'd say no to one either."

Turning to Hilary, Gran continued. "Perhaps you'd take the little ones to see Aunty Sarah. You'll have to wake her up but she's been so looking forward to seeing you all."

"Can I have a drink of water first, please?" Asked Hilary. "I'm so thirsty, I couldn't spit sixpence." She passed the handle of the pram to Pat, as she rushed inside to open the pantry door where full to the brim, stood a jug of fresh well water. "That's better," she said, wiping her mouth with the back of her hand as she took control of the pram once again. "I'm ready for anything now."

Sally, needing no second bidding, rushed down to the piggeries and saw Granpy leaning on a besom broom chatting to another old man. "As yu's come to zee yer Granpee? I ken tell 'e now, e's grimed up to is eyebrews, 'e is. Looks as thew he jest swip a chimney," said the old man that Sally took to be Fred, the person mentioned by her gran. And he chuckled wickedly at her discomfiture. "Now yer dad, 'e kep pigs one toime there, en when 'e took em to be kewd, owd 'Olmes 'e said, Christ! Ems the leanest pigs I ever sawed in me life. Musta bin all thet thar 'scaping them did from yer fiewd. End awl the chasin 'em got owf dem dere gardens in der village.' Dugged ep a few choice plants em pigs did, end fowks weren't 'appy, no 'ow."

Roughly translated, this bit of old Sussex referred to the fact that her Dad's pigs were always escaping and doing untold damage in the village until it became too embarrassing to keep pigs there any longer.

Not knowing quite how to reply, Sally turned to her uncle. "Do you want a cup of tea? Gran sent me down here to ask you." Then not waiting for a reply, she rushed off to explore the pig-pens, now awash with the water that had been slopped into them, plus the inevitable bit of slurry that always stayed stubbornly around, no matter how meticulous the cleaning process had been. As she moved around the pens, the grunts and snuffles from so many excited pigs delighted her. She sighed contentedly. They were the reason she loved this place. Plus her gran of course, she was a bit special. So were the thick chunks of bread and dripping she gave them, each with its generous layer of salty jelly that always lurked in the bottom of the bowl, the residue of the delicious meat juices. Then there was the garden. That was something else.

By the time she returned to the bungalow, everyone was in the front garden. Granpy and old Fred, noisily slurping their tea, stood apart from the others preferring discussions about Battle Market and the price of pigs, to the idle chatter of women and children.

Jacky, perched on Aunty Sarah's lap, squealed with delight as Dorothy and Pat played games around the bench. Then she struggled to get down to take an active part in what was becoming an even noisier, more physical game. As Sally and Hilary tried to calm the little ones, gran disappeared inside the cottage. Within a few minutes she was back out in the garden again, clutching two large potatoes into which she had stuck a few chicken feathers.

"Here you go then you two. Here's two little birds for you to play with."

She placed them carefully into Dorothy and Jacky's chubby little hands. Then from her large overall pocket, she withdrew a further handful of assorted feathers, which she gave to Pat. "You can pick the big ones out of this lot and give them a few tail feathers if you want to. Or you can get yourself a potato from the kitchen and make your own bird to play with," she said sitting down on the bench beside her sister. "Blow, I left my cup of tea indoors," she said just as she had made herself comfortable. "Will one of you girls fetch it back out here for me please? And while you're at it, perhaps you'd top it up with what's left in the tea-pot on the side table."

Both Hilary and Sally moved at the same time, eager to free themselves from the demands of the little ones. Once inside the kitchen, it took them a while to locate the misplaced cup and saucer. The tidiness of gran's garden did not extend further than the doorstep. Every surface was filled to overflowing with pots, pans, jars and all sorts of kitchen utensils, while concealed beneath bits of clean cloth, were plates and other receptacles filled with foodstuffs in various stages of preparation.

On the window ledge, jam jars filled with sweet Williams and fading wallflowers, were interspersed with pot plants, mostly cacti. The old shallow sink on which Sally leaned to get a better view of the plants and back garden, was covered with the stains of countless years of slops that no one had cared to remove, and it was impossible to guess what its original colour had been. As for the lavatory, which lurked within sniffing distance of the kitchen area, the less said the better. 'A flush lavatory' it was called, the only trouble being that the flushing system never seemed to be working.

While Hilary was replenishing gran's teacup, Sally could not resist the temptation of peeping into the front room where to her delight, she could see numerous dust-laden glass domes filled with stuffed birds. Ornaments, vases, photos and pictures adorned every flat surface and wall space. And still the same old cracked leather arm chairs with the crocheted covers that were supposed to hide the bits of horse-hair that were poking through here and there. This room had looked like this for as long as she could remember. She sighed as she touched a bit of the old faded wallpaper, then reluctantly she turned to join her friend. Before she left the kitchen however, she could not resist the temptation to lift the piece of cloth that covered the freshly cut bread and sniff appreciatively. Then she moved her nose sideways to sniff into a flat tin where a layer of dripping hid the delicious gelatinous meat juices, which lay beneath its fatty surface.

"You're like a dust 'ole fairy, you are," Hilary tutt-tutted as Sally moved towards the window to take another look at the cacti. "This tea'll be stone cold by the time gran gets it. I don't know why you have to flit about all over the place. You've seen it all before. Come on, poor old gran and Aunty Sarah will be pulling their hair out by now." She stepped out into the back garden, carefully holding the cup and saucer with both hands.

As they turned the corner of the bungalow, and the garden seat came into view, they noticed that Jacky was sitting on Aunty Sarah's lap once again, watching Pat and Dorothy, playing close by with the feather stuffed potatoes. These make believe birds, with the attention of twenty little fingers and ever more inventive imaginations, had taken on a look of manic improbability. Bald in places, with thick tufts of feathers sticking up at all angles in others, these poor creatures looked as though they might have had a close encounter with the old crow from Mr Rudge's garden.

"So," said gran as she pulled herself up from where she had been scrabbling around amongst her precious flowers. "You've brought me out my tea at last have you. I could be forgiven for thinking you had run all the way down to Caves Café for it. What kept you? Don't tell me, I can guess. It was that Sally rummaging around in there. That nose of yours will get you into trouble one of these fine days my girl," she said wagging her finger at Sally who was far more interested in what was going on around the bench than in what her gran had to say.

"Come on gran, come and sit over here and drink your tea," said Sally, ignoring the mild reprimand. "When you've drunk it you can tell us a story. What about telling us the one about the old headless woman," she suggested, and smiled when Pat and Dorothy looked up with an expression of fear on their faces. Normally this story would also have put the fear of God in her but standing here in the bright, late morning sunshine, she was full of bravado. Night-time, and especially when she was laying in a pitch black bedroom, would be different, but then she would have to make sure that this particular story did not follow her there.

"Well first off, it isn't a story, my girl. It's something that happened to me and something similar had already happened to some other youngsters as well, though I hadn't believed them until I saw it with my own eyes," said gran settling herself down on the seat next to Aunty Sarah and Jacky. "It was when me and Louie, were walking home from our uncles farm. The King family have been farming around Bicester - Ambrosden, Launton, that area, for as far back as anyone can remember. Lots of land they had there and so us kids always had somewhere to play. When we got the chance you understand. When we were not at school or doing jobs, which was most of the time, not like you youngsters these days. Always gallivanting all over the place you are. Well as I say, it was because our Louie was with me, she being the oldest of us girls, that we stayed at the farm until it was dark. It had been an overcast and blustery winters day but by the time we made our way along that lane, the wind had dropped. Uncanny it was how it suddenly went quiet, when I think about it now, though I didn't think anything of it at the time. Anyway, we were about half way home, and black as the ace of spades it was by this time, when Louie whispered that there was somebody following us. I just froze and felt my skin prickle all over. I couldn't have run if I'd tried. Then as we stood there, absolutely rigid with fear we were, she was right beside us. This woman without a head, her black cloak streaming out behind her."

"How could you see anything if it was that dark?" asked Pat fearfully. "And how did you know it was a woman if it hadn't got a head?"

"Ah, that shows how little you know about ghosts, my girl. You don't just see them with your eyes, you feel them, become part of them for a split second. She didn't just pass by us, oh no. She went right through us," replied gran, her forehead all wrinkled up as she struggled to explain her paranormal experience to her open mouthed audience. "Her fear and desperation went right through me and Louie. Then we both fell over. As I lay there, a feeling of weightlessness came over me and I swear I floated above the ground. Just a momentary thing it was, but it drained all the energy out of me, right down to the last scrap. She took something out of us, something she needed to release her from what was keeping her a prisoner on this earth. I swear it. She'd been a victim see, an innocent one, of some religious purge that was going on in the olden days, and do you know, the old axe man never even managed to cut her head off first go. Wasn't that dreadful?" She paused here for a few seconds to allow the full significance of what she had experienced to sink in, and then she continued. "It was a woman, definitely a woman and a young one at that, and she was trying to escape from her terrifying experience. I never heard that she'd appeared again after we saw her so perhaps she got what she needed from me and Louie. I hope so."

"Freda and Betty have seen a ghost too, gran." said Hilary, breaking the momentary silence that followed Granny Sansom's tale. "It wasn't like your one though, and they reckoned it was a man. We worked it out that it was probably a soldier killed in the Battle of Hastings or even old Harold himself. I've never seen a ghost meself and I never want to," she added shivering fearfully. Then instinctively, she placed her arms around Dorothy and Pat's shoulders.

"Now that's quite enough about ghosts and things," said Aunty Sarah sternly. "You'll have nightmares the lot of you, and that includes you Alice," she added wagging her finger at her sister. "You should know better at your age. I've never heard such nonsense, ghosts of headless women and old soldiers, whatever next. Now, how about a game of cats cradle? All we need for that is a length or two of wool. You'll find your grandma's knitting bag beside one of the chairs in the front room, Sally," she added briskly. "There's lots of odds and ends in there and I can still manage to hold the wool even with these bent old fingers. This baby can sit here beside me and watch," she continued, placing the little one down beside her in readiness for the task ahead.

The two old men were long gone by the time they assembled themselves for the serious game of cat's cradle, and apart from Jacky they all had a go. Even Aunty Sarah, though confined to the bench, still took a turn to weave, with just her forefingers and thumbs, one intricate pattern into another. Now and then, through carelessness or lack of tension on the wool, the whole thing collapsed and the procedure had to be started all over again. And once, when Dorothy's inexperienced wobbly fingers caused the whole thing to disintegrate into a tangle of knots, they all fell about laughing. The patterns they created were often much of a muchness. Occasionally however, someone came up with a fresh example of interwoven magic. Then there would be a unanimous, 'wow,' from the little group.

"Now, how about you two giving me a hand with a bit of weeding for a change," said gran, as she pointed towards Hilary and Sally. "The others can carry on playing for as long as they want to, but I haven't got any more time for this nonsense."

"Can we have our bread and dripping first please gran?" asked Sally. "I'm starving."

Later, as they were about to leave, gran came over to the pram with a loaf, also some duck eggs individually wrapped in bits of newspaper, which she placed on the bottom of the pram. "Don't put them there, that's where Dorothy sits," said Hilary picking up the offending objects and holding them at arms length. "Here, you'd better carry them," she said, passing them to Sally. "Can we have a bag for them, please gran?" she asked.

"Well I'll go to Stoke," gran replied, turning back towards the kitchen to seek out one of her precious carrier bags. "You'll be wanting the top brick off the chimney next!"

As they hurried up the road on the first leg of their journey home, Hilary was pushing the pram and Dorothy was already sitting on the bottom end. As they passed beneath the old bridge, Sally looked back over her shoulder, then turned to take another look at this example of early Victorian craftsmanship.

"What are those black crosses up there for?" She asked, halting the pram with her one free hand and then pointing upwards once they had all come to a standstill.

"They're tie bars- metal rods- and they've been put up there to strengthen the bridge or I should say, to hold those loose bricks in place, so's the bridge doesn't fall down," replied Hilary. "It's been there for a long time, this old bridge I should think. I wonder how they got it to arch like this, the men who built it? It's got to be done just about right otherwise it'd fall down straight away. It's quite clever really when you think about it and it's neatly done. Come on then, it's all down hill from now on, or very nearly anyway. We'll soon be home," she added briskly as she set her sights on the downward road ahead. As they walked down the long drawn out Ebdon's Hill, Sally began to think ahead to next weekend when her sister Betty would be home.

Betty lived in London now, working as a dressmaker and could only afford to come home every other weekend. Next Friday evening Sally knew that she and Pat, unable to contain their excitement, would be to and fro the window like dust hole fairies looking for their sister. They would be ready to dash down the field the moment she came into view, with her familiar homemade canvas bag slung casually across her shoulder. Having walked all the way from Battle station, she would always be hungry and thirsty by the time she arrived home. The first thing she always did however, once she had greeted them all was to disappear into the back bedroom and with her elbows on the window-sill, gaze out across the fields and into the distant woodland. She was homesick, and although she enjoyed the work she did, she said she could not wait to get back to Sylvian. She felt claustrophobic in the City. Even though rebuilding was taking place, she still found the piles of rubble and the bomb craters all cordoned off with red tape, depressing.

Sally came to as they reached the bottom of Ebdens Hill. In spite of her thoughts, she had still managed to listen with half an ear and even to participate in some of the conversation. "Do you mind if we cross over here and have a quick look along Moat Lane?" she asked, looking up and down the road as she prepared to cross over. "There's lots of wild flowers along here. I saw them when I came here with dad and Hazel the other day. We went to see old Mrs Peppler to pick up a clutch of eggs for mum to put under one of the broody hens. She, Mrs Peppler is always the first one anywhere around here to hear the cuckoo. Or so she says, and she always writes to the paper about it. Anyway, dad was in too much of a hurry to let us stop and look at anything at the time and I've been dying to have a close look at what's here. You can get off the pram for a while Dotty, then you can pick some flowers to take home for mum," she added as she lifted her little sister uncomplainingly from her comfortable seat with her one free arm.

There was a proliferation of ragged robin, which Dorothy immediately set upon with her eager little fingers, pulling them up by the roots. "No don't do it like that, you'll kill the plants," said Sally. "Hold the bottom of the stem with one hand and break the flower off with the other. Like this, see?" and after putting her carrier to one side, she proceeded to instruct her sister in the gentle art of flower plucking. "Don't touch those, she added pointing into the hedge where the Lords and Ladies with their spotted leaves and hooded flower spikes were growing in abundance. "They're poisonous."

Here too were oxe-eye daisies, red campion and long stemmed buttercups, their flower heads straining to reach above the tall grasses, to collect a fair share of sun and pollinating bees and other insects. Then she moved forward to examine more closely the vetch, clover and herb Robert and then, almost eclipsed by its bolder neighbours, she saw the gentle scarlet Pimpernel, its tiny flower head opened up to absorb the dappled sunlight. She sighed contentedly, then leaned over into the hedge and bent a dog rose towards her nose, sniffing deeply into its centre. "I just love this time of the year," she said, for the umpteenth time.

There was no sign of the swallows that had decorated the skyline with their highly aerobatic flight that they had seen on their outward journey. Or even the cows if it came to that, which apart from the occasional flicking tail, had seemed oblivious to the presence of birds and insects. They, the cows that is, were probably in the milking sheds chewing on their ration of cow cake by this time Sally reckoned.

As they reached the top of Whydown Hill, they all breathed a sigh of relief. "Hop back on then," said Hilary and she bent over, picked Dorothy up and sat her up on the pram again. "It's definitely all down hill from now on. Except for the field that is. Whew, I feel a bit like old Pilgrim retracing his footsteps," she said grinning around at the other girls. "Beat you to the lane you lot," she called over her shoulder as, having got her second wind, she began the last lap of the journey at a brisk pace.

CHAPTER 9

"Can I lend your rucksack please dad?" Sally called across the field to her dad as he came out of one of the chicken coops carrying a clutch of eggs. "We're going strawberry picking up Kent Street today and I need something to carry my drink and sandwiches in."

"No you're not having my best one, not to take into the fields you're not. There's my old one hanging up behind the scullery door. You can take that with you. And it's borrow, by the way my girl, not lend," he called back to her, then turned away to resume his rustic chores.

"What?" she replied, then as she stood there with a puzzled expression on her face he turned round again.

"Ah, before you go, perhaps you'd give me a hand to move the old door that's leaning up against the wall in there," he said and pointed towards the partitioned brick building that was grandly referred to as the garage. "It's not that heavy but it's a bit awkward on your own. Open the gate for me will you," he said and as he walked from field to garden, he half turned. "Just give me a minute to put these 'ere eggs in the copper house, will you. They should be safe enough in there for the time being."

"Now, you'd better go down the far end," he said as he scurried back, now empty handed and they moved forward to tackle the job. "Better let me walk backwards while we get the thing out, don't want you tripping over or anything like that, do we. I need it for that shed near the sycamores by the way, the one I've just got round to moving over there, so it's not far. I've divided that shed up into two rooms now and with any luck, I'll have made the opening just the right size to take this ere door. It'd better fit. I haven't got time to go around altering things," he added, then sniffed and brushed the back of his hand beneath his nostrils as he moved purposely forward.

As they began to ease the recumbent door away from the wall, there was an ominous soft squelching sound as the mesh of cobwebs, spun and re-spun over aeons, began to disintegrate. Then as they stooped, knees bent and began to lift the door up and away from its resting place, Sally saw it. The biggest, ugliest most terrifying spider she had seen in all her life was scurrying back and forth like a thing in torment, and in the split second before she dropped the door, she saw it making a bee line for her right hand. Then she shrieked.

"What the bloody hell!" shouted dad as the corner of the door shot upwards, narrowly missing his chin. Then he swore again as he struggled to control the bucking door, his little legs moving so fast that it looked for all the world as though old St Vitus himself had gotten hold of them.

"It's that spider, that huge, hairy thing over there!" said Sally in a shrill voice, pointing to where the spider was just disappearing behind a stack of wood in the corner of the room. "It nearly got me. It was right on my hand and I couldn't get away from it," she added with a shudder. Then she rubbed the back of her hand down the side of her skirt as though to wipe away the horror of her experience.

"You stupid child, just look at the size of you compared to that thing!" he shouted, pointing in the direction of the vanishing spider. "It's only a spider for God's sake, not a bloody tiger. What a stupid bloody fuss about nothing. Now get a grip of this door right this minute, before I really lose my temper. Don't you realise I've got better things to do than pander to your cranky, infantile behaviour."

As she bent to pick up her end of the door, she ran her eye anxiously over the webby surface, looking for any movement, however slight, which would suggest the presence of any other oversized arachnid like the one that had just terrified the living daylights out of her. However, although she would rather deal with her father's rage than risk another encounter with such a monster, she still kept a peripheral eye on him and what was happening at his end of the door.

As they walked slowly through the doorway, Sally saw Pat and Dorothy, brought out of doors no doubt by the commotion, standing by the side of the scullery wall, watching the procession in solemn silence.

"Now just turn round a bit here so's I can walk forward with the thing same as you. Yes that'll do, that's far enough," said dad as he steadied the wobbling door. "And straighten up. You'll do your back in if you stoop like that." With that they made their way towards the sycamores with Pat and Dorothy following behind but keeping a safe distance.

When they reached the shed, dad lifted his end of the door up and over the step. As he shuffled himself around it and through the opening, he said, "I've got a decent bronze knocker to put on the outer door you know. It's a miniature horseshoe with the shapes of a horse and rider inside. And there's a fox in there somewhere. Don't worry about him though, there's no hounds in the thing to chase him to kingdom come." As he was talking, he was moving the door around to lean against the inner wall. As Sally moved away to join her two sisters, he called out after her. "Now don't go upsetting that old spider in there, will you. Its big and ugly enough to catch all the flies within spitting distance of its den, then it can come indoors and mop up the ones that compete for my food. Save me a fortune in those sticky old fly papers that you girls are always moaning about. Come to think of it, it's big enough to catch a mouse or two and that'd give old Nuggly a bit of help. She's an old lady now. The old mice are beginning to run rings round her." Sally turned and smiled wryly towards her father who having closed the outer door of the shed, was now walking towards the copperhouse to retrieve his eggs.

As he drew level with the girls, he said, "I'll go and get that old rucksack for you."

"Mum, have you seen that top of mine, the yellow one?" Called out Sally.

"I want to wear it strawberry picking today." She walked up to her mum who was bending over the sink, busy with the last few bits of washing up.

"Well yes I have, it's in the pile of clean washing on the sideboard in there," replied mum pointing through the scullery door with one wet hand. "But it really is getting past it you know. It's really untidy and not even fit for the fields. Yes, I know it's your favourite and that you've patched and mended the thing very neatly but nothing lasts forever," she said, anticipating her daughter's reaction. "You wear things to death, that's your trouble. Now, what's wrong with the one you're wearing at the moment. It's a lovely shade of blue and Mrs Linch brought it up here specially for you. Apart from the colour it's just the same as your yellow one anyway."

"No I don't like this one half as much and look, it's too big anyway. "I'll wear it when this one's really past it," she replied, as she held up her beloved top, having retrieved it from the pile of washing on the sideboard. As she shrugged herself into the top, a satisfied grin spread across her face. "That's better, I'm ready for anything now. And here comes Hilary, I'd better get my sandwiches sorted out. I'll get her to come across the field with me first, we'll have plenty of time to look at some flowers and things before we go up to Kent Street," she added.

***

The two girls walked shoulder to shoulder across the field towards the stile in the far corner. The sun well risen now, had broken through the early heat haze and was glowing warmly on their backs. The landscape, decked out in its summer garb, was showing off in the dappled sunshine of this early summer morning, sporting countless shades of green. From the dark, sombre hue of the ancient ivy through to the most delicate shade of aquamarine, where the tall beach trees decorated the far horizon. The green was interspersed here and there, with the soft glow of a copper beech, where Mother Nature had selected the perfect foil for her chosen colour.

Sally's gaze moved instinctively from the far and middle distance to the grass around her feet as she sought out one of the clumps of bird's foot trefoil, which flowered in and around the field year on year. As her practised eye focussed on a cluster within spitting distance of the stile, she hastened her step then stooped and brushed her hand lightly across its springy surface. For some reason, she found both the appearance and the feel of these delicate pea-like flowers strangely satisfying. They looked and felt just like fairies bonnets.

As she stood up, Hilary caught hold of her arm. "Look over there," she said pointing towards the hedge where, as though splashed carelessly from the palette of some impressionist artist, little blobs of red decorated the lush green grass. The scarlet pimpernel was sunning itself in the morning sunshine, its petals wide open and turned towards its warmth. The heart shaped leaves growing side by side along its long slender stems, looked just like little wings. "On the way back, if they're still open like this, I'm going to pick some and press them," said Hilary. "I've got lots of flowers, daisies, primroses that kind of thing now, but I haven't got any of these and they're such a lovely colour. I wonder how flowers get to be the colours they are."

"I expect God lined them all up and decorated them just like he did with the birds," replied Sally solemnly. " The only problem with them is, if the sun goes in, they go in. Now lets get a move on or we'll be late, it's a tidy old walk from here."

As Sally looked towards Horseman's farm, she spotted Mr Gay's Caterpillar tractor in the distance and could just make out the chug, chug of its old engine. It was an American machine with the name CLETRAC printed along its bulky side and was Mr Gay's pride and joy. He was the first farmer for miles around to have purchased such a powerful and labour saving device. Often he would pass his hand lovingly across its shiny yellow surface whenever it came within touching distance, seemingly oblivious to the puff of thin, oily smoke that issued from its smoke stack.

Mr Freeman would be driving it for sure. He was almost as proud of the thing as was the old farmer himself. He, Mr Freeman, was one of several men who worked on the farm from time to time, and the only one who could get the hang of steering a track-laying vehicle. Sally had heard older men say it was a bit like driving a tank but without getting shot at.

Sid Puxty also worked for Mr Gay. He was particularly skilled in the art of pruning and oversaw the pest control of the various fruit crops on this farm.

As they walked briskly along the lane, they took turns to recite a little ditty, which at the moment was their favourite bit of nonsense. The trick was to recite it as fast as possible without tripping over the words. Hilary had bagged first go and then before Sally could get a word in edgeways, she took another go but faster this time.

"I said he was mad, he said mad? I said yes. He said, who? I said you, he said me? I said yes. He said oh," she giggled, word perfect both times. When it came to Sally's turn however, her mouth refused to keep pace with her brain and they both fell about laughing as the words spewed out all jumbled up and bearing little if any resemblance to the verse.

"I've got to get it right, give me a chance, give me a chance," said Sally impatiently as Hilary, having regained her composure, took a deep breath in readiness for another attempt. "There, I'm as good as you," she said triumphantly when after her third attempt she managed to get the words out fast and in the right order. "Give us another go, just to make sure, then it's your turn again," she said.

They were still reciting the same nonsense as they walked briskly up Whydown Hill, stopping now and then to examine the flowers in the grassy verge. When they reached the spot where, summer or winter, a steady stream of pure, cool water bubbled from a pipe embedded in the bank, they stooped and with cupped hands, caught and slurped a few handfuls of this nectar.

The water here was derived from a cluster of natural springs which had their origins somewhere deep within the hillside, they had been told. Over the years the steady flow of water had gouged out a depression in the bank and they stood either side of the indentation for a few seconds, watching the water as it trickled slowly down the hill. It was this spring that Ellen Brown visited every day with her little galvanized bucket to fetch her supply of drinking water. She lived with her father on their smallholding, which was situated on the western side of the hill.

Although Ellen was considered 'simple' by some of the local folk, their dad reckoned she could teach them a thing or two when it came to common sense. As Sally stood there, she was overcome by a sense of shame at the way she and other children had teased this mild mannered and friendly lady.

She remembered the anger of her parents when they had been appraised of the way the youngsters, Sally included, had followed Ellen, giggling as they imitated her curious gait and the apparent holding up of her knickers with the back of her left hand. Rarely, if ever had they seen their mum so angry and Sally's cheeks glowed with shame even now when she remembered the ticking off they had received. She had learned how to deal with her father's anger but her mother's apparent distress had made her feel very uncomfortable. It had taken a while for Ellen to accept their overtures of friendship and even now eyed them with a measure of suspicion whenever their paths crossed. But then, Sally had to acknowledge, they had never exactly apologised to her.

By the time they reached the strawberry field, several women were already at work, squatting or kneeling between the lines of ripening fruit. She was sure she could see Glad Fuller and Ruby Selmes amongst them. All the women seemed to pick with a similar two-handed rhythm, sometimes moving the foliage around with rapid hand movements as they sought out any fruits that might be lurking beneath the leaves. As they filled each punnet, it was placed in a tray. When full, these would be collected by one of the men and taken into the weighing and packing shed. For some reason, the younger fruit pickers used cardboard baskets with tin handles to pick the strawberries into. These came flat packed and, in experienced hands, took only a few seconds to assemble.

As Sally's eye moved to the side of the strawberry field, she spotted old Jim Croft, a white hankie knotted at its four corners on top of his bald head.

He was pushing a massive handcart, or more precisely, a thick rectangular plank of wood balanced on two wheels, with a length of iron girder bent to serve as a handle. There were piles of empty trays perched precariously on it. They wobbled alarmingly as he pushed the cart over the uneven ground. He whistled as he propelled the light but precarious load forward, seemingly oblivious to anything but the task in hand. Sally and Hilary watched as he moved off the path and down the field.

Jim was short and bandy legged, with a ruddy brown complexion. A cross between Mr Garner and Mr Linch, Sally reckoned, in build anyway. Unlike the other two garrulous old men though, he was a man of few words. His motto being 'why use twenty words when two'll do.' And his favourite word was 'yip.' As Sally thought about Mr Garner now, she realised how much she missed him and his family since they had moved away from Blackbrooks. That was a long while ago and she knew her mum and dad missed them as well.

Mrs Garner, a self-taught but first class seamstress, had always been on the lookout for odd pieces of material or discarded dresses, which she ran up into pretty dresses for 'Dolly's girls' as she called them. Freda had reason to be grateful to her on one occasion in particular. She had been tree climbing and had ripped her dress from waist to hem. Mrs Garner had woven the torn pieces together with the neatest of stitches and Freda had continued to wear the dress until, as she said, it fell off her back. The old couple now ran a small bakery business somewhere in Kent.

As the two girls walked through the large opening into the packing shed, there was Mrs Clements. She was responsible for the weighing of the fruit and the payment of the women's wages. She was standing beside the massive weighing machine, which dominated the workbench just inside the doorway, making entries into a ledger. She was wearing a floral, bib-fronted apron, edged with red bias binding over her frock and looked as she always did, neat, tidy and fresh as a new pin. She looked up as they entered, then laid down her pen.

"I've got you down in the book already, I knew you'd be here," she said in her cultured voice. "You'll find Mr Croft down in the field, he'll show you where to pick. Here, take these baskets I've just made up. They'll do to start you off with."

As she passed the rigid cardboard containers with their shiny tin handles into the hands of the two girls, the smile that accompanied the gesture, transformed her face from its normal serious expression, to one of friendly inclusion and put them immediately at their ease. There was only one other person in the packing shed and, although Sally had seen her before, she did not know her name. At the moment she was down at the far end of the shed, sorting through a stack of empty wooden crates. Totally absorbed in her work, she seemed not to have noticed the two girls. Mind you, appearances could be deceptive, as Sally knew to her cost. On one occasion she had been walking down through the garden away from Horseman's farmhouse when, thinking herself unobserved, she had picked a couple of Mr Gay's luscious dessert gooseberries, which grew on well pruned bushes right beside the pathway. As she popped the first sweet yellow delight into her mouth, he had called out to her from the open doorway and she had dropped the second one in fright and embarrassment. He had not shouted at her, but the experience had taught her a lesson. Not everything was always what it appeared to be on the surface.

It took old Jim a second or two to halt the progression of his ancient cart as Hilary and Sally came up beside him and they moved along at the same pace until he had the thing under control. As he turned to acknowledge them, he grinned revealing a pair of oversized false teeth of which he was inordinately proud and which he flashed around at every opportunity. As Sally looked at him she thought, not for the first time, that he looked the image of Mr Budgen's old cart-horse.

"Over dare den," he said balancing his cart with one hand while with the other he pointed across the field to where two women knelt, heads down among the strawberries. "Yip, next to dem two dare," he added as the girls followed the direction of his pointing finger. His top plate flapped up and down as he spoke. The girls found it difficult to suppress their mirth.

"Lets leave our bags there with the others," said Sally, heaving the borrowed rucksack off her shoulder as she spoke, at the same time moving over to where a pile of assorted bags flopped in the shade of a stack of wooden boxes. "It's not far away if we need a drink. Those teeth of his are out of control," she whispered as an aside. They walked off, giggling and swinging their baskets to and fro.

Vera and Gran Powell looked up as they approached and re-arranged their baskets to accommodate the two extra bodies.

"Where's Amy," asked Hilary? "I thought she was coming strawberry picking today? I even brought along a book she wanted to lend, it's in my bag down there." And she pointed in the general direction of the pile of assorted wooden crates.

"She's looking after Janet for me this morning, then she'll be bringing her here to meet us when we've finished this afternoon," replied Vera. "We've not been here long, picked just a couple of pounds at the most, so you'll soon catch up, unless you succumb to temptation that is. I always reckon that if you can resist the first strawberry, then the temptation goes away after a while."

Sally felt her mouth begin to water as she started to pick the strawberries and the desire to pop that really fat, juicy one she'd just picked, into her mouth was almost overwhelming. However, remembering what Vera had just told her, she dragged her eye away from the object of desire. Squatting comfortably on her haunches, she began to part the ripe strawberries carefully from the mother plant, making sure that a small section of stem and the calyx remained connected to the fruit.

After a while, vaguely aware of the voices around them, which had now conjoined and descended into a low hum, the girls got into their stride, chatting sporadically about this and that. Sally missed the quick and easy wit of Mrs Winchester and Mrs Freeman who would have kept them all in stitches throughout the day. They were finishing off a job on another farm today, she had been told. Perhaps for Mr Farrow at Luff's farm or even at Mr Gosse's place. She smiled to herself as she thought about these two women, aspen thin in their light cotton frocks, who usually worked within hailing distance of one another. Although of different content and effect, their witticisms seemed to complement one another.

Mrs Freeman's acerbic wit had caused more than one person to remark that she must have had vinegar for breakfast and she was rather rude at times. Sally remembered the time a horse fly had landed on her arm. As she had brushed the thing off, she had said, 'can't you tell the difference between my arm and a horse's arse? No, I thought not. Well bugger off and get your bloody eyes tested then.' And she always seemed to be out of humour with her husband. Mrs Winchester's humour on the other hand, though equally amusing, was rather more gentle, denoting her keen observation and understanding of human nature, Sally reckoned. She was very fond of this lady. She could be a bit irreverent though and only the other day, when she had tripped over her front door-step, had said 'bugger' in a very loud voice. Then, as she had turned around and noticed the youngsters, had added quick as a flash, 'Our Father who art in Heaven, put up six and knocked down seven.' Sally, although she had smiled at the time, had still not puzzled out the connection between the curse and the joke. It would come to her in time no doubt.

Gran Powell made up for the absence of these two women with her own words of wisdom, her down to earth approach to life and her understanding of peoples strengths and weaknesses. One of her sayings, oft repeated was, 'don't put your wishbone where your backbone ought to be.' Another was, 'I was doing this before your backside was big as a ha'penny.' Then there was the one about mince pies that was quoted by her and also by their mum. That for each one eaten at Christmas time, a happy month would follow. That was definitely Sally's favourite.

And as far back as Sally could remember, Gran Powell had always used the same broken old table knife to clean between the cracks in her pathway, as well as the weeding of her borders. She also used it to despatch, swiftly and expertly, the many and various pests in her beloved garden.

Then of course, there was Glad Fuller, who could also be depended upon to get a few chuckles from the other women with her wit and her comments on the goings on in the village, in particular around the East View Terrace area, where she lived. She was 'quite a lass' herself, according to Mrs Freeman who would tap the side of her nose with her forefinger if anyone sought further gossip on that particular subject. She was, mum said, a good sort, kind-hearted and very generous.

At long last came the call they had all been waiting for: the summons to eat and drink. Part filled punnets were hastily stuffed beneath the big floppy leaves of the strawberry plants. Then the women, moving like clockwork, made their way to the edge of the field. Bags and baskets found their way, as if by magic, into eager hands. Bums were plonked onto hastily positioned wooden crates and bushel boxes.

Before they partook of their victuals however, they all lifted bottles of water to their parched lips and sighed with relief as the lukewarm liquid, gurgling as it passed from bottle to throat, began to assuage their thirst.

Hilary and Sally did not bother with wooden boxes. They sat on the grass, legs stretched out in front of them and having slurped their water, they dragged their bags onto their knees and began to unravel the greaseproof paper in which their sandwiches were wrapped.

Once her hunger had been partly satisfied, Sally looked around her. As she munched, she looked with interest at the diversity of size, shape and facial features of the women around her. Even Barbara and Stella Holman, who were sisters, were totally different from one another, she reckoned. And there was not one hessian apron to be seen, which was very unusual. She was careful now to keep her eyes above waist level for, from where she was sitting, had a birds eye view of bloomers of various size and colour and an occasional flash of pink suspenders belonging mostly to the older women who sat, knees wide apart, chatting and relaxing before the afternoon shift began.

The steady rhythm of the morning's operations extended into the afternoon until at going home time, they all traipsed wearily across the field into the weighing shed. As they waited while their tally of fruit was converted into cash, Sally and Hilary wandered outside and were just in time to see a procession of youngsters coming up the road.

Patty Winchester was there with two of her brothers, Raymond and Brian. Amy was also there, with Janet walking along beside her and holding on tightly to her hand. The two girls, forgetful for the moment of collecting their hard earned shilling, ran the short distance towards the slow moving bunch and together they chatted their way back up to the shed. Brian was rather quiet but Raymond was a replica of Basil, quick witted, mischievous and good fun. At the moment, he was talking to Janet and as she listened to his words, which were lost on the rest of the group, her face lit up and she began to giggle. There was something special about this little girl with her fringe drawn back off her face with a large, pink hairgrip. Behind her gentle demeanour, so like her mother's and grandmother's, was a look of wisdom that was way beyond her years. 'An old head on young shoulders,' as mum might have said.

Vera was waiting outside the packing shed, watching the slow moving procession. Then she moved towards them, holding her arms out to her little daughter. "Bet you've missed your mum, haven't you? She's missed you anyway," she said, kissing Janet on the cheek. "Thanks Aym," she added, patting her sister on the shoulder. Then she turned and joined the other women in the shed.

"Better take this book, Amy, I nearly forgot about it," said Hilary. Then she fished about in her bag and pulled out a package wrapped in brown paper.

"I've been carrying it around all day," she added. Sally knew that was a bit of an exaggeration, and smiled inwardly.

When they had collected their earnings, they all dispersed in little groups. Hilary, Sally, Amy, Patty, Raymond and Brian made their way home together, chattering wildly. Their voices rose steadily as each one tried to get in edgeways.

As they passed Gotway's farm, they saw Ken Edwards. These days they tried to remember to call him 'Cornelius,' a name given him by their Headmaster and which he preferred to his old nick-name of 'Gaggy.' "Could hear you lot coming a mile off," he said. "It's a good job I weren't old Puff-Puff Beezle, or I'd have caught you good and proper." He tutt-tutted, moving his head from side to side as he did so. Then he grinned at them and Sally thought, not for the first time what a kindly youth he was, so different from that Denis Crow. Ken was someone you could rely on somehow.

"Tell that little sister of yours there's a new foal, back of the farm here," he said looking in Sally's direction. "She'll be tickled pink by it. It's all legs and ockerdness at the moment but it'll soon grow up, so you'd best get her here before long. She'll not want to miss this one. I'll be around the farm tomorrow morning if you come this way. I'll take you round there myself." Then he turned on his heels and walked away.

When they reached the entrance to Trickly Hollow, they stood there for a while, reluctant to part company. "I know, let's go up to the farm, to Porky and John's place, we've got time," suggested Hilary. "It's not far and it'll be milking time soon. That's if they haven't already started."

There was a unanimous 'yes,' and without any hesitation, they turned and hurried along the lane towards Beanford farm. By the time they had turned the corner at the bottom of the slope, Porky and John Partridge, having rounded up the cows, were driving them towards the milking shed.

"Can we watch please, while you get them in? We'll be ever so quiet, honest," Raymond called out breathlessly to the two men. Porky and John nodded their assent without looking up, concentrating instead on the gentle, almost casual guiding with their sticks, of their herd of Friesian cows.

The animals seemed to find their way by instinct into their own stalls, where rope halters, fixed to the inner wall, were slipped loosely over their heads. Then they began to munch contentedly on their rations of cow cake left in readiness for them.

The youngsters watched in silent fascination as John, starting at the far end of the shed, began to work his way up the stalls, wiping off the cows' teats with a large cotton cloth. Porky followed behind with a tin of special disinfectant called 'Udsall', into which he dipped his fingers and smeared onto the cleaned teats. Then the two men, each with a pail in one hand and a three legged stool in the other, set themselves to tackle the job in hand. They squatted on the low seats, knees apart, angled pail held firmly between legs and booted feet and, with their foreheads against the cows flanks, began to extract the milk. As if by magic, gallons of foaming milk began to fill their pails, light spirals of steam visible even in this warm early summer weather. Every so often, one or other of the men rose carefully to his feet and went next door to the dairy to empty his fresh and foaming pail of milk into a large container. Their affinity with animals as well as nature in general, was apparent even to the youngest member of the group.

Mrs Partridge was in charge in the dairy. They could hear her moving around in preparation for the processing of the milk and the churning of the butter, amongst other things. After a while, she came through the open doorway, a ladle filled to the brim with milk in one hand and a tall nursery rhyme mug in the other. As she passed the warm fresh milk around to each one in turn, she asked after their parents and younger siblings. She seemed to know a lot about their families. As Sally took her share from the work-roughened hand of this kindly lady, she looked with interest at the shape and pleasing proportions of the milk ladle, identical to the ones used by the Collins,' and nearly empty now. Its deep cylindrical shape was balanced by its long handle, looped over at the top. When not in use, it would be hanging on the rim of the milk container, along with several others. Their shiny metal surfaces were always kept scrupulously clean though this one was now dulled here and there by the residue of milk, which stuck to its surface. She was also fascinated by the implement, which was used to skim the thick layer of cream from some of the rested milk. Though just a circle of thick metal, slightly dished with evenly spaced holes on its surface and a circular handle to one side, it had a kind of harmony about it somehow. It was rather nice Sally reckoned that utilitarian objects like this should also look so good. There were always milk churns in and around the dairy, massive containers with thick handles on their sides and these would be filled with milk in readiness for the lorry, which made its way along the bumpy track every day to collect them.

A while later, they took their leave reluctantly and began to make their way down the pathway towards home, the two boys messing about and running ahead of the girls. As they neared the bend in the track, Amy remarked on the difference between this smelly, cow patted pathway and the shiny cleanliness of the Partridges' dairy. "How come that smelly creatures like cows can produce something that tastes so good, like milk anyway," she concluded. "And cream and butter of course."

A mental picture of the Lawrence's old lavatory, which put the fear of God in her, sprung immediately into Sally's mind. If a comparison with that and the house it belonged to, all spick and span and shiny, was not comparable with cows and milk and the Partridges dairy, then she did not know what was. She could not think of a better comparison anyway. "Yes, and meat I suppose when you come to think about it," she replied hastily as Amy looked towards her for some kind of reaction. "And I reckon the smells got something to do with their milk and pancakes coming out of different holes, that's all."

Raymond, now not far in front of the girls and obviously interested in the current conversation, turned and walked back towards them. "If you think cows stink, then what about old Mill's pig farm then? He's got a pile of muck behind the sties that stinks to high heaven and come autumn, he'll be spreading the stuff all over his fields. I know it's miles away from here but you'd smell that stuff from here to Scotland, at least I reckon." And he grabbed his sister by the arm as though to emphasise the potency of the offensive smell. "It's good for the ground it is, I reckon your dad should use some of it on his garden," he added turning around, now directing his spoken thoughts towards where Sally was standing. "Mind you, your place does pong a bit at times so he probably does. Hey when's he going to get that old cow he's been talking about then?" He asked. After a short pause and when he realized that no answer was forthcoming, he looked around at the little group his twinkling eyes an indication of humorous thoughts. "Here have you heard this one? I really don't know what made me think of it!

There's a little yellow idol to the east of Kathmandu.
There's a meadow to the side of it where the donkeys do their poo.

I reckon donkeys stink more than pigs or cows any old how," he said, grinning around at them all. Then he grabbed Brian by the arm and the two boys ran off again along the lane.

When they got to the holly tree they stopped and as Raymond looked up into it, he shouted back to the girls. "What do you call that old tree house of yours up there then? Cotton Reel Castle?"

The girls did not bother to reply. By this time, perhaps because of Raymond's poetic intervention, they had swung into a recitation of their own little ditties. Their first literary contribution started by Patty had now been now taken up by the four of them and, walking side by side, they chanted the words in a sing song fashion:

"There was an old woman tossed up in a basket, twenty times as high as the moon.
Where she was going I feared but to ask it, for in her hand she carried a broom.

Old woman, old woman, old woman quothe I. Oh whither, oh whither, oh whither so high.
To sweep the cobwebs off the sky.
Can I come with you?
Ah, bye and bye."

"Winken , Blinken and Nod next, I bags," said Sally and before the others had time to disagree, had giggled her way into the first line:

"Winken Blinken and Nod one night, sailed off in a wooden shoe.
Sailed in a river of crystal light, into a sea of blue.
Where are you going and what do you wish? The old moon asked the three.
We have come to fish for the herring fish that live in this beautiful sea.
Nets of silver and gold have we, said Winken, Blinken and Nod."

The old moon laughed and sang a song as they rocked in the wooden shoe.
And the wind that sped them all night long, ruffled the waves of dew.
The little stars were the herring fish that lived in that beautiful sea.
Now cast your nets wherever you wish, but never a feared are we.
So cried the stars to the fishermen three, Winken, Blinken and Nod.

Winken and Blinken are two little eyes and Nod is a little head.
And the wooden shoe that sailed the skies is the wee one's trundle bed.
So shut your eyes while your mother sings of wonderful sights that be.
And you shall see the beautiful things as you rock in the misty sea.
And the old shoe rocked the fishermen three, Winken, Blinken and Nod."

After a pause Hilary said, "I know, lets sing the one we've just learned at school, the Lassies and Lads song. I like that one." And re-positioning her bag on her back, linked arms with the others and began to sing:

"Come Lassies and Lads get leave of your dads and away to the Maypole hie.
Where every he has got him a she with the minstrels standing by.
For Willy has got his Jill and Johnny has got his Joan.
To trip it, trip it, trip it, trip it, trip it up and down.
To trip it, trip it, trip it, trip it, trip it up and down

You're out said Dick, not I said Nick, 'twas the fiddler played it wrong.
Tis true said Sue and so said Hugh and so said everyone.
The fiddler then began, to play the tune again.
And every girl did trip it, trip it, trip it to the men.
And every girl did trip it, trip it, trip it to the men

Good night said Harry, goodnight said Mary. Goodnight said Poll to John.
Goodnight said Sue to her sweetheart Hugh, goodnight said everyone.

Some walked and some did run, some loitered on the way.
And bound themselves by kisses twelve to meet the next holiday.
And bound themselves by kisses twelve to meet the next holiday."

They were singing 'The Drunken Sailor' when they got to the gate at the bottom of the field and stood still until they had finished the song. As they said their goodbyes and Amy, Patty, Raymond and Basil moved away from them, Hilary called out to them. "We'll see you later Patty. Sals staying at my place tonight, we'll get the skipping ropes out, shall we? Basils got a long rope hasn't he so we can do some two sided skipping as well. Pity you can't come Amy, but you're going out, aren't you? You're going to miss all the fun."

As she and Sally turned their noses towards Sylvian, in anticipation of the food that awaited them, they saw Pat coming through the top gate and before they knew it, she was rushing down the field to meet them. Then as they reached the top gate, they saw Dorothy peeping through the kitchen window, her little face bright with happiness.

***

"I'm bringing 'Hiawatha' down to your place with me Hilary," said Sally as, having eaten their dinner, they were now out in the scullery doing some of the washing up. "It's really good, he talks to animals and trees and all sorts of other things. I suppose you'd call it magic really."

"Just leave the water when you've magicked away all that washing up out there," mum called to them from the kitchen. "I need to give the sink a bit of a clean up." Sally's eye went immediately to the drum of Vim sitting on the narrow window ledge, a bit of old rag screwed up beside it. It was used for all sorts of cleaning jobs around the house and this one, like its predecessors, was decorated with skeins of dried up dirty water. She had never used the stuff and wasn't about to change the habit of a lifetime by offering to do this wearisome task.

"Yes mum," she replied.

"Can Pat come down with us Mum?" asked Hilary who always called Sally's mother, Mum. "We'll only be down in Crazy Lane with the Winch's, doing some skipping and that sort of thing. We'll bring her all the way back before it gets too late, promise." As mum nodded, Hilary turned to Sally. "Have you got all your bits and pieces together then," she asked. "Now don't forget that book of yours or we'll never hear the last of it, or those short bits of rope. We can use that long bit of rope Basil's got for when we want to play two sided skipping, can't we." When Sally returned with the rucksack on her shoulder, she whispered. "Does dad know you've got his rucksack again? I bet you haven't asked him." As Sally shook her head and put her finger to her lip, she said, "best be on our way then before he comes in."

By the time the girls had divested themselves of bags and baggage's at Hilary's house, gathered up Ronald and made their way with a jumble of ropes, across the back gardens into Crazy Lane, Patty, Basil and Raymond were already waiting for them.

"What time do you call this?" asked Basil, taking a coil of ancient rope from his shoulder as they drew level with him. Then, not waiting for or expecting an answer, he passed one knotted end to Ronald then trotted across the lane with the other. "Right you lot, who wants to start off then?" He asked as he and Ronald began to turn the line vigorously, using both hands. At first it bucked and rolled and it took the boys a few seconds to co-ordinate their timing and get the thing under control. Hilary moved forward and the others watched silently as she turned sideways on to the arcing rope, rocking back and forth a couple of times before, with split second timing, she jumped into the rotating line. As she jumped up and down in time with the swish and whack of the rope, the others began to chant one of their favourite skipping rhymes:

"Sitting in the kitchen, doing a bit of knitting.
In comes a bogey man and out goes I."

On the last word, Hilary jumped nimbly out on the opposite side to be immediately replaced by Patty, followed one after the other by the other children. And the chanting continued, getting louder as the game progressed.

After a while, the two rope operatives slackened the pace, and brought the skipping to a close. "Blow this for a game of soldiers," said Ronald. "My arms feel like they're ready to drop off. How about someone else having a go."

"Give it here," said Hilary. "Here you can take the other end Sal," she added handing the other end of the knotted rope to her friend. After a couple of false starts, and a lot of confusion the game, with its minor adjustment finally got under way and the chanting began. The rhyme this time was one that they also used for finger games:

"Here is the Church and here is the steeple, you open the door and you see all the people.
Here's the choir boys going upstairs, here's the parson saying his prayers,"

This rhyme needed a measure of concentration for the words and footwork to co-ordinate, and their voices rose higher and higher as they strove to force some discipline into the game.

At last, breathless and giggling, they all collapsed down onto the grass verge. The rope, now abandoned, lay across the lane looking for all the world like some undernourished snake. The boys lay flat out on their backs, while the girls sat with their chins on crooked knees, legs loosely enfolded by weary arms. Once they had got their breath back, they began to chat amongst themselves. Then, one by one they got to their feet.

"Hey, I know, lets make some skeletons," said Sally and she rushed across the lane and began to pick a fist full of hazel leaves. As she passed them around she said, "now don't worry if you mess one or two up, there's plenty more where they came from."

There was silence for a while as they concentrated on the painstaking task of separating the flesh of the leaf from its delicate skeleton. Now and again however, an impatient curse escaped the lips of one or other of them when, in spite of their efforts, the tracery of fine strands was shattered by over eager fingers and they were obliged to reach for yet another hairy, oval leaf to fashion.

After a while the boys began to fidget, moving from one foot to the other as a collection of spoiled skeletons, in various degrees of completion, lay discarded around their feet. "It's no good, I can't get the hang of this," said Ronald crossly. "It's something girls do not boys," he added as he threw yet another ruined masterpiece down in frustration. "I know, let's sit down for a while and have a game of 'I Spy,' shall we?"

***

Later, with the sun dipping towards the horizon, they wandered along Crazy Lane to take Pat home. "Bloody 'ell, here comes Denis," exclaimed Sally, pointing towards Paygate Corner and then instinctively ducking behind Basil. "What's he been up to I wonder?"

"Don't fess yourself about him, he wont be no trouble, not with us lot against him he wont," said Basil and he turned his head and grinned into the face that was close up against his neck. "Watch this." Then he turned around and waited until the youth had drawn level with him. "Hey Denis, what's the Gypsy cure for cold sores then?" He asked grinning all over his face. As boy and bicycle came to a halt, he replied, "Kiss my arse, that's what" Without a word, Denis flicked his right hand peddle upwards, bore down heavily on the thing and pushed himself and his bike off to tackle the rest of Whydown Hill. As he rode away, he lifted his bum off the seat and farted. Then he half turned, and treated them all to a very rude hand signal.

"Well I'll be blowed, what do you think he did that for," said Raymond in mock indignation, pitching his voice to over-ride the chattering and giggling now going on around him. Then as they crossed the road and began to walk along the dusty lane leading to Sylvian, he asked. "Has he lost weight or something? Looks like a wet racing dog he does." Before anyone had the time or the inclination to reply, he continued. "Here how about this then. This crow saw a snake and asked him what two and two was. The old snake raised his head and said, how should know, I'm a grass snake not an adder." Basil groaned as Sally giggled. She found the Winchesters sense of humour, from Molly downwards, really funny.

As they passed through the top gate, Basil pointed towards the underground tank. "That's a bit of luck. I see you've got your hop scotch pitch still marked out on your old underground tank over there, and just by chance I happen to have a few bits of slate in my pocket. There's plenty here to go round," he added as he lifted an assorted fistful of the dark grey stuff from his pocket. "If we get a shift on, we can get a couple of games in before it gets dark. Better let your mum know you're home, by the way Patsy," he added, falling back into her old, familiar infant name.

"As if she didn't already know with all the row we've been making," said Hilary. "But, I'll just pop inside to let her know anyway, just to make sure."

As she came back through the scullery door, she held out her hand. "Come on then, give us the aimers Basil," she said. "Now who's having first go? It had better be you Pat," she said answering her own question. "The first few are easy, you can just drop them in." Then they stood and watched in silence as Pat hopped and wobbled herself into the game.

A couple of games later, Basil gathered up his bits of slate and slipped them carefully into his trouser pocket. "There, was I right or was I right?" he said smugly. "Two games I said and that's all we had time for. Right you lot, lets get home then and see what's to eat. I'm starving. Come on then, beat you to the bottom of the field."

As the boys moved towards the gate, Sally ran inside with Pat to say goodnight to her mum once again. Then, almost instinctively, she skipped up onto the underground tank for one last look around, before she joined the others. As she stood there, she saw the sun disappearing down below the horizon with a rosy, hazy glow, which was an indication of continued settled weather, according to Mr Collins.

We've got bread and cheese for supper tonight with old Buttons special butter," said Hilary as they were walking along Crazy Lane towards the Winchesters house. "I can smell it from here, well the bread I can. I reckon Gregory's bread's the best in the world and so are his dough-nuts. And we've got plenty of milk so we can have a mug of cocoa as well, how about that then you two?" She said, touching her brother and her friend lightly on their shoulders. "And we'll all stay up as long as we like, because mum won't be home until at least midnight, I reckon." As they came up to the gateway leading into Brookside, she stooped and picked up the tangle of rope that, earlier on, they had carelessly abandoned onto the grassy pathway. "Here, these bit are yours Basil," she said, as having pulled the mess of ropes apart with great difficulty, she passed a bundle of loosely and unevenly looped line, to him. He took the burden silently from her into crooked arms then tucked it under his left armpit, holding up the long, unruly bits with his right hand.

As they stepped over the low wire netting fence at the top of the garden and made their way hurriedly towards the back end of Windy Ridge, Sally's mouth began to water. "Yummy, I can taste that grub already, I'm starved, " she said.

***

Once they had eaten their supper and done the washing up, they sat at the kitchen table, slowly sipping their steaming cocoa. They had left the back door ajar and every now and again, a current of air stirred the tablecloth overhang, and played gently around their ankles. Ronald was speaking now, his thoughts spilling out into the comparative silence of the room.

"I reckon the old smugglers were all around here you know," he announced suddenly as though the two girls had been privy to his thought processes. "Some of 'em would've come through here on their way to Hawkhurst, that's where one of the biggest smuggling gangs lived. And they were a blood thirsty lot, leastways that's what's in the book I've just read. You didn't dare tell on 'em or they'd have cut your throat, or worse. The smugglers round here had all sorts of secret tunnels, passages that sort of thing to hide the stuff in. Well they had something called Excise men, policemen sort of, after them all the time, so they had to be careful where they kept the stuff and how they moved it around. I'd love to find some of those old tunnels, wouldn't you?" he said putting his mug firmly down onto the table and wriggling around in his seat as he began to get really into his subject. "Some of these tunnels were under pubs and I reckon most of them are still there, if you know where to look. My friend reckons the best place to look would be all round Pevensey, because there's lots of old pubs there. When we're allowed, we're going to ride over there and have a look round."

"Well you won't be allowed into any of the pubs yet, that's for sure. You're much too young," said Hilary.

"Tell you what then, I'll have a word with dad, perhaps he can find something out for us," he replied. "Or mum if it comes to that. She works in the Queens Head after all and that pubs old as the hills. Just imagine finding a secret passage here in the village!"

"Well, anyway that'll give you and your friends something to do when it's not bird-nesting time," said Sally.

"The last time we went bird-nesting, along Hurst Lane it was, we saw some of the bigger boys setting light to a robins nest in the hedge along there," said Ronald completely forgetting for the moment about smugglers and their dubious habits. "We shouted at them, but there were only the two of us and they just laughed at us. They said they were going to burn all the nests they could find and told us to mind our own business. That's bloody cruel that is and none of our lot would do a thing like that, would we? We might've taken an egg or two here and there ages ago, but that's all and we always made sure it wasn't addled. Just imagine if there'd been babies in there. They'd all have been killed. Anyway they hopped up through a gap in the hedge and we followed them for a while at a distance, but they suddenly disappeared and we never saw them again that afternoon. I wanted to go back to check on that nest but I was scared to. I was too frightened of finding dead babies in there." And he shuddered. "We just cut across the fields and back into the village that way."

Hilary and Sally shook their heads sadly clearly upset by this disturbing revelation. They sighed in unison.

"Let's talk about something else, shall we," said Hilary, quickly changing the subject, "else we'll all have nightmares Tell you what, lets get our pyjamas on just in case mum comes back early, then if she does, as soon as we hear that front gate click, we can dive into bed. We'll have plenty of time."

Before Hilary sat back down again, with her freshly washed and ironed pyjamas on, she picked up the empty mugs, took them over to the sink and ran a bit of water into them. "There, they can wait till morning. It'll probably be us lot who'll have to do the washing up anyway," she said. Then she settled herself comfortably back down again and looked at Ronald and Sally. "How about a game of 'I Spy then?' Bags first go.

Ronald was the first to hear the click of the gate but before he had had time to move his finger up to his lips, the girls were up onto their feet and were making for the bedroom door. They dived under the bed covers and lay there in silence, only realising when it was too late that they had left the back door open. They held their breath as Mrs Elkins came towards the bedroom, opened the door and then spoke softly to Hilary. Hilary stirred, pretended to yawn and then sat up in bed and replied to her mother, in as convincing a sleepy voice as she could muster. Mrs Elkins was not fooled by it however, and when the girls left their beds to go to the lavvy, having been too engrossed in their game to think about it before, remarked on the lack of creases in Hilary's pyjamas. They were then reminded that it was now well past midnight and that they should have been in bed two hours ago.

"We'll just have to be a bit more careful in future and not leave any clues around," said Hilary as they climbed back into bed again. It was not that easy to fool grownups after all, they decided.

two of the Playford boys
Bangy Smith's relatives

Albert Soan

more of Bangy Smith's relatives
hop picking

old cottages on Church Hill

Gregory's staff
left to right:
Mrs E Taylor, Bill Kyle,
Evie Thomas, Mrs E Honeyset
Nancy Stuart, Dora Stuart,
Ernie Elkins and Mrs Stuart

Sally, Dom and Jackie

Freda

Hazel

Betty

Betty and Freda
at Wayside

Uncle Frank Johnson

Great Aunty Sarah Sylvia (on knee)

Celia and Hetty

at Wayside

Granny Cotton early days at Sylvian

Granny and Grandad Sansom with sons Jack and Tom

V.E. day parade through Sedlescombe Village by the Queens Head

George (Porky) Partridge

John and George (Porky) Partridge

Margery Freeman and Sylvia Glyde with house pig

Janet Powell

Derek Thomas

Ethel Thomas

Hilary Elkins

Sally Cotton

Jacky Cotton

Pat Cotton

Top row left to right:
Patty Winchester, Marjorie Freeman, Sally Cotton, Hilary Elkins, Anne Pope, Dorothy Simmons

Jumbo James

Next row:
Ron (Wangy) Hudson, Jim Leaney, Rosemary Wilmshurst, Diana Woollett, June Padgham, Frankie Richmond, Basil Beeching

Next row:

Alan Turner, Gordon Winchester, Harry Haddock, Michael Clements, Peter Clements, John Soan, Basil Winchester

Next row:
Gerald Ansett, Amy Powell, Ivy Simmons, Joan Jarvis

An outing to Croydon Aerodrome

*George Taylor, Mr Cooper, Mrs Dudley
Fred Soan, Mr Tingle, Charlie Soan,
Reg Phillips, Mrs Sellens, Jean Gasson,
John Gasson, Mrs Hayward, Doris Taylor (killed
by doodlebug), Mrs Ern Taylor, Mrs Gasson,
Charlie Taylor, Derek Wilton, Mrs Charlie Taylor,
Mr Gasson, Albert Soan, Mr Dudley,
Mrs Dawson, Mr Ern Taylor, Nelson Dawson,
Ethel Soan, Freddie Phillips,
Mrs Maud Soan, Fred Taylor*

*From right to left:
Bob Robinson - shunting driver
Fred Breach - shed operative
Nobby Russel, George Baldock, Aubrey
Woollet - main line drivers*

Dolly and Pop Cotton's wedding

CHAPTER 10

Hilary, Pat and Sally were on their way to Poppinghole Lane. The main object of the exercise was to give Pat a bit of practice on the little bike, which had just come into her possession. They rode in tandem, Pat in the middle, concentration written plain as a pike staff on her face as she struggled to control this newly acquired, useful but awkward vehicle of conveyance. Sally had managed to borrow her dad's old rucksack yet again to house her own and Pats iron rations, and had slung it over her shoulder, where it was now resting comfortably on her back. They felt the strength of the sun as it emerged from behind the white fluffy clouds, suggesting that summer had really got into its stride.

"That's Henry Maplesden, I'm sure it is," puffed Hilary as they cycled up through the village. Then she slowed right down, bringing her bicycle to a halt with the other two girls pulling up just behind her. "I didn't know he had a bike," she whispered. "Wonder where he got that thing from." They stood, watching in silence as the youth turned from Brede Lane, down onto the main road towards them. He was sitting bolt upright on an old fashioned, heavy framed ladies bicycle that would have been the envy of any District Nurse, and was puffing away on an old clay pipe that looked as though it had been passed down through generations of village folk. It would not have looked out of place in any museum of antiquities. He freewheeled slowly past them, the fingers of his left hand hovering around the lever on the handle bar, controlling the brake on the back wheel with the lightest of touches.

"Well I'll be blowed," exclaimed Pat as he passed within a few feet of them, with never so much as a glance in their direction. "I've never seen him on a bike before but he's a lot better at it than I am. Wonder who taught him to ride? Tell you one thing that's for sure, it wasn't old Fraggles. He rides his bike all over the place with his hands behind his back he does, have you seen him? As he passed Mrs Phillips the other day he called out to her, 'Hey Pat, look, no bloody 'ands,' and she couldn't help smiling. 'Don't be too cocky young Alfie. Pride comes before a fall, remember,' she called out after him. But he just laughed. Funny she's got the same name as me, isn't it?"

"Not really" said Sally, "Lots of people have got the same names. Come on then, this won't get the poe's emptied," she added, her right foot already poised at the top of her peddle, bum in the air, in readiness for a further push up the hill. And she waited for the other two girls to move forward.

"Whew, I'm sweating," I'd forgotten how hilly it was round here," said Sally as they dismounted once again and began to walk the short distance to the top of Church Hill. "Never mind, once we get round the next corner, it'll all be plain sailing, well more or less."

As she was speaking, she noticed and recognised straight away, a large blue car, which was turning the corner just beyond the Church and heading towards them. It was an Alvis Firefly, belonging to Mrs Bentham, Puff, Puff' Beezle's sister and seemed to be taking up most of the road. She was immediately reminded of an altercation she had had with this lady while on her way to school.

Being on her own, which was very unusual she had accepted a lift on Margery Freeman's bicycle. Instead of sitting on the seat however, she had sat cockily on the handlebars, legs stretched out in front of her singing, 'keep right on to the end of the road.' Suddenly, this blue car coming from behind, had swung round in front of them causing Sally to dismount in a bit of a hurry. As she had slid off the handlebars, she had caught the bottom of her spine on the spur of thick metal which, when travelling in the dark, would be used to house Marjory's squat, black torch. The pain as it shot up her back was indescribable and had rendered her speechless. She had just stood there holding her breath while Mrs Bentham's passenger, Miss McKeen from Asselton House, had scolded her for behaving in such a dangerous and irresponsible manner. Even now, after all this time, she still experienced discomfort in her nether regions but had not complained either at the time or since. She reckoned that it had been her own fault and it would be rather stupid to risk another telling off for her recklessness. She had however, treated the two ladies with a degree of caution ever since and now began to feel the familiar rapid heart beating that she associated with fear rather than physical exertion. "Get in, get in, there's a car coming," she shouted out in a high pitched voice.

"For goodness sake, it's on the other side of the road. It's nowhere near us," Hilary replied. "What's got into you all of a sudden? Anyone would think you'd not seen a car before. It's only old Mrs Bentham anyway, with a fag in her mouth as usual. Perhaps I should call it a cigarette. After all she does smoke 'Craven A's,' and she's a bit posh." And she giggled. "There she's gone now, we'll soon be able to get back on our bike's again, once we're passed the Church. Pity we haven't got time to look around the old place, but there you go, you can't do everything in a day."

"I'm so thirsty I couldn't spit sixpence," continued Hilary as they rounded the bend and into Cripps Corner. Then she pointed towards a sign just beyond the corner, which said, 'Claude Brann, Staplecross 281.' "Tell you what, we'll save our water and I'll treat you to some lemonade from the grocery shop here. I think he makes it himself or perhaps his wife does but whoever, it's the best I've ever tasted anyway. His wife's called Bessie and before she was married, her surname was Winchester. She's not related to Patty, Basil and the others though or that's what mum told me anyway."

They leant their bikes carefully against the hedge and walked the short distance to the shop, passing through its open doorway. Sally sniffed appreciatively. It smelled just like the two grocery shops in Sedlescombe, reminding her of the first six items always on her mum's weekly grocery order list- Butter, marge, lard, cheese, bacon, sugar. Mr Brann was standing behind the counter, a box of groceries at his elbow and was adding up a column of figures in a thickly lined notebook. He looked up and smiled, recognising Hilary immediately. She had used this shop on a regular basis when she and her family had first moved to the area and had lived nearby. He was wearing a full length fawn overall with the sleeves rolled up to the elbows, and the buttons that held the flaps together, were removable ones. These funny buttons, had a round loop of wire at the back, and this was inserted into a small opening and then fastened into place with an oddly shaped piece of metal. It was a pity that not all buttons were removable, Sally thought to herself. It would have made the job of mangling shirts, blouses, cardigans and that sort of thing, so much easier.

"What can I do for you then, young lady?" asked the shop-keeper, putting his pencil to one side and placing his hands on to the counter as he looked up at Hilary.

"Have you got some lemonade please? We're going on a long bike ride and we're thirsty already," replied Hilary. "We've got some water with us but if we drink it all now, we'll have none left for later on. We can all share the same glass, don't worry," she added as he turned towards the doorway at the back of the shop. "Save you washing up, that's all," she shouted to his retreating back.

When he returned with the liquid refreshment, they noticed that he had brought in two bottles, one larger than the other. As he began to pour the first measure of lemonade from the larger of the two bottles into the glass, he said without looking up, "There's a bit extra here, reckon it could come in useful later on. It's hot already and set to get even hotter if my seaweed's anything to go by! Looks like you've got a bit of spare capacity in that old bag of yours," he added, pointing to the rucksack slung carelessly over Sally's shoulder. "Here, turn round and I'll find a space for it," Then he shuffled the contents of her bag around, carefully placing the small bottle where it would be cushioned amongst all the other paraphernalia in there. "There, that'll do, your turn next then," he said as he moved back to the counter. Then he filled the glass once again and passed it to Sally. "That'll be tuppence ha'penny then, a special rate for you girls," he said to Hilary and added. "If you come back this way and you're thirsty, call back in here and you can have a lemonade on the house. That means you can have it for nothing."

***

"Don't look now but here comes old Cokey Coleman," said Hilary as they stepped across the grass verge to retrieve their bicycles from the hedge. "Quick, let's get across the road and down the lane before he gets here or we'll never get away from him."

Ignoring her friend's plea for discretion, Sally looked along the road and saw a little old man walking towards them. He was wearing a tweed jacket and on his head was perched a cap that seemed several sizes too big for his little head. Riding comfortably on his left shoulder was a garden fork, while in the crook of his right arm and held firmly in place at his side, was an old wicker basket. As they hurried across the road and turned into the lane that would lead them into Poppinghole Lane, Hilary whispered, "My dad reckons he's got a screw loose. He always carries that stuff around with him and he's always going on about what he's been doing and that he's not afraid of hard work. But as dad says, as far as he knows, he's never gotten close enough to it to find out. He just carries it around for show. Right, on your bike's then and let's get away from here pretty darned quick, he's gaining on us. Poor Mr Brann, he'll be stuck with him for ages now I reckon," she added, pushing down hard on her peddle. "I hope he puts that blooming fork down before he goes in the shop though, that's all," she added as she grinned around at the other two.

"Make an interesting pub sign that, 'The Fork and Basket,' said Sally. Her observation however, fell on deaf ears. The other two girls, Pat in second place, were too intent on beating a hasty retreat to appreciate her remark, and she felt a bit miffed.

"Who said it would be all plain sailing once we'd passed the Church," said Pat as she puffed to a standstill half way up a steep incline. "I reckon this bit here's as steep as Church Hill and it's hotter now than it was when we did that bit. "I'll need another drink before long."

"It's not that bad really, they're only little hills around here. You haven't been here before though have you, so you didn't know what to expect. Now me and Sal, we know this lane like the back of our hands. Well we've been here at least a couple of times before anyway, haven't we Sal?" replied Hilary looking back over her shoulder as she brought her own bicycle to a stand still. "Tell you what, once we get down the other side of this hill, we'll stop and have another drink and a bit of mum's fruit cake, how about that then. You okay then Sal?" she asked as she turned around. And then she turned back to concentrate on the work in hand, and began to propel herself and her bicycle towards the brow of the hill.

As they freewheeled down the next hill, squeezing their brakes ever so gently to control the speed of their bicycles, Sally looked around at the rolling fields, interspersed here and there with small copses of trees. Distance and the rays of the sun as it climbed lazily up into the Heavens, gave the scenery a soft, impressionistic glow. The cows, some grazing while others sat, legs tucked comfortably around their enormous stomachs, chewing the cud, swished their tails as they sought to dislodge the persistent flies. Every now and again, she instinctively checked her position in the lane as she took in the wonder of her surroundings. Then she watched as the birds dipped and dived over the landscape, their colours neutralized by the sun's glow. She thought again and for the umpteenth time, how difficult it was to decide what was really her favourite time of the year. As the seasons metamorphosed, they produced a fresh journey of discovery.

When they reached the bottom of the hill, they stopped and straddled their bicycles, as they looked around for a site suitable for a short respite and where they could participate in a spot of light refreshment. "Right, if we pop through this hedge, we can sit on that bank over there and have our drink and a bit of cake," said Hilary pointing towards a narrow stream, which trickled its leisurely way down the slight incline. We'll just dump our bikes here by the roadside. They won't be in anybody's way. Look there's celandines down there still. And there's some silverweed there as well. Must be the dampness they like."

As they sat down amongst the greenery, their wriggling bottoms released the strong and pungent sap from the cow parsley, which proliferated there, making Pat sneeze. "I've forgotten to bring a hankie with me," she said as she brushed her hand beneath her nose. "And sneezing always makes my nose run."

"Here use mine, running noses make me feel sick" said Sally, handing over her clean piece of rag grudgingly to her sister, turning her head as she did so, to avoid an affront to her sensibilities. "Now, mind you bring your own hankie next time, it's unhealthy to share things like this. Now, where did I put the cake?" she asked, as she rummaged around in the rucksack. "Mr Brann moved everything around when he put that bottle in here, but never mind, lemonade's a bit more tasty than water is, so I'm not really complaining like." Then she paused and her right hand moved from bag to mouth in a split second as she tried to contain the most enormous sneeze that forced itself from between her pursed lips and down her nose. "Quick, give my hankie back," she said, one open hand covering the front of her face as, with the other she snatched the piece of rag from her sisters outstretch hand. "This wild parsley stuff really gets up your nose, doesn't it? " she said as she began to mop her face from chin to brow. "It's always around, that stuff, even in winter, though it does get a bit scruffy then."

"Bit like good and evil really I suppose, when you come to think about it. They're always around," replied Hilary. "Now I wonder what made me say that? Yes, I remember it was what your dad said the other day. He was looking at the paper at the time and there were some old pictures of the war in it. There was one there that I'd seen before, where the bombed buildings and trees were sticking up like broken teeth. I think it was Hiroshima or that other place in Japan that the Atom Bomb destroyed. It was the pictures I think that started him off talking to mum, and then he said something like wars bringing out the best and the worst in people. That good and evil are around all the time and are often there, side by side, or something. Then he started talking about things that I didn't understand and I lost interest. Don't you remember Sal? I'm sure you were there at the time. Anyway, if you've finished scrubbing your face, how about giving us a bit of that cake?" she added, without pausing to allow Sally the time to answer. "I'll have my drink afterwards. Bags we use the water first and save the lemonade for later on."

As they stood up, fed and watered, and brushed the bits of flotsam and jetsam off their skirts, Sally passed the back of her hand across her forehead. "Blimey, is it hot or is it hot," she asked. "Maybe it's because there's no breeze down here, but I'm sweltering. I'm not riding up this next hill, no way. I'm walking. I'd melt by the time I got to the top if I did. Here, I've just been watching those birds flying in and out of those trees over there," she said pointing towards a clump of mature trees silhouetted against the skyline. "How the hell do you think they manage to dive helter-skelter through all those branches and things, without knocking themselves out? Now if they were bats I could understand it because they've got something in their heads that lets them know when they're close to danger, but birds haven't got it. Well, as far as I know, they haven't. They must have bloody good eye sight and quick reflexes, that's all I can think of."

"Well I reckon birds and animals and so forth are a lot cleverer than us lot can understand," said Hilary. "Some birds, like swallows and things, fly for miles and miles to get from one part of the world to another and I haven't got a clue how they do it. A lot of birds find their way across oceans, deserts and even mountains and land up exactly where they need to be, year after year. How do they know where they're going without having a compass, that's what I'd like to know? The only thing I can think of is that one generation passes the knowledge on to the next one and so forth, but it's very clever when you think about it. Anyway, we'd best be on our way then," she said and she turned and moved back towards the gap in the hedge. As she squeezed her way through, followed closely by the other two girls, she added. "You'll have to move your bike Sal, so's Pat and me can get to ours. I reckon we can walk side by side up the road here. The only thing we're liable to see around this 'ere lane is a tractor or a horse and we'd hear them coming a mile off."

They continued their journey along the lane their view partially obscured from time to time by hedges and the undulating fields and wooded areas around them. Sometimes the hedges disappeared altogether and a wire netting fence, anchored by thick chestnut stakes was used to mark boundaries and line the roadway. When this happened and the seemingly endless and tranquil landscape was opened up to her, Sally was reminded of something she had read in a book quite recently. 'And indelibly printed upon the whole is the hand of man.' When she had mentioned it to her dad, he had told her that mankind had been changing the countryside for thousands of years and the way it looked now was different from how it would have looked even fifty years ago. What was the title of that book? She was darned if she could remember and there were lots of other interesting things in it as well. She was the same with poetry. She could remember lots of it but hardly ever remembered who had written it.

"I've been bitten on my arm, and it's coming up just like a horse fly bite," said Pat, breaking into Sally's thoughts. And she stopped and straddled her bicycle as she rubbed the offending area. "I bet I got it back down there, while we were sitting in all that grass, though I didn't see any flies or mosquitoes around us, did you? I don't suppose one of you thought to bring a bit of calamine lotion with you, did you? It'll have driven me mad by the time I get home," she said, wrinkling her forehead to express the discomfiture she was feeling.

"No, sorry Pat, I didn't give it a thought," said Hilary. "And anyway, what would we have carried it in? We couldn't bring the whole bottle with us, could we? Tell you what though, try some of this," she suggested as she stooped and grabbed a handful of thick, sappy dandelion leaves from the grassy verge. "Better still, try some of the flower stems, they've got more juice in them. There, that might help a bit. Should keep you going till we get home anyway," she said as she began to smear the milky sap onto Pats arm that was now all puffy, red and swollen. "We'll soon be coming out onto the road now and from then on it's all plain sailing. We'll have some more grub soon, that'll take your mind off your bite. I'm parched though, I don't know about you two. Lets have some of that lemonade Mr Brann gave us. Turn around then Sal and I'll get it out of your bag," she said abandoning her bicycle on the grass verge as she moved to extract the precious bottle of drink from Sally's back pack.

"I'm sure Molly and Alma Woodgate live around here somewhere, but I'm darned if I know exactly where. We only see then at school or down in the village, don't we," said Hilary as they cycled down the Whatlington road. "We aught to find out really, they're good for a laugh those two. Trouble is, we don't come this way very often. Now, how about turning into one of the lanes down here? We're sure to find a decent spot where we can sit and eat our sandwiches. Don't worry we'll all keep an eye out for stinging insects this time, and stinging nettles if it comes to that Pat. Woops, I nearly wobbled out in front of you, sorry Pat," she said as she struggled to bring her bicycle under control again. "I think I'd better concentrate on where I'm going for a bit, don't you and make sure we don't miss the turning into one of these 'ere lanes along here."

"I haven't seen one rabbit this morning and we've been out for ages," said Pat chewing away on a thick cheese sandwich as she sat with the other two girls, making the most of the shade afforded by a small copse of scrub oak trees. "There's plenty of them around, you can tell that by all the droppings and the burrows. Look over there, the bank's full of holes. I bet there's hundreds and thousands in there," she said taking another bite into her sandwich as she turned around and pointed towards the side of the field.

"You won't see them, not when it's hot like this and anyway, they do most of their eating first thing in the morning and in the evenings," said Sally. "When they do come out, they have to keep an eye out for the old foxes who'd just love a nice succulent rabbit for their breakfast or supper. Bit like us lot really except we don't eat 'em raw, we have 'em cooked for dinner with potatoes and greens and things. Sylvia Glyde was talking to us the other about her and her dad going rabbiting, do you remember? They take ferrets with them. Sylvia's not the least bit frightened of holding the things, but their teeth alone would put me off. Evil things they are. She has to carry the nets that they put over all the holes to trap the rabbits, well not all the holes. They keep just one open to put the ferret down. Then when he chases the rabbits out, they tangle up in the nets over the holes and Mr Freeman runs around hitting them over the head, the rabbits that is. He wouldn't do that to his ferrets, would he? They cost money and take a lot of training they do."

"Yes I remember her talking to us about that and also about her and her dad going to watch the fox hunt people when they meet in front of Battle Abbey," said Hilary. I wouldn't mind going up there myself sometime. Just to have a look mind, not to go killing foxes or anything like that. They'd be too much blood. She reckons it's quite exciting, and colourful and noisy. The riders all wear bright red coats and have black hats on and blow bugles to keep the dogs in order. Well you know that of course because you've seen pictures of it all. Anyway, she said that they usually have a glass of wine or something before they start, the hunts people that is. Her gran sometimes goes with them to see it all, especially on Boxing Day when she's staying with them. She loves it. She lives in Robertsbridge by the way, her gran. Just down the road from Poppinghole Lane where we've just come from. I don't know where exactly though.

"I like Sylvia and Margie, and yes I do remember Sylvia talking about rabbiting and fox hunting and things," said Sally drowsily. She was now leaning back against one of the trunks of the trees with her arms folded across her chest, and her legs, folded at the ankles, sticking straight out in front of her. As she looked up, the dappled sunlight played across her face, distorting the leaves into weird and wonderful shapes of improbable hues and she blinked to bring a semblance of normality to the fantastical images. As her eyes began to water, she looked away from the Heavens and down into the valley where the fields merged into woodland that went off to the right, and stretched as far as the eye could see.

There's a wood around here somewhere called Bodgers wood," she said sitting up, wide awake now and completely changing the subject. "Leastways that's what I think dad called it. He definitely said bodgers not badgers. Funny name that. We went through it one Sunday morning ages ago when he took us all for a walk. Well you weren't there Hilary for some reason but I know Hazel was. He nearly always takes us along Marley Lane so's he can have a chat with Mr Freeman and old Bunny Finch, doesn't he? But I reckon he wanted a change that day. That reminds me, he hasn't taken us out for a while now, probably because we're always gallivanting some place else. And he's always busy. Anyway, he told us that it got its name from what went on there in the olden days, making chairs and other bits of furniture. He reckons that all sorts of things went on in these woods years ago, like iron workings and that sort of things. And charcoal making, but we know all about that, don't we? He's quite interesting once you get him talking, is dad."

"I don't know about Bodgers Wood but Petley Wood's down there somewhere," said Hilary, pointing over the fields to the wooded area in the distance. "A Doodlebug came down in there during the war, so I've been told. I wasn't here at the time so I don't remember it, but I think it was Mr Linch who told me about it when he was talking about the one that came down near Magazine Farm. I reckon we should look around sometime and see if we can find any holes. Mind you, they'll all be overgrown by now I expect." After a slight pause, she lifted her right arm and began to move it side to side, roughly describing the area that dipped away in front and to the right of where they were sitting, before continuing. "It's hard to imagine that these fields just below us here, were all used for growing hops at one time. The bines were grown up poles in those days, and there had to be pole pullers to get the things on to the bins. It's much easier these days now the bines grow up string, isn't it? You can just pull one when you're ready for it, and the old measurer comes along later and makes a note of how many bushels you've picked," she added as she settled back against her chosen trunk.

"There were hop fields along Poppinghole Lane where we've just come from, as well," said Sally. "In the olden days, a lot of farmers used disk things, tokens they were called, as a tally of what pickers had earned and in some cases they, the pickers, could only spend their tokens in the farmer's own shops. That was ages ago though. People get paid real money these days. Were you there when Mr Linch showed us the tokens he's got, Hilary? Yes of course you were. They look a bit like real money don't they? Except they're tinny and a bit rough looking, and they've got all sorts of different writing and numbers on them. He even had one that was three cornered, now that was strange. It's hard to imagine now, but there were hop fields all around Sedlescome at one time. There was even one just behind old Gregory's Place," she continued after a short pause. "What the hell did they do with all the hops I wonder? They must have drunk a lot of beer in those days, that's all I can think of. The Farrows at Luffs farm grew them and Mr Linch reckons he can remember how it looked up there before the old Oast Houses were pulled down, but he can't be that old surely."

"Talking about Luffs Farm," said Hilary grinning and leaning forward again as she warmed to her subject. "Did you know that the Home Guard, Defence Volunteers or whatever they were called, used to have their meetings up there during the war? Well one dark evening when they'd left the place, they wandered off in the wrong direction and some of them ended up in the sewer. I think Charlie Taylor the Blacksmith, Mr English from Beech Farm and Harold Horsely from Carpenters Barn were amongst them. Mr Farrow said he grabbed his torch and rushed out there when he heard a commotion, realising straight away what must have happened. Pitch black it was he said but in the beam of his torch he picked out these blokes, up to their knees in muck and mischief as he called it, and spitting tin tacks. Why didn't they bring a torch with them, I'd like to know? But anyway, he said that he had to take them into one of the cow sheds and got buckets of water to clean them up with. Then Mrs Farrow insisted on taking them into the kitchen for a warm up and another hot drink before they went home. I hope she put newspapers or something on the floor before she let them in. I bet they didn't half stink."

"They're ever so kind, Mr and Mrs Farrow," said Sally. "Do you remember the time we scrumped some of their apples? By the time we got back into Chapel Hill to pick up our bikes they were waiting for us, weren't they? We were frightened to death I remember but they just told us that they had more than enough fruit for their own needs, and that we were welcome fill a bag or two at any time. They did say that they'd prefer it if we'd just let them know we were there though, so's they knew what was going on, but I suppose you can understand that, can't you? Do you know what Mr Farrows nickname is?" she asked and paused for a moment as she looked around at the other two.

"Neil Farrow, wheelbarrow, you told me that ages ago," replied Pat, before Sally had time to tell them. "Anyway, I was just thinking about Penny Farrow while you two were talking. She fell into all those stinging nettles round the back of the farm, not far from that cesspool you were talking about. Mrs Collins told me all about it when I went up to collect the milk the other day. She said that the poor little thing was covered from head to toe in all these stings and blains and things and that she yelled her head off. Well so would I have done, wouldn't you? Anyway, her mum smothered her in calamine lotion but it took ages to calm her down. Pity she didn't think about dock leaves but perhaps she couldn't find enough of them around there for so many stings," said Pat reflectively. "She was only just getting over being attacked by the old mother goose up there as well. She's a vicious old thing that goose of their's but then most geese are vicious if you ask me." Penny, the daughter of Josie and Neil Farrow, though christened Penelope had, from the moment the Reverend Noble had crossed her brow with holy water, been referred to as Penny.

As they sat there in the warm sunshine, Sally thought back to the time when she, Pat and their mum, had walked all the way from Sylvian to the fields just below where they were sitting, to bring sandwiches, pies and drinks to her older sisters, who had shared a bin in the hop fields there. She could still remember the pungent smell of the hops and feel the tickle of smoke in her nostrils from the brushwood fires, fuelled up to brew the strong, sweet smoky tea that was the best in the world. Then she thought about the rough and tumbles she had enjoyed with Gordon, Patty and Basil Winchester, and smiled to herself as she recalled the quick but gentle wit of their Mother. This lady, this rasher of wind as Gordon called her, always brought a ray of sunshine to any gathering. She was one of life's colourful but gentle characters. "Were those big things they stored the hops in called pokes or was it pockets?" She asked out of the blue, drawing her knees up under her chin and folding her arms around them, as she asked the question.

"Either or both," replied Hilary a little puzzled by the sudden and unexpected question. "Some called them one thing and some the other, that's all. Anyway, we'd best be on our way, we've been sitting here for ages and ages."

As Sally rose to her feet, she looked over to where a lightning tree stood out, skeletal and boney white against the living, breathing greenery of high summer. For some unaccountable reason it evoked the same strange feeling of unease in her as had that 'disoriented goat' picture at Wayside all those years ago. Though different in content, composition and even medium, they seemed somehow connected by and imbued with the same strange melancholy imagery. When, only the other day she had told her dad that she quite enjoyed feeling a bit sad, he had quietly told her that she did not know the real meaning of sadness. Before he had turned and walked away from her, she had seen such a look of sadness in his eyes that it had made her want to cry.

As she turned and absentmindedly brushed down the skirt of her dress, she noticed with concern, a holly tree like the one at the bottom of their field, being choked and slowly devoured by thick, sinuous ivy. Mother Nature worked in mysterious ways, she reckoned and both gave and took away life. Her generosity was incalculable and overlay every aspect of existence. She was obliging, waving a magic wand to produce trees for them to climb, grass to run on and nuts and berries to eat. Then there were all the flowers and fruit she provided, the list was endless. Though undoubtedly red in tooth and claw as her dad had observed, her works of art were everywhere, affecting all the senses. And somehow through it all was this seemingly harmonious balance.

"Hark," said Hilary, one hand cradling the back of her ear and Sally jumped a foot into the air, so engrossed had she been in her own thoughts. "Look, it's over there," she said and pointed to where an aeroplane, still low on the horizon was heading towards them. They all looked skyward and stood perfectly still and silent as the familiar sound of a solitary Spitfire hit their ears. Above the clatter of the propeller blades, they could hear the characteristic whirr of its Merlin engine and as it came closer, they could see, silhouetted against the azure blue of the summer sky, this symbol of blessed deliverance. They watched its progress across the Heavens, standing to attention as a mark of respect for this special aeroplane that all through the years of the war had given them hope.

"I wonder where that's off to," said Sally once the sound and sight of the aeroplane of such satisfying shape and proportions had disappeared into the wide blue yonder. "It's funny isn't it that all through the war there were so many of them about that we sort of took them for granted. Now that we only see one here and there, they seem so much more special. Do you know, I'll recognise the sound of a Spitfire until the day I die. I know I will. It gave you a bit of hope when you didn't know what the hell else was going on, didn't it? I reckon that some things just stay with you for ever and ever. Like your skin I suppose."

"I thought for a moment there you said sting," said Pat rubbing her arm and wincing as she stirred back into life the area inflamed by the insect bite. "Trust you to remind me. I'll be glad to get home and get some calamine on this sting before it drives me crazy. It's not far now, is it? She asked looking anxiously at her sister. Then without waiting for an answer, she stooped to retie the lace on one of her plimsolls, before making her way over to the hedge to retrieve her bicycle. As they freewheeled down the hill towards the entrance to Marley Lane, she began to chant a favourite rhyme of hers. "To market to market to buy a fat pig, home again home again jiggerty jig. To market to market to buy a fat hog, home again home again jiggerty jog."

Thank God she's forgotten about her itchy arm, for the moment at least, Sally thought to herself.

"When did you say your cousins from Oxford were coming down?" Hilary asked as they walked wearily up the hill with Horseman's Farmland to their right and the Brooks on their left. "I can't remember if you said next week or next month."

"I don't think I did say exactly when but I know they'll be here in time for hop picking," replied Sally. "They're only here for a couple of weeks so I expect they'll share a bin with us. You don't mind, do you? I'm really looking forward to seeing them. Peggy really makes me laugh, and Eddie's clever and good at mending punctures as well," she continued. She thought back to their last visit, just after the war in Europe had finished. They had arrived amidst great excitement with Aunty Nellie, mums sister, Uncle Tom and their baby sister Ann. They were referred to as 'The Doe family,' by one and all. Peggy hardly ever stopped talking, and she had the same infectious laugh as her mum.

"By the way, next Friday I'm going to stay the night with Eileen Lawrence," said Sally, her mind grass-hopping from one subject to another with ease. "Her mum and dad are going out and they won't be home until after midnight. I've stayed there once or twice before. We always play 'I spy,' and then when we get fed up with that, we sing and tell stories. Eileen always sings, 'I'm leaning on the lamppost at the corner of the street in case a certain little lady comes by.' That's her favourite song. She sings it at least three times during the evening. The worst thing is, we always end up giggling about something then I have to use their lavvy. I still can't for the life of me, fathom out why it's so moth eaten when the house itself is so spick and span. I don't think Mrs Lawrence ever goes up there. She's far too finicky. And she wouldn't risk catching her bum on that cracked old seat, I know. No, I reckon she's got a secret lavvy some place else. She's ever so tiny, isn't she? She could hide up in any old nook or cranny. Right, on your bikes then," she commanded bossily, as they came to the Bee House. "We're nearly home now. Look, you can see our house from here."

"There's Frankie Richmond," said Hilary interrupting Sally and pointing towards Paygate Corner. "Quick, call out to him before he gets to his house." The tall, gangly youth stopped in his tracks as the girls called his name and waited until they drew up beside him. "What you up to then Frankie?" asked Hilary. "Don't tell me, you've been out collecting rabbit food and now you've got the kindling wood to chop. Don't you ever stop working?"

"Well you know what its like, there's always something needs doing," he replied looking anxiously towards the little bungalow where he lived. "I'm allowed out this evening if I get all my jobs done, and once I've fed the rabbits and got the coal in, I think I'll have just about finished. I've just seen Ellen, Ellen Brown you know, up the hill there. She'd got her little pail with her and was trying to fill it up with water from that spring in the bank up there. She wasn't having much luck though, there's not much water comes out of there at this time of year. I stood talking to her for a few minutes. You can't help feeling sorry for her, can you? She was wearing that enormous brown beret of hers, even in this hot weather. How about you girls then, where've you been?" He asked as he scanned their faces with his bespectacled, intelligent eyes.

"We've been to Poppinghole Lane. It's ever such a long way," said Pat. "And I've been stung by a horsefly or something so we're going home to get some calamine lotion." With that, she put one foot through the frame of the bicycle and on to the peddle, propelled the thing forward and wobbled off up the road.

Frankie lived with Mrs Wintergreen Edwards and her son Owen, in one of the bungalows near Paygate Corner. As far as Sally knew, he was not related to them in any way and guessed that he must have lost his family during the war. Though kind to Frankie in her own way, Mrs Edwards allowed him only the minimum of freedom. He had chores to perform before and after school, and others at weekends. He was however, always allowed to go to Sunday school and it was when they were walking to and from the little Chapel, that the girls managed to get him to talk and mess about. As soon as they discovered that he was as good a mimic as Basil Winchester, they egged him on and his imitation of old Puff, Puff Beasle, had them in fits of laughter. He would never however, talk about his family and what his life had been like prior to his arrival at Blackbrooks. It was a bit sad somehow and puzzling. There was always a chance though that when he knew them better, he might unwind a bit.

As they walked wearily up the field, Sally paused for a few moments to watch the hens as they scratched about in an area that their dexterous feet had worried into a dustbowl. She smiled as she watched them flapping their wings and puffing out their breast feathers as they kicked up and scrabbled about in the dry soil. One old hen with her puffed out breast on the ground and her bum in the air was paddling furiously with her little feet, creating a miniature dust storm all of her own. As Sally watched, she began to flick the fine soil over and under her feathers and then she cocked her head back and a sound like the signal from a distant train, emerged from her wide open beak. Sally grinned to herself as she turned away but before she began to tackle the short distance to the top gate, she leant her bicycle against her hip and stooped and carefully plucked a dandy clock from between its green protective leaves. As she began to blow its top not off, she chanted quietly to herself, "One o'clock, Two o'clock, Three o'clock, four." Then she paused and as she looked at the other two girls added. "Why is it that nearly all the umbrellas come off in the first blow, then you're left with this one bit that just won't give itself up?"

"Give it here," said Hilary and as she took it from Sally's hand, took a deep breath then expelled it, removing the stubborn seed from its protective cushion.

***

"Just cut up some more newspapers for the lavvy before you go. We're nearly out in both of them and I just haven't had time to do it," said mum. It was now early evening and Sally was making her preparations to spend the night at Hilary's place.

"Where are they then, the newspapers?" asked Sally. I don't want to cut up anything dad hasn't finished with or he'll go mad. You know what he's like about reading them from cover to cover. Takes him ages it does."

"Don't worry about your dad. If there's any here that he's not finished with, he'll have to catch up with them while he's doing his business out there," replied mum. "Anyway, there're right here, I've got them all ready for you and here's a big blunt knife that you can use to cut them up with. Pass them here when you've done that and I'll pierce the edges with the meat skewer, so's you can thread the string through. Those skewers are sharp and if you put too much pressure on them, they'll really bite you. I don't want any accidents thank you. I've got enough to think about."

"I love this job," said Hilary, as they sat at the kitchen table ready to take it in turns to cut the thick paper up into a usable size. "You always come across something interesting that you've missed before. Look, there's an advert here for those thick, lisle stockings, like the ones old Mrs Marsden wears. I couldn't help noticing hers when we went strawberry picking a while ago. They only reached to just above her knees, and when she sat down on that box to eat her sandwiches, you could see that huge lump of flesh bulging out between her stockings and her knickerlegs."

Sally grinned and nodded. She remembered it well and the lady in question's apparent indifference to the exposure of her person and underwear. She had just sat there with her belly in her lap, munching away at her sandwiches, seemingly oblivious to the covert attention of the youngsters.

"Ah, now this is more serious. There's something here about some kids getting injured in a house that collapsed, somewhere in London by the look of it," said Hilary. "It says here that there'd been a 'keep out' notice on the place and it was all boarded up but these kids had managed to get in somehow. That's the trouble with youngsters. They don't seem to see danger until it's too late," she added seriously, quite unaware of the look of amusement that passed momentarily over mum's face. "Well, we'd better get a move on or we'll never get away," she said shuffling the papers together again and reaching for the knife. "I'll start cutting it up and you can tidy up the rest of the papers if you like, then you can have a go."

"What annoys me, is when you pull a bit of paper off the string while you're in the lav, start to read something really interesting, and then can't find the matching bit. After all they're all cut up together, aren't they?" Said Sally as she started to straighten out the pile of newspapers. "You always wonder how you could have missed the article in the first place then think that the bit you want has got to be there somewhere. I've spent ages sometimes looking for something in particular that I've just got to read, but I've never yet found even one missing bit. I reckon there's got to be some place, up in the sky or wherever, where all the things you ever lose, end up. Hey, I wonder if my old yellow top's up there? It's suddenly disappeared," she added looking up anxiously as the thought struck her, causing genuine concern. "I'll never see it again if that's what's happened, then what'll I do?"

"You'll manage, it was falling to bits anyway," said Hilary. "Like mum says, that blue one of yours looks a lot better on you anyway. I was just trying to think though what the word is for things that disappear without trace and all those other things that happen that you just can't account for. Like when you drop a bit of bread on the floor and it always lands butter side down, and that sort of thing. I wish I could remember what it's called. Not to worry, I'll probably remember it soon enough, when I'm in bed and trying to get off to sleep. I wouldn't be surprised. Anyway, don't forget that Willie and Roy are coming round this evening. They said they'd be here at about half past seven, so we'd best get a move on. Here mum, there's quite a pile here for you to skewer and so forth, I'll pass them over shall I?" she asked. Then as she lifted the neat piles of paper across the table, she passed her hand across her forehead, leaving a smudged streak of newspaper print from brow to hairline.

Later, as the two girls walked briskly down the field, mum called out after them. "Don't forget your dad wants to cut your hair tomorrow morning Sally, so don't be late up here, will you?" Sally's hand went instinctively to her head and then she felt around the back of her neck, before she turned and waved to her mum. She hated having her hair cut, especially the tidying up bit where her dad used a pair of clippers up the back of her neck. Not only did it tickle, making her squirm and hunch her shoulders, but it always snagged, viciously pulling out single strands of hair that really made her scalp tingle. Why couldn't it be left alone to grow to its hearts content? Then all she would need to do would be to tie it back with a ribbon or even a piece of string to keep it tidy. That made good common sense she reckoned especially as dad disliked the rigmarole as much as she and her sisters did. She knew that by the way he moaned throughout the whole operation. So she got nits from time to time, but longer hair would not make that much difference, surely. Never mind, that ordeal was tomorrow morning, ages away. She still had this evening to look forward to.

As she fell into step beside her friend, and they linked arms, she said, "lets sing The Dream Ship, I love that song." And after taking a deep breath, they began to sing-

Come for a sail in the Dream Ship, O come with us tonight.
Round the moon and twinkling stars, all shining with silvery light.
Come, come in the Dream Ship, it holds your dreams of joy.
Call, call to the Dream Ship. Dream Ship ahoy!

First we will go to the cold lands, the lands of ice and snow.
Into home of polar bear and frosty Eskimo.
Come, come in the Dream Ship, it holds your dreams of joy.
Call, call to the Dream Ship. Dream Ship ahoy!

Now we will go to the warm lands, where hungry tigers roam.
Through the jungle we will go, and visit an Indian home.
Come, come in the Dream Ship, it holds your dreams of joy.
Call, call to the Dream Ship. Dream Ship ahoy!"

"Look they're there already, they're early," said Hilary pointing towards her house. As Sally followed her pointed finger, she saw the two boys sitting comfortably on the steps leading up to the front door. They were deep in conversation and showed no sign of having seen the girls. "Shush, if we push through the hedge here by the stream, we can come round the back way and make them jump," she whispered. "I'm pretty sure they haven't seen us." As they pushed their way through the thick hedge, Sally caught the top of her arm on a bramble, and winced, "Shush, they'll hear you," said Hilary, for once seemingly unsympathetic to Sally's discomfort. "This is our chance to get our own back on them. They're always frightening us." They jumped the narrow stream, skirted around the Winchesters garden and made their way silently towards the back garden of Windy Ridge. Then they crept down the side of the house and were within a whisker of the corner, when the boys suddenly leapt out on them frightening them nearly to death.

"Gotcha," said Roy, amusement and satisfaction written all over his face. "We saw you coming right from when you left your top gate. We timed you coming down the field and along the lane and then when you suddenly disappeared through that hedge, we knew exactly what you were up to. You were pretty quiet coming down the side of the house here, we'll give you that, and if we'd not known what you were up to, you'd have got us good and proper. As it was though, we were listening and just heard a slight rustle, so we knew exactly when to jump out on you. Here, what's happened to your arm," he asked, coming over to examine Sally's wound more closely. "It's a fresh scratch, so you must have done it when you jumped through that hedge down there, tut tut. It's still bleeding but not very much. Never mind, I've got a clean hankie here, I'll clean it up a bit for you." Then he wound the white cotton handkerchief around his forefinger, spat on the covered digit and cleaned away the offending blood from around the wound. "There, that's better, you'll live to see another day I reckon," he added.

"Thanks," said Sally turning her head to one side. "It's a bit sore but spit's supposed to clean wounds and things and it stops them going bad, doesn't it?"

"Not if someone who spits on you has got rabies, it doesn't," said Willie dryly.

"Talking about rabies, look who's coming along the road then," whispered Hilary, ducking back behind the wall and pulling Sally with her. "It's old Denis, wonder what he's been up to? I bet he's been round East View Terrace, winding up the kids round there," she added answering her own question. "Mind you, he gets on alright with some of them, your brother thinks he's quite funny, doesn't he Roy? And even Dorothy and Enid Simmons don't seem to mind him. They must be a lot more tolerant than us lot that's all I can say and have a jolly good sense of humour as well. They'd need it with him. He's got the brains of a rocking horse."

"Not that good surely," replied Roy with a grin.

"Right, who's for a game of hide and seek then?" asked Sally once Denis and his bicycle had been swallowed up by the hedge, and the contours of the undulating hill. Now, having fully regained her composure, she was keen not to waste any more time in idle chit, chat especially on someone as innocuous as Denis. She already had the first hiding place for herself and Hilary lined up. It was in no mans land behind some clumps of thick, course grass, not far from the old well. She reckoned it would take the boys ages to find them there. "We'll go first then if you like," she suggested and grabbed Hilary by the arm. "No peeping now and count up to fifty, that'll give us time to hide properly."

So well hidden were they that the boys had to resort to the old and trusted signal of 'oller if you're far away, whistle if you're near.' As Sally tried to whistle, she giggled, giving the game and their hiding place away and they returned reluctantly to the side of the house to count for the boys. After a while it became increasingly difficult to find a fresh hiding place and when it was the boy's turn to hide, they ventured into forbidden territory. The first the girls knew about this was when they heard a sudden cry of distress from the bottom of the garden where a line of dwarf fir trees masked the area where the overflow from the sewer seeped into the lush green grass down there. "Bugger," was the one word Roy uttered, followed by a few seconds of unnatural silence. Then he spoke again, more urgently this time. "Well, don't just stand there gawping, pull me out of here for Gods sake."

The girls rushed to where Willie, while struggling to keep his own person uncontaminated, was doing his best to retrieve his friend from the quagmire.

"Just grab my hand will you and give us a pull," he said extending his one free arm out towards them as they approached the odorous region. "I've gone in as far as I dare, but it stinks to high Heaven down here. Look, he's up to his knees in it."

"Hilary told you not to go down there, you two," said Sally wrinkling her nose as she leaned forward and extended a helping hand to Willie. Then she started giggling. She remembered a bit of nonsense that she had heard as she and Hilary had come out of Wilton's, the paper shop the other day. Mr Budgen had been leading his horses up through the village at the time and one of them had left behind a goodly pile of steaming manure. As this had been swiftly shovelled up by one of the men for his allotment, Bunny Finch, who had been standing by the village pump watching the show, had shouted out to him, 'after the Lord Mayors Show comes the shit cart, eh Fred?' To which Fred had replied, 'I'd liefer brung 'osses duvers to me oynuns en soot, you ewld faggit.' And the two old men had fallen about laughing. There had to be a parallel between that occasion and the here and now, she reckoned if only because of the stench that accompanied both happenings. And she swiftly covered her face, her nose in particular with her free arm.

"I don't know, we always seem to be rescuing you from something or somewhere Roy," said Hilary as half an hour or so later they all sat around the kitchen table eating bread and dripping. "You won't be able to put your socks back on, you know that don't you? They're still sopping wet but at least they smell a bit sweeter. I gave them a good old rub with that carbolic soap over there, and so forth. As for your shoes, well I've washed them inside and out and dried them best as I can, but you'll have to stuff them with newspaper when you get home. If your mum asks what you've been up to, tell her you fell in the Brooks. Tell you what, to save you having to tell her a lie, get Willie to push you in there on the way home."

"I suppose you think that's funny," said Roy not looking in the least amused. "Look at the bottoms of me trousers, they're still wet and they're really uncomfortable. They keep sticking round my legs. And your blasted cat keeps licking my feet," he added wriggling around on his bottom to emphasise his discomfort.

"Cat? We haven't got a cat," said Hilary jumping up from her seat and bending down to look beneath the table. Then as a tabby moggy shot out, dived between her legs and disappeared through the open door, she added. "How on earth did Mrs Wintergreen's cat get in here? I like cats but I don't encourage that one. Old Mrs Edwards got me into trouble once. She saw me combing out one of my rabbits, that angora one, and reported me for skinning a rabbit alive of all things. As if I would do such a thing. I don't even bend down to stroke that cat these days in case she thinks I'm planning to skin the thing. I wonder sometimes what goes on in that mind of hers. Never mind, I've just thought of something else, a bit of a coincidence if you like. Do you remember us talking earlier on today, about those blokes falling in the Farrows cesspool during the war Sal? Well don't you think it's strange that Roy should get stuck in this one on the same day? Do you think that perhaps us talking and laughing about it had a kind of influence on him, sort of compelled him to walk over to that one and fill his boots up? Now wouldn't that be something?

"Don't be daft," replied Sally. Then she paused for a moment to think about it before continuing. "Hang on a bit, you could be right you know. He did jump out on us and frighten us half to death, didn't he so it could be that fear sort of took over and made our minds really powerful and vengeful. I like that," she added grinning away like a Cheshire cat.

"Yes but Willie jumped out on you same as I did and nothing's happened to him, well not so far," said Roy a little nervously. "And don't forget that you were going to do the same thing to us except we got in first, that's all. You two weren't creeping down beside that wall for nothing."

"Don't try and make excuses Roy. No, that was your punishment for jumping out on us. I've made up my mind about that," replied Sally. And nobody in their right mind would dare to argue with her when she adopted that tone of voice.

CHAPTER 11

Pat, Hilary and Sally sat on the underground tank, up to their eyebrows in vegetables. Well, peas, carrots and potatoes to be exact. Pat was shelling peas into a metal colander, while Sally peeled potatoes. Hilary had the messy job of scraping the carrots, frequently dipping them into the bowl of water, balanced precariously on her lap and which was getting muddier and bittier by the minute.

"If you keep eating those peas we'll have none left for dinner," said Sally sternly as Pat popped yet another handful of the miniature, sweet orbs into her mouth. "You know there's extra for dinner today, don't you? There'll be Aunty Nellie, Uncle Tom, Peggy, Eddie and Ann.

"That makes five extra, yes I know," replied Pat. "So what? "I don't care if I don't get any cooked ones. I prefer them raw anyway. Here pass me a bit of that carrot Hilary. I like that better raw as well. And I'm going indoors in a minute to cadge a bit of raw cabbage stalk off mum, and she grinned as she glanced sideways at her sister. You aren't half getting bossy," she added as she munched her way through the chunk of crisp orange flesh that Hilary had passed to her. "Our Dinner's going to be late today, because they're coming all the way from Oxford and I'm starving hungry already."

"Well you did have a bit of bread and marmite earlier on, same as Hilary and me did," replied Sally. "And don't worry, mum said that didn't count as eating between meals because dinner was going to be late today and we'd be half starved before the others got here otherwise. I can't wait to see Peggy and Eddie again, can you?"

As they chatted, they glanced instinctively towards Paygate Corner from time to time even though they knew that it would be an hour or two at least before their cousins would arrive. For some reason though, they did not see a short, stocky figure as it passed the Bee House and Paygate Corner. It was only when the gate at the bottom of the field opened with its characteristic click, that the girls looked up in expectation.

"Hey look, here comes old Bunny Finch, I wonder what he's got in that old sack he's carrying?" said Sally. "The last time I saw him was a few weeks ago, up by the pump in the village." As he came through the top gate, he smiled at the girls then turned his attention towards the scullery door where mum had just appeared.

"Got a few pigeons here for you Doll," he said as he walked up the pathway towards her. "Only just been shot they have, so they'll keep for a day or two. Get Pop to hang 'em up in one of his sheds, in the shade like."

"Well I didn't expect pigeons, not at this time of the year anyway," replied mum. "But you don't look a gift horse in the mouth do you? Talking of mouths I've got a few extra to feed for the next week or two as I've got my sister and her family coming to stay. They should be here any time as a matter of fact. These birds'll do us a meal or two by the weight of this bag. They go a long way if you cook them slowly in the oven and strip all the meat off the bones," she added as she took the Hessian sack from him.

"Yes, and they'd have gone more of a long way if I hadn't up and shot 'em," he replied dryly.

Sally remembered the last time he had supplied mum with a sack full of pigeons, and his reply when she had asked him how he managed to get so many. 'Well now, all you have to do is stand around on freezing cold morning and make a sound like a cabbage,' he'd said. Then he had just walked off down the field.

The rest of the day passed in a flurry of noise and activity interspersed with meals, and countless cups of tea accompanied by thick chunks of fruit-cake. Most of the bags that had been abandoned in doorways, gradually found their way into one or other of the two sheds where Aunty Nellie and her family would be sleeping, the contents to be sorted through at leisure. The other bags that had held the food and drink for the journey, had been sorted, the brown paper bags and bits of greaseproof paper, carefully smoothed out to be used again and again.

Later that evening, the girls and Eddie sat on the underground tank planning the next day's activities.

"Mum says we don't have to go to Sunday school tomorrow, I've already asked her," said Sally. "That means we can take the bikes and go as far as we like. You'll have to ride a girl's bike by the way Eddie. I hope you don't mind but dad's got the only boys one and he won't let you lend his. Shall we try and get as far as Eastbourne, do you think? It's not that far and we can take a map with us. You can be in charge of that Eddie and we'll give you the puncture mending kit as well, so's we don't forget it."

"That sounds like a good idea, even though I've no idea how far Eastbourne is from here," said Peggy with a grin. "We're going to be hop picking for the rest of the week so I don't care how far we go tomorrow. Don't forget though, I'll need a bike that you can put the seat down on. I've only got little legs, remember." And she giggled as she stretched her legs out as far as they would go, which was not very far.

The next day they were up bright and early. Eddie was checking the bicycles over, testing the tyres and the brakes with a critical eye, while Hilary and Sally were on their way to fetch the milk from Battle Barn Farm. As they scurried across the field, Pat called out to them, "now don't hang about, will you. No stopping for scones and things like that today. We've got to make an early start if we're to get all the way to Eastbourne." Then as the two girls turned and waved their acknowledgement, she turned on her heel and walked back through the scullery door and into the kitchen. Pat and Peggy were in charge of the food and already a pile of sandwiches was building up as Peggy cut the bread and spread the slices with an assortment of fillings, including smelly fish paste. "Pass me those bits of greaseproof and I'll wrap some of these sandwiches up before they all topple over," Pat said, and she pointed towards the bits of paper in question, which were just out of her reach. Then she began to wrap the sandwiches up carefully before placing them into brown paper bags. "Tidy old doorsteps some of these," she added as she lifted them up for inspection. "Never mind, by the time we get to eat them, we'll be hungry enough to eat a scabby donkey. By the way, we mustn't forget to take some of dad's tomatoes with us. His ones taste better than any others you've ever tasted in your life. They're sweet and savoury at the same time. He's got some secret ingredient that he feeds them with and he's promised to tell me what it is, one of these days."

"We've got to take some of Aunty Doll's fruit cake with us as well, that'll give us energy," said Peggy. "I'll pick out the bits of greaseproof to put them in. We don't want them wrapped in bits that have got brown sauce on, do we? And what about drink, have you got plenty of bottles to fill with water or something? They'll be heavy so we'll give them to Eddie to carry. He won't mind. Talking about Eddie, we'd better make sure he takes the map with him. He's the only one who can follow the blooming things and also if we get lost, we can blame him for it, can't we?"

As they peddled along Marley Lane, bicycles and bodies laden with food and other necessities, they were full of energy and enthusiasm. They were negotiating the sharp bend around Rutherford's corner, when they saw Margie and Sylvia walking towards them. They stopped and talked to the two girls who were on their way to the farm to see Granny Partridge, hoping that some at least of her pears would be ripe enough to eat. They were going to branch off just round the corner and make their way past the marshy area where the kingcups grew in such profusion, through the field and wood and on to the farm that way. If they managed to catch a glimpse of Deffy and Bill, so much the better. They were also trying to get out of going to Sunday School, which they thought was a waste of time on a day like this. Margie's mum reckoned however, that they needed to go to Church at least once a week to ask God's forgiveness for all the mischief they got up to. Sally thought that was a bit unfair, knowing the girls as well as she did. Although they were always laughing, it just did not seem to enter their heads to look for mischief. Not like some kids she could mention, and she grinned as she mentally included herself in this.

After telling them that they were planning to ride all the way to Eastbourne and back with Eddie as chief map reader and puncture mender, they straddled their bicycles in readiness to resume their journey. They all chuckled at Sylvia's parting comment on the amount of food they were carrying. "How many weeks did you say you were going for?" she asked.

When they reached the end of Marley Lane, Eddie stopped and after consulting his map pointed to the left, to road that would take them past the Cinema. "That's our best way," he said. " There's a lane to the right down there that'll take us past the back of Battle Abbey. Dad'n I are going there one day next week. I've only been there once but I didn't get chance to find the spot where Harold got that arrow in his eye that time, so that'll be the first thing I do when I get there with dad. I'm not going hop picking every day, you know."

With Eddie in the lead, they made their way along the lane, stopping briefly at his request to take a look at the back view of the Abbey. He seemed surprised and a little taken aback by the sheer scale and attention to detail at the rear of this impressive building. The beauty yet simplicity of the architecture here as he put it. He would be hard put he reckoned, to choose between this view and the more familiar frontal gateway into the Abbey. Sally, who also was not familiar with this view of the Abbey, decided there and then that her vote would definitely go to this one. Though not as ornate as the main entrance with its lofty crenulations, the balance here was right somehow.

They pressed on along the lane, which followed the contours of the landscape and divided up ancient farms and woodland. When they came to a wide opening in the hedge, which edged this country lane and led directly into a densely wooded area, Peggy decided it was time to take a break. As she was quick to remind them, she and Pat only had little legs. They wheeled their bicycles through the gap and laid them down while they looked around for somewhere to sit amongst the rough foliage.

As Sally sat down, she put her hand out to steady herself and sucked her breath in sharply as she felt a sharp pain in her finger. As she examined the area where a thorn had pierced the skin, she saw a small blob of bright red blood oozing through, and was reminded of a little rhyme she had heard somewhere. 'Not half so big as a round little worm, pricked from the lazy finger of a maid.' And she grinned to herself. The little ditty seemed to work some kind of healing power for within a couple of minutes the soreness had quite disappeared. She could not resist the urge to exact a little sympathy from the others however, and held up her finger, blood and all for inspection.

"Just suck it for a few seconds, it'll soon stop bleeding," said Peggy. Look, there's some dock leaves here. They're good for wounds as well as nettle stings, or so Granny Sansom reckons. She said you could use plantains as well if I remember rightly but I'm not sure what they look like." And she leaned forward and plucked a few succulent leaves of the prolific dock and passed them to Sally who made a feeble attempt to wind them around her finger.

Eddie just sat there, elbows on knees sucking on a long piece of grass, completely oblivious to Sally's injury and when he began to speak, the girls looked at him in puzzlement. "Master Huggett and Roman John. They did cast the first can-non." He said. Then with the grass still dangling from his mouth, he looked around at the girls. "I can't remember where I read that but do you know what made me think about it?" He asked. "It was looking into this wood where you can see dips and things, where the ground's been disturbed. I had a good look before I sat down. That's usually a sign that there's been iron workings going on here, and I know for a fact, it was going on all around this area. There's a stream not far away from here. That was important as well. A lot of the biggest guns on the battle ships were made in this part of Sussex, you know. There were always wars going on somewhere or other, mostly against the French it seems, so iron was really important because it was ideal for guns, bullets that sort of thing. It wasn't just used to make guns though. Iron was used for all sorts of other things. You ask your Blacksmith in the village, Mr Taylor. He'll tell you," he said spitting out the piece of chewed grass before continuing.

"Can you imagine what it must have been like in the olden days though, with all that cutting down and burning of trees to feed the forges and the making of charcoal and such like. They must have been pretty strong, the men who worked in these woods, don't you reckon. And what about the gunpowder? That was important as well. They needed charcoal for that and a couple or so other things as well. Salt Peter was one of them. There were some tidy old explosions where they made that gunpowder, I can tell you and a lot of people were killed or badly injured. Can you imagine it, being burned like those men must have been? And boys like me worked there as well, don't forget that. It must have been really grim. It's a wonder that anyone would work somewhere where they could be blown to bits at any time. I wouldn't have," he added hastily. And he shivered. Then as he paused to inwardly contemplate the fate of those hapless victims, he picked up another piece of grass and began chewing it.

"Hey don't drink all that water, leave some for me. And don't forget we've got the rest of the day to think about as well," he said suddenly sitting bolt upright, his lecture on iron, explosions and weapons of war coming to an abrupt end. Then he leaned over and took the bottle of liquid from Peggy. As he lifted it up to his mouth, there was silence as the girls sat and watched as he slaked his thirst, his Adams apple moving up and down rhythmically. "I didn't see you take that bottle from my bag Peg," he said as he passed the back of his hand across his mouth. Then he reached out and took the stopper from his sister, replaced it on the bottle and popped the container back into his rucksack.

"Right on your feet then, we've got a long way to go," said Hilary standing up. "How's your finger then Sal?" she asked and examined the punctured skin, free now from its covering of greenstuff. "That looks okay now. That won't be no trouble, but how on earth do you manage to get your hands so grubby? Don't tell me, it's because you're such a fidgety britches. You're always scrabbling about in the ground or up a tree or investigating some interesting bit of flotsam or jetsam. I can't imagine what you're hoping to find most of the time."

"Hark who's talking!" said Sally in mock indignation. "Talk about the coal calling the chimney black. You're as bad if not worse than me. Let's have a look at your hands shall we? There, I thought so. Look everyone, her hands are every bit as grubby as mine, though I have to admit her finger nails are not quite as dirty as mine are."

While they were talking, Pat moved over to the pile of bicycles. "It's the pot calling the kettle black. It's nothing to do with chimneys and things," she said seriously as she stooped to extricate her little bike from the others. Then she examined the bag fixed to the pannier on her back mudguard. Having made sure that it was still firmly attached, she looked more closely at the carrier. "Here I wonder if this grid thing here is made of iron? She said moving the bicycle around to examine the thing more closely. "Perhaps it was made with the iron they got from this wood, you never know."

"No that's not iron, well not just iron on its own anyway. It's got something else mixed up in it, some other kind of metal," said Eddie, coming over to examine the thing more closely. "It's a kind of steel, you can see that by the colour of it. Iron on its own rusts like mad and it's very heavy, so it's nearly always mixed up with something else. It's like the frame here, that's mostly iron but that's mixed up with other metals as well. It's really clever when you think about it, and it makes you wonder who discovered how to make all these things."

"Well, it's a bit like making a cake really I suppose," said Peggy. "You just put in a few ingredients, give it a stir, then cook it and hope for the best. If it tastes okay, you do it again. If not, you throw the whole lot out of the window and try something else. So I reckon it's just the same with all these metals and things. I reckon they, the people in the olden days, tried umpteen different concoctions before they came up with something useful. We've no idea how long it took them, have we? Or perhaps they just discovered the best things by accident, you never know. Bit like the old cake making really. It's all trial and error and hoping for the best, kind of thing. Hey wait for us," she called out, suddenly aware that her brother had left the little group and was already several yards away from them as he peddled off along the country lane.

"I'm only going to the end of this lane here to see where we go to after that," he called out over his shoulder. "I told you what I was doing but you were too busy talking. I'll wait for you lot at the end there," he said as he pointed ahead. Then he quickly placed his hand back onto his handlebar to steady his bicycle, which was wobbling alarmingly by this time.

The girls wheeled their bicycles back onto the lane again, and rode off two by two. By the time they reached the crossroads, Eddie was sitting astride his bicycle studying his map. "It's this way," he said pointing to his left and pushed off with the girls following behind. After a mile or so, he indicated left again and then almost immediately, he crossed the road to where a very narrow lane snaked off to the right. "Ah, this is it, this is what I'm looking for, it's got to be down here," he said.

"Are you sure? It's not very wide this lane, its hardly wide enough for a tractor if you ask me," said Hilary. Still you're the one with the map so you're in charge I suppose. We'll have to ride in single file down here and if we do meet up with a tractor, we'll have to dive into a ditch or some such thing."

They rode down the narrow lane in comparative silence for a while. Eddie was still out in front, looking to the right and left anxiously as though he sought an answer to his whereabouts from the thick hedges that towered above them. Then suddenly the hedges gave way to an ancient wire netting fence and a vast area of marshland was revealed, rolling away to a distant horizon. "Now, I wonder how we get from here to there," said Eddie almost to himself, and with an audible sigh of relief. "That's where we need to be, we've got to go through there to get to Eastbourne. Tell you what, there's a house over there. If it's in this lane and we can get to it, we'll ask someone for directions," he said and he pushed down on his pedal and continued off along the lane.

"Ah, there it is," he said as, after a few bends in the lane, he spotted the cottage squatting in quiet decay in a garden dominated by wild parsley, dock and giant hogweed. "You wait here then, and I'll see if anyone lives here," he said pointing to where a gate would have been if there had ever been one. Then propping his bicycle up against the hedge, he ventured along the overgrown pathway. As he knocked on the flaking wooden door, a dog barked and he jumped backwards as though he had been shot. After what seemed an age, the door opened slowly and an old lady peered short-sightedly through the narrow opening, a growling dog right behind her. "We want to get to Eastbourne, we think the road's down here somewhere," Eddie said nervously, standing well back from the doorway just in case the dog had designs on his person.

"Oyl be back drackly, I'll jest see to me dawg," said the old lady closing the door on him and he just stood there moving from one foot to the other, clearly uncertain about what he should do. "Eastbun, yer say? She asked coming through the door way now and peering at Eddie, closely and unselfconsciously. As he nodded his head she said. "Wall it be down 'ere en turn roit over tham thar marshes en on threw Pavensy. Eastbun ain't fer from ther and good luck to 'e," she said and then she turned and before Eddie could thank her, had disappeared through the doorway.

"Well, what do you make of that then," said Eddie as he walked back down the overgrown pathway. "She seemed a nice old lady but I couldn't make out half of what she said."

"Don't worry about that as long as we're on the right road and going in the right direction," said Sally. "For a moment there I thought she was going to let that old dog loose on you and we just getting ready to run for it. By the time it had finished with you we'd have been halfway to Eastbourne." And she grinned at him. "No, we wouldn't do that to you, would we. We'd have sent Hilary up there to save you. She's good with dogs. I've never seen one get the better of her yet. That old lady was so short sighted, she didn't notice us standing at the end of her garden, did she? I bet her old dog saw us though. I wouldn't have wanted him snapping at my ankles. He sounded like the hound of the Baskervilles he did. He could have eaten the lot of us at one go, us being right out here in the wilds." And she shuddered.

"For goodness sake, it was only an old mongrel and about the same age as she is, give or take a century or two, and toothless" replied Eddie. "Anyway, let's be on the safe side shall we and get away from here, right now." And he moved his rucksack onto his back, got onto his bicycle and rode off down the track.

As they rode slowly over the meandering marsh road, Sally looked around at the rushes, tall and graceful that lined the lane on which they were travelling. The occasional pollarded willow that grew alongside, and the ditches cut away at irregular intervals to drain the water from this marshy area, reminded her of the brooks near their home. There was the obvious difference in dimension of course. But as far as she could see, their watery playground was a replica, in miniature, of this vast expanse of flat marshland. As she looked further a field, she saw the sea birds riding the currents in the far and middle distance while above their heads, the white fluffy clouds moved slowly across the azure blue sky. At times like this she felt that she wanted to live forever.

After a while, Eddie pulled into a siding at the side of the lane and laying down his bicycle, moved towards the overgrown ditch. "There used to be a village somewhere through here according to this book," he said as he extricated a dog-eared manual from his pocket. "Yes look, it was over there somewhere, back where we've just come from. You can't imagine anyone living out here like this, with just sheep for company, can you? But then I suppose that old lady in the cottage back there was out on her own a bit so to speak and it's not the olden days now. Looks like it wasn't the only village over here though. There's another one mentioned and it's on the other side. They were built on little islands or something, these villages so I expect they got washed away in a storm or something, I'll have a look later to see if it tells you in this book what happened to them. Mind you it's all different here now because it's been drained and the sea doesn't come right in like it used to. It's funny isn't it that although Sylvian, where you live, is on its own, it's not lonely. It's not what you would call isolated. There's always movement of some kind. There's always something going on and something to be seen from where ever you're standing."

Sally thought about this and as she got back on to her bicycle and cycled off with the others, she saw in her minds eye the field with Sylvian stuck in the middle of it. It was on its own but, as Eddie had observed, not lonely. It was always lively and bustling and there was always movement along the bottom lane and up and down the Battle Barn Farm track. And Paygate corner was just about within hailing distance. Then there were the sheep that more often than not grazed the field, enlivening and decorating the place in more ways than one. The cow that dad had promised them had not yet materialised but she was quite certain that one fine day she would come home from school and it would be there, just cropping the grass as though it had been there forever. Would it be a brown or a black and white one, she wondered. And who would have the dubious honour of being the first to milk the thing. Now if by any chance it happened to be one of those shaggy Highland cows, like the ones in the pictures in the front room at home, she'd be the first to volunteer for milking duties. But they were used to living amongst hills and snow covered mountains and would most likely feel lost and homesick if they came to this lowland area. Though engrossed in her own thoughts, she still had one ear tuned into the monosyllabic conversation going on around her. But it was not until Hilary called out, 'there's Pevensey Castle,' that she realized that the marshland had metamorphosed into an area of sedate and ancient civilization.

Pat wobbled to a standstill and she pointed just ahead to where the walls of the old Castle, built of impossibly large stones, towered above them. As they all came to a standstill beside her to admire this majestic ruin, she said, "It looks ever so old and it's huge isn't it? It must have been very important in the olden days to have been built as big as this. This is a lovely Castle, this is."

Or what's left of it," said Peggy solemnly as she got off her bicycle and began to inspect the remains of this once dominant citadel. "You just can't imagine how big it must have been before it started falling down like this, can you? Just look at the thickness of these walls by the gateway here," she added laying down her bicycle on the pathway and stepping through the gaping arch to examine more closely, the depth of the brickwork there. "How on earth did they get all these stones to fit together like this? And how did they manage to get them on top of one another, they're huge these stones. Remember it was much taller than this before it began to fall down. Did it fall though or was it pushed? You should know Eddie."

"I know more about Battle Abbey than I do about this Castle," replied Eddie. "Old William had that built of course, to celebrate his win over Harold and to show off a bit I expect. Well you know all about that and the battle of Hastings, don't you? Well you aught to, you live close enough. Tell you what, we'll go inside and see if we can find out something about this place, there's bound to be a plaque up somewhere or we could ask someone. Hang on, I'll have a word with this bloke coming along here," he said and he put his bicycle carefully down and walked towards an old man, flat cap perched on top of his thick crop of steel grey hair, body thin as a lathe, who was coming from the direction of the nearby Church.

"Well, there be a building o' sorts 'ere from Roman toimes and dem owd geezers knew ow to build fer persterity loik," he replied in answer to Eddie's question. Tham thar Saxons norked it abart a bit. Then owd Queen Elizabeth, she ad a mind to its destruction, same as Cromwell did. Not ersel mind, she were too busy tryin to ang on ter er throne. But 'ere it be and 'ere it'or stay, frayed aroond its edges, fer another tharsen yer, you mark me woyds. En if yer want a really owd Church ter look at, ther be one a bit along der road ere. Ther be owd ouses galore noo thet es well. Well, good day to ye," he said and he tipped his cap as he walked away from them.

"Thanks," Eddie called out after him and then he turned back to where the girls were standing. "Did you get that?" He asked. "At least we know a bit more about it than we did before we asked him. He looked ancient enough to have been around when the first brick was put into place. Anyway, let's go inside and have a look round shall we? We'll leave our bikes here."

"Can we have a quick look round this church first?" asked Sally, pointing to another old stone building that had just caught her eye. "It looks a bit like Sedlescombe Church, except the stone's different and ours hasn't got a clock on it. Leastways, I don't think it has." As there was no word of dissent from the others, she bent down to retrieve her rucksack, slung it casually across her shoulder and began to walk away. As they passed through the wrought iron gateway, she looked upwards and then pointed towards the weather vane, which topped the Church steeple. "Look there's a bird up there. It looks a bit like a cockerel. I wonder what its doing up there? Minding its own business like what we should be doing, I reckon," she said answering her own question.

"That's a weather vane," replied Hilary. "They have them on lots of tall buildings." Then as they walked in tandem down the cobbled pathway towards the open doorway, she whispered. "Listen, it sounds like there's still a service going on in there. We'll have to wait a bit." And she put out her arms as though to bar their progress.

"What's happened to your voice?" asked Peggy. "You don't have to whisper, they can't hear you from here. I wanted to have a look round the outside first anyway. I love Churches, especially looking at the old gravestones in Churchyards, they tell such a story they do. I often wonder what sort of life the people who're buried underneath these old mounds lived and what they looked like. Life was pretty tough for most of them in the olden days, you know." And she bent down to inspect a particularly ancient lichen covered stone whose inscription was undecipherable. "I don't even know if this was a man or a woman buried under here. Or it could be a whole family I suppose, one on top of the other."

After a while, they moved away from contemplation of long departed village folk and their monuments, towards the old Church itself. As they walked around its walls, they stopped now and again to comment on the thickness of the buttresses that supported this impressive building. Then they looked more closely at the stones with which this Church had been built and decorated.

Where the stones had been knapped, the depth and subtlety of colour was still as vibrant as the day some ancient Artisan had painstakingly placed them there.

"Don't mention 'Gray's Elegy," whispered Pat into Hilary's ear and they grinned as they looked in Sally's direction. She however, was in her own little world. Then a movement by the doorway caught Pat's eye. "They're coming out!" She exclaimed, moving instinctively behind Sally who, deep in thought, was brought rudely back to the here and now by the pronouncement. Then holding on to Sally's rucksack with one hand and her upper arm with the other, she peered out to observe the progress of this little group of worshippers. Eddie and the girls just stood and watched as the congregation, preceded by the Parson, emerged from the inner sanctum of the Church and out into the brightness of the late morning sunshine. Each worshipper paused briefly to bid farewell to the robed and dignified man of God who shook each one by the hand, bending forward ever so slightly as he performed this duty. Then they made their way in two's and three's along the cobbled pathway, through the gateway and disappeared amongst the narrow streets. The scene reminded Sally of a picture in 'The English Spy,' one of the books in the front room at home except these participants seemed rather less furtive than the ones depicted in that particular Churchyard scene.

After a while, the Parson emerged and hurried off along the same pathway, his robes dragging along behind him. His arms, folded across his chest, were tucked comfortably into his surplus and he was obviously deep in thought.

"He looks like a wounded bean-stick and hark, he's talking to himself," said Eddie. "You can hear him from here and you can see his cheeks moving up and down, look." And he pointed towards the fast retreating back of the Holy man. "Well you could see it before he disappeared like that," he added turning back to look at the girls. "I reckon he's rehearsing his evening lecture, that's what or perhaps he's praying for the souls of that flock of his. They were a bit like sheep if you think about it, those people, following each other along the path just like a lot of sheep would."

"Well considering that seems to be the only way out of here, then they would be following each other, wouldn't they," said Peggy dryly. "Anyway, now he's gone it'll give us a chance to look inside the Church itself, come on." Then leading the way, she passed through the studded oak panelled door and into the dark interior of the old Church, followed closely by the others.

The first thing Sally noticed as she entered was the characteristic smell, common to all the Churches that she had ever been into, a mixture of stone and wood and dust and just old age. Then as she looked around she noticed one or two curious crosses that had been crudely etched into the stonework and wondered whose hand had formed these ancient symbols of Christianity, and when. The age softened contours of the etched stone suggested that the identity of the artist along with his artistry were, as her sister Hazel would have said, lost in the mists of time. After a moment of quiet contemplation, she looked upwards and ahead of her, to where a Saintly figure, immortalised by some long dead artist, gazed benevolently down on her. After moving on, she noticed a similar visage this time picked out in silks and embroideries and reckoned that this must be the Saint after whom this old Church had been named. There were various 'Coats of Arms' dotted here and there, similar to the ones in Sedlescombe Church except for a slight variation in detail. They were all dedicated to the memory of some family, ecclesiastical or otherwise, whose members had obviously been the prominent citizens of their time.

"It says something about 'Corbel heads' here, I wonder what on earth they are," whispered Hilary looking up from the page of the pamphlet she was reading. "They're supposed to be on the wall outside somewhere."

"They're just heads made out of stone, you can see them on lots of old buildings like Church's, Cathedrals that sort of thing," said Eddie. "I've just read about them in that book myself as a matter of fact. They're often likenesses or effigies of people who were around at the time, and were knocked out, the images I mean, by the old Stonemasons. Mind you if that's the case, some of the people in the olden days weren't half bloody ugly. No I'm joking, the really ugly ones are called gargoyles or some such thing. Who knows what or who they're likenesses of."

"Shush, there's somebody coming," said Pat looking fearfully towards the doorway. "I hope we're allowed to be in here." As they watched, a young woman walked through the open doorway, tying the ends of a black headscarf beneath her chin as she entered the Church. Totally ignoring them, she glided towards the altar, genuflected and crossed herself before kneeling down in the front pew where she began to pray.

Realising instinctively this lady's need for solitude, they tip toed silently towards the doorway and out into the fresh air. It was a while before anyone spoke, choosing instead to wander over the soft, undulating grass of the Churchyard, quietly contemplating the memorials to the forefathers of this place. Although Sally had only seen the woman's face in profile, she was moved by what she saw. An aura of sadness seemed to surround this young woman, and she could not even hazard a guess as to what had caused her grief.

"She was so sad, that lady," said Pat, the first to break the self imposed silence. "I didn't exactly see her face but you could tell, couldn't you by the way she moved up the aisle like that as though she was under some kind of spell. I expect she feels that only a prayer can make her feel better. I wonder what's happened to make her so unhappy?"

I don't suppose we'll ever know," said Peggy sadly. "One thing's for sure though, I don't want to be around when she comes out of there. Perhaps it's about time we moved on from here. Let's see what the Castle looks like, shall we? I don't think I want to look at the other Church, the one that the old man told us about. I'm not in the mood."

Needing no second bidding, the little group moved from the Churchyard towards the entrance to the ancient Castle.

"Our bikes won't be in the way here, not if we move them a bit further up the bank," said Hilary. "We'd better take our food with us though because I for one could do with a bite to eat, I'm starved."

As they were sitting within the ancient stone walls eating their sandwiches, a tall bespectacled man approached them. Sally recognised him at once. She had noticed him leaving the Church after the service there a while ago, and as he had walked down the pathway, he had been head and shoulders above any other member of the congregation.

"Have you been here before?" he asked them politely, bending forward slightly and raising his trilby hat in salutation. As they all answered in the negative, he said. "Well if you're interested, I can tell you a little bit about this place. It's very old as you can see and some of it has been here from the time of the Romans. It was a Fort then rather than a Castle and in those days the sea came right up to the walls. There were bits of high ground here and there of course that even at high tide would remain dry, and these became little villages. They always had 'eye' or a similar pronunciation at the end of their names, meaning island you see. Now the sea has receded and the marshes are drained, and very little remains of those old dwellings, mores the pity.

Anyway, this area was known as Anderida in the early days, it was all part of the Roman Empire, as you probably already know. It was the Saxons who renamed these parts, Pefele spelt p-e-f-e l-e, to start with, which eventually became what it's known by these days, Pevensey. When the Normans came along, they built up the Castle. The inner Bailey at the eastern end and other structures are all down to them. One man called Robert De Montain was responsible for a lot of it." He paused for a moment, enjoying their obvious interest before continuing. "There was also a Chapel in here at one time but only the foundations are left. This place had its share of sieges mind you and it's hard to imagine on a day like this, the bloodshed and horrors that occurred here as elsewhere in the country if it comes to that. Those old times were pretty violent I can tell you. Anyway, old Queen Elizabeth had a go at it and a bit later on, so did old Cromwell but happily it's still here to tell its story. I never tire of the place nor do I tire of telling all those that'll listen, the bit I know about it, especially when they're as quiet and attentive as you are. Thankfully it will see me out and there'll be others to carry on telling the tale when I'm dead and gone."

"See that old cannon over there," he said crouching down now and pointing towards a large gun mounted on a stand, just a few yards away from where they were sitting. "Well that was made at Ashburnam, a place not very far away from here. All the best iron came from Sussex and it was a thriving industry for a long while, especially so in the time of the Tudors and Stuarts. Many a battle would have been won on the quality of the guns and cannon made in these parts. And the invasion by the Spanish Armada was defeated or should I say repelled, mainly on the strength and quality of the iron used in the making of our guns. With a bit of a hand perhaps from the weather and the shape of the Spanish ships, which were a bit tall and ungainly by all accounts. And Sussex iron was used for lots of other things beside guns and cannon of course. Well you can see all manner of articles made of the stuff if you look around you and the Blacksmith's shacks are full of it in various stages of construction. It must have been incredibly noisy and smelly in those days if you think about it. There was the burning of wood, masses of it for the charcoal that powered the furnaces and forges, for a start. Then there was all that water power needed to drive the huge bellows for the furnaces which smelted the iron. The relentless noise of those trip hammers, day and night must have driven folks nearly mad."

The children nodded in agreement and screwed up their faces, imagining how horrid it must have been in the old days.

"Of course, there's another thing the area all around here is famous or perhaps I should say infamous for," he continued as he levered himself up awkwardly from the ground. "Smuggling. It would have gone on in just about every village and hamlet for miles around, and you would be surprised at the number of seemingly respectable folk involved in this illegal trade. It seems the Clergy and even the Magistrates were indirectly involved in that they would, at the very least, turn a blind eye to what was going on, so to speak. Old Kipling even wrote a poem about it. It goes something like this.

Five and twenty ponies trotting through the dark.
Brandy for the Parson, baccy for the Clerk.
Laces for a lady, letters for a spy.
And watch the wall my darling, while the gentlemen go by.

Anyway, it was very well organised this smuggling, with numerous hiding places for the contraband and a system of signals was formulated to warn them when the excise men were on the prowl. Tradition has it that the excise men were the villains of the piece, that the smugglers were victims of the tax system if you like, but that wasn't the whole story. One group of smugglers, known as the 'Hawkhurst gang,' were real villains. They'd stop at nothing, even the most gruesome murders, if anyone got between them and their booty. This smuggling business though started well before their time and it has always been a two way thing.

"Anyway, I take it those bikes by the gate over there belong to you," he continued pointing towards the Castle entrance. "If so and if you've got the time, you might be interested in cycling up to a place called Hooe, which is not all that far from here. The old pub there called the Red Lion is reputed to harbour its share of ghosts and could tell a tale or two about smugglers. It was a favourite haunt of their's as was the Lamb Inn, which is not that far away from here either. Another place that's worth looking around if you're interested in smugglers, and you've got the time, is Wartling. Now there's a place that could tell a tale or two. Well, I'd best be on my way then, mustn't be late for my dinner, must I? Have an interesting afternoon all of you and enjoy your bike ride," he added as he turned and began to move away from them.

"Thanks," they called out in unison.

"That was really interesting," shouted Eddie scrambling to his feet and projecting his voice towards the man's fast retreating back. Then he brushed himself off and turned back to the girls. "He was really interesting that man. He doesn't half know what he's talking about, doesn't he? Anyway, I don't know about you but I can't see us getting all the way to Eastbourne and back, not if we want to have a good look around here we won't. We'll make sure we've got enough time to see Wartling though and those other places the man mentioned. You don't mind do you? As they nodded in agreement, he reached into his pocket, took out his map which he unfolded and spread out in front of them.

"Look, Wartling's here and so is Hooe," he said, moving his fore-finger around the relevant area. They're both on our way home if we make a slight detour, that is. It doesn't look like we'll see the Lamb Inn though going that way. It's here look, back the way we came." And he pointed back along the marsh road. "I don't remember seeing it on the way here for some reason, though we must have cycled right passed it." And he scratched his head in puzzlement. "It's funny, I don't usually miss something as important as that. I expect someone was talking to me at the time. Never mind, we're bound to come this way again sometime. Lets take a look round this place first though," he said as he refolded his map and popped it back into his pocket. Then he stooped and began to gather up the remnants of their meal.

"I wish Ronald had come with us," said Hilary. "He's always talking about smugglers and things and he's wanted to come to Pevensey for ages now. He'd have been really interested in what that man was telling us. Never mind, I expect as you say, that we'll come back here again sometime."

***

It was some time later when Peggy, the first to wilt sank down on to the soft grass followed closely by the others. "Whew, I'm worn to a frazzle," she said stretching her legs out in front of her and propping herself up with her arms angled backwards. There had been so much to explore within this relic of a bye gone era, and so absorbed had they been in what they were seeing that they had not paused for one moment, not even for a sip of their precious water. They had moved seamlessly from a thorough examination of the huge gun, through passages and dungeons and up and down spiral staircases. And they had inspected with interest, the ruins of an old chapel that had once stood within these ancient walls. They had gazed in breathless wonder at the views from the top of the ancient walls and spent precious time searching in vain for the old well, which they knew would have been crucial to the survival of its ancient inhabitants. Now, suddenly aware of their thirst, they reached eagerly for the bottles of water, passing them round from person to person and gurgling the contents noisily down their parched throats. By the time they had assuaged their thirst, only a dribble of water remained in one bottle, and that was quickly downed by Eddie.

"Don't worry, if we can't find a water fountain around here anywhere, I'll knock on one of the doors down in the village. Someone'll fill our bottles back up for us," he said as he lifted the remaining dregs of water up to his mouth. Then he wiped his mouth with the back of his hand before replacing the stopper on the empty bottle. "Pity we haven't got time to look around the other Church that man was telling us about but never mind. We'll just have to come back here before me and Peg go back home. It's not that far and there's a lot more besides that other Church to look at around here. Come on, let's go and find our bikes."

"I'll try here for some water," said Eddie stopping and propping his bicycle up against a low brick wall. "You never know, that old man who was talking to us back in the Castle may live here. He'll fill our bottles back up for us I know he will." And he walked towards the ancient wooden door, raised the round black knocker on its surface and brought it down smartly on to the circle of iron beneath its bottom edge. As they stood on the narrow pavement, Sally looked across the road and noticed an old poster in one of the windows. It said, 'Join the Women's Land Army. Food comes first.' Then underneath, 'for a healthy, happy job.' There was another one there that she did not remember having seen anywhere before. It sported a flag and the initials M F on it and the caption, 'Food is a munition of war. Don't waste it.' Suddenly, the war, which was now mostly just a distant memory, came back into sharp focus. A thousand and one images flashed across her minds eye, bombarding her with memories both personal and multi-faceted, connected to those eventful years. She was brought back suddenly to the here and now by the sound of a door opening, and as she looked around she saw an elderly lady standing in the doorway, looking enquiringly at Eddie. As he spoke and then passed the empty bottles to her, Sally sighed with relief. They might well experience a few hunger pangs on the long journey home but at least they would not be thirsty.

"It's this other road we take if we want to go to Wartling," said Eddie, pointing to where the road veered away to the left. "Least I hope it is. It's a bit narrow this road and by the state of it, it doesn't look like many people use it," he added. "There used to be salt workings all around here you know," he called out as they cycled two by two along this narrow lane, with the marshland now stretching away as far as the eye could see. "I don't know much about them, how they worked and that sort of thing and it doesn't look like there's much to tell you where they were. Perhaps we'll find someone to ask when we get to Wartling."

"Look at the leaves on that butterfly over there, aren't they're beautiful?" said Sally pointing to the side of the track where the flashy insect hovered over the tall grasses, its wings iridescent in the late summer sunshine. "What are you laughing at," she asked looking around as one by one the other girls started giggling.

"Well you said leaves and butterflies don't have leaves, they have wings," said Pat as they all brought their bicycles to a standstill to admire the little creature.

"I did not," replied Sally indignantly. Then as they all looked at her, still grinning, she said. "Well anyone can make a mistake, can't they? You all say silly things at times, everyone does. It is lovely though isn't it," she asked as, leaning on her handlebars and visibly relaxing, she looked towards this object of wonder. "You couldn't paint anything like that, now could you? Not even the best artist like Constable could get those colours right."

They did not see another soul on this long, meandering road. There were just a few farm animals dotted around, their shape and colour muted by distance and the faint mist that hung over this lonely stretch of marshland. Here and there, occasional clumps of bushes, dwarfed and shaped by the prevailing wind, rose at intervals to decorate the flat landscape. Sally thought, not for the first time that while within the dark, hallowed walls of an old church, God was in control. Here in the wide open spaces of the countryside, Mother Nature was well and truly the boss. It was nonsense to think that these two superior beings could ever be one and the same person, as the old Rector would have you believe. No, she reckoned that while God sat on a gold throne up in the Heavens and did his bit with a magic wand, Mother Nature had her hands, dirty finger nails and all, in the soil. Sally had always envisaged her as a cross between Gran Powell and Mercy Dengate with a broken old knife in one hand and a garden fork in the other. And she was always wearing a long, kaki coloured pinny, which covered the tops but not the feet of her old black wellies.

As they approached Wartling, Eddie brought his bicycle to a standstill and, straddling the machine, looked back over his shoulder. "I can just imagine how it would have been all around here in the olden days, can't you, with all that smuggling and stuff going on," he said. "There'd have been covered wagons coming along here at dead of night full of stuff the smugglers had got off the ships that crept into the bays around the coast here. And there'd have been pack horses as well, laden down with all kinds of things," he added, warming to his subject. "They, the men, tied bits of rag or hessian or anything they could lay their hands on around the feet of the horses to muffle the sound, so's not to give themselves away. They knew these lanes like the backs of their hands of course, ruts and all and they certainly needed to. The old excise men were always on the prowl and there was always a chance that someone would have snitched on them. Mind you, the old smugglers dealt pretty severely with people who informed on them and I certainly wouldn't have dared to," he added shivering as he paused to contemplate the punishments dealt out to miscreants. "Anyway, it must have been worth the risks they took when you come to think about it. There was so much poverty in the seventeen and eighteen hundreds. It seemed that as the landed gentry got richer the poor got poorer. So the higher the taxes imposed by the King for stuff coming into and going out of the country, the more incentive there was for people to smuggle the stuff to and fro without paying that duty. Makes sense really, when you come to think about it. There was even a tax on windows there at one time, can you imagine that?"

"They had secret passages and hidey holes all over the place, the smugglers," said Hilary. "That man said so. And they used look out's with special signals to warn them if the agents were about, he told us that as well. They even had pretend ghosts to frighten off anyone who might get too close and see what they were doing. They thought of everything those old smugglers did. Anyway, best be on our way again, it's a long way home and all our grub's gone. After you then Eddie," she added as she stepped through the frame of her bicycle and placed her foot on the peddle in readiness for the off. Then they set off two by two along the narrow roadway.

"There it is, there's the Red Lion Inn," exclaimed Eddie skidding to a standstill and pointing sideways to a building set just back off the main highway. "That's where a lot of smuggling went on. It looks really, really old doesn't it and I bet there's secret passages and all sorts of things in there if you know where to look. Ghosts as well, like the one in Marley House you lot were telling me and Peg about on the way here. Or Granny Sansom's one, you know the one about the lady in a long white dress and no head. Gran must have told you about her, surely. She always used to tell us about that one at bedtime, didn't she Peg. On purpose I reckon. Frightened the life out of us it did."

"Yes, she told us lot about her as well, but not when it was dark thank goodness," said Sally. "But listen, I've just remembered what old Mr Kenward told us. You know, that bloke who helped dad to build Sylvian. I didn't really understand what he was talking about at the time, but it makes sense now. Anyway, he said that his Grandfather or Great Grandfather had been a smuggler, made a decent living out of it he reckoned. He didn't actually say whether he'd been a member of the Hawkhurst gang but he did mention them at the same time come to think of it. He said they, the Hawkhurst Gang were a nasty bunch and that a lot of them had been hanged. That's awful isn't it? That's probably why I'd forgotten about it till now. Things like that give me nightmares, so I always push them right to the back of my mind."

"Well, I reckon we've heard just about enough of smugglers and ghosts and that sort of thing. You're scaring Pat to bits, and me too," said Hilary, shuffling forward awkwardly, the frame of her bicycle between her legs. "Look there's a Rowan tree over there. That's supposed to be the tree of life, isn't it?" She said pointing ahead to where the characteristic shape of the Rowan, stood head and shoulders above the hedge lining this section of the lane, just where the roadway began to veer slightly away to the left. "I'm much more interested in living things."

"Well I was only going to tell you about Owler's, wool smugglers," said Eddie looking a bit crest fallen. "Though for the life of me I can't think why they were called that. But if you're not interested, I won't bother." He paused here for a short while as he looked around to gauge their reaction and noting their puzzled expressions, decided to continue. "Well perhaps then I'll just tell you a bit about them because it's interesting and you aught to learn about these things," he said getting off his bicycle and moving a bit closer to the old Inn. "Well it was like this, the flocks of sheep around the coast here grew the best wool in the world so it was in great demand both in this country but especially in Europe. The weavers over there, especially the Flemish ones who were the best in the world, couldn't get enough of it. So being the best meant of course that there was a lot of tax on it, enough to make these Owler's risk life and limb to smuggle it out of England and they smuggled stacks of it out of the country. How they managed to avoid the old Excise men most of the time, I'll never know. Crafty, devious lot they were. Taxes worked both ways you know, both in and out of the country, but that's beside the point. Well it was as that old chap was telling us, and he seemed so knowledgeable about all these things. I wish I knew half a she much as he does. And another thing…"

"Well that's as may be, but I'm with Hilary on this one. I've had a belly full of smugglers," interrupted Sally hurriedly. These law breakers and their nefarious doings had dominated the conversation for far too long as far as she was concerned and it was time to move on anyway. "Which way then Eddie, just carry on along this lane, do we?" she asked, as she stepped back through the frame of her bicycle in readiness for the next step of their journey. She felt a bit guilty about stopping him in full flow, but enough was enough. "How far is it to Battle from here do you think?"

"About a mile or two as the crow flies, four or five times that distance by road I would think," said Eddie moving reluctantly away from the old Inn. "You've heard the rhyme haven't you?"

"Before the Romans came to Rye or down to Severn strode.
The rolling English drunkard made the rolling English road.
A reeling road, a rolling road that rambled round the Shire.
And after him the Parson ran, the Sexton and the Squire."

"Bugger the English drunkard," Sally muttered having recited this piece of poetry to herself so many times before. But within a split second, she had rearranged her thoughts. If all the roads had been made by the Romans she thought, life and more especially travelling from place to place, wouldn't be half so much fun. Take their journey today for instance with its twists and turns along lanes that snaked first this way and then that. That special feeling of quiet anticipation for what lay around the next bend, like the old Crones cottage that had appeared out of nowhere this morning, would not be there. Then there were the smugglers to think about. How on earth would they have found hiding places for themselves and all that contraband or avoided the Excise men along a straight old Roman road? That bit of mental re-adjustment out of the way, she felt refreshed and ready to face the next stage of the journey, with renewed energy.

By the time they reached the ancient town of Battle, they were ready for a rest. Having propped their bicycles against a low wall in the market place, they sank down gratefully onto a long wooden bench. "What does that clock over there say?" asked Pat, squinting as she pointed in the direction of an ancient time-piece.

"Tick Tock," answered Peggy and giggled as Pat clicked her tongue and gave her cousin a dirty look.

"You know what I mean, what's the time I want to know," said Pat. "I can't make out whether it's half past four or half past five from here."

"Well you're the same distance as us from the clock so how do you expect us to see what time it is if you can't," replied Peggy. "Don't worry, we're not that far from home now and no matter what time we get home, mum and Aunt Doll will find us something to eat. Here, hand us over some of that water," she said, leaning towards her brother who having already bent to retrieve the water bottle from the bag down by his feet, handed it over to her without a word. He watched the clear liquid disappearing down her throat for a few seconds, then bent and retrieved a piece of wood that had been carelessly discarded beside the bench. Then he stood up, turned around to face them and as he held the unwieldy implement aloft, said:

"Old Brown is dead, that good old man. We ne'er shall see him more.

For what he drank for H2o was H2so4.

We just learned that at school, in science lesson. H2o is water and H2so4 is sulphuric acid of course. It must be water you're drinking or we'd all be dead by now," he added grinning down at them.

"I've heard that one before," said Hilary. "Old Jumbo James told it to us."

***

Later, as they walked with their bicycles down through the high street, they stopped to look in the window of a newsagents come sweet shop. The shop itself was closed, the shutter down over the glass fronted door. A piece of cardboard with the word 'closed' written on it was hanging by a thin piece of string from a nail that had been driven into the top of the wooden frame between the glass and the shuttering. Sally looked through the window and as she shaded her eyes with one hand, saw copies of 'The Picture Post' laying beside old newspapers, comics and various magazines, on a bench that ran the length of the shop. If the shop had been open, she could not have resisted the temptation to look at this latest edition of her favourite publication and would have held a copy in her hands as though she had every intention of purchasing it. Then, just as casually, she would have returned it pristine, to its rightful position as though it had not been touched by human hands.

As her eyes moved up from the bench towards the shelving where jars and boxes were neatly arranged, her attention was drawn towards a box of little black 'imps,' in their cellophane wrappers and she shuddered. Of all the things she had ever tasted in her life, dandelion sap included, these little black monstrosities had to be the most repellent. As she quickly averted her eyes, her attention was drawn to two faded old posters, still adhering stubbornly to the distempered wall at the back of the shop. On one was 'Potato Pete,' with the caption, still just about readable on its dusty surface, 'I make good soup.' On the other was 'Dr Carrot, the children's best friend.' He was looking as cheerful as ever in his top hat and glasses and was still carrying that big black bag effortlessly on one arm. Puzzlingly, the word 'Vita' was clearly visible on this poster though for the life of her, she had no idea what it meant. She wondered if this shop was the one that had been owned by Mr and Mrs Eldridge, until they were killed in the war by one of Hitler's bombs. They had owned a sweet shop, she was sure of that. Mr and Mrs Tickner had also been killed in the war and she remembered how upset Sylvia Glyde and Margery Freeman had been at the time. They were a kindly couple, who often gave the two girls a lift into Battle in their little old motor car. When it was raining this was especially appreciated. She turned as Hilary, equally curious and absorbed in this interesting array of assorted paraphernalia, jumped as the front wheel and handlebars of her bicycle suddenly slewed around her body, the machine landing at her feet with a clatter.

"Sorry," she said as Peggy stepped smartly to one side to avoid contact with the jumble of writhing metal, its back wheel spinning furiously and out of control. "I don't know what happened there. I'd better check to see that nothing's broken. I haven't got any tools much with me." Then she stooped and man handled the bicycle to an upward position, bending it this way and that, as she checked for any bent or broken parts. As she stood upright, satisfied that her precious machine was none the worse for its tumble, she pointed across the road. "Look, there's Len Partridge over there, I'm sure it is," she said. "I wonder why they call him Tusker? And if you think about it, Porky's a funny name to call his brother George as well. He's not exactly fat, is he? I think it's got something to do with names of characters in comics, least ways that's what Albert reckons. Mrs Partridge calls Tony Powell, Spider which has got changed to Spidder for some peculiar reason, but that's got nothing to do with comic characters. It's because he used to be so thin. All arms and legs and no bum, that's what she used to say. Well he wouldn't have got into that milk churn back in the war there if there'd been any fat on him, would he?

"You lot seem to have nick names for just about everyone," said Eddie. "There's Wangy and Wimpy and Willie and Bangy and Gaggy and all those others you've just mentioned and they're only the ones I can think of, off the top of me head. You're a funny lot down here and no mistake. The only nick-name we've got for anybody is 'Creeping Jesus,' that's what we call the Verger in the Church near us. He comes up behind you without making a sound, and scares you half to death he does. We get told off though if anyone hears us say it."

"I should think so," replied Peggy. "You shouldn't take Jesus' name in vain, he was a good man, he was. Mind you, if he died to make men good and to stop suffering in the world as the Bible says, then it sort of didn't work did it? People have still carried on killing one another and there's still hunger and disease all over the world. And I reckon nobody knows how many wars there've been since then. It makes you wonder doesn't it, what this God and religion thing is all about. It doesn't make sense to me. Anyway, I don't know about you lot, but I'm tired and I'm hungry and we've still got a long way to go. Well not that far now I suppose but far enough. You know what they say about the last mile home being the longest."

As they cycled up the slight incline past the entrance to Dodd's farm and began to free wheel down the next hill, Sally looked ahead to where Marley House crouched behind a thick layer of trees and shrubs. As its top windows stared blankly back at her, she thought of the ghost associated with the place and wondered if he still wandered the gloomy corridors, or if his spirit had now found rest. The latter she hoped, for his sake and for her own peace of mind. That this one was male rather than female she felt with the same conviction as the knowledge that Granny Sansom's headless ghost had been a lady. She took a deep breath as they approached the scary area. On one side, slowly rotting away into Mother Earth amongst the rusting farm implements and lush vegetation, lay the old barn. On the other side, behind the trees and bushes, squatted her nemesis, Marley House. She took another deep breath as she prepared herself for the feeling of unease that she had experienced from this house ever since she had heard the tale about the ghost. To her surprise however, that old heart pumping sensation was not there, it had been replaced by a feeling of easy familiarity. Just like it had been in the old days.

"The ghost's gone, it's not here any more," she shouted startling the others to a standstill. "Can't you tell? It's not spooky around here now. It's just like any other old place, well mostly. It's still a bit gloomy but there's no restless spirit here now, I'm sure of it."

"Well thank you for that bit of information I'm sure. There was no need to frighten us half to death telling us though," replied Peggy. "I nearly fell off my bike when you shouted out like that, and Pat didn't half wobble too. I can't tell any difference around here myself, but then I didn't hear the tale in the first place from a story teller as good as Betty. When's she coming home again by the way? It's ages since I last saw her."

"Soon I hope," all the other girls said in unison and giggled. Then as one, they hopped onto their saddles and began to peddle off along the lane, followed by Eddie who had been relegated to last place now that they were on familiar ground and were not reliant upon his map reading skills. They were unnaturally quiet for the rest of the journey, each seemingly absorbed in singular contemplation of the day's events.

As they turned the corner at the end of Marley Lane, Sally looked instinctively across the brooks to where the pollarded willows decorated the flat landscape and sighed. They were very nearly home now and the familiarity of this landscape, which she knew like the back of her hand, almost brought a lump to her throat. As she walked wearily up the field a few minutes later, she noticed dad and Uncle Tom in the top end of the garden digging the last of the potatoes which, along with the hessian sacks full of ones dug earlier would with any luck last the family until next years first early's could be harvested.

As they came through the scullery door, they saw Dora kneeling on a chair beside the kitchen table, moulding a bit of pastry, which was a putty shade of grey from contact with mucky fingers. Sally prayed silently to herself that her little sister would not cover the revolting mess with jam, then insist on it being baked and eaten by her sisters as had happened on a previous occasion. She shuddered. The only thing worse than that she reckoned, was Mrs Moon's rock cakes.

"Let's see if there's a cup of tea in this ere pot, I'm parched," said Peggy lifting the cosy from the squat brown tea-pot which was resting on a tray at the side of the kitchen table. She ignored the 'you'll be lucky' followed by the characteristic giggle from Aunty Nellie who was helping mum with the dinner. "There's a clean cup over there, pass it here will you Sally." She lifted the pot into the air, carefully tilting the thing at the right angle, and watched critically as the pale, lukewarm liquid dribbled into the cup. "Huh, I might have known. Water bewitched and tea begrudged," she said as she replaced the tea-pot. "Daft I calls it, putting a cosy on a pot that's worn out like this one is." Then she sniffed. "Something doesn't half smell good," she said appreciatively. "And come to think of it, I'm more hungry than thirsty anyway."

"Call your dad and your Uncle Pop, will you Peg?" said Aunty Nellie as, having laid the table, she was now helping mum to dish up the dinner.

Long before the plates, piled high with meat, roast potatoes and as many other vegetables as could be squeezed onto them, were handed around the table, Sally's mouth had began to water. By the time dad and Uncle Tom came into the scullery to wash their hands at the sink, she, along with the other youngsters had already silently devoured a decent half of their meal and were tucking into the rest with relish.

"Never known you lot to be so quiet, thought we'd come to the wrong house," said Uncle Tom as he came through the doorway, wiping his damp hands down his trousers. "Hope they've left some for us Pop. We deserve it after all the gardening we've done today. Don't know how you and Dolly manage all the work that's to be done on this place, I really don't. I feel like two men, one dead and one dying right now and I've only been here for a day. I feel like I need a gallon of Sloan's Liniment and that's on me back alone.

"Don't mention that stuff," replied dad with a sideways glance at mum. Then he grinned. "Tell you what, I reckon it's all down to the lovely grub we get here that keeps us healthy, isn't that it you girls. It's your mum's cooking that makes us so fit. You know what Hypocrites say, he say let food be your medicine. And the food don't get no better, nowhere and that's a fact." They all looked up at him in uncomprehending silence. He was a funny old stick was their dad and no mistake. When he was good he was very, very good but when he was bad he was horrid, as the saying went.

As the two men sat down at the kitchen table, knives and forks at the ready, mum stooped down in front of the stove. With an old tea cloth stretched out between her hands, she withdrew from the oven two plates filled to overflowing with food and set them out in front of the men. As they began to eat, she turned back to the stove and this time lifted from its top shelf, a rhubarb pie, its surface liberally sprinkled with some of the sugar that Aunty Nellie had brought down with her, and carefully placed the large dish onto the enamelled tray next to the primus stove. Sally's mouth began to water as the delicious creamy custard to go with it, steam rising lazily from its surface, was brought over to join its companion. There was an anticipatory silence as mum ladled the contents into dishes and brought them over to the table where eager hands reached out to claim their share.

The washing up seemed to go on for ever and each time the girls thought that was it, mum would come through from the kitchen, and with a 'sorry ducks,' pop a few more items onto the draining board. "Blow this for a game of soldiers," said Sally after the umpteenth time. "It's never ending this washing up. Are you sure you're not picking up the stuff we've already washed and making us do it again?" she asked crossly to mum's retreating back.

"You can't make a cake without cracking an egg," Aunty Nellie called from the kitchen with a chuckle, which Sally reckoned was a curious thing to say and no help at all.

When at last they had finished this tiresome chore, they wandered off outside and on to the underground tank. "I know, let's do some cotton reel knitting, we've got enough nailed up for all of us, Eddie as well if he wants," said Sally. And she jumped back off the tank, ran indoors and started rummaging through the sideboard. "Ah that's it," she exclaimed as she pulled out a bag of assorted wool and cotton reels, while holding back the rest of the flotsam and jetsam with well practiced hands. This cupboard was always packed to the gunnels with arts and crafts of varying degrees of complexity and in varying stages of completion. One opened it at ones peril. "There's enough for all of us here," she said standing up with a satisfied grin on her face. As she made for the doorway with her arms full, she noticed Aunty Nellie scraping every last bit of fat from some margarine and lard wrappers and putting it into a large bowl on top of a mound of flour and the larger lumps of fat already in there. Then as she stepped outside, she glanced across the garden to where her dad, her uncle and Eddie, who had declined to joined them, were picking up the now dry potatoes, and packing them into hessian sacks. That's one job we've got out of, she thought to herself gratefully.

As the girls sat on the underground tank absorbed in their craft, they chatted intermittently, lulled by the gentle rhythm of the task. They passed the wool around the four small nails which had been hammered evenly into the tops of the reels, and passed the lower loops over the newly wound ones, fascinated by the slow but steady growth of the narrow woolly tube. From time to time, they fed new colours onto the reel, and watched excitedly as that colour emerged from the bottom of the reel.

After a while, mum came through the doorway wiping her hands on her pinny. "Don't forget you've got hop picking in the morning and it's an early start remember. You've got your clothes and things to get ready. I've just cut you some sandwiches and Aunty Nellie has made an apple pie for you. It's in the oven cooking right now. And I really should have got you to do some pumping this evening. Let's just hope it lasts out until you get home tomorrow."

"Course it will," replied Sally optimistically. She paused for a moment then and as mum turned, she called out to her retreating back. "Can we take some of that condensed milk that Aunty Nellie brought down with her as well please? We can pull a few sticks of rhubarb and dip them in the stuff. That'll be much nicer than the little bags of sugar we usually take with us. And don't worry about clothes and things. Any old thing'll do out there."

"I really should be getting home now," said Hilary putting aside her knitting reluctantly. "I've still got my stuff to get ready and it'll soon be dark." Then she half turned. "Look at that, isn't that just beautiful?" she added as she pointed over towards the village where a faint mist hung suspended over the ground. "That's an indication of continued settled weather that is, according to Mr Collins. I think we're in luck for the next few days at least."

Pat, Sally and Peggy watched from the underground tank as Hilary walked down the field, along the lane and were still there when she turned and waved as she got to Paygate corner. As they stood there, the last of the suns rays glowed on the horizon, lighting up their faces and accentuated the light mist that hung over the hollow. Then they turned back to the table, gathered up their handiwork and bundled it into the large brown bag from whence it had come. "Come on then," said Peggy. "Aunt Doll's right, we've still got things to do before we get to bed tonight and I'm beginning to feel tired now. It's been a long day. I'm glad us girls are allowed to sleep upstairs tonight. I'll be able to tell you some good old ghostly bed time stories, how about that?"

"Don't you dare, you'll give me and Sally nightmares. "You know we've got to be up early in the morning, we need a good nights sleep," replied Pat sternly sounding just like a grownup. "Come on let's get our stuff ready and then mum'll do us some cocoa before we go to bed."

***

Later as they lay on the big mattress in the attic, elbows bent with open hands beneath their heads, they talked for a while. Soon however, the activities of the day caught up with them and Pat and Sally began to yawn. "Blow the candle out will you Peg," asked Sally sleepily, sitting up and balancing herself on one elbow. As she lay down again, Peggy leaned over the flame and, still chatting away, drew a deep breath. Then she began to cough and splutter. Sally shot up and began to hit her on the back. Then she quickly removed her hankie from beneath her pillow and thrust it into Peggy's hand.

"I've swallowed a moth," squeaked Peggy and then she began to cough again. "It was right by the candle and I didn't see it until it was too late." As Pat and Sally began to giggle uncontrollably, she began to cough again. "Shut up you two, it's nothing to laugh at. I could have choked." Then after a few seconds, her natural sense of humour got the better of her and she began to giggle. "There was an old woman who swallowed a fly, I don't know why she swallowed a fly. Perhaps she'll die," she croaked.

"Shall I go back downstairs and get you a drink of water," asked Pat, having regained her composure. "That's all you need to make you better."

"What, and go arse over head down the stairs in the dark. Not bloody likely," replied Sally. "No I'll go, I'm older than what you are and with all the carrots I eat, I reckon I can see in the dark."

"There's no need, it's gone now. It's probably drowning in all that cocoa I had earlier," said Peggy, her voice still husky. They'll never believe you anyway or worse still, if they do, I'll never hear the last of it. You know what mums like, she'd laugh to see a pudden crawl, she would. And I don't expect Ed's gone to bed yet. Imagine what he'd make of it. No we'd best keep quiet about this. Tell you what you can have a go at blowing the candle out this time Sally. See if there's another moth that wants to commit suicide."

Sally leaned across the mattress and looked around carefully before committing herself. Then she took a quick, deep breath and exhaled it in a split second through pursed lips, plunging the room into sudden darkness. For quite a while afterwards the faint smell of molten wax that Sally had always found somehow pleasing, hung around the room.

"God bless you, goodnight, see you in the morning, Hope you sleep well and don't dream of ghost's," said Pat sleepily.

"Same to you, thank you," replied Sally, automatically responding to the nightly ritual.

Sally lay for a while thinking about the days events, her thoughts returning again and again to the little cottage up the narrow lane with its two ancient inhabitants. Just before she drifted off to sleep however, a vision of the Lady in the Church floated across her minds eye and her dreams were all of shadowy figures. Like Old Father Time with his scythe, at the front of dad's book, 'The English Spy,' in the front room.

CHAPTER 12

Sally looked through the kitchen window and up into a sky which was grey on grey, then as she watched, it took on a curious glow as a wintery sun tried to break through. "Let's go up and get the milk before we have our breakfast. It doesn't take long and then once we've done the pumping we can go down and call for Hilary," she said, moving away from the window. "We'll need our wellies. It's very wet out there. Can I wear your mack please Hazel?" she asked moving through the scullery door and reaching up to remove the gabardine rain coat from the hook behind the back door. "Mine's too small for me now and you haven't worn yours for ages." Hazel, her attention taken with administering food to the little ones, just nodded as Sally knew she would. Their mum was not feeling too good this morning and Hazel, always in tune with the needs of others, was quietly working through the early morning chores.

Pat and Sally walked across the field to inspect the old oak tree on the way. Tony Powell used this tree for target practice with his air gun and they wanted to inspect any fresh slugs he might have introduced to their favourite tree. At the last count, made a couple of weeks ago, the score had been twenty eight. It was still the same, which meant that he had not been back since then. He was a very good shot and there would have been fresh evidence of this newly acquired skill of his had he been practicing. Why he needed this string to his bow when he had other, and as far as Sally was concerned, more interesting hobbies, she had no idea. He could yodel like no other person she had ever heard and played the melodeon with as much skill as a professional musician, she reckoned. It was a joy to listen to him. When he and Johnny Gain, crippled from birth as far as she could make out, played their music in the Coach and Horses, practically the whole population of the village turned out to listen to them.

They walked up the track towards Battle Barn farmhouse and as they shuffled through the leaves blown down in the recent autumn gales, Pat and Sally began to chant.

> *"I've a broom, a broom cried the autumn wind, and I'll blow all the leaves away.*
>
> > *I'll harry them, scarry them rush them along, and they'll sing me a crickly crackly song.*
>
> *I'll give them a fright tonight.*
>
> > *So off he set with his great big broom and SWISH, all the leaves on the ground went hurrying, scurrying rushing along.*

Some scampering high, some whispering low, with a crickerly, crackerly sound.
Down by the hedge and into the moss grown ditch the wind swept the leaves. Brown, yellow and red.
Then tired, put down his broom and fled.
Who rides on it now?
Why, a Witch."

"I love that poem," said Pat. Then she stooped down and picked up a large sweet chestnut leaf. "What does this remind you of?" she asked holding the light brown leaf beneath Sally's nose for inspection. "A kipper," she said and grinned at her sisters' puzzled expression. "I'm taking this home to show to mum. She's not very well is she? It might cheer her up a bit. Look there's some really pretty yellow and orange leaves over there. I think I'll take those as well. Dora and Jacky will love those to play with. Look I'll pop them under this bit of wood and pick them up on the way back down."

They did not linger at the farm today but taking heed of Mrs Collins's warning that the geese, accompanied by the gander, were making their way towards the fence, hurried back down the track making as little noise as possible. Pat handed her container of milk to Sally as she bent to pick up her precious leaves, and then they hurried towards and over the stile and made their way down the field. As they walked into the kitchen with the churns of milk, dad was leaning over the primus table with two large cotton reels and a long screw in his hand. The handle on one of their kettles had broken and he was in the process of giving the old thing a new lease of life. As Sally watched, she could see that he had already neatly sawn off one end from each of the reels and was slotting the screw through, keeping the cut ends in the middle, the uncut parts flush against the side of the handle. It fitted perfectly.

"There, all I've got to do now is to screw on these two nuts and then it'll be as good as new," he said as he lifted the kettle up to inspect his handy work. Then he looked anxiously across at mum. "Not feeling any better by the looks of things." he said. "It'll get worse before it gets better, that's the trouble," he added mysteriously. Then after a pause, he continued. "Better tell 'em what's up I suppose," and he turned to face them. "It's like this, your Mother is expecting another baby and she's feeling very tired and unwell at the moment, so make sure you all do all you can to help her. You Sally can probably remember how unwell she was when she was expecting Jacky, though she never complained like she's not complaining now."

Sally looked at her mum who did not reply but who's eyes had filled with tears. And she felt her own eyes begin to water. She had noticed that her mum had been tired for a while now, but had not really paid much attention. She, like most of her sisters, just took mum for granted. There was always food on the table when they were hungry, their clothes were always washed, their beds made up and she was always there for them with a sympathetic ear whatever their problems, real or just perceived. Then there were the times when they would go to bed leaving the kitchen looking like a bomb site. When they got up in the morning and remarked on its transformation into orderliness, mum would say, 'yes the fairies have been here again.' And Sally would imagine the little creatures rushing around the kitchen, flexing their tiny muscles, bringing order out of chaos to the place. She would try, she would really try to be more helpful, more understanding, but she knew how thoughtless she often was. That she often moaned and groaned when asked to perform the simplest of tasks and knew that her mum would often do them herself rather than wait for the inevitable excuses.

"We're going along the village once we've called for Hilary. We'll get you some shopping if you like," said Sally her conscience pricking her now that she had come face to face with her shortcomings. "That's after we've done the pumping, that is." And she relaxed as her mum smiled at her, both of them accepting that she would fall back into her old habits in a very short space of time.

"As a matter of fact I do need a few bits and pieces. I'll make you a list," mum replied. "And you never know, it could be a boy this time. Now wouldn't that make a change? Not that we'd love him any more than we do you girls of course," she added hastily.

Pat and Sally called for Hilary and the three girls walked across the piece of waste ground adjacent to Windy Ridge, into the twitten and up and into Crazy Lane. This was the route favoured by them when they had plenty of time on their hands. They were all wearing wellies, which was essential footwear at this time of the year especially with what they had in mind. They had not been further along Brede Lane than East View terrace for ages now nor had they explored the fields that lay on either side, and they planned to remedy this.

When they walked into the shop, Mr Phillips was nowhere to be seen. Joy however, was behind the counter and they deposited the shopping list along with the string bag with her. She was the daughter of this lively household and, like her parents always made time to talk and joke with them no matter how busy she happened to be. She was already taller than her parents and very slim, but her sense of humour was already on a par with theirs. There was a time when she had spent a lot of time in and around Sylvian, playing and getting into mischief with Sally's older sisters, but they all had other commitments these days it seemed.

As they stood there, Mr Phillips bounced nimbly up the few steps from the lower deck. This General Store come Post Office, also housed a switchboard, which connected incoming calls with local telephone lines, and Sally reckoned that he had been busy taking care of this puzzling contraption. There was never a free moment or a dull one here it seemed. Reg, Joy's older brother had been absent from the village for a long time along with many other young men and also women, a part of the enormous war effort. He had been in the Navy and she shivered when she thought about the shelling and sinking of so many ships during the war and how many of those on board had gone to a watery grave. Sally had one lingering memory of him however. On one memorable occasion years ago, he had helped her carefully and safely down from a tree in his back garden, into which she had got herself truly and very firmly stuck. She had been terrified at the time, which she found quite surprising these days with so many other and more challenging climbs now under her belt. But then she had been very young at the time. Hilary was asking for three sherbet dabs by this time and had put a few coins on the counter to pay for them. As she took the three little packages from Joy, she passed one to Pat and another to Sally. The third one she held up, tweaked out bits of the wrapping paper here and there, and likened the thing to a long tailed tit, which Mr Phillips found quite amusing. Sally could not for the life of her, see any resemblance to any bird she had ever seen, but that was Hilary for you. Mad on birds she was. However, she was quick to alert her friend to the loss of precious sherbet, which was beginning to seep through the housing.

As they walked up beside the village green, sucking away on their sherbet dabs, they talked about the changes that someone from the council had suggested should be made to this area. As far as they were concerned, the village green and the surrounding area was fine just the way it was and that was that. They were grateful however, that the barbed wire had been removed from around the allotment plots, allowing them access to pull a carrot or two for immediate consumption, when they were in season.

Shortly after they turned into Brede Lane, Pat spotted Mr Gammon across the field with his old horse Boxer, and pointed in their direction. The relationship between these two was on a par with Mr Budgen and his old shire horses. There was the usual 'whoa, whoa' and 'steady, steady there,' always with that slow but firm intonation in their voices. And when they flicked the reigns against the horse's thighs, it was nearly always as a guidance rather than as a reprimand. Working horses were worth their weight in gold and the men who used them realized this. The girls stopped for a while to observe the pair in operation. They watched as the steady grinding up of the ground brought with it the inevitable flocks of birds, rising and falling as they competed with one another to gobble up as many worms and grubs as their crops could cope with.

As they moved reluctantly away from this satisfying scene, Sally thought about David Gammon and how little they saw of him outside school. Being the only boy and the youngest member of the family, he probably helped out on the farm as most farmer's sons were expected to do, she reckoned. He was also rather shy. His sister Sheila, the younger of the two girls, had a heart condition, she had heard. Another child, a boy called Geoffrey had died while very young, from a similar complaint. She had seen his grave stone up in the churchyard recently, with 'Little Geoff,' chiselled on the stone, and had felt quite sad when she had looked at it. Sheila was a musician of some note, though her skill with the viola left much to be desired. Once when she had stood up to do a solo on stage in the village hall with this particular instrument, Ken Drury had shouted out, 'O Christ,' and had caused a few giggles as well shushes from some members of the audience. Rowena, the eldest child in this family and a few years older than they were, was a very confident girl. Sally thought the name 'Rowena' was beautiful probably because she has always loved the tree with a similar name, which always conjured up visions of wild inaccessible places. Both girls went to private schools for some reason and did not seem to mix with many of the village children.

Just as they reached the top of the incline, Hilary bent down and picked up a match box, from where it had been discarded beside the pathway. It was soggy and limp but still intact and had obviously not been parted from its careless owner for any length of time.

"Look, here's a new one for your collection Sal," she said as she passed the damp receptacle over to her friend for inspection. "It was laying face up on the pathway over there. I know you've got some boxes with ships on similar to this but you can see straight away that this one's a bit different from those. They're all part of a series like the cigarette cards are and after a while you get to know what you've got and what you haven't, don't you."

Sally took the box from Hilary's hand and examined it critically. Her friend knew as much about her collection of these precious boxes as she did herself and for that she was very grateful. Having noticed this one with her eagle eye, meant that her collection of this particular series with its simplistically styled ship, was now almost complete. Hilary was as enthusiastic about these boxes that Sally was so keen on as she was about the cigarette cards that she and Ronald collected. She seemed to know who smoked any particular brand of cigarette and the matches with which they lit the things. She was always on the look out for swops as well, and got quite excited when they were only one away from completing a particular set. As she stowed the precious box away in the pocket of her, or rather Hazels, gabardine mackintosh, she felt very contented.

As they approached the entrance to East View Terrace, they spotted a group of young men and boys clustered around the front end of an old motor. They stopped in their tracks, curiosity getting the better of them and watched as one by one, the men and boys tried cranking the old motor up into life with a starting handle, for all they were worth. After a while one of the men took the handle out of the starting dog and laid it across the bonnet of the car. Then he passed around a packet of Woodbine cigarettes, struck a match and shielding the flame with his cupped hand, lit the white tubes, one by one as those who felt the need to partake in this ritual, leaned towards the meagre flame.

"Can I have that match box when you've finished with it?" Asked Sally having eyed up this interesting and potential addition to her collection. "You can give it to Willie or Roy. You'll pass it on to me when it's empty, won't you?" she added turning to the two boys who were standing to one side of the motor.

The man nodded vaguely, his mind and concentration on other, and to him more important things, while Willie and Roy, who had only just become aware of their presence, came over to chat with them, along with Ron Hudson, Wangy as they used to call him, and Trev. Roy's brother Jack they noticed, was amongst the tight knit bunch standing around the motor along with one or two other boys from the village. They, however, were all engrossed in this diseased, terminally ill old motor

Have you seen Denis lately?" asked Ron. "He's had his hair cut and whoever did it must have had St Vitus' dance. He looks like a cow with scabies, he does. What was he was thinking about, letting a mad barber do that to him?"

"Think? He hasn't got room in his brain to think His heads full up with sawdust or cotton wool," said Sally. A rocking horse's has got more brains that he's got. I wonder why he's like it, how he got to be the way he is?"

"It's the way is mam put is 'at on when he was a kid, that's what's done it," replied Trev with a grin. "Meself like, I've never let anyone anywhere near me head, just in case. Except the old nitty nurse when I was at school of course. Anyway, where're you lot off to?" he asked. "Looks like you mean business. All togged up like that, wellies and all. All you need is a gun tucked under you arm and an old sack over your shoulder, and I'd think you were going out to catch yourself a bit of fresh meat for your dinner. There's plenty of tasty little old rabbits around here you know and they're all free. Ask old Mercy Dengate."

"Free did you say? You mean free until you shoot 'em," replied Hilary dryly. No, you're the one with the gun. Us lot just use bows and arrows and catapults now and again. And some of us are better than others at shooting out windows and things with catapults, I can tell you." And she grinned across at Sally, both remembering Hilary's attempt to rattle Mrs Wintergreen Edwards' chimney pots with her stone, only to hear the tinkle of glass as it ricocheted off the wall and through one of the windows of Windy Ridge. "We've had to scarper a few times when our aim's been like not what it should have been and so forth if you know what I mean," she said, still grinning at the memory of this particular incident. Then she paused for a few seconds, her attention caught by a movement along the lane, and as the others followed her gaze, they saw a familiar figure puffing and peddling up the lane towards them.

"Well blow me down, if it ain't old Beelzebub. He don't normally come this way," whispered Roy instinctively catching Sally by the shoulder and pulling her towards him.

"Looks more like a wet racing dog every time I sees him, blowed if he don't," said Trev standing there bravely, hands on hips, feet set wide apart watching and listening as the mad cyclist approached them at a rate of knots.

"A whippet you mean," replied Roy. "A whippet with legs like a bloody pantomime horse. I've never seen owt like him, never before in my whole life."

"Shush, he'll hear you," whispered Sally, disengaging herself from Roy and trying to hide behind his back as the apparition drew closer at an alarming rate.

"Don't you dare call out puff, puff Beazle, or he'll kill us," she added. Then unable to contain her curiosity, she peered cautiously around his shoulder, just in time to see this cantankerous old cyclist pass by with out as much as a glance in their direction. Then they watched in silence until he disappeared around the bend in the road.

"Well I'll be blowed, what do you think of that then," said Roy, visibly relaxing and moving forward for a better look along the lane to make sure that man and bicycle had really gone. "I quite expected him to jump off that bike of his and give us a piece of his mind just for the sheer hell of it. We have name-called him a few times in the past, haven't we? But not lately, not in the last few months at least," he added hastily. Perhaps he saw you there Trev, imagined you'd got your gun with you and thought better of it. Us lot, we only travel light, with bows and arrows and catapults and things as Hilary was saying and you don't have time to load and shoot them when you're in a bit of a hurry to get away from a madman like him. No we just have to rely on shanks' pony when he's after us, we do. Anyway, me and Willie are off to the village. We only stopped to have a look at what was going on with that old car over there, but it don't look like it's going to live a normal life ever again, so we'll be on our way. You never know, we may see you girls on the way back. We'll look for you anyway."

As the girls parted company with Willie, Roy and Trev and began to make their way down the lane, they saw Edgar Boxall walking towards them. His long legs were encased in muddy Wellington boots and his two dogs, running freely up and down and to and fro the lane, were the colour of a newly ploughed field. He and his family had been the first to move into East View Terrace when the building work had commenced there back in 1929, and as he said, had watched the growth of the estate from small beginnings to what it had now become. And very proud of the place he was too. They stopped for a while to pass the time of day with him and for Hilary to stroke the animated dogs without getting covered with the mud that the animals had obviously been revelling in. Sally especially was trying to protect Hazel's gabardine mackintosh from the ravages of muddy claws and slobbery lips, without much success. She was the first to move away from the muddy trio for this reason, even though she found what this elderly man was talking about, really interesting. He knew the local area inside out and had made a fair study of the folk in the village and surrounding area as well. His keen appraisal, his observations of the rich variety within the human race were both humorous and astute, with folk like Mrs Brooman becoming almost caricatures of themselves. As he talked, the person to whom he was referring came instantly to life, in front of your very eyes. And yet he was never unkind.

As they continued on their way, they talked about this and that, often about the people whose names had come up in conversation with Mr Boxall. Mrs Brooman whose lifestyle seemed mostly to be stuck in the past, was one of them and they chuckled when they began to imagine what effect on her old lavvy her habit of taking syrup of figs on a weekly basis would be. They reckoned this was another reason for her having cut that trap door at the back of the hut, housing her privy That it had not been put there for the sole purpose of making emptying of the thing that much easier on her old back. Having sampled the stuff on one or two occasions, they would even go as far as to say that the syrup of figs would have been the first consideration.

After a while, their conversation slipped naturally from personality appraisals to other topics.

"I'm glad I didn't pass the eleven plus," Sally was saying. "I did try but I didn't really want to, not really, and if you didn't pass it Hilary, then sure as hell I wasn't going to. I'm surprised that Patty Winchester and Anne Pope didn't pass though. They're both good at arithmetic and things, like you are Hilary and they're nearly always top of the class. So was Cynthia Morrison but then she got through, didn't she? I'm sorry we phoned her that time. We were a bit rude to her weren't we? If the truth be known, it was partly an excuse to use that new phone box and it had to be her really, because there's not many people we know who've got a phone, is there? I don't know about you but I feel really nervous using those damned things. I just get lost for words. Anyway, that's no excuse for being rude, but there you go. It was Barbara Swift I should have been rude to. She passed as well didn't she? I'll never forget the time she put that bogey on my desk. Made me feel really sick it did. But anyway, I couldn't have gone to another school, not without you two. And there's another thing, what about the food then? I bet the old Grammar School hasn't got anyone half as good as Mrs Bishop to cook the dinners. In fact I don't suppose anyone anywhere's gets dinners as good as we get at school."

"I didn't wan to pass it either," said Hilary. "Before we moved to Sedlescombe, I'd been to so many schools I lost count of them. I vowed ages ago that as I liked this one and liked you lot even more, I'd stay put until they kicked me out to work. And I must say, I did think about the food, just like you did Sal. We learn enough from Jumbo James anyway. We're even doing a bit of science and quite interesting it is too. That's where we learned that poem about old Brown. You know, 'Old Brown is dead' and so forth."

"Yes I learned it off by heart when Eddie told it to us," replied Sally. "It's got a good rhythm to it."

Much further down the lane, they came to a small cottage, which was almost as isolated as the one they had seen on the way to Pevensey. Emily Philpott lived here and as they looked over the low hedge, they could see her pottering about in her garden. Another Mother Nature in a pinny, just like Mercy Dengate, thought Sally. She lived here with her brother, but he was nowhere to be seen. When she saw them, she came over to the gate to talk to them and after a few minutes invited them in for a drink.

"It be a bit isolated around these parts," she said wiping the mud off her trowel onto the grass, then popping it into her apron pocket. "All I see are them farm workers, mostly at a distance, course they be too busy for idle chit chat, especially at this time of year when there be so few hours of daylight to work in." Then she opened the gate and they all trooped through and walked slowly up the garden path.

In a few months time Sally knew, the whole front garden would be carpeted with daffodils, a mass of waving bright yellow from the gate right up to the wall of the cottage. She had seen it last spring when she had walked through the lane with Hilary and it had almost taken her breath away. As they passed through the squat doorway and into the low slung interior with its black beams, she could see the rickety old stairs with their lethal tilt, which lead up into the two bedrooms above. How this elderly couple managed to negotiate this death trap with just a candle to light their way, she could not imagine. The handle that had been fixed to the wall with long iron nails, now hung away from its anchor and wobbled precariously at the slightest touch. It was about as much use as a chocolate teapot. The little cottage however, was clean and fresh as a new pin, just like the Lawrence's abode. Whether their outdoor lavvy resembled the one in the Lawrence's back garden, she had no idea nor was she in any hurry to find out.

As they moved through to the kitchen, Sally looked out of the window and saw a dozen or so hens pecking away in the back garden. They were a mixture of Light Sussex and Rhode Island Red, the same kind as the ones at home. Miss Philpott, following her gaze, smiled and patted her on the shoulder.

"Don't they be in fine fettle, me old hens?" she said. "They can get a bit scruffy this time of year, going on winter Then they look awful sorry for 'emselves. Mind you they've had a good lot of sunflower seeds in their crops this autumn and now there be the stems of the old sprout plants coming along. They be nice and juicy and full of what helps to keep them healthy. Course, come springtime, there's nothing they like better than to peck around in them old anthills over there. They specially like their little white eggs, and you should see the way they gobble them up. Ants used to be bred specially to feed pheasant chicks at one time you know, and lots of folk aren't too happy that they've sort of invaded their gardens. There's plenty of 'em around in these parts, I can tell you. But It's an ill wind that blows no one no good I says, and my old hens ain't complaining. Is it some of me special well water you'll be wanting then or a cup of tea? I reckon I could just about stretch the milk out to three extra cups."

"Water please," the girl's replied in chorus remembering the 'water bewitched and tea begrudged' stuff that had been dished up to them on one of their earlier excursions. They would not refuse a piece of her cake however. Her cooking, unlike her beverages, was almost on a par with Sally's mum's.

"We'd best be on our way then," said Hilary after while. "We've got some shopping to pick up on the way home. Thanks for the cake and everything," she added and Pat and Sally hastily added their words of thanks and appreciation as they made their way towards the low doorway.

As they walked back along the lane, Sally glanced across the fields to where a tractor was grinding up the ground. There were flocks of greyish birds, ducking and diving as they followed the plough and their cries echoed strangely in the moist autumnal air. Then she sniffed. Above the smell of wet soil, there was another, unmistakable smell. Someone had been cutting the hedge and the heady, green aroma overwhelmed the smell of tractor and its craft. "I love this time of year," she said for the umpteenth time, not expecting nor getting a reply from the other girls.

Sally glanced sideways as they passed the entrance to East View Terrace. The clapped out old motor was still there with to one side of it, a rainbow coloured puddle where oil from the thing had leaked and combined with water, to decorate the pavement.

By the time they reached the village, Willie and Roy were nowhere to be seen. Bunny Finch and old Fred were there however. They were standing together on the green, close to the entrance to the allotments. Fred was leaning on the handle of his spade, his foot resting lightly on the working part. That he was on his way from and not to his plot they could tell by the state of his boots and the contents of the old bucket standing beside him. There were huge parsnips in the bucket, roughly washed and showing signs of canker here and there. On top of these monsters but by no means concealing them, were sprout tops, nibbled here and there and with a few white fly fluttering aimlessly above them. The two men turned as the girls drew level with them and grinned, seemingly unfazed by the sudden interruption of what had seemed quite an animated conversation.

"Old Fred reckons that the river here was still wide enough for boats when smuggling was rife around these parts," said Bunny pointing downwards. "He says that a lot of stuff was smuggled in and out that way. You reckon that some of the toffs houses were used to store the stuff in an all, don't you Fred. And that the old church up on the hill there could tell a tale or two if it chose, as could the Old Gun House and some of the big old houses around the place as well. Course, he gets a lot of his knowledge from old Jessie Kenward, who's granddad was a smuggler by all accounts."

Old Fred, realising that he was being side lined by his friend, butted in determined to get his penny's worth. Bunny, he reckoned liked the sound of his own voice more even than the ale that they consumed and argued over in the Coach and Horses on a Friday evening and he was unable to contain himself any longer.

"E don't arf chipe, talk ind leg orf a donkey, e do. Now loiks of me, I be a doer mornan a chiper. Look at soize of em ere persneeps in me bucket en me oynuns be soize of footballs. Thar, ye ewld faggit," he said grinning now and lightly punching his friend on the arm. "Ye caint do better en thet, cans ye. En what I tells e bout smugglerers, be as true as what I be standing ere en all. So I'll tek no argifying from loiks o you."

"Aye Fred, it's a wise old sage what knows his onions," replied Bunny, winking and grinning at the girls before turning back to his old mate. "And anyway, I wouldn't dream of argifying with you."

The girls stood for a while, reluctant to take their leave of these two interesting old men with their good humoured bickering and their tales from a bygone era. That they contradicted one another all the time was an accepted part of their relationship. As Bunny had told them from time to time, 'the time we stops arguing is when we's in a box and buried deep in that old churchyard up yonder. And we ain't planning to pop our clogs for a wee while yet.'

After picking up the shopping, the girls made their way across the bridge and out of the village. As Sally looked up, she watched the sun as it struggled to break through, changed its mind then snuggled back behind the rolling grey clouds. It reminded her of Mr Collins' prediction of an extra cold winter this year. She had better check that her Liberty bodices still fitted and that all the buttons were in place. She hoped that Jumbo James would order enough coal for the school fires this winter as well. She found it so difficult to concentrate on even the most interesting of subjects when icy draughts whistled through the gaps in the casement windows and forced their way beneath the ill fitting doors. Then not even her thick grey socks, Liberty bodice and succession of top layers stopped her from shivering. Nor, if she really thought about it, did the meagre warmth that emanated from the one fire at the side of the classroom, no matter how often the old caretaker banked it up. She sighed. She loved the winter, she really did. Except of course for the chilblains that plagued her. And if she were honest, the dash from the scullery door to the little hut that housed the lavvy, when it was bitterly cold and the wind threatened to cut her body in half, was a daunting prospect. Only undertaken out of dire necessity. But there again, she loved sitting in their cosy kitchen or laying snuggled up in bed at night, listening to the sound of the cold north east winds as they rattled the windows of the house and forced their way down the chimney. And when it snowed, covering the fields and cloaking the anxious trees in a mantle of the purest white, she reckoned that fairyland or even Heaven, did not get any better than this.

"Bags we go main road way home," said Pat calling over her shoulder as she ran on ahead, causing Sally to jump out of her skin at the sudden interruption. "I want to have a slide down Farrow's steps."

"Well don't blame me then if you rag out your knickers and mum tells you off," Sally called back to her sternly, forgetting her own enjoyment of this childish game, not so very long ago.

As Pat ran on ahead, Hilary and Sally started talking about the clothes and shoes they had purchased from money earned in the hop fields back in the late summer. They were still discussing this interesting subject when they caught up with the littlest one and sat down, one above the other, on Farrow's cold concrete steps.

" I like that floral material we chose to make our dresses with and I'm glad we've nearly finished them. Mrs Moon reckons we're making a good job of them as well. The only thing is that if we want to wear them at this time of year, we'll have to wear two or three Liberty bodices underneath and those cardigans we've just made on top, but I don't mind that, do you? We'll wear them at Christmas and for my party on Boxing Day anyway, that's for sure. We'll have finished them by then with any luck."

Sally thought, with a certain amount of pride about the dresses she and Hilary were making. This was definitely the most ambitious bit of sewing she had ever undertaken and she had needed a lot of help from her teacher to get the curiously shaped bits of material pinned then tacked together in the right order, ready for the sewing machine. The old Singer, which could be used as a treadle as well as a hand machine, had also presented her with problems. It was difficult to guide and control the material with one hand while turning the handle with the other. How the devil her dad managed to coordinate hands and feet as he did with ease when stitching up leather or rexine or any other material on his old treadle machine, she could not fathom. She would never ever get the hang of that. The dress though with its flared skirt and closely fitting bodice, was very stylish. She still needed to fit and carefully stitch the puff sleeves into place then fix the two long strips of material, which would circle the waist and tie in at the back of the dress with a bow. For this, she and Hilary had already prepared an oval shape of the same material. The very last bit would be to measure then neatly turn and hem up the bottom of the dress and then it would be ready to wear. She could not wait for the next sewing lesson.

All the while they were talking, Pat, oblivious to their idle chatter, continued to run up the steps then slide down the slope with rhythmic monotony. She was hampered somewhat by her wellies which slowed her descent, but she did not let that small detail detract from her enjoyment. At other times her low laughter would have been accompanied by a shower of sparks shooting out in all directions from her blakey studded shoes, as she propelled herself downward. The two older girls were thankful for small mercies, forgetting their own enjoyment of this simple pleasure, not so very long ago.

After a while, Hilary and Sally rose slowly to their feet rubbing their cold, numb bums. It was Hilary who stooped to retrieve the shopping which, contained only loosely within the confines of the old string bag, had spread itself higgledy piggledy onto the grass. "Righto, lets get home then. Come on Pat, you've done enough sliding for one day," she said as she stepped lightly out into the road. "Time and tide wait for no man. And my stomach tells me, its time we weren't here anyway. Here, take one of these handles will you Sal. This bag seems a lot heavier now than it did when I put it down," she added as Sally took one of the thickly crocheted handles silently from her friend.

When they reached Uplyme, they stopped out of sheer curiosity, and leaned on the gate to scan the large front garden. At the side of the rectangular shed, a large buddleia tree dominated the area, its scorched elongated blossoms looking for all the world as though they had been breathed on by an angry dragon. The hydrangea bushes dotted here and there also still sported some of their summer foliage. The leaves however, were now brown edged and the faded flower heads were already taking on a desiccated transparency. The overlong grass on the lawn was still green and lush but coarser now as though preparing itself for the ravages of winter. Sally sighed as she turned away from contemplation of this interesting garden, experiencing a glow of satisfaction as she thought about their day's activities. And suddenly a short ditty came unbidden into her mind and she began to hum it softly to herself.

Store away your happy hours, for they shall be Decembers flowers.
Store away you happy hours, for they shall be Dece-embers flowers.
Man does fairest garlands find, in the treasures o o of his mind.
Store away your happy hours, for they shall be Decembers flowers.
Store away your happy hours, for they shall be Dece-embers flowers.

Sally grinned as she looked ahead. Mrs Paygate Edwards had been doing her washing, and it hung limp and grey from the line, which stretched from one side of her garden to the other. Then she looked across the road to see Frankie Richmond coming down Mrs Wintergreen Edward's steps, carefully bumping his small hand cart down after him.

"Where're you off to Frankie?" Hilary called out to him.

"I'm going along to Farrows to get some bits of wood," he replied. "Neil, that's Mr Farrow, has just been cutting some branches and things off his old apple trees and he says we can have what we want. Here, did you know they got their back door blown out by an explosion during the war then? Well they did because Mrs Farrow told me about it the last time I went there. Anyway, I'd best be careful how I go this time, and look where I put me feet. Last time I went up there, I fell in the outfall of their old sewer. Well it's all covered up with stinging nettles and things and I couldn't see it and nobody told me it was there. I'd got my wellies and long trousers on so a few nettles wouldn't bother me and that's all I thought it was. But it went right up over me boots that stuff, nearly to my waist it was and it didn't half pong. Mrs Farrow sorted me out as much as she could but I still got a bloody good ticking off when I got home and I had to take my clothes outside and wash them off in an old bucket." Then he paused for a few seconds and a grin spread across his face. "Hey, do you know what they call Mr Farrow then?" he asked. He paused again while they looked back at him in uncomprehending silence. "They call him wheelbarrow, get it? Neil Farrow, wheelbarrow. Don't you think that's funny?"

"Yes, we knew that anyway," replied Hilary. "And it's not as funny as something Sal and I worked out. Well I don't think so anyway. There's families called Cotton, Soan and Button in the village. Yes? So you take your button and sew it on with a bit of cotton. Well we thought it was funny anyway, didn't we Sal? In fact it kept us going for a whole day." As Frankie grinned back at her, clearly amused by the observation, Hilary said, "If we weren't so tired and hungry, we'd walk back with you, just to make sure you don't fall in that sewer again. You were not the first to fall in it though. Penny's fallen in there and she got badly stung as well. And some of the men from the Home Guard kind of lost their sense of direction after one of their meetings up there during the war and landed up covered in the stuff. Mrs Farrow must be getting used to cleaning off people who fall in the thing. I expect she always keeps a bucket of water ready, just in case.

Anyway, you'd best be on your way and remember, just go up Farrows steps, across the yard and the orchard's at the back there. We should know, we've pinched a few windfalls from there a time or two, haven't we Sal?" she said as she stooped to pick up the bag of groceries once again. "Look, the wind's blowing the smoke from your chimney about a bit," she added and they all looked up into the field where spirals of smoke emerged from the chimney only to be extinguished in their prime by the rising wind. "Mum must have got a bit of wood on there I reckon. I bet she's cooking something that needs a hot oven. I'm starved." And she absentmindedly passed one handle of the bag to Sally, and the three girls set off on the last leg of their journey home.

The smell of the dinner cooking assailed their noses as they walked across the field and they all sniffed appreciatively. She never let them down, their mum. No matter how she felt, there was always a delicious meal and freshly washed clothes for them. And Sally had to admit that this morning her mum had looked really poorly. Never mind, they would give her a hand to make up the mixture for the Christmas puddings tomorrow morning and she would even volunteer to grate the carrots. A job she disliked with a vengeance. No matter how careful she tried to be, she always seemed to grate a bit of her knuckle into the mixture and had to finish the job with a bit of rag tied round her hand. The best bit of the whole job of course, was the addition of the silver thruppenny bits followed by the ritual stirring of the thick, glupey mixture. It was at this last stage that you closed your eyes tightly and made a very special and secret wish. It had to be secret, for if you were foolish enough to reveal what you had wished for to even one other person, then that wish would never come true.

Later that evening, when Sally was on her way to visit 'the little hut,' she looked upward to where a few stars blinked then disappeared behind a mass of rolling grey clouds. Autumn was drifting imperceptibly into winter when the wind would veer from a warm westerly direction, to an icy north, north easterly one. And Jack Frost would creep through the countryside and around the houses, painting intricate patterns on every available surface. It was on these cold mornings that she and her sisters would rush shivering to the warmth of the old kitchen range to get dressed. She shivered, not with cold but with anticipation of the season ahead with all its ups and downs.

CHAPTER 13

Accounts of the outcome of the Nuremberg trials of Nazi war criminals, had dominated the news recently. Once again the front pages of the News Chronicle had been full of smudged images of condemned men with accompanying extensive analyses on these long, protracted trials. The news bulletins on the wireless had been extended to cover the complexities of detail of this trial with the newsreaders' tone even more solemn than usual.

Bormann it seemed had disappeared and questions were being asked as to why and how Goering had managed to cheat the hang man by committing suicide, also why Von Papen had got off so lightly. Sally had also heard other names mentioned like Speer, Jodl, Ribbentrop, Hess, Himmler, Goebbels but could not make out quite who had been condemned and who had managed to escape the hangman's rope. The background to all this, the years of suffering that had brought about this trial, were just too painful for her to think about, like a nightmare that would not go away. How the presiding Judge, Hartley Shawcross had managed to remain calm and seemingly dispassionate while evaluating the evidence put before him, she had no idea. As to the fate of the condemned men, she would not allow her imagination to go down that road. Hitler, the leader of these seemingly ruthless, unscrupulous men, had of course put himself out of reach of any kind of earthly justice.

Another disturbing news item that had been around for several weeks now was the trial and execution of a man called Neville Heath. The grey images of this man had stared out from the newspaper day after day, with lengthy debates on the state of mind of this gruesome murderer. Was he insane or just plain evil? Sally along with most people did not know the answer to this, but from the little bit of evidence that she had been privy to, the answer had to be 'both.' He had now been hanged, with debates still going on as to whether this man should have been hanged or whether he should have been detained for life at his Majesty's pleasure.

She turned her thoughts determinedly away from these morbid reflections and on to the day ahead. Although it had turned cold now, it was certainly not cold enough to keep her indoors, and she and Hilary were going to call for Margery, then walk through the wood to Sylvia's place and explore Battle big wood together.

The two girls set off, passing Deffy and Bill's little hut on the way, pausing just long enough to sniff the characteristic smell of wood smoke emanating from the narrow tin chimney, and being scattered in all directions by the cold east wind. Sally did not envy them in there, not when this cold wind would be finding its way through every crack and crevasse, creating draughts and stirring up the fuggy air within, and she pulled her balaclava more closely around her ears. She hoped they had had their porridge this morning, as she had, and she smiled as she recalled their breakfast and dad's reaction to it. As he had walked over to the stove when she had been stirring the thick bubbling stuff, he had leaned over and said, 'what you got in there then? Looks like some primeval magma to me.' And then he had walked away again and out into the scullery without another word. She wondered about him sometimes, she really did.

As they moved further into the wood, Sally looked up into the bare trees, their branches bending stiffly in the wind. "Look, there's some of those lolly on a stick birds up there," she said pointing to where a small flock of birds fluttered and twittered amongst the top most branches of the trees. "What did you say they were called?"

"Long tailed tits, that's what they are," replied Hilary coming to a standstill to gaze upward the better to examine these quaint, asymmetrical little birds. "That's one good thing about this time of the year, nearly all the leaves have gone so you can see birds and things so much easier. Look, there's masses of them up there now, they're all over the place. I wonder what they get to eat at this time of the year?"

"Bread and pullet," said Sally without pausing to think. "I'm sorry," she added after a few seconds thought, directing her words up into the trees. The objects of her facetious remark however, quite unfazed by her words, just ignored her and carried on doing what birds do best.

After a while, Hilary and Sally lapsed into a companionable silence, which was broken only by the occasional rustle of some creature as it rooted around amongst the dead leaves, and in the background, the sporadic twitter of small birds. As they walked the deserted pathways, the words of a little poem she had heard somewhere, came into her mind. The poem, which began with the words: 'lonely woods, with paths dim and silent. O haunt of peace for weary hearted,' seemed kind of appropriate somehow. Not that she was weary hearted but she could appreciate the effect that a place like this would have on someone with overwhelming problems, like the lady in the Church at Pevensey for instance. She had read on a plaque somewhere, the words: 'one is nearer God's heart in a garden than anywhere else on earth' but she reckoned that a wood like this one, was just as near to God's heart as any garden anywhere.

By the time they had called for Margery and were walking the short distance along the lane towards the muddy track that lead back into the wood again, the wind seemed to have increased in volume. It rustled the dead leaves around their feet and they instinctively walked faster to reach the comparative calm of the big wood. As Sally looked along the hedgerow, she noticed one or two silver birch trees dotted here and there. There were still one or two pale yellow and brown triangular leaves on their twiggy branches and from their straight silvery white trunks, paper thin shards of skin were peeling away from the bark. She had read somewhere that these trees had been considered sacred in the olden days and, looking at them now she could understand why.

Sylvia was out in the garden, all dressed up and ready to go, as they walked towards Keepers Cottage. She was talking and laughing with Jean and Mick Pallett who lived in the other half of the clapboard cottage. Sally could not remember ever having seen Mr Pallett. All she knew was that he had been in the Home Guard during the war, while Mr Glyde had done his stint in the fire service, and also that his piano playing was second to none. She had also heard that he made chestnut palings and stakes, amongst many other things, mostly to do with wood. But then he would, wouldn't he she thought, living in a place like this.

"Here, guess what Mick did with his new wellies when he got them last week?" Sylvia was saying. "He filled 'em with water didn't he, to find out if they were water tight or not. His mum wasn't half cross and she's still not quite got them dry for him yet. What's wrong with trying them out in the kingcup pond, we were just asking him. That's just about deep enough and a lot more fun. He doesn't agree. He says he spent ages dipping them in and out of that water tank round the back there and giving our old pig a much needed bath."

As they stood there, Mr Glyde came round the side of the house with Spot, his little dog at his heels. He was tall and muscular with the most enormous hands and he always wore a hat. By the sound of the grunting and scuffling noises coming from the back garden, they guessed he had been feeding the pig, which was being fattened up for pork, and she knew the poor things days were numbered. Mr Glyde had repeated what she had heard other folks say, that you could eat every part of the pig bar its squeak. A vision of Granny Sansom in an old pinny, holding a basin under the cut throat of her old pig to catch the blood for her black pudding, came to mind to be instantly rejected. She just wished that her imagination did not conjure everything up in such graphic detail. It was not much fun being an animal she reckoned, and if she ever came back as anything other than a human, it would be as a tree. Maybe an oak or an ash or a beech or any tree really. She turned round at the sound of a sash window being lifted, and saw Mrs Glyde's head poking through the bottom half of the cavity.

"I've just made some mince pies. I can spare you youngsters one each if you want and then I'll put the rest away for Christmas," she said. "Come round the back, then you won't have to traipse right through the house with those dirty wellies."

As she made to close the window down, Mr Glyde called out, "hang on a bit, does that include me? I'm only a youngster you know, especially if you compare me with old Fred. And you remember the saying about each mince pie you eat giving you a months worth of luck right through the year? Well I could do with a bit of luck right now. Maybe I'll have a couple then, just to make sure I gets meself off to a good start," he added before taking a good long draw on his ancient pipe. Then he followed the youngsters around to the back of the house.

They stood around in the kitchen, eating and listening to Mr Glyde's plans for the afternoon, which included getting a Christmas tree for himself and his family. "I usually take a decent branch off one of the old pines at the side of the wood here, but I was talking to old Bailey yesterday and he reckons he knows where there's some real shapely ones," he said. "It means going a bit further a field than I normally do but it'll be worth it."

The Bailey family lived and farmed along Stream Lane. It was Mr Bailey who had said to them once that birds eat your fruit and then shit on your washing, which Sally thought was quite funny at the time and true really. He also referred to Beelzebub as 'a gorn off wasp,' which was obviously a reference to the way he buzzed here there and everywhere on that old bike of his. That, plus the fact that he often wore a dull yellow and black striped jacket as he invaded the countryside. That observation had made her really chuckle.

After a while, they left the warmth of the kitchen and made their way along the pathway and deeper into the wood. "It ain't half cold out here," said Sally, shivering as she pulled her coat around her. "I wish I'd worn a scarf now as well as a balaclava. Your dad reckons it's going to be a cold winter this year, just like old Mr Collins told us, Sylv," she added. "I hope it doesn't get much colder than this, or we'll all freeze half to death." She thought about Sylvian, which was exposed and sensitive to all weathers, particularly the cold north-easterly, which howled its rage at the windows and doors. Also the frosts that iced up the windows, inside and out, creating the most intricate patterns and causing their breath to evaporate into puffs of steam as they lay in bed. It wasn't that she minded the winter, she liked it in fact, but if it was going to be extra cold, then they had best be prepared for it.

They paused for a while beneath the old beech tree to soak up its ancient tranquillity and to re-read the many signatures and messages engraved around its thick trunk. Then they moved towards the far side of the wood, to where the tall Scots pines towered head and shoulders above the other trees, smelling their characteristic resinous odour, long before they got there. As they leaned their backs against the deeply fissured bark, Sally examined the long trunks, scarred here and there, where the lower branches had been removed, either by the woodsman or by old Mother Nature herself. Then she looked even higher to where the topmost branches formed individual canopies of dark green foliage. These trees were so different from all the other trees within this wood but were just as interesting in their own way. As she looked around her, she saw other trees with trunks decorated by dark green sinuous ivy, which in some cases had wound itself almost to the top of the naked trees. In spring and summer, this ivy would be heavily camouflaged by the growth of fresh, green leaves on the parent tree, and would regain a measure of anonymity.

Suddenly, the sun peeped through and they all looked instinctively upward to extract every last bit of warmth from this thin wintry glow. Then they fell silent as shafts of sunlight, slanting through the trees, shimmered in a glow of thin, glistening mist, before disappearing as suddenly as it had come into being. Sally blinked, instinctively seeking to recreate the magical phenomenon, but the greyness of the winters day, had once again settled itself around them.

As they eased themselves away from the trunks of the tall pine trees, Margery bent down and began picking up cones and cramming them into her pockets, and the other girls followed suit. "They spit and splutter when you put them on the fire but they don't half give out some heat," she said. "Here, how does that song about the little doves go? The only bit I remember is, 'coo said the little dove, coo said she. In the strong shady branches of the dark pine tree."

"Now the young turtle doves never quarrelled in their nest. They loved each other dearly though they loved their mother best." Replied Sally. There's more I think but I can't quite remember it. I wonder what made you think of that," she replied, grinning as though she had made some kind of joke. "I like the one, I love the fitful gust that shakes a casement all the day. And from the glossy elm trees, takes the faded leaves away. I think that's lovely. You can imagine that happening, can't you?"

As they walked back through the wood, they made arrangements to meet up in the village the following Saturday, either by the bridge or if Pat had anything to do with it, by the old Blacksmiths shed.

***

Sally seemed to be developing the winter snots but there was no way this was going to put her off going to the village to meet Sylvia and Margery. The fresh air would do her good and a large bit of rag would take care of her runny nose.

When Pat, Hilary and Sally got to Paygate Corner, they saw Mrs Wintergreen Edwards coming slowly down the steps from her front garden. As the girls drew level with her, they were very much aware of the smelly ointment, which emanated from her, even through the thick layers of clothes she was wearing.

"Where're you girls off to?" she asked. "If it's to the village then I hope it's to get some shopping for your mother, she's feeling poorly you know. I expect you'll take your time. You're all the same you youngster's, you think you've got all the time in the world."

"Where's Frankie?" asked Hilary. I thought I saw him in the garden as we came down the field just now."

"He's just chopped some fire wood for me, then he's off to the village to do my shopping. I gave him a jar of elbow grease for his breakfast," she replied, and smiled one of her rare smiles. "He won't hang about, he won't. Not in this freezing cold weather. Now get along with you before I freeze to death in this icy wind." And she turned and made her way across the road to Paygate Cottage.

"Wow, she's got a sense of humour after all," said Hilary. "And talking about grease, aren't you glad she uses the stuff she does and not goose grease?" And they all giggled as they made their way along the main road.

By the time they reached the village, Sylvia and Margery were already there. They were leaning on the stile beside the Tithe Barn and looking out across the fields, discussing the merits or otherwise of using this muddy pathway as a short cut to East View Terrace. They turned as the other girls approached and as Margery walked towards them, she began to wind the thick scarf, borrowed from her dad, more closely around her neck.

"Sylv's dying to see what's in Gregory's window. We thought we'd wait till you got here before we went to have a look though," she said as she began to cross to the other side of the road, followed closely by the other girls.

They followed the aroma of freshly baked bread and doughnuts, and stood in line, their noses pressed up against the window of the high class bakery shop, staring silently at the display within. There were Christmas cakes galore, all beautifully and individually decorated by Mrs Gregory's practiced hand. On some were hand made roses, their petals delicately sculptured with attention to the finest detail, and looking as though they had just been plucked from some fairy garden. Others were sedately decorated with scrolls and shells with the odd Christmas feature dotted here and there. The girls' favourites however, were the snow scenes, where the soft icing was peaked up to unnatural heights with the aid of a pallet knife, and then jam pack filled with miniature figures and forms of every description. There were smiling figures standing, legs akimbo, and with arms raised ready to release a snowball from their loosely clenched fists. Other figures were either sliding down miniature slides, with flailing arms and legs in the air, or were sitting on their bottoms at the bottom of the slide, one arm raised to nurse a bumped head. There were snowmen, complete with top hats and long scarves and with buttons adorning their fat bellies. There were smiling Father Christmas's with sacks of toys on their backs, the leads connecting them with their reindeer and sleds, falling loosely between man and beast. The Christmas trees, dotted here and there, were decorated with a dusting of fine snow and with every one the bottom of its little trunk had been carefully inserted into a bright red pot.

In the centre of the display, as it had been from as far back as any of them could remember, was the nodding Father Christmas. What kind of mechanism was in place to animate the figure, or what it was made of, they neither knew nor cared. It just stood there fat and smiling, nodding and waving at the passers by, unfazed by the look of astonishment on the faces of those observing this work of art for the first time.

"Well, what do you think of that then Sylv? I told you it was special, didn't I," said Margery. Then she paused for a few seconds before pointing to a notice pinned up at the back of the display. "Look, it says 'Toys for good girls and boys up there.' Wonder why I've not seen that before? I expect they've only just put it up there. That's it, that's why I've not noticed it before. But where are the toys I wonder?" Without allowing the others to reply, she turned and began to stamp her feet. "Not to worry, lets get going, shall we? My feet are freezing and Dorothy is half expecting us."

The other girls turned reluctantly away from the window with its captivating display and they all hurried up the road, chatting in between blowing on their mitten covered hands. As they walked passed the Queens head, the sign creaked on its hinges and they instinctively moved away from it, increasing their pace as they entered Brede Lane. By the time they reached East View Terrace, their blood was circulating around their bodies and had even reached and warmed their hands and feet. The only person they could see from the end of the terrace was Henry Maplesden. He was leaning on his gate, puffing away on his old clay pipe, oblivious to them or the cold east wind. As they passed by and said 'hello,' he just grunted without moving a muscle and they hurried on down to the end to see if Dorothy Simmons and her sister Enid, who lived at Number 29 were at home. Before they reached the house however, they spotted the two girls in the field at the back of the houses and they walked over to the swings on which they were sitting.

"Aren't you cold, sitting there like that?" asked Hilary. As though in answer to her question the two girls began to propel themselves backwards and forwards, swinging higher and higher until the chains holding the swing, began to buck and jink.

"That better?" asked Dorothy, bringing the swing to a sudden stop with a bit of expert footwork. "We were just waiting for you lot to get here, see. You did say you thought you might be coming round, and we hoped you'd get here early if you did. Enid feels the cold, but then she would do wouldn't she. There's not enough fat on her to keep a mouse warm." And she smiled across at her little flaxen haired sister. Rumour had it that when Enid was a baby, the nurse had tripped whilst descending the stairs and had dropped her, and as a result of this her growth had been affected. Whether this was actually true or not, Sally had no idea. Enid was dainty that was for sure, but she seemed lively and healthy enough.

While they were playing on the swings and slide, they saw Jimmie coming along the footpath from the direction of the Tithe Barn. As he walked towards them, they watched fascinated as he drew deeply on his Wills Woodbine cigarette, exhaling the smoke through his nose as well as his mouth. Then he began to cough and splutter and hurriedly withdrew a hankie from his pocket into which he blew noisily. "I don't know, me nose runs and me feet smell, I must be upside down," he said with a runny eyed grin. "Now don't you girls ever get into this smoking lark, it just ain't worth it." Then he paused to take a few more long drags on his cigarette before dropping the butt onto the ground and grinding it out with the heel of his boot. "I've just been talking to old George, in the village like, and he made me chuckle he did. It went something like this. 'Owld Tom up Kent Street way, 'e reckon 'e be avin one orv them checkens thet scraggle around thet yard o thers fer Christmas. E dent ave preper chickuns I tells im, 'yer only 'as skinny owld boilers, thet yer don't get owt from bet a bit o thin browth thet goes right thru 'e, jest loik a lazy wind. Thet's what I tells 'im.' Sorry, I can't talk like he does. He's got a right gladsome way with words, he has, but I had to laugh," said Jimmie. "He was serious an all." There was silence for a few seconds as he looked around and then he continued. "Hey, did you know that he uses a warming pan as well to warm his bed up when it's cold like this?" Well he does. Then when he gets into bed he puts the thing down onto his piddle pot. He said if he put it down onto the lino, he'd scorch the stuff, and that'd never do."

The girls chuckled as they pictured the old Boy with his particular idiosyncrasies and rare sense of humour. As they continued to chat about this and that, Sally smiled to herself, remembering the many times she and the other girls had stopped to speak to the old man. She also thought about old Tom, the butt of George's latest discourse. As he was unable to read or write, he was forced to enlist the help of a friend on the rare occasion when a letter dropped through his letter-box. When this happened, he always said, 'put your fingers in your ears when you read this. It's private and I don't want you to know what it says.' He also owned a small dog, a mongrel with a bit of spaniel in it. On the odd occasion when she and her sisters had called on him in his little cottage up Kent Street way, the dank unpleasant doggy smell that had invaded their nostrils as they entered the place had made them feel sick. He was a funny old boy, like his mates George and Fred from the village. They were garrulous old men but with a countryman's understanding of the natural world. Unfortunately, none of them had much sense of smell and seemed to eschew the act of washing or bathing. 'A right lot of old Rustics,' as dad had called them on more than one occasion.

Sally came to as Jimmie began to walk away and then she noticed that the girls seemed to be making preparations for their departure. As they stood there chatting, three dogs came bounding over to them from the direction of the fields, and by the look of them, they had been out for some time. They were caked in mud from their paws to their eyebrows and the girls shrieked and ran for what little cover was available. Jimmie, hearing the commotion turned and called the dogs over to him, scolding them for going into the brooks itself on a day like this. "Don't worry, they'll find their way home from here," he called out to them. "They do this every day."

Once Sally had made sure the dogs had gone for good, she took her hankie out of her sleeve and gave her nose a good blow. Then she tried, not altogether successfully, to rub the mud off her coat with a bit of added spittle. If the dogs had managed to get much closer to her, she'd have needed a whole packet of Rinso to rid her coat of the mud, she reckoned.

"Can I have a drink of water before we go?" Hilary asked Dorothy, and they trooped along to her house all now with the same thought in mind. Hilary was the first to reach the sink and leaned over, cup in hand, towards the tap. As she turned it on with her other hand, the water gushed into the cup and then shot out again like a fountain, covering her from waist to eyebrows in heavy spray. She shot back as though she had been shot, the shock of the cold water temporarily knocking the breath out of her. The other girls fell about laughing, all secretly thanking their lucky stars that they had not been the one to receive that unexpected shower.

"Sorry," spluttered Dorothy, not even attempting to keep a straight face. "I forgot to warn you that there's something wrong with the water supply here. We seem to have more than we want and other people in the road can only get a trickle through their taps. I expect they'll do something about it sometime."

"The sooner the better," replied Hilary, mopping her face with the hankie that Sally had passed hurriedly over to her. "We're used to waiting ages for our water to come through. I didn't expect to get nearly drowned when I turned your tap on. You aught to pin a warning notice up somewhere. Anyway, I don't think I'm thirsty anymore, I'll wait till I get home to get a drink, thank you. How about you lot?" she asked looking around her. The other girls however, declined and turned away from the sink, unwilling to take the risk of a cold shower on a day like this. "Right then, you ready?" she asked. We'll go across the field this time, shall we? As Margie said earlier on, it's a lot quicker that way."

As they hurried along the pathway and over the stile beside the Tithe Barn, they saw little Mrs Dawson coming out of Mr Phillip's shop. They watched as she paused just outside, placed her large shopping bag down on to the damp pavement, and rummaged around in her handbag. After a few seconds she clicked the twin clasps together and then pushed the bag into the crook of her arm. Then she stooped to retrieve her shopping and hurried off up the road, her little legs going nineteen to the dozen. They would have known who she was by her characteristic hop, skip and jump walk even if they had not seen her face. And the hat she was wearing, generously studded with hat pins, was one that came out every November and stayed on her head until the end of May. Sally could not imagine anyone not liking her. She had an impish grin and she had never heard her utter one word of complaint against anyone.

They continued watching until she was well past the bottom pub and on her way towards the pump and thence to her house, and then they crossed the road and began to walk towards the Waterfall, the stile and the Brooks.

CHAPTER 14

Although it was the beginning of January now, the weather was not as cold as it had been towards the end of the old year. Hilary and Sally had managed to finish making their dresses, just in time for the festive season and had worn them on Christmas day and again for Hilary's party on Boxing day. They were now sitting in a jam packed village hall with Pat and Patty, waiting for the Pantomime to begin. It was Cinderella this year.

While they waited they talked about an alternative interpretation of The Christmas Carol that Jumbo James had arranged at the School, just before the Christmas break. He decided that those taking part should stand up and just read the words from a script, rather than acting the whole thing out on a stage. This would have worked very well had not the part of Scrooge been allocated to Basil Winchester who, with his natural gift for mimicry and absurd sense of humour, had them all in stitches and rendered some children unable to read out their own lines. When this happened, he just carried on, improvising as he went, changing his accent and demeanour to suit the part. By the end of the pseudo concert, Scrooge had almost lost his voice and just managed to croak out the last few lines before taking a bow and passing his lines over to Jumbo James with a grin. The Headmaster, who had tried unsuccessfully to intervene a couple of times, just took the papers from him and patted him on the back, and after a while everything returned to normal. Except for Basil's voice that is, which took a day or two to recover.

The curtains were opening now and a hush came over the audience as the stage was exposed revealing Cinderella kneeling in front of an old fashioned fire place, brushing out the remains of an imaginary fire. A bass broom was propped up against the wall on one side and a black and white cat sat grinning or rather grimacing, on the other. Three overstuffed mice lurked to one side of the stage, half hidden by the folds of the long curtain. As she rose slowly to her feet, someone at the back of the hall called out, "she's got Minnie Mouse's shoes on."

The giggling that ensued was quickly shushed by Mrs Moon, who was standing with her sister Mrs Vallor at the side of the hall. These conscientious and hard working teachers had co produced this pantomime and having put in so many hours of rehearsals, were not about to let it be high jacked by some callow youth.

When the ugly sisters made their debut, there was buzz of low key murmurings accompanied by the occasional giggle as the actors were identified as two of the older boys from the school. As they looked out over the mass of faces, an embarrassed grin spread across their shiney, highly rouged cheeks before they tottered uncomfortably forward on their high heeled shoes and proceeded to put on very convincing performances. The wicked step mother, sounding suspiciously like Jumbo James, also seemed to find her footwear uncomfortable.

As she staggered for the second time on stage, someone sitting just behind the girls hissed, "drunk in charge of two legs, 'e is." And several people sniggered. It was when 'she' suddenly flicked open her fan however, that the girls nearly jumped out of their seats. It cracked so loudly they thought they had been shot.

Later, when the coach, magic ked up by the sparkling wand of the Fairy Godmother was revealed, it was a pram, decorated up to the nines in tinsel and ribbon, in which more than one infant had been carted to and from and around the village over the past decade or two.

There were oo's and aa's from the grown ups in the last scene when Cinderella floated around the stage in the arms of Prince Charming. Some of the younger ones amongst them however, were less impressed and there were sniggers and low key murmurings from them, albeit with an eye to the side of the stage where the two teachers watched both stage and audience with critical eyes.

At the end of the show, as the players bowed to loud applause from a satisfied audience, the ugly sisters whisked off their curly wigs and waved them high in the air to the delight of the youngsters. Even the teachers and the grown ups seemed to find this amusing and clapped as long and enthusiastically as the younger audience.

As they filed outside, Sally spotted Eileen Lawrence and her mum and they all enthused about the performances of the cast. "Do you remember when Freda had a part in one of the pantomimes? A Midsummer Nights Dream I think it was," said Eileen. "She didn't have a suitable frock did she, so she borrowed a nightdress from Mrs Griffin. It looked alright on her though and not at all out of place. They did the show in Saville's place as well as the village hall and I bet it was even better in the gardens there. We only saw it in the hall though."

Yes I remember," replied Sally. "I remember her telling us about the time Miss Yates took her to The White Rock Pavilion to see Babes in the Wood as well. She reckoned it was just like being in fairyland. She wasn't very old then, that was years ago. Miss Yates's been dead for ages and ages. She owned Caves Café, where mum used to work, you know."

They walked in a group as far as the top of Crazy Lane and before they parted, the girls arranged to meet up the following week. Sally was sorry Mr Lawrence was not with them. She had not seen him for ages now and missed the little ditties he sang. The one uppermost in her mind as she thought about it, was one that began with, 'Isn't it a pity that the loiks of 'er should put upon the loiks of 'im.' Then there was this particular habit he had of extracting his hob watch from his top pocket and examining the thing with singular concentration while holding it, chain and all, in the palm of his hand. Granpy had had one just like it, and she wondered what had happened to it since his death. He had been a funny old man, Granpy but she missed him somehow, as she also missed her great Aunt Sarah who had also died. They had lived at Wayside for more years than she could even imagine and she and her sisters had just taken them for granted. Granny Sansom was still around though so they were still able to visit Wayside from time to time.

As they walked up the field, they could see Doro and Jacky waving from the window. They had probably been on the look out for a while now, eager to hear all about the Pantomime. Perhaps after tea, they would have a game or two of snakes and ladders. Doro was beginning to get the hang of it now, though she still argued and complained when her counter landed on a snake and she had to go down the board. 'I hate snakes,' she always said and sulked until her next throw of the dice. Jacky just watched for a while until her attention was taken up with something more interesting, then she was off. She was a bit young for games like this of course.

***

The weather had changed yet again. The brief mild spell had been replaced almost over night by biting winds that seemed, even for mid January, to be excessively cold. The browns and faded greens had now assumed a lack lustre hue, and all life seemed to be shivering beneath the bleak, snow threatening sky. The winter had returned with a vengeance.

Hilary and Sally were on their way to meet Sylvia and Margery and had just walked briskly up alongside Beanford farm. Sally had managed to find a pair of rabbit skin mittens that still fitted her and her hands were warm as toast. She sent up a silent prayer of thanks for these, or more to the point to her dad for this self-sufficient ethic of his. She wished he would come up with an equivalent covering for her feet. She was still suffering from these blasted chilblains. The two girls were calling for Sylvia first, then on to Margery's house and if everything went according to plan, they would walk into Battle. Today was not a day for dawdling and the two girls walked smartly up to then through the wood, arriving at Sylvia's house in record time. Then they called for Margery and set off at a brisk pace along Marley Lane, towards the little market town.

As they passed Coronation Gardens, Sally looked instinctively for any sign of the youngsters, who during the war, had treated them as some kind of a threat and had bombarded them with all kinds of missiles, but there was no sign of any enemy ambush. As they walked they talked nineteen to the dozen, their chatter seeming in direct relation to the pace of their feet, their breath coming out in little bursts of steam which vaporized immediately into the cold air. They paused for a while to admire the shape and proportions of Battle Abbey and marvelled at the sheer age of the place. As Eddie had remarked back in the summer, it was as impressive viewed from the front as it was from the back.

Sylvia and Margery had attended the Hunt Meeting here on Boxing Day and they now enthused about the spectacle of it all. They talked about the riders in their scarlet coats and the friendly dogs that they had been allowed to stroke. And Sylvia's Grandma who had been with them, had even been offered a glass of wine. They planned to repeat the experience again next year.

Sally thought back to Boxing Day and although the thought of a Hunt Meeting was alluring with all its colour and spectacle, she did not regret having missed it. She had seen it from time to time, and yes it was exciting. But as dad had said, and she had to agree with his sentiments, chasing a little fox around the countryside did not seem quite right somehow. Anyway, she had been at Hilary's birthday party to which they had both worn their new dresses. She smiled as she thought about the games they had played. Musical chairs, always with the same Military marches played on the HMV Gramophone to accompany the games, had been so much fun. Especially when Mr Forrest, a long standing family friend, forgot to wind the thing up at regular intervals and the music deteriorated into a slow dirge. Ronald had won those games. He was even quicker, more agile than Basil was, and that was saying something. Blind mans buff had deteriorated into an undisciplined rabble, with the boys all trying to push one or other of the girls into the arms of the unfortunate person wearing the blindfold. The giggling and screaming that had accompanied this game, was stopped eventually by Mrs Elkins who thought that a quiet game of I Spy was to be recommended. This had been opposed until she threw the offer of a nice glass of lemonade into the equation. The shove ha'penny board had been put into operation once again, as a platform for the little ones to experience the sensation of riding to great heights with the aid of Mr Elkins and Mr Forrest's shaking arms, only to realise when their blindfolds had been removed that they were only a few inches off the ground.

She pricked up her ears now as she heard Sylvia talking about Christmas. "I only bent over the tree to straighten up one of the candles and one of the others caught my hair alight," she was saying. "Frightened the life out of me it did, and Spot as well. He hates the smell of burning. Dad rushed over and put it out with his bare hands and then he got a wet towel and put it round my head. It didn't do much damage thank goodness. Mum just had to trim it a bit here and there, that's all. She said it was a good job I've got plenty of hair and could afford to lose a bit."

"That's funny, our Christmas tree nearly caught on fire Christmas day," said Sally. "Freda was the only one in the front room at the time. One of the candles fell over sideways and set one of the branches alight and then she ran out screaming. Good job dad wasn't far away when it happened. He went running in there like a bat out of hell and put it out and all the other candles as well. He wouldn't let us light them again until both him and mum were in the room." She paused here, stamped her feet, then linked arms with Hilary. "I'm getting cold again now, let's get going shall we."

As they walked they talked about Carol singing. Sylvia and Margery had sung their Carols at several houses along the High Street where they seemed to know most of the inhabitants. They were very pleased with the donation of five shillings from Mrs Elphic, whose shop they were just passing. And that was not all. If this kindly lady happened to be driving through the lane in her little red van when Sylvia was on her way to school, she always stopped and gave her a lift - as did the drivers of Gregory's vans as they drove between the shop in Sedlescombe and the one in Battle. As Sylvia's mother also often timed her shopping trips to Battle to coincide with the time her daughter started school, Sally reckoned that her friend hardly ever made the journey on shank's pony. Sylvia's mother had even fixed a rack over the back mudguard with a soft cushion on it to lessen the jarring from the lumps and bumps in the lane.

The only lift Sally ever got to school was on the saddle of Margery's bike on the rare occasion when she was on her own. She did not dare risk riding on the handle bars these days. Not since her encounter with Miss Mckeen and Mrs Bentham, when their unwelcome intervention had caused her to jump off suddenly, catching the bottom of her spine on Margery's lamp holder. As she thought about it, she instinctively rubbed gingerly around the area, which still gave her a bit of pain now and again.

Hilary was talking now about their own recent Carol singing experiences when she and Sally had been joined by Amy and Patty for a musical tour of the village and Kent Street. They all knew the words of the most popular Carols and Hilary and Sally could sing passably well. Patty and Amy however, were the true songbirds and could and very often did, charm the hardest heart. The girls had received several donations of half a crown and little Mrs Edwards from Kent Street, who had invited them indoors to sing, had given them three shillings. For the most part they relied on luck and instinct to get them from place to place, rarely resorting to the use of the torch that one or other of them would be carrying. On one occasion however, when the were on their way towards Waterfall House to sing, they had been so engrossed in a discussion of their favourites wireless programmes, that they had strayed perilously close to the edge of the Brooks. It was as they were harmonising to, 'we three in Happydrome, working for the BBC. Ramsbottom and Enoch and Me,' that they suddenly noticed the dull tract of water looming in front of them and had giggled their way back on to the footpath.

She grinned when she remembered how nervous they had been as they had made their way along the driveway towards Highfields, the big house tucked away behind the old Rectory. They had failed to actually sing there, partly because they could not decide where to position themselves where their voices might penetrate into the vast interior but mostly because nerves had taken over and they had failed to pluck up the courage to do so. They had however, looked through one of the un-curtained windows where in the centre of a large circular table, stood a masterpiece in green and white glass. Fluted, trumpet shaped flowers sprouted as if by magic from its ornately decorated bowl, while pale green leaves snaked sensuously up and through the whole display. It looked exquisite in the subdued light cast by a solitary bulb. It would not have looked out of place in the palace of the Fairy Queen, Sally reckoned. Freda, Betty and Hazel had mentioned Highfield from time to time, and the Christmas parties that the lady of the house had organised for the village children many years ago. They had commented on with a kind of wry humour, the disparity between the small notebooks handed out to the poorer children, while those from more affluent families received gifts more appropriate to their status. Usually dolls for the girls and boxes of assorted soldiers for the boys. It did not detract from their enjoyment of the parties however, far from it. The large kitchen table, piled high with an assortment of sandwiches, pies, cakes and jellies, always more than made up for it. And each child received a cracker containing a small trinket and a paper hat. She came too as Hilary patted her on the arm.

"Here, guess what Sal got for Christmas then?" she said grinning as she remembered her friend's reaction to the thing. "She got a Jack in the box, and it frightened the life out of her - and Dora and Jacky as well. They screamed when it shot up in the box, grinning like a mad thing and I must say it made me jump the first time I saw it. It's got a big red mouth that looks like its been painted with blood and its body looked just like a skeleton with St Vitus Dance. She's put it away now, right at the back of one of the cupboards in the scullery, with as much stuff as she could find to pile in front of it. God help anyone who comes upon it unawares, that's what I say. You loved those pink sugar mice you got in you stocking though, didn't you," she added as an afterthought. "And I enjoyed sharing them with you."

As Sally opened her mouth to add her penny's worth, Sylvia pointed up the road, towards the entrance to the market place, where a couple of boys were playing a game of 'tin can Tommy.'

"They go to my school those two boys, and they're always getting into trouble. I expect someone will come out before long and move them away from there and serve the right," she said. "They give the monkey man a hard time when he comes to the market. He dresses his little animal up in a red coat with a fez and things and they tease the living daylights out of it. They keep creeping up on the pair of them and offering the monkey bits of food when it's sitting on his shoulder. They've got the measure of the length of chain the old bloke keeps the monkey on by now and always manage to stay just out of reach when the monkey jumps down and tries to get to them. He doesn't half get angry the bloke as you can imagine, and they've been chased out of the market a few times." Then she paused bringing the other girls to a standstill beside her while she pointed out the shop where Mr and Mrs Tickner had lived and worked until their sudden death during the war. They all fell silent for a few moments recalling other wartime tragedies before moving on again. Tills double fronted shop then caught Sally's eye. Not for nothing was it reputed to sell everything. They even sold gun powder she had been told.

"Do you mind if we go this way?" asked Margery when they reached Mount Street. "Molly Daley lives along here and her dad's got pigs, just like my dad has. It's a bit of a walk, but once you get to Virgins Lane, you're a good half way and then it's all countrified from then on. And it'll warm us up a bit. I don't know about you lot but my toes and fingers are freezing."

As they walked briskly along the lane, Sally glanced into the handful of cottage gardens scattered along the side of the roadway. The ground in these gardens, as elsewhere, looked frost hardened and unyielding, the plant life reduced to a few shrubs and hardy perennials. A poem she had once learned came suddenly into her head and she mouthed it silently into the frosty air:

> *'Under the ground in a million places, bulbs are hiding their little brown faces.*
> *Pushing out roots to hold themselves tight, working away in the long winter night.'*

As she recited the poem, she looked out over the countryside, at the vast expanse of land that opened up in the countryside every winter, once the leaves had fallen from the trees. They were naked these trees, skeletal even and she could almost feel them shivering as they waited patiently for spring to dress their branches with a fresh green garment. They were in for a bit of a wait she reckoned, she could feel it in her bones. But it would happen. She, or rather Old Mother Nature, never let them down.

The little cottage they were looking for was tucked away down a narrow track, flanked on either side by a tall straggly hedge, which was interspersed here and there by even taller ivy covered trees. The cottage itself was old with a brick foundation, and the red tiles that decorated the top half of the wall, were echoed in those, which made up its low skilling roof.

As they reached the door and Margery was about to lift the heavy black knocker, it opened suddenly and her friend stood there looking rather surprised.

She stepped aside to let them in, remarking on their bravery or foolhardiness for having made the journey here on a day like this. Her Mother had gone shopping, she told them and that was why she was in the throes of making a suet pudding. Then she walked through to the kitchen beckoning them through with her flour covered hands.

"If you hang on a sec, I'll put some milk on for a cup of Horlicks, that's if we've got any Horlicks left. If not you'll have to have cocoa. Just sit down in here somewhere then while I finish off this pud."

It was warm in the kitchen and before the girls sat down they moved instinctively towards the old black range, taking off their gloves and holding their hands over the hot plate, on which a pan of water was bubbling away in readiness to receive the rag wrapped suet pudding. Before Sally sat down, she looked through the window and out across the fields. What took her eye straight away was the scarecrow, which had been propped up at an angle, against the hedge in the nearest stubble covered field. It was still wearing an old jacket and a pair of tatty shorts, and knotted around its neck, was what had once been a multicoloured scarf but which had now faded to a dull discoloration. What gave him character and charm however, was the charcoal coloured trilby, set at a jaunty angle on his straw straggled head, and she grinned to herself.

After a while, Molly came over to the table and handed round the mugs of steaming Horlicks, which they reached out for enthusiastically, holding them in a two handed embrace and downing the liquid in little delicious sips. The mugs were decorated with nursery rhyme characters, just like the ones in which their hot Horlicks at school was served. It was delicious and Sally was reminded of an expression her mum often used, 'that'll warm the cockles of your heart.' And she smiled again.

Molly was going to be a Bridesmaid and as she sat down at the table with them, she began to propound on the occasion with great enthusiasm. Her cousin was getting married in the spring and she and two other cousins were being measured for their dresses, which her mother would be making. Getting enough of the right material had been a bit of a problem, she said until a member of the family somewhere, had managed to track down enough pink satin for all the dresses. Molly declared that this was the colour she would have chosen anyway, and that as satin was very much her favourite material, she was more than satisfied. She had no doubts about her mother's ability to make the dresses. As she said, her mum was the best dressmaker for miles around.

Then she grinned, noticing Hilary and Sally's eyes forever straying to a brightly coloured clock, which hung suspended from a nail high up on the kitchen wall. It was designed as a house with a sloping roof, with two doors taking up most of its front surface. "That's our weather clock up there," she said. "When the man comes out, it's going to rain and when the lady comes out it's going to be fine."

"What happens when it's going to snow then?" asked Sally.

"Ah, then they both stand in the doorway, shivering and rubbing their hands together," said Sylvia, quick as a flash. As they chuckled, Sally was thinking that whenever she happened to be in the company of Sylvia and Margery, it was always a laugh a minute.

As they chatted away, Sally was thinking about her own experience as a bridesmaid to Lily Linch when Lily had married Chick Fowler. It must have been two or even three years ago she reckoned, but she could remember it as though it were yesterday. The Church service had been quite a sombre affair, but the reception in the Village Hall had been anything but. Chick Fowler was a born tease if ever there was one and nobody escaped his ready wit. He was totally unselfconscious, loved an audience and had kept everyone around him in fits of laughter. She had managed to keep out of his reach thankfully, for if or when he ever managed to grab hold of her, he tickled her mercilessly and she hated it. As a present for being their Bridesmaid, she had been given a narrow, gold wire bangle, with three blue stones in the centre. When she was not wearing it, which was most of the time, it resided in the little chest of drawers, given to her by the nurses in the Buchanan Hospital all those years ago. She would keep these treasures forever and ever.

When it was time to leave, they donned their top clothes and moved reluctantly towards the front door. As Hilary opened it, a shaft of cold air whipped through and they shivered. "Rather you than me," said Molly standing well back from the open doorway. "I'll be thinking about you lot for the next hour or two. It'll take you at least that long to get home from here, I reckon. Me? Well I think I'll just stay here and keep an eye on me suet pudding like."

"Trust you to rub it in," said Margery. "We're peckish already and Hilary and Sally have got even further to go than us two have. Any way, I can tell you now, that if it's cold as this tomorrow, me and Sylv won't be going to Sunday School will we Syl, she said." Sylvia and Margery went to Battle Church Sunday School, while Hilary, Sally and most of the youngsters from BlackBrooks, still made their way up Crazy Lane to the little Chapel on the hill. Although they still missed Mrs Brockway who had retired and moved away some time ago, Mr and Mrs Smith who sometimes conducted the services in the little Chapel, more than made up for the loss of their old teacher. It was rumoured that they and their family would move into the Manse at some time in the not too distant future, and Sally for one could not wait for that to happen.

On the way home, they paused momentarily, to look once again at the Abbey, before heading off towards Marley Lane. There was now a pink tinge to the grey, snow laden sky and the wind, though not quite as strong as it had been earlier, was if anything, more biting. They could even smell the snow, and every so often an intake of breath would be followed by a sharp pain in the nostrils, making their eyes water and their noses, run. In spite of this, once they were well down Marley Lane, they linked arms and began to sing, and before long their blood was circulating right around their bodies, even down to the tips of their toes. And by the time they got to Sylvia's cottage where Margery was spending the rest of the day with her friend, their faces were glowing. As Sylvia opened the gate and stepped aside to let her friend through, she commented in a good imitation of old George, "I be farly sartin we be in fer a bita snow afer long." Then they began to make their way around to the back door.

Hilary and Sally did not linger, they were now impatient to reach the comfort and comparative warmth of home where they knew a hearty meal would be waiting for them. They chatted for a while, and chuckled as they recalled the witty interactions between Sylvia and Margery, the laughs they had shared. By the time they reached Deffy and Bill's little hut however, their chatter became more sporadic, stopping altogether by the time they approached Beanford Farm.

As they walked down the track on the last lap of their journey, Sally looked out over the fields to where, not that long ago she had watched the starlings, huge flocks of them, dipping and diving, morphing into ever more intricate and unbelievable shapes. Then she thought about the geese, skein upon skein of them, with their strange haunting cry, that she had watched flying high over the countryside recently. How birds communicated with one another she had no idea. That they did however, there was not a shadow of doubt in her mind. Since she and her mum and Hilary had talked about it, she had witnessed it time and time again. They could teach humans a thing or two about co-operation she reckoned.

***

Early the next morning, Sally awoke to an unmistakable glow lightening the darkness of the cold dawn, and moving swiftly from bed to window, she gazed out into a dazzling white silence. Nothing stirred in this winter wonderland and Sally shivered with excitement in anticipation of the day ahead.

CHAPTER 15

Sally was roused from a deep dreamless sleep by the sound of muffles voices coming from the other bedroom. Though low pitched, there was an urgency to them that made her turn from her side onto her back, straining her ears to catch a word here and there, that would give her some idea of what was happening. Pat was awake in the bed beside her, she was sure of that even though there was no word or movement from her. There was tension in the silent stillness of her sister, rather than the sound of relaxed, even breathing associated with sleep. It was freezing cold but before she pulled the covers up over her chin, she raised her head off the pillow, looked across the room and could just make out the bed in which her older sisters slept. It was now empty.

After a while, a door opened and she heard her father's voice giving some kind of instruction or message to her mum and older sisters before it clicked shut again. After a few seconds she heard the two dull thuds of the outer door being pulled to and then there was silence for a while. It was not long however, before she could hear movement and sporadic conversation coming from the next room, then one or both of her sisters went through to the kitchen. Much later, she heard the return of her father and shortly afterwards a sharp instruction to her sisters with again the two toned dull thud of the outer door being closed. She spent the rest of the night in and out of sleep, dreams and reality merging until she could not differentiate between the two.

She came to with a start the next morning. It was still dark and freezing cold, but with the familiar snow induced glow lightening up and showing the contours of the bedroom. Pat was already up and the other bed across the room was still empty. She swung her legs out of the bed, picked up the coat which had slipped from bed to floor at some time during the long night, shrugged it around her shoulders and hurried through to the kitchen. Her dad was sitting at the kitchen table with Freda, Hazel and Pat and as they looked towards her as she came through the doorway, she could tell from their red rimmed eyes, that something very serious had happened. As she joined them at the table, dad began to tell her, as gently as he knew how, about the events of the long, long night.

"Your mother had the baby during the night, a little girl but she didn't survive," he began. "Beautiful little thing she is, a perfect little baby just like you all were," and his eyes brimmed with fresh tears as he struggled to control the tremor in his voice. Sally felt a sudden, painful constriction in her throat and as her own eyes began to brim with tears, her sisters looked at her, compassion and understanding in their eyes. "She struggled so hard to survive, poor little mite but in the end she died of exposure. What a waste, such a dreadful waste of a little life," he said almost to himself, and paused before continuing. "Your mum didn't feel too good when she went to bed last night but as the baby wasn't due until mid April, according to old Hollin's, she ignored the first signs. It was obvious though after a while what was happening and I left Freda and Hazel here with your mum while I went to get the Doctor. It was a nightmare getting to the village. The roads were just sheets of ice and even the grass verges were covered in packed down, frozen snow and a devil of a job to walk on. Well you know what they're like. Old Hollins had only just got back from another call out and after listening to the symptoms, reckoned your mum would be okay until the morning. I wasn't happy I can tell you but I just wanted to get back by then and I had it in my mind that if things hadn't improved by the time I got home, I'd have to use the Tanner's phone next time. They've always told us we could. They've not been down the garage there for long but they are just as helpful as the Griffin's always were. Your mum still misses Griff, she'd probably have been able to help out if she'd still been here. Anyway, by the time I got back the baby was being born and I sent the girls down straight away down to the Tanner's to call the Doctor. He couldn't attend but he did phone the Mid-wife in Brede for assistance. Nurse Kenward, who brought most of you into the world, only lived at the top of the hill here but she's retired now of course. I'd have got her here in no time at all. As it was, it took this lady best part of four hours to get here, the lanes were so treacherous and by the time she got here, the baby had died.

Your mum is very weak and upset at the moment. She's had a dreadful time and it was touch and go for her at one time. It's so cold and I just couldn't keep her and the baby warm enough until the mid-wife got here. She's still in the bedroom with your mum, the mid-wife, by the way." As he lapsed into silence, Sally looked at his strong, work worn hands, laying palm down on the table and his now bowed head and she was struck by the gesture of weary helplessness, so unlike her Father.

There was silence around the table for a while and then Freda got to her feet, followed by Hazel and between them they began to make preparations for a fresh pot of tea. Shortly afterwards, the Mid-wife came through from the bedroom and quietly closed the door behind her as she came on into the kitchen. As Freda poured then passed her a cup of tea, she told them that their Mother was comfortable and that perhaps they would like to go in to see her now.

"I don't know how to thank you," dad began as she sank wearily down onto the nearest chair. "If you hadn't have got here when you did, Dolly wouldn't have made it, that's for certain. I couldn't keep them warm, not Dolly or the baby, that was the thing. And I didn't dare try to cut the cord or anything like that. Those bedrooms are not warm at the best of times and these past few weeks they've been freezing. And there's no way of heating them even if we could get the coal. We've had the devils own job to get enough even for the fire in the kitchen here. We've had to supplement it with what we could find in the wood up there. All we could do was cover them up as best we could. The baby, wasn't due until towards the end of April, or so the Doctor thought."

"Don't worry Mr Cotton, your wife make it now," she replied. "She's a remarkable woman that wife of yours. I'm sorry about the baby, it was already too late by the time I got here and such a perfect little girl she is too. The date was obviously wrong, no doubt about that. She's a full term baby, you can tell that by her fully formed finger-nails, amongst other things. But anyway, I'll let the Doctor know what's happened, and he'll most likely be along sometime this morning. The two little ones are still asleep by the way, but no doubt they'll be up and about any time now. I'm sure your older girls will look after them for you. You've certainly got your hands full, you and your wife, but you seem to have a healthy, supportive family that many people would envy. Including me," she added and, as she smiled at the girls, they rose from the table and began to move towards the bedroom door. "Don't forget to take your mother through a cup of tea now with lot's of sugar in it," she reminded them and they turned around automatically, Hazel setting a cup onto its saucer as Freda poured in the liquid.

As they entered the bedroom, Mum struggled to sit up and in spite of her obvious weakness, smiled at them as she took the tea from Hazel's shaking hand. She was unnaturally pale and her fine wavy hair looked limp and lifeless. After a few sips of tea, she passed the cup back to Hazel and sank back down onto the pillows again, closing her eyes for a few seconds. A moment later, she beckoned towards the cot on the far side of the bed where even from where they stood, they could see a little swaddled bundle, laying unnaturally still within its folds. As Freda, Hazel and Pat moved slowly around the bed towards it, Sally hung back, suddenly gripped by a fear that she could not explain. She moved instead towards her mother who took her hand and as she squeezed it, looked at her with such a depth of understanding within her kind blue eyes, that Sally began to cry silently. As she looked over to where her sisters stood, looking over and downward into the cot, she knew that they were also in tears.

"She's so beautiful," whispered Hazel as she drew the covering gently away from the little white face.

"She looks just like she's sleeping. I just can't bear that she's believe she's not ever going to wake up," said Freda. And for a while there was silence in the room.

"Yes she's a lovely little girl, but everything was against her," replied mum, her gaze hardly straying from the little bundle in the cot. "For a start it must have been the coldest night of this freezing cold winter. Then of course the mid-wife had to get here from Brede through all that ice and snow and it took her best part of four hours. But she got here eventually bless her and I'm so grateful for that. She's been so kind to me. If Nurse Kenward had still been around though, she'd have been here in less than half an hour. Your dad would have fetched her and got her here safely. She only lived up in New England Lane, didn't she? But she's retired, bless her and not before time. How we all miss that wonderful lady. She wasn't just a nurse and first class Mid-wife, she was a friend to us all." Mum paused here for a few seconds and withdrew her eyes from the cot. "We're calling her Ann, this little baby," she said looking at each one of the girls in turn. "That's the name you wanted as well, isn't it?" she asked, looking towards Pat who stood beside the bed, her face pale and set but who had as yet not uttered one word. "She's very special."

As they stood there, the sound of chattering and scuffling reached their ears and Dorothy and Jacky ran towards the bed, bringing normality into the room with their bright morning faces.

"Mum's not well, give her a kiss and then we'll take you through and get you some breakfast," said Freda, trying to prise their reluctant bodies from the bed on which there was a very real danger that they would make themselves too comfortable. "We'll all have shredded wheat this morning with lots of milk, shall we? That's your favourite isn't it? Then we'll have stodgy porridge tomorrow morning, because that's your next best favourite." They clung to mum for several seconds as though sensing that something was amiss, before allowing their older sister to herd them out of the room.

Sally and Pat heard later from their sisters what a nightmare it had been during the night. They had slipped and fallen several times trying to get down the field, along the icy lane and down the slope to the Griffin's house in the dark. The torch they carried only accentuated the ice-covered surface, making them feel even more nervous and insecure. Then they had had to wake the sleeping occupants, explain what was happening and it seemed to have taken forever for Mr Tanner to get through to the Doctor. Then the wait while he phoned the Mid-wife in Brede and the call back confirming that she would do her level best to attend. After that, there was the hazardous walk back home, the agonising wait for the Mid-wife to arrive, and not really knowing if she'd be able to get there at all. Worst of all they said, was trying to keep mum and the baby warm and seeing the distress of their dad, which was something they had never seen before. Freda had wanted to get into the bed to add her warmth to the baby but dad for some reason had considered it too risky. The arrival of the Mid-wife brought with it a relief that just could not be described. She summed up the situation straight away, took charge and concentrated on saving their mum, knowing that it was already too late for the baby. The two girls looked exhausted by this time but knowing that they would be unable to sleep, refused to go to bed.

Pat was the first to see the Doctor. She had taken up her position of vigil beside the kitchen window just after breakfast and as she saw him struggling along the lane towards the bottom gate, she called out to her dad. The other girls rushed to the window as dad hurriedly donned his jacket and shrugged his feet into his old boots. He was down the field and had relieved the Doctor of his big black bag before the man of medicine had even begun his ascent of the snow and ice covered field. As the two men came through the top gate, the girls jumped down from the window and Freda went out through the scullery door and opened the outer door for them. After nodding briefly to the girls, the Doctor with dad close on his heels, went through to the bedroom.

Later that day, the Rector came to see mum and dad to arrange the funeral of the baby. The arrangements took place in the bedroom so the girls were not privy to what was said. However, the cold anger of their Father as he escorted the man of God from the house, left them in no doubt about his reaction to the dictates of the Church of England.

"Original sin, what sin I ask you?" he fumed as he came back through the scullery door. "This poor little mite cannot be buried in sanctified ground because she's supposed to have something called original sin. She only breathed for an hour or two at the most, what sin could there be in such a defenceless little child. What did God say? Suffer the little children to come unto me, that's what the bible tells us God said." He paused here to take a breath and as he looked from one startled face to another, he seemed to make a conscious effort to moderate his voice before continuing. "I shouldn't be so surprised. I was aware of this insane doctrine of the Church of England, but if this is what organised religion is all about, then they can keep it. Anyway, I must go and see your mum. She's upset same as I am."

As he went through to the bedroom once again, Dorothy pressed a book into Hazel's hand. "Tell me a story," she said looking at her older sister with a puzzled expression in her large brown eyes. Hazel opened the book at random and began to recite the words in front of her in parrot fashion:

"The owl and the pussy cat went to sea, in a beautiful pea green boat.
They took some honey and plenty of money, wrapped up in a five pond note.
The owl looked up to the stars above and sang to a small guitar.
O lovely pussy, o pussy my love.
What a beautiful pussy you are, you are. What a beautiful pussy you are.

Pussy said to the owl, you elegant fowl, how charming sweetly you sing.
O let us get married, too long we have tarried, but what shall we do for a ring?
They sailed away for a year and a day, to the land where the bong tree grows.
And there in a wood a piggy-wig stood, with a ring at the end of his nose, his nose.
With a ring at the end of his nose.

Dear pig, are you willing to sell for a shilling, your ring? Said the piggy, I will.

So they took it away and were married next day, by the turkey who lives on the hill.
They dined on mince and slices of quince, which they ate with a runcible spoon.
And hand in hand, on the edge of the sand, they danced by the light of the moon, the moon.
They danced by the light of the moon."

For the little ones, the telling of a story or a rhyme or two, was enough to transport their minds away from this bewildering situation in which they found themselves. For the other girls, the day was spent mechanically going about the business of performing chores, just like any other day. Except it wasn't just any other day.

Mum, still pale and tired looking was nevertheless up and about again and taking charge within a few days and life got back to a kind of normality. She had been quite badly affected by a remark made by the Doctor while he was examining the baby. 'Well, it's only another girl,' he had said, and mum had cried then. For a while Granny Sansom came through from Wayside as often as the weather and availability of buses permitted, and Little Mrs Edwards and Mrs Lawrence came in from time to time to lend a hand. Their help was invaluable.

For Freda and Hazel, it was work as usual. Freda now worked in Battle and the journey too and from there was a rather hazardous one as she struggled through the snow gripped lane. For the first three months after leaving school she had taken a temporary job, working for Mr Gay at Horseman's farm, hoeing through his long fields of fruit bushes. Although the work was hard and gave her as she said woefully, muscles on her muscles, it was well paid and the farmer always made sure she took regular breaks. After the three months were up, she scrubbed her nails and applied for and got a job working for Plummer Roddis in Robertson Street, Hastings. By the time she had taken her bus fares of 7/6 out of the 10/- she earned per week however, she was left with precious little cash with which to pay her way. She then applied for and got a job away from home as Nanny to three children and although happy with the arrangement, was homesick.

Within a few months she was home again with the proviso that if she were to change her mind, the family would be happy to reinstate her. Ever vigilant, she spotted an advertisement in a local paper for a job as a shop assistant at the International Stores in Battle, for which she applied and was accepted. She was quite happy to change her smart suit for a white overall if it meant being able to cycle to work, thus saving money on expensive bus fares. Most days she even cycled home for her dinner, but not at the moment with the weather conditions the way they were. Every Friday dinner time however, she took herself off to Gregory's little tea rooms in the High Street and indulged herself in a generous helping of beans on toast, which cost her 10d.

Hazel walked to the village every day through the stubbornly persistent covering of snow and ice, catching hold of the hedges every now and again for support. She had started her working life with Mr and Mrs Phillips, working not in the shop but in the house. She was quite happy there until the offer of an office job came her way. Mr Thomas the builder, offered her a job in his office in Bohemia Road Hastings, with the chance of transferring to the office in Sedlescombe at the earliest opportunity. She accepted and after a few months of commuting to Hastings on a daily basis, found herself working within walking distance of home.

The younger girls quickly adapted to the slippery, ice and snow covered surfaces of the paths and roadways on their way to and from school. They were still occasionally caught off guard by a particularly hazardous tract of solid ice, and would quickly grab hold of one another, grabbing any part of the anatomy within reach and giggle their way to a standstill. Now and again however, their concentration would be lost in a gaggle of excited chatter and in spite of their newly acquired skills, would slip and in a split second, find themselves in an untidy heap on the ground.

Once having developed the skill of keeping their balance on ice and snow to their satisfaction though, they inevitably took the next step and created their own slippery surfaces. Any slope commanded their undivided and expert attention but an area near the top of Chapel Hill soon became their favourite ski slope. Not just the girls but soon other youngsters in the area joined in the fun, following each another down its slippery surface until they created an elongated stretch of icy insecurity that gleamed like polished glass. Their fun was brought to a temporary halt by the Police Constable who lived in one of the houses just above the Chapel. Unfortunately he did not share their enthusiasm for ice and snow and his skill in dealing with these hazards turned out to be abysmal.

As he walked over to chastise them for their lack of consideration for other road users, he suddenly lost his footing and slid down the whole length of their precious slide on his back. His efforts to get up in a dignified manner, proved unsuccessful and as he scrabbled around, some of the youngsters went quickly to his aid. Sally however, moved in the other direction, trying unsuccessfully to contain her convulsive laughter. The look on his face as the ground came up towards him and the way he had bounced a couple of times before settling into free fall, was an image that had imprinted itself once and for all upon her vivid, warped imagination. As she turned around again to face the inevitable reprimand, she was overcome by a fresh attack of the giggles. His red face had upon it that embarrassed look of someone who had just made a rude sound in Church. She wiped the back of her mitten covered hands across her eyes and mouth to cover her mirth.

One morning after a slight thaw during the night was followed immediately by yet another serious drop in temperature, walking up Crazy Lane was like walking through fairyland. Icicles, some as long as a man's arm hung from the trees on either side of the narrow lane, bowing and distorting their skeletal branches into weird and wonderful shapes. The little cottages dotted here and there along the lane were also similarly decorated, their eaves festooned with strange icy stalactites. It was graveyard still, and the only sound to break the silence, was the creak of protesting branches. It was just like being in some kind of a time warp.

A pathway had been made up through the village street and the girls walked in single file along its length, avoiding the banks of snow piled high on either side.

The fire in the infants classroom was well alight, the wood and glowing coals hissing and sending showers of sparks and puffs of smoke up the wide chimney, when the children arrived for school that day. As soon as they had removed their outer garments, they were ushered through to where Mrs Baker and Mrs Bishop had set out trays laden with beakers, full to the brim with hot Horlicks. The children moved instinctively towards the guard protected fire, both hands clasped firmly around the steaming mugs and there were low murmurings of appreciation as they sipped the milky drink.

All too soon it was time for lessons to begin and they made their way reluctantly towards their own classrooms. The old black boiler was positioned at the side of the Headmasters classroom where, separated by just a narrow gangway, both Hilary and Sally now took their lessons. As they entered, he was dipping his fountain pen into the inkwell, sucking up enough of the blue, black liquid to last for the whole day's markings. He always used a Waterman's pen of which he seemed inordinately proud, and the box that housed the thing, was always carefully stowed away in the top drawer of his desk. Mrs Moon also used a fountain pen, but hers was marbled, brown and green not black like the Headmasters and its box had long since disappeared.

"First lesson today's arithmetic as you know, but I've got a bit of Shakespeare here that's kind of appropriate to today's weather. Any volunteers to read it out aloud to the rest of the class?" Asked Jumbo James looking up and around for a willing volunteer. Several hands shot up among them Anne Pope's and she was chosen to read the passage. She walked to the front of the class, picked up the book that the headmaster held out to her and began to read:

"When icicles hand from the wall, and Dick the shepherd blows his nail.
And Tom bears logs into the hall, and milk comes frozen home in pail.
When blood is nipped, and ways be foul, then nightly sings the staring owl,
To-whit! To-whit! To-who! – a merry note.
While greasy Joan doth keel the pot.

When all around the wind doth blow, and coughing drowns the Parson's saw.

And birds sit brooding in the snow, and Marion's nose looks red and raw.
When roasted crabs hiss in the bowl, then nightly sings the staring owl,
To-whit! To-whit! To-who! – a merry note.
While greasy Joan doth keel the pot."

"Well done," he said as Anne sat back down again. "While you're at break, I'll write this poem down on one side of the blackboard and before we start the next lesson, you can write it down in your exercise books and learn it in time for the next English lesson. Now if you'd all get your arithmetic books out, well get on straight away with the lesson we're supposed to be doing." As he moved towards the blackboard and picked up the piece of chalk from its ledge, there was a creaking of hinges as every desktop was raised in unison.

As Sally moved all her paraphernalia on to the desktop, she looked at her gold coloured pen nib that had started to cross over at the ends and frowned. She had used this one for ages now and it was her all time favourite. With it she had been able to get the thin upward strokes and the much thicker downward ones that she had been taught were the hallmark of good writing. She feared the nib would soon be unusable. She would have to search carefully through the box of assorted nibs in the store cupboard and try to replicate this little bit of metal that was worth its weight in gold.

The first lesson of the afternoon was spelling, and the columns of words chalked onto the blackboard, had to be copied into their exercise books to be learned by heart. As Sally struggled with her pen, a couple of the boys started snickering and after a while, passed a piece of paper over to her on which was written one of the words from the blackboard, 'attitude' followed by 'is 'at 'e chewed. At the time she did not find it the least bit funny but just passed it on down the line. Later however, when she thought about it without the stress of trying to protect a much loved pen nib, she giggled. Trust the boys to come up with something like this. There was definitely something wrong with their minds, she reckoned.

When it was time to go home, the youngsters shivered back into their outer garments, making sure their scarves and headgear left no gaps for the freezing cold air to sneak in. Then they made their way to the front of the school, through the heavy oak door and dispersed in little groups. Sally and Pat positioned themselves one on each side of Hilary, clinging tightly on to her arms, until they reached the dug out section of the road. Then it was single file once again with Hilary in the lead followed closely by Pat and Sally, always at the ready to grab the nearest bit of anatomy of the one in front, if or when the going became especially hazardous. Basil, Ronald and a few other boys ran on ahead, seemingly unfazed by the slippery surfaces. The girls continued to walk with a well practiced gait, knees bent and with their upper bodies angled ever so slightly forward.

As they passed Mrs Brooman's cottage, the old lady was nowhere to be seen. Her bass broom however, was leaning up against the wall at the side of her cottage, its whiskers frozen solidly into the ice and snow. It was going nowhere for the time being, that was for sure. Just like its owner most likely. The only grown ups they saw as they walked through he village was Miss Lucas, who was coming out of the Gregory's shop, walking stick in one hand and a big shopping bag in the other. She looked more like a worried prune than ever, Sally thought to herself. So engaged was she with negotiating a safe passage way for herself and her shopping, she seemed not to have noticed the girls as they passed by. The other was Wig at River Bridge Cottages who, having scattered sand onto his pathway, was now trying unsuccessfully to brush it and the accumulation of snow and ice away with an old broom. He looked just like a cow with a musket - in a woolly hat.

As they passed cow shit corner, Sally looked briefly towards the corner of the field, wondering if the sweet smelling violets would survive this prolonged spell of arctic weather. She hoped so. She really hoped so. As soon as spring got here, she would search them out and pick two bunches, one for mum and another for dad. They had both looked so tired lately. She would like to pick some to put on the baby's grave except she had no idea where it was, and was too afraid of upsetting her parents to mention it.

In spite of a bit of wintry sun that forced its way momentarily through the grey cloud as they walked up Chapel Hill, there was still a pinching rawness to the air. They did not dally, but moved along at as brisk a pace as the ice beneath their feet allowed. By the time they reached Patty's bungalow the sun had long gone, the sky gun metal grey and just as snow threatening as ever.

Early the next morning, Sally looked through the bedroom window and out into a whirling mass of whiteness. The dense grey cloud of the day before was fulfilling its promise of more snow - with a vengeance. She rushed through to the kitchen where her older sisters were already sitting at the table eating breakfast. She had forgotten momentarily that although it was Saturday and a day off for her, they still had to get through to the village for work. She reckoned the snow would be above their wellies before they were even half way down the field. The realisation that she and Pat would also have to negotiate the field on their way to Battle Barn to fetch the milk did not faze her one bit. She was filled with a feeling of sheer excitement, exhilarated at the thought of battling her way through the drifting snow. They would have to wait until Hilary got here, that was for sure. She would be very upset if they went without her.

Hilary did accompany them to the farm and so thankfully did their dad. He had already been out to feed the chickens in their coops, but the tracks he had made just that short while ago, were rapidly being masked by fresh snow. Now, head down against the whirling snowflakes and with his trouser legs tucked securely into his long, black wellies, he forced a pathway through the thick snow for the girls to follow. The snow in the field was deep enough but around the hedges and particularly by the stile it had accumulated in huge drifts and was only gotten through with great difficulty. It was in these places that he used the short handled spade that he had brought along with him, holding it with both hands as he shovelled a narrow pathway through the piled up snow. Sally had no idea why he had brought a rolled up hessian sack along with him, passed hastily over to her when he had started digging. No doubt she would find out sooner or later.

They stopped in the farmhouse for a chat and a warm up before setting off for home again, supplied with extra milk to see them over the weekend. They walked gingerly back down the farm track and when they reached the top of the field, dad leaned carefully over the stile and placed the sack over the thick snow. Then they passed the churns of milk to and fro as they negotiated the tricky manoeuvre of crossing the snow smothered stile and down onto the sack subdued drifts that had accumulated on the other side.

By the time they got home, the tops of the girls legs were mottled, the whole area covered in blotchy, red and blue patches. In spite of the slight discomfort however, they had thoroughly enjoyed the experience. Their bright red and shiny faces bore witness to this. They had a sneaking feeling that dad had not found the experience altogether unpleasing either. 'A bit of a challenge,' was the way he summed it up.

As they came through the door, mum was at the sink in the scullery rubbing a few bits of washing through using a bar of sunlight soap. After quickly rinsing then wringing them out with a well practised twist of her wrists, she placed them on the draining board, wiped her hands on her pinny then carried them through to the kitchen. As she hung them over the line above the fireplace to dry, she moved a saucepan of milk from the side of the stove onto the hot plate before gathering together the beakers that would contain their cocoa.

"It'll have to be half and half milk and water I'm afraid," she said stirring the cocoa to a thick paste with a drop of hot water. "We'd best go easy on the milk We don't know how long we'll have to make it last, not with the weather the way it is. I'm doing liver and bacon for dinner by the way, and you can thank your dad for picking the sprouts to go with it. He got all the vegetables sorted out yesterday, he did. Just as well, he wouldn't have got near them today. And yes that is a suet pudding," she added noticing Sally glance towards a large saucepan simmering away on the stove. "It's a plain one so you can have butter and brown sugar with it. Satisfied?" she asked smiling around at the girls. Sally was even more grateful for her mum's smile than she was at the thought of her favourite pudding, and that was saying something. Her mum had been looking so pale and weary lately.

After dinner, the older girls cleared a space on the kitchen table and sat for a while, mending the holes in the heels of their thick socks. Sally had never been able to get the hang of using one of those new fangled wooden mushroom things that had been designed for this purpose, finding that cupping her left hand beneath the hole and then weaving it away with her right hand, was the easier option. Now and again Dorothy or Jacky would suddenly get up from the table and rush to the window to check the fall and density of the snow. The weather reports that followed, though met with oo's and aa's, were irrelevant. They could all see the snow as it dipped and eddied across the window-panes, perfectly well from where they were sitting.

After a while however, the little ones grew tired of their forays to and from the window and became restless. They ran around the room then dived beneath the table, alternately swinging on the rails and grabbing their sister's legs and giggling when they were scolded by one or other of the girls. At last Pat had had enough and, jumping off her chair scrabbled beneath the table and pulled Jacky out by her legs.

"You're a fidgety breeches that's what you are," she scolded the pair of them when Dorothy had joined her little sister. "Go on then, go and get the snakes and ladders out and we'll have a game of that. That'll keep you out of mischief. And don't moan when you get on a snakes head and have to come all the way down again, like you usually do, that's all."

Dorothy shot across the room and flung open the doors of sideboard. There was a crash as all the games and books and general clutter came cascading out all over the floor, and she shot backwards as though she had been shot.

"For goodness sake, can't you be more careful," said Sally crossly, scraping her chair back and moving swiftly towards the scene of devastation. "You know what that cupboard's like, it's always got too much stuff in it. People keep poking more and more in there and this is what happens when you just open the door like that," she added forgetting that she was probably responsible for most of it. Then she paused as her hand came in contact with a paper bag, which she opened. Then she began to rummage around in the mess of brass curtain rings and small balls of brightly coloured wool contained within. "Wow, I'd forgotten all about this," she said standing up and moving back towards the table, ignoring the rest of the clutter on the floor. "Look here's one I've nearly finished. I started this one ages ago." And she held up a ring, neatly blanket stitched around its periphery and with the beginnings of a pattern in its centre. "I've just got to finish this one and make it into a brooch then mum can wear it"

"How about giving a hand with tidying up first, then we can all have a go," said Hilary from her crouched position beside the sideboard. "It's a good job we tied up some of these boxes, else all the counters and dice and things would have gone all over the place and got lost. Mind you there's some odd bits and pieces here that have escaped from somewhere," she added, now on her hands and knees and scrabbling around the floor and under the table. "It'll take ages to sort all this lot out properly."

"Where's the snakes and ladders box. We want a game of snakes and ladders, don't we Jack," said Dorothy in a small voice. "It wasn't my fault they came out like that all over the place. I only opened the door."

"It's alright Doro, it wasn't your fault. Don't worry, me and Pat'll give you a game of snakes and ladders, but we've got to get this lot back in the cupboard first," said Hilary. "Here you go then, here's what you want," she said a few moments later, as she passed up an oblong box into Dorothy's eager hands. Though tatty around its edges, it was still colourful, its lid covered with pictures of snakes and ladders superimposed on a gaudy background. The mesmeric eyes of the snakes seemed to leap out of the picture as they twined their elongated bodies sinuously around and in and out of the ladders. Dorothy beamed as she took the box from Hilary's hand. Then she placed it on the kitchen table, opened out the folded card, which was inscribed with a replica of the picture on its lid, sorted out the counters and began to shake the dice around in its bakelite tube.

Later, when dad came down the stairs from the attic, the girls looked up from their sedentary activities and watched as he blew a bit of warm breath through his frozen hands.

"It's no good Doll, it's too cold to work up there," he said. "I've managed to cut out the leather for a couple more bags and I've stitched some lengths of piping up already. I just tried to get some oil into the machine, but it's thickened up with this cold and I've had to leave it to soak in for a bit. Dad's handbags were much sought after and several women in the village and surrounding area sported one. Although he stuck to a few basic pattern designs, there was always a slight variation in the finished product, a bit of personalisation as he called it. He used coloured leather, like green and red as well as the usual brown, and the former were by far the more popular.

"Any chance of a cup of tea?" he asked looking expectantly towards the kettle. Mum however, had anticipated his request and the boiling water had already been added to the tea leaves in the now cosy covered tea pot. "What's the time then? It must be getting on a bit," he asked. As there was no immediate response to his question, he muttered to himself, "about now, getting on for presently I suppose," and moved over to the old kitchen range for a bit of immediate warmth. As he took the cup and saucer with its steaming liquid from mum's hand, he thanked her then moved away from the fireplace towards his favourite chair and sat down, indulging in a rare bit of relaxation.

"I've got some dripping in the larder with a nice bit of jelly underneath, and I've got some marmite as well," said mum. "If we get that long fork out of the front room, we should be able to toast some bread to go with it. Best leave that to me though, or your dad. It's a bit tricky doing it on this fire in the kitchen here. If you don't fix and hold it right, it'll fall down into the fire and you'll never see it again. I hope this weather eases up a bit before long," she added looking anxiously towards the window. "We're getting seriously low on coal and there's no way we can get any more wood with the weather this bad, not even with Mr Budgen's old cart horses we wouldn't be able to. It can't go on for much longer surely."

"I wouldn't count on it," replied dad getting out of his chair and moving over to the window. "The sky's still full of it. I did manage to get a couple more buckets of coal into the copper-house before it got this bad, but you're right, there's precious little out there in the hopper. I know I've always gone on about needing a cold spell to kill off germs and pests and things, but this is ridiculous. It's the little old birds and mammals I feel sorry for. They don't stand a chance in a prolonged spell of freezing cold weather like this. Not with all this snow they don't." As he turned back into the room again, he started to rub his ear. "I don't know, I'm deaf in one ear and can't hear out of the other. It'll be wax I reckon, like it was with you Sally," he said looking over to where she was sitting, busily stitching a rose into the centre of her curtain ring with knicker pink wool.

"I wouldn't go to the Doctors if I were you," she replied. "Get mum to put a bit of olive oil in your ears and then when the wax's softened, you can hoik it out carefully with a hair grip."

How well she remembered her trip to the Doctor's to have her ears syringed and how noisy and uncomfortable the procedure had been. Most of all she remembered the Doctors reaction when she had asked him how much it would cost. In a very loud, cross voice, which could have been heard beyond the waiting room and down through the village she would not be surprised, he said, 'why, are you paying?' When she had shaken her head, feeling very uncomfortable, he had replied, 'seven and six.' She had shot out of the surgery as fast as she could and moved even more quickly through the waiting room where she could sense the eyes of the ailing villager's following her. Her thoughts however, soon returned to the toast and dripping for tea and her mouth began to water in anticipation. The thick slices of bread would be toasted crisp and crunchy on the outside and soft in the middle. Then they would be spread liberally with a mixture of the fat and meaty substances and topped with a thin layer of marmite. She could not wait.

***

"Mum, we're going over the Brooks," announced Sally a few days later as she burst through the door from school. "It's still all iced up over there and we want to make some slides and things. Lots of kids are going over there. We've got to get a move on, it'll be dark in an hour or two and we've got to call for Hilary, and Basil and Patty. Don't worry, we'll be careful," she added anticipating her mum's usual pronouncement. "Where's my other wellie?" She asked scrabbling noisily through the pile of footwear in the cupboard. "Ah, here it is and here's yours Pat," she added passing over the pair that she herself had been the owner of not that long ago.

Pat and Sally could see the other youngsters waiting for them by Paygate corner as they hurried down the short path towards the top gate and into the field. As Sally looked around, she was struck afresh by the vast expanse of whiteness that went on for as far as the eye could see. It was interspersed here and there with petrified trees and in the distance, the isolated houses stood dwarfed and metamorphosed into an indifferent shade of grey by the horizontal blending of their snow topped roofs with the surrounding whitened countryside. They joined the waiting group at Paygate corner, fell into step with them and headed off towards the Brooks. As Sally climbed over the stile she spotted someone standing head and shoulders above other revellers, milling around on the ice covered meadow. "Look, there's old eyebrows over there," she announced nodding in the direction of a man referred to by the grown ups as 'Big Jim.' "I wonder why he's so wrinkled? He's got even more lines on his forehead than old Miss Lucas has and that's saying something."

"Well it's obvious isn't it, they're there for his hat to screw on to, aren't they," replied Basil quick as a flash. "When your heads as far from the ground as his is it catches the wind, see? So he's got to anchor his old hat on somehow or other or he'd be everlastingly chasing after it. They go right round his head they do, those wrinkles, just like a bloody spinning top," and he grinned. "Tell you what, just tell him his shoe lace is undone then when he bends down to tie it, knock his hat off and have a look."

"Don't be daft, he's wearing wellies," replied Sally dryly.

Most of the youngsters were playing at the far side of the flooded, ice-covered meadow, shouting and name calling as they competed with one another to perform the most spectacularly athletic slide show. They had honed the area on which they were skating into a surface that shone like polished glass. Sally watched them for a while as they crouched, knees bent, outstretched arms carefully controlling their balance. Then with their bodies zig-zagging this way and that with split second timing, they propelled themselves through the cold air following one another down the slippery surface. She could easily pick out the figure of Arthur Puxty or Pucker as they called him, from amongst them. He stood out not only because of his height but being naturally athletic, he rode the ice with ease. He possessed a talent for games of all kinds, football in particular in which he excelled. The last time she had seen him, he had been riding his bicycle down through the village with the same easy skill even though Amy had been sitting sideways on the crossbar at the time.

Tony Taylor, or Ticker as they called him, was also there, following Pucker across the ice with the same consummate skill. She could also see Len Larkin, but he was standing on the edge of the ice, calling and waving his arms around as though trying to control a herd of cows. As she watched, he suddenly moved towards the slide and propelled himself with ease across its icy surface, still name calling and agitating his arms. Standing to one side and just looking on was a youth unmistakably familiar to Sally even from this distance. "Look, there's Denis over there, she said grabbing hold of Hilary's sleeve and pointing across the ice. "Still forewarned is for armed, I suppose. At least we've seen him before he's seen us for a change."

"I wouldn't bank on that," replied Basil with a grin. "He's got eyes everywhere that one. But don't worry, he won't be no trouble. He's all mouth and trousers he is. Couldn't even knock the skin off a rice pudding, he couldn't." Sally however was not convinced. She had seen him in action a few times and was determined to stay up wind of him at all times, rice pudding not withstanding.

As they looked around, they spotted Cynthia Cummings, tall and slim weaving graceful figures of eight on the ice. She was one of a small band of intrepid skaters, brave or foolhardy enough to defy gravity and all else by putting their faith in and their weight onto, a pair of boots with impossibly thin blades. She also owned a couple of horses, and was as confident and competent around them as she was around this ice covered pond. These skaters were surrounded by an admiring group of mostly older spectators, and a cheer went up as Cynthia performed a particularly difficult manoeuvre.

"Well what did you make of that then," said Hilary admiringly. "I couldn't do that on roller skates let alone on those things. They're lethal they are."

"Nor me neither. Blow that for a game of soldiers," replied Sally emphatically. She had watched Hilary perform some tricky manoeuvres on her roller skates from time to time and had always envied her determination and perseverance to succeed with the death defying things. She was terrified of them and each time she had been persuaded, against her better judgement to don the hideous things, she had been petrified, unable to move unless held firmly on either side by strong hands. If you could imagine anything more lethal than roller skates to trust your very life with, then it had to be those things with the long, thin blades, which Cynthia seemed to be floating gracefully around on with the greatest of ease. It defied all the laws of gravity and common sense, she reckoned.

As she dragged her eyes away from this most spectacular and daring of spectator sports, she spotted old Mr Playford, spats and all, talking to Bunny Finch. He, Mr Playford worked at Hart's Green farm on a casual basis, working in the fields and orchards or doing maintenance work, according to the seasons. On Sunday's however, he donned his barbers hat and plied his trade in a small wooden building alongside the village green. He specialised in the short back and sides style and when he came to the finishing touches, he always held the head of his victim firmly with one splayed fingered hand while with the other, he clipped swiftly and expertly up the backs of their necks with his old, squeaky hair clippers. Now again someone would wince as a hair or two, having escaped the blade would be pulled painfully out of its socket as it got stuck at the base of the instrument. How well Sally understood their discomfort. She wondered if he were related to Bangy Smith whose nephews, famous or infamous for their expertise in hunting with their old ferrets, shared the same surname. They were always referred to as the Playford boys even though they were grown men and well known for their hunting and handling of their old ferrets. As Playford was a relatively uncommon surname, it was a distinct possibility she reckoned.

As they passed by, she hung back ever so slightly when she heard him refer to the Thames and the number of people who had thronged its ice covered waters in past freezing cold winters, remembering that her Granddad had witnessed one of these events when he had been quite a young man. He was holding his arms out, as he tried to describe the scale and magnitude of the event and looked for all the world like an angler who had caught a fish, 'this big.' Evidently, alongside the innumerable bodies gathered together on the ice, had been shops and stalls selling anything from hot chestnuts and baked potatoes to muffs and mittens. She tried to imagine how thick the ice must have been to bear the weight of the people and all those transient structures and shuddered when she considered the dire consequences had there been a miscalculation on the strength of the stuff. It did not bear thinking about. She also hoped that there had been no miscalculation about the thickness of the ice on which she was about to step. At least the water across the Brooks here, though freezing cold, was nothing like as deep as the river Thames would have been.

They had spotted Willie and Roy a while ago and now made their way towards them. They were with a separate group of youngsters, whose slide though not as long and wide as the one fashioned by the older boys, was just as highly polished and mean looking. Dorothy Simmons was with them, speeding across the ice with her scarf streaming out behind her, showing not the slightest sign of fear or trepidation. She seemed confident in most things, and most especially when it came to the game of stool ball, remembered Sally ruefully. When sides were chosen for this game, she always hoped and prayed and kept her fingers crossed that she would be with Dorothy's team thus avoiding the ordeal of having to face that girls' fearsome bowling. Thankfully, she was mostly lucky on this score. She remembered however, only too well the times she had stood quaking at the wicket, waiting fearfully for the long run up, the backward thrust of that powerful arm before the hard ball was released with a speed and accuracy that even David would have been proud of. She was not the only one by any means to have suffered the indignity of leaving the pitch without scoring off Dorothy's bowling. She had seen many a girl leave the field - with a duck, and Anne Pope who was now sliding along with the rest of the youngsters, was one of them. A few girls however, seemed to have got her measure and used the speed of her delivery to propel the ball into the open field, and make a decent score.

The next hour or two passed by in a flash. There was a lot of slipping and sliding, ducking and diving and shouting as a well aimed snow ball found its mark. Usually around the neck area when a small area between scarf and collar became exposed. After a while, people started to stamp their feet and flap their arms about as the cold began to penetrate their thick clothing, shivering their flesh. Eventually they to started to drift away in two's and three's.

As they walked back around the ice, they passed Mr Pope, Anne's dad who was standing beside an elderly man. He was leaning over and listening intently to what the old man was saying She smiled to herself as she caught part of the conversation.

"Nature she be obliging, she be. She gives yer snow'n ice thicker'n a grewl 'o pottage, what kills orf them germs, en all the while she be busy working away to git things aready fer the Spring. Jobbery ol' biddy she be." Sally would liked to have stayed around to hear more of the conversation, especially Mr Pope's response to the old man's observations. The others however, were moving off towards the stile and she hurried to catch up with them, conscious of the fact that she was just too nosey for her own good. As she caught up and fell into step with them, she took Pat's arm and joined in the rhyme they were reciting over and over again, parrot fashion and began to march in time with the absurd jingle.

'To market to market to buy a fat pig, home again home again jiggerty jig. To market to market to buy a fat hog, home again home again jiggerty jog."

"Slow down, there's old three miles to the pint up ahead," said Basil suddenly, pointing towards Paygate corner. "If he sees us, we'll never get away from him and I don't fancy hanging about in this weather. He's come from the Coach and Horses I bet, and he's still got to walk all the way up through Kent Street. Mr Pollard says he only lets him have three pints of beer at a time these days, reckons that's enough to get him home even if he does lose his way and goes via Hastings. Nah, he didn't really say that. I made that one up," he added with a grin. "He's a funny old bloke old three miles, but there's not much harm in him me mum says, except he's got such a big gob on him. Still looks like we're in luck, he's already passed Lavender Cottage and he hasn't looked back once."

As they came through the scullery door, they saw mum and Granny Cotton sitting at the kitchen table with a pile of odd socks stacked up in front of them. As Sally looked over her mum's shoulder, she noted with satisfaction and a sense of pride that her mum used the same method with this chore as she did. Her left hand was inside the sock, cupping the hole while she wove a neat miniature basket weave repair in the heel of one of dad's old socks with her very capable right hand. That it was from mum as well as Betty that she had learned this chore, and not the other way round, did not for one moment occur to her. A stitch in time saves nine however, was the saying that shot quickly through her mind.

As Sally walked up to the table, she noticed the small bottle containing Granny's smelling salts standing to one side of the pile of mending, and she picked it up absentmindedly and read the label. 'A little whiff relieves that faintness,' was the instruction written in thick bold capitals on the front of the bottle. As she turned it round, she could just about make out a few words on the back written in tiny print. Most of these however, had been rendered indecipherable by constant handling. Even though Granny seldom actually used the stuff, she often picked the bottle up and cradled it in her hands as though the mere feel of the thing gave her a measure of comfort. Sally had bought the stuff for her ages ago, from a little shop in Battle. She remembered also, that it was in this shop that Pat had pointed out a notice, which stated, 'Bottes of Ice Cremola Foam Drinks sold here.' And she and Hilary had chuckled when she had added with a straight face, 'look no L. It must be Christmas.

Sally snapped out of her reverie at the mention of toast, a rare treat and she suddenly realised how hungry she was. "I've cut the bread nice and thick and I've found that long handled toasting fork at last. It'd fallen down behind the dresser in the scullery," said mum. "The short one is alright for the front room fire, but we'll need this longer one for the fire in here. I'll do it," she added hastily as both Hilary and Sally moved towards the pile of bread. "Don't want any accidents do we. Not with you two or the toast. It comes off the fork if you're not really careful and you can so easy to burn yourself on the side of the range if you don't watch out. Now what do you want on yours then Sally? She asked a few minutes later as she picked up a plate full of nicely toasted bread from the hearth. "As if I need to ask. It'll be dripping with a nice bit of jelly, same as always. And the same for the rest of you I expect. Blow, I've left it in the scullery," she added looking around her. "Go and get it for me will you please Sally, before this toast gets cold."

As mum began to ladle out the contents of the basin, with just the right balance of fat versus jelly, Sally's mouth began to water. As she sank her teeth through the crisp outer layer, dripping already melting on its surface, then down into the soft centre, she sighed with contentment. Mum grinned as, with her mouth full, she mumbled. "This is the best thing I've ever tasted in all my life."

While they were laying in bed that night, Pat told Hilary and Sally that when she had asked dad if he would take her to the church and show her the burial site of the baby, he had taken her the very next day. He had shown her the tiny grave very close to the stile over looking the footpath leading from the church to Balcombe Green, where their little sister had been buried. The same footpath they had used so many times in the past, especially when they were making their way home after having searched out the best chestnuts in the churchyard. Sally found it very difficult to analyse her feelings about the resting place of her little sister. Unsanctified ground it may be she thought to herself, yet the birds sang as sweetly here and the wild flowers and grasses that decorated the pathway were echoed in and around the old, angled, neglected grave stones that slumbered within the churchyard itself. Also, alongside the old stile and very near to the little grave, a Rowan tree stood head and shoulders above the other bushes in the hedgerow. The tree of life so called, and was symbolic in a way she could feel but did not fully understand. It was as tranquil and blessed a resting place as any within the so called sanctified ground. The sudden lump in her throat however, prevented her from replying and she was grateful to Hilary for her immediate and sympathetic response, her natural ability to empathise with the grief of others.

CHAPTER 16

A few weeks later, the cold northeast wind that had held the countryside in its grip forever it seemed, gave way quite suddenly to a warm westerly, which carried the winter away. Catkins soon decorated the hedgerows with their elongated fruits and the goat willow tree, not to be outdone, soon revealed its presence in a pale yellow halo of pussy willow. Down in the lane, wild flowers, celandine, buttercup, dandelion and a little pink flower that grew in abundance down there but nowhere else roundabouts as far as Sally knew, were turning their little faces up to the warm sunshine. And the silverweed was already creeping furtively across the lane, its edible roots lurking just below the surface. Sally also knew that up in the big wood the ground would be carpeted in a sea of wood anemone's their green mantled white flowers, nodding gently in the light breeze. The rise in temperature after the unusually cold winter had awoken Mother Nature from her slumber. The cycle of life was once again and thankfully, under her control.

"I'm going to need a hand emptying out the soil in the greenhouse and putting some fresh stuff in there," said Dad as he came through the scullery door and into the kitchen. "It's been such a long cold winter, I've not had chance to do the job myself until now. I don't normally need to do it every year but there were a couple of ant's nests in there last year and they're a devil of a job to get rid of. They always seem to get in and around the roots of the tomato plants, and they play havoc with them they do. I'll spread that old soil over the garden and if there's any grubs and things in it, my little old friend the robin will soon winkle them out. Alf and Fred gave me a hand with it last year, had it done in no time they did, but I can't leave it till they come down again more's the pity. Anyway, I'll put the wheelbarrow and the spade just outside, and when you've filled the barrow, I'll come along and empty it on the garden. It won't take long."

Apart from the tinkle of spoons on china, there was silence from the girls as they sat at the table munching away on their shredded wheat. Sally had never done the job before, but remembered how the older girls had grumbled when having to help with this particular task. It had always looked too much like hard work for her to volunteer her services. She had always stayed well away from that area until the work was well and truly done.

"Cat got your tongue then?" he asked as his gaze went from one to the other.

"Well, I'm working this morning and so's Hazel," replied Freda, rising from the table, dish in hand and with a satisfied edge to her voice. "And I reckon we've done our share of that job even if we never do it again. It's about time somebody else took a turn. It's blooming hard work"

"Sally and I'll do it," volunteered Hilary ignoring Sally's frown. "I'm used to using a spade, I use one all the time on my garden. I'll make a start on it now. You can come out when you're ready," she added patting Sally on the shoulder as she rose from the table. "Good job it's a spade and not a fork we'll be using," she said reminding Sally of the time she had driven a garden fork through her wellie and into her foot. She still bore the scar, probably would for the rest of her life, she didn't wonder.

The worse part of the job as far as Sally was concerned were the worms that had over wintered in the soil. They were pale and desiccated looking, as though the exceptionally low temperatures had mummified them. And yet they were not dead, not quite and she shuddered and averted her eyes when they moved their sluggish, elongated bodies around as though in some kind of stupor. Horrid, horrid things, she thought to herself, and very nearly as nasty as slugs. At least these particular ones were.

On their way up to the farm to fetch the milk, they took a slight detour, curious and anxious to get a glimpse of the man who had moved a caravan into the edge of the big wood recently. There was smoke curling up and out of a tin chimney stack on the side of the caravan so they guessed that the occupant, a Mr Greenwood had already taken up residence there. They crept silently and as close up to the caravan as they dared, trying to get a glimpse of this man through the window on the side of the caravan, but could see no movement from inside. After a few moments, they decided that caution was the better part of valour, and began to retrace their footsteps. As they made their way back to the farm track, they pontificated on what he would look like and on his whereabouts. Hilary and Pat reckoned that he was probably very old, like Deffy and Bill and that he was either eating a late breakfast or was out gathering wood for his fire. Sally however, was keeping an open mind on the subject. It could have been down to her over active imagination, but she felt sure that they had been observed. She had definitely got the impression that a pair of eyes was watching them silently and with probably as much curiosity as their own. Whether the inspection came from within the caravan or from behind one or other clump of ivy covered vegetation thereabouts, she could not make up her mind. Of one thing she was certain however, there had been no malevolence in that observation. If there had been, she would have sensed it.

As they walked back down the farm track after collecting the milk from the farm, Sally glanced towards the edge of the field adjacent to Sylvian, where a row of beehives stood sentinel along the hedgerow. Four of these curious cone shaped hives had decorated the edge of this field for as far back as Sally could remember, possibly even before the Collins family had taken up residence in

Battle Barn Farm. Every so often, Mrs Collins would produce a jar of honey from her pantry and as she passed it to one or other of the girls would always say, 'that's for your Mother.' As far as Sally could make out, the hives were not there just for the excellent honey the bees produced but also because they pollinated the fruit trees on this and adjacent farms.

She looked for signs of these fascinating little creatures around the entrance to the hive, but there was very little if any activity there. Some were probably in there at this very moment she thought, busily cleaning out the hives ready for the onslaught. She knew for sure though, that in a few weeks there would be a constant to-ing and fro-ing as some of the bees brought back pollen, nectar and water for the growing larvae, doing a bit of housework and nursery-maiding while they were about it. Mr Collins had told her that some of the bees guarded the hives and that some of them even fanned the air with their little wings to ensure good air circulation inside the hives. They did not live for very long, which was probably the reason why they worked so hard. They had so much to do and so little time to do it in, she thought to herself.

"Look at those stringy bits of clouds up there, they're a sign that rain's on the way. Mr Collins told me so while we were waiting for the milk just now," said Pat, breaking into Sally's thoughts. "He showed me what to look out for and he even told me the name of them but I can't for the life of me remember what it is. Never mind, it may not get here for a couple of days, the rain I mean. What are we doing today by the way?"

"We're going down to Wayside. Gran's got some duck eggs for us, and they'll tide us over until the pullets start to lay," replied Sally. "Mum say's we can go swimming down in Hastings first if we want to, then we can walk back to Wayside and catch the bus back home again from there. Look, mum's already pegged out the washing," she added pointing down towards the back garden where a gentle breeze was stirring the lines of assorted washing. "I bet she's used up all her pegs getting that lot out but never mind, I expect the Gypsy's will be around again with some more soon."

As they passed Wayside on the way down to Hastings, they spotted Gran in the garden and waved to her. Although she seemed to be looking towards the top of the bus and directly onto the front seat where they were sitting, she appeared not to have seen them. Her eyes were not so good these days, Sally thought and she tutted to herself. You couldn't wonder at it really. She was ever so old.

***

They did not leave the bus at the Pier as did most of the youngsters from the village, who were also on their way to the swimming baths. They stayed on until the bus reached its destination in Wellington Square for Hilary to purchase a few bits and pieces for her mum from Woolworth's. And then they would double back to the Pool. As they walked across the Square, they saw old Mr Dimarco in the doorway of his café and waved as he smiled at them. Mum had known him for ages, probably from way back to the time when she had worked as a waitress in Caves Café most likely Sally reckoned, and she always went to see him on her rare excursions into the town.

Once Hilary had made her purchases, they quickly made their way to and then through the back exit of this large store and on to the sea front. Apart from the huge blocks of concrete that had been hastily placed at regular intervals along there during the war, the whole promenade was now clear of war time debris. The tangles of wire netting, that had decorated the beaches for all those long years had disappeared, and the stony beach and lapping waves were once again free to people and were not the exclusive domain of the wild sea birds, the countless gulls that squawked over its ever changing surface.

They paused when they reached the pool and looked briefly over at the Pier, which had been made safe and was open again after the long years of war. A small group of youngsters were running around outside, and as the girls stood and watched, they disappeared into one of the buildings, which housed the penny machines. As they stood there, the sound of thumping and banging reached their ears, when presumably the loss of a precious coin without gaining a prize proved too frustrating. That feet as well as fists were being used to attack the machines was obvious by the increasing din. As they hovered, unsure whether to investigate further or to mind their own business, the door on the entrance booth opened with a loud click and out stepped a stocky man who moved purposefully in the direction of the ever increasing racket. The girls hung around just long enough to hear a loud bellow followed immediately by a cessation of the banging and thumping before moving swiftly away from the kafuffle.

As they made their way down into the underground swimming pool, they noticed several youngsters clustered around at the bottom of the stairs, none of whom they recognised. They moved aside as the girls approached and allowed them access, still laughing and chatting amongst themselves. After paying their entrance fee, they snatched up their locker keys and hurried off to the changing rooms to don their costumes. Sally was still struggling into her tight fitting, obligatory rubber bathing hat as they made their way to the side of the pool and was the last of the three to enter the water. Hilary with her eagle eye had spotted Dorothy and Enid Simmonds and Diana Woolett on the other side of the pool and was already working her way towards them. They were all learning to swim under the watchful eye of Jumbo James, not in this pool but in the open air one in Bexhill - weather permitting. They were all taking their time to master the skill, finding the breast stroke somewhat tricky and the crawl with its un-coordinated rhythm of legs and arms, virtually impossible. It was more fun anyway, to practice the lesson with one foot on the bottom of the pool and then to splash about in the shallow end for the rest of the time.

After playing around for a while, they pulled themselves out of the water and watched as a continuous procession of youngsters moved from water to diving platforms via the open steps at the side of the tall structure. As they looked towards the top platform, they saw one or two familiar faces, and watched in silence as one of them, Ted Smissen, moved towards the edge of the platform. He bounced a couple of times then at the top of the third bounce, he launched himself off, touching his toes with his finger tips as he fell through the air. Then in a split second he had straightened himself out and entered the deep water with scarcely a splash. As Sally watched this skilful display, she remembered how Mr lee their ex headmaster, had had a down on Ted for some peculiar reason and had singled him out for the cane on the flimsiest of excuses and certainly more times than he deserved it or were good for him. Ted however, never gave him the satisfaction of crying out in pain, not once, and he never complained. Sally had found that very difficult to understand. Ted was outwardly confident and articulate and must have been aware of the injustice towards him. He must have breathed a huge sigh of relief, along with several other children when Mr Lee had been replaced by Jumbo James as their Head Master.

Len Larkin, who followed Ted down into the water, omitted the acrobatics and just shot through the air like a dart. After larking around in the water for a few seconds, the two tall, handsome, athletic youths followed one another back up the steps to have another go.

"What I wouldn't give to be able to do that," said Sally admiringly, a mixture of awe and admiration in her voice. "Trouble is we've got to learn to swim first. Then we'll only be allowed to use the lowest board for ages and ages. Mind you, I don't know if I'd ever have the nerve to dive off any platform and down into all that water. It's pretty deep over there I reckon."

"Well it'd have to be deep. You'd give yourself a tidy old headache if you tried to do dive in at the shallow end, especially from that top board up there," replied Dorothy. "What I do know is that once I've mastered this swimming lark, I'll be up there like a flash, right to the top. I can't wait."

Sally grinned, not doubting her words for one moment. She remembered with trepidation, Dorothy's prowess and daring on the stool ball field, especially that deadly and mostly accurate aim as she propelled the hard as a nut, deceptively small ball in the direction of the batsman.

After spending the best part of another hour, playing in the water and doing the doggy paddle, Hilary reminded Pat and Sally that they had to call in at Wayside on the way home to pick up the duck eggs. If they were prepared to walk as far as Christ Church, a designated fare stage to catch the bus, she would pay for the journey to Wayside, she told them as she peeled off her tight rubber hat with a sigh of relief. It was a long old haul all the way to gran's place, and although they had planned to walk, they all liked the idea of catching a bus even better. They walked through to the changing rooms and after giving themselves a perfunctory rub down, they wrung out their wet costumes and wrapped them up in the damp towels with which they had partially dried themselves.

Although it was quite warm for the time of year, they shivered as they emerged from the building and out into the fresh air, and they hugged their coats closely to their bodies as they walked briskly along the promenade. By the time they reached bottle alley however, they were warm enough to slow down and admire this work of art, appreciating the hour upon hour of patient dedication that must have gone into this awesome project.

"Mum was telling us that the people of Hastings and roundabouts collected all this glass," said Sally. "They saved up all their bottles, like Marmite, milk of magnesia, lemonade and such like and washed them, then the dustmen collected it all and took it to some depot somewhere to sort it." She paused here as she tried to imagine just how long the job of sorting all these bottles into their various hues would have taken, let alone the painstaking task of setting the myriad, various shaped and coloured pieces of glass into those horizontal columns of concrete. As to whether this was the work of one individual or of many, she had no idea. Same as she was no nearer to solving the mystery of the identity of the potter who had fashioned mum's old brown pig with its upturned nose and enigmatic smile.

When they reached the bottom of London Road, they paused and looked towards the West Pier, which even before the war had been slowly decaying away. Now, having been further breached by military action, storm and fire, it looked really dilapidated. As Hilary and Sally discussed its appearance and contemplated its likely future, Pat suddenly and very loudly proclaimed the approach of the Westfield bus, and they all crossed the road and sprinted up the steep slope towards Christ Church, piers and their problems suddenly forgotten. Pat and Sally shot up the stairs of the double-decker bus with Hilary not far behind and made straight for the front seats. The Conductor followed soon after and as Hilary handed over the correct money for the fares to him, he adjusted a couple of buttons on his machine, turned the handle at the side and one by one the tickets plopped out into his open hand. As he passed the tickets over, he dropped the coins into a thick leather shoulder bag at his side.

They alighted from the bus outside Towner's the Stone Masons and walked the short distance to Wayside. As they opened the gate they saw Mary and Jill in the garden and as the two girls skipped towards them, Mary, the elder of the two called out over her shoulder, "They're here gran." And they all made their way around the side of the house and in through the open kitchen door.

These cousins of theirs, daughters of mum's brother Uncle Jack and his wife Aunty Ivy, had recently moved into the area with their brother Ian and were living just down the road at the Willows. Peter, the eldest of the four had moved here some time ago to live with gran at Wayside, but the girls very rarely saw him. He was nearly always missing, either intentionally or by chance when they called. Tall and nice looking like his siblings, he was the apple of her eye and she would not hear a word said against him. But then gran preferred boys to girls any old day. Sally had always known that.

Sally was looking forward to seeing mum's other brother Uncle Tom again in the not too distant future. He, Auntie Annie and their cousin June, lived in a little village near Bicester and although letters passed between the two families on a regular basis, their visits were very few and far between, which was a pity Sally thought. On the one visit of theirs that she could remember, they had made quite an impression on her.

"You got here then, and about time too. I thought you'd have got here a bit earlier than this," said gran wiping her hands down her overall and pushing a few wisps of grey hair off her forehead. "Pop next door and see if Mrs Beresford's got a bit of milk I can have, will you Sally," she added after a short pause. "I'm getting a bit low on the stuff and I'd be right out by the time I made you all a drink. And don't take all day. You know what she's like. She could talk the hind leg off a donkey she could."

Sally did not hesitate. She found Mrs Beresford's house nearly as interesting as Wayside, especially the kitchen. She ran the short distance to the little house, leaned forward and knocked on the open back door and almost immediately the old lady appeared with a bright smile on her face.

"Can gran have some milk, she's getting a bit short of the stuff and she wants to make us a drink," she said.

Then as Mrs Beresford busied herself with the practicalities of obtaining a container for the liquid, she looked towards the dark old dresser on the far side of the kitchen, which was greasy with age and neglect. She felt an acute sense of satisfaction and relief as she examined the contents and noted that not one item had been removed or even moved from the higher shelves since she had last visited this house. There it was, her favourite tin still in pride of place. The now slightly fading but still readable words, 'Huntley and Palmers Biscuits, 1911. Reading and London,' was written on its flat surface. Then better still, beneath this writing was the picture of a little elf sitting on a toadstool playing a ukulele and its colours were still as bright and fresh as the day it had been fashioned. How she just loved that picture.

Perched on the next shelf down was yet another tin, yellow in colour and boldly written on its surface were the words, 'Macfarlane Lang's Fine Water Biscuits.' Though not as decorative as the one above, it still had a kind of functional appeal. The two fat Toby jugs that sat either side of this tin eyeing one another with a malevolent glint in their eyes, reminded her somehow of two of the characters in Alice in Wonderland. They would have quarrelled had they been placed eye ball to eye ball, she was sure of that. Many and various were the other items that decorated these shelves, and her gaze now fell upon one in particular. It was a curiously shaped piece of china with a moat shaped gully around its irregular surface, and was decorated with flowers of highly improbable hues. She had pondered the possible use of such a curiosity but had never been able to come up with a satisfactory answer. She could always ask Mrs Beresford she supposed, but it was a lot more fun to guess at its purpose in life, if indeed it had one. There were several vases on these shelves and one in particular had always fascinated her. The design on its cracked, glazed surface was of a rural scene, painted in dull ochre yellow, green and brown. With its scrolled handles on either side, it looked very old. It also had an air of mystery about it somehow. The Jersey cow cream jug on the same shelf, always made her smile to herself. The handle, fashioned from its tail looked for all the world as though the poor animal had flipped its tail over its back to dislodge a fly, and got it stuck there for eternity. There was something a bit 'Lot and the pillar of salt' around this one. She hardly noticed the every day things on the bottom shelf. They were just a haphazard collection of utilitarian items, mostly plates, cups and saucers and dishes with some nondescript crocks of indeterminate usage among them - with a Spong mincer placed upside down on the far side. And what was the shaving mug and the wooden box of assorted clay pipes doing there, she wondered. Still listening with half an ear to what the old lady was saying to her and making responses in what she hoped were the right places, she moved towards the doorway of the front room to check the contents within.

Her eyes went straight to the fireplace, to the old brass fender with the little padded seats on either side. Though not quite as ornate as the one next door, it never the less endowed the old fireplace with an air of functional dignity, making it the focal point of the room, and rightly so, Sally thought to herself. A companion set and coal scuttle sat in the hearth, somewhat battered and scratched from years of service, but according to her dad's philosophy, still with plenty of use to be got from the old things. There was an old oval mirror over the fireplace with a black and gold rim, and on the mantle piece underneath was a collection of dusty ornaments.

The other walls were decorated with the same old paintings that had hung there from as far back as she could remember and a long time before that even she reckoned. A few of them were allegorical pictures, similar to those next door that Granpy had collected all those years ago, the ones that she had always found rather disturbing. And she knew that beneath each one, the wallpaper would be as fresh as the day it had been placed there. She knew this for sure having lifted each one to marvel at the contrast between the covered and the exposed wall covering. She visibly jumped as Mrs Beresford appeared at her elbow, so engrossed was she in her contemplation of all these artefacts.

"Sorry, did I make you jump," she asked rather unnecessary Sally thought. "I was just saying about your old Granpy and how I still miss him about the place. Always through here he was to get to those pigs of his and he always stopped for a bit of a chat with me and Mr Beresford he did, when he got the time of course. If he weren't among those pigs of his he was off to Battle, picking up this and that from the market up there. Always on the look out he were for old stuff that other folks wanted to be rid of. That place in there still be full to overflowing with it. Poor Sarah, bless her soul, she just put up with all his funny ways. Never complained she didn't, even towards the end when she was suffering so with all those rheumatics and things.

He had a horse and cart at one time, your Granpy you know," she continued after a short contemplative pause. "Went all round the hotels and places with it he did afore the war to pick up the swill for his old pigs. And proud as a peacock he was of that old horse of his. He had an old Beatrice down in them piggery's there at one time. Still there somewhere as far as I know. Brewed up his tea many's the time, as well as his old swill on that thing. It won't be there for long if that Peter gets his way. He's talking about him and Ian turning the place down there into some sort of track for cycling around or something. Your gran hasn't said yay or nay yet as far as I know, but he'll get his way in the end, you mark my words. She loves that boy, she can't deny him anything for long."

Then she sighed and paused for a few contemplative seconds before continuing. "They were good old days they were, when folks took their time. Not like today when they havn't got time to wipe their noses. You wouldn't remember all the things I've been talking about, would you? You was hardly born then. Anyway, you'd best get back with this milk before your Grandma comes looking for you," she said as she held out the milk jug and placed it into Sally's hands. "Looks like we'll be getting a drop of rain afore long," she said as she peered through the back door and up into the heavens. Then, "Finished your inspection, have you?" she added with a grin.

As Sally made her way along the back path towards Gran's kitchen with the jug balanced carefully between cupped hands, she thought about Mrs Beresford who's soft brogue was similar to Mercy Dengate's. She also had the same weather beaten face and large, work worn hands as the other old lady, an indication of a life spent in the open air. She was a mine of information she was and Sally would normally have enjoyed listening to her tales of long ago and far away. They had a bus to catch however, and hopefully a mug of cocoa or Camp coffee to drink before that and if she did not get a move on, one or other would be in jeopardy.

"You took your time, we thought you'd got lost. I was about to send the girls round to find you," said gran as Sally walked through the kitchen door. "I'd as well gone up to Harrow farm and milked the cow meself in the time it took you to go next door. Give it here then before we all die of thirst," she added taking the jug from Sally's hands and pouring some of the contents into a pan. "I won't make it too hot or you'll be hard put to it to drink it before the bus comes along. It'll have to be Camp coffee I'm afraid. I'm right out of cocoa. And make sure you stay a bit longer the next time you come here. Mary and Jill've been really looking forward to seeing you, you know. There now, drink up and get along to that bus stop or you'll have to walk home," she said as she passed around the steaming mugs. And don't forget the eggs either," she called out to them as a short while later they headed towards the door. "They're over there on the draining board, look. In that old canvas bag of your uncles. Best let Hilary carry them. She's a bit more careful than you other two. They'll keep you going until pop's pullets come into lay."

They dawdled ever so slightly as they walked down the pathways, admiring the mass of crocus, daffodils and hyacinths that decorated gran's early spring garden. Then as they reached the gate, they saw the bus turning the corner at the bottom of the road, and as it made its way steadily up the hill towards them, they rushed towards the stop waving their hands wildly to catch the attention of the driver.

"Whew, that was close," said Hilary as they clambered on board, sitting on the lower deck this time. Then as the bus moved off, they turned and waved to Mary and Jill, vowing to meet up with them again very soon.

As they walked up the field, Sally noticed that the washing was still out on the line, with a light wind playing with it just as it had been when they had walked down the field from Battle Barn this morning. It was nice to go travelling but it was even nicer to come home, she reckoned, especially when the homecoming was accompanied by the smell of cooking.

A couple of days later as predicted by Pat, the budding weather forecaster, the heavens opened and in spite of gabardine raincoats and a shared umbrella, Hilary's of course, the girls arrived at school looking like drowned rats in a thunderstorm.

***

Pat, Hilary and Sally were walking up Crazy Lane chatting and listening with half an ear to the tree top conversations of an assortment of birds. There was a magpie in there somewhere, causing trouble with its harassment of other birds as usual, Sally was sure of that. All magpies were bullies she reckoned, it was just their nature. They not only attacked dad's chicks, they also raided the eggs and babies from smaller birds nests given half a chance. Still this time it seemed that they were being given a run for their money. By the racket up there, they were not getting all their own way, and as she looked, there was a flutter of black and white followed by an angry and vociferous flock of sparrows. At least these bullies knew when to beat a hasty retreat.

The girls were on their way to Gosse's farm to give a helping hand with the somewhat delicate task of egg washing. Hope, normally the main stay with this exacting job of work, was out of action having fallen from her horse and broken her collar bone a few days previously. Having offered their services the day before, the girls had rushed through their chores this morning, collecting the milk from the farm in record time. Then Sally, her mouth crammed full with the last of her Weetabix, had taken over the pumping from Pat and had worked away until the tank rumbled, its belly full and near to over flowing. She grinned as she recalled her dad's words when she had mentioned, exaggerating ever so slightly, the mountains of eggs desperately needing beauty treatment up at Gosse's farm. 'Well, I reckon if you stuck a feather in a tater at this time of year, it'd lay you an egg,' he had said. Then he had spoiled the effect of the quip for her somewhat by reminding her that there were plenty of grubby eggs in the copper-house awaiting the same treatment. She had not replied but had thought that with luck and a good wind behind them, they would be able to get out of that chore until tomorrow at least. It was not just a question of cleaning the eggs up at the Gosse's farm, Hilary had also promised to exercise Hope's ponies for her and that took time. And if she remembered rightly, Caroline Keelings horse, also stabled with the Gosse's at the moment, would need some attention.

Caroline was abroad somewhere with her mother and Hope had volunteered to take care of the creature. It was a fine looking animal, all sleek and glossy brown. Just like a highly polished conker. They had also planned to go to the Picture House in Battle this afternoon, paying partly for this treat with the money promised to them by Mrs Gosse. By the time they had eaten their dinner, there would be no time left at all to deal with the eggs in the copper-house. They would just have to spend an extra day in there with a coating of muck and bits of feathers on their shells.

They arrived at the farmhouse, and once seated around the massive old table in the barn, they rubbed away with bits of wet rag at the stains set solid on the surface of the eggs, unable to press too hard for fear of cracking the delicate shells. The chickens on this farm were the same as those at Sylvian, Rhode Island red and Light Sussex, and Sally remembered her dad saying that as far as he was concerned, they were the most versatile breeds. The Rhode Islands in particular, he reckoned, produced the best flesh as well as supplying a regular and reliable crop of eggs. Mrs Gosse had provided them with a jug of lemonade and glasses, and from time to time they reached out to pour themselves a measure, smacking their lips with satisfaction as they downed the home made brew. From time to time they stood up to rinse out their cloths in the bucket of water, standing at one end of the table, making sure the rag was well wrung out before they continued with the chore. They worked away, chatting comfortably amongst themselves, and gradually the baskets of grubby eggs were transformed into neat trays of clean ones.

When they had finished cleaning the eggs, they went back into the farmhouse kitchen and washed their hands at the kitchen sink, sharing the piece of Sunlight soap, which they found on the draining board. It was as hard as Newgate's knocker, a sure sign that Mrs Gosse believed in the efficacy of storing the stuff for a year or two before use. It was an old trick, practised by many a frugal housewife. As they turned to walk back through the kitchen door after wiping their hands on a piece of roller towelling, Hope appeared right on cue.

"I'm ready when you are," she said in that rather posh voice of hers. "Sorry I can't help you with the saddles and bridles, you'll have to put them on yourselves. Or rather, on the horses yourselves," she corrected herself with a grin.

It was left mostly to Hilary and Pat to exercise the horses, taking them over low jumps and trotting them around the bottom field, close to the stream. Sally did pluck up the courage to mount one of Hope's ponies however, rising to the trot as the animal made its way obediently across the field watched critically by its owner. To steady her nerves she mumbled under her breath, a bit a bit of nonsense she had heard recently:

Horsey keep your tail up keep your tail up, keep your tail up.
Horsey keep your tail up why don't you make it rise?
Tell me how you get that way, you mean yes and say neigh, neigh.
O horsey keep your tail up keep the sun out of my eyes.

By the time she had recited this ditty a few times she reckoned she had just about done her duty by the horse and by its owner. She was therefore quick to remind the other two that it was close on dinner time and they had promised Amy they would call for her promptly at one thirty to walk to the picture house in Battle with her.

They almost had to drag Pat away from the horses, reminding her that the picture house opened its doors at two fifteen for the two thirty showing of the film, and that most likely they would have to queue up to get in. It was a Tarzan film after all, and very popular with boys and girls alike. Johnny Weissmuller performed the most unbelievable acrobatics, swinging from tree to tree on a succession of strategically placed ropes, and always seemed to be in the right place to accomplish the most heroic of rescues. And his swimming prowess had to be seen to be believed. No one, not even Ted Smisson could swim as well as he could.

Once they had freed the horses from their shackles and stored the tackle carefully away in the barn, they decided to take the short cut home, jumping over Staffords stream at its narrowest point before heading along the track and into the lower end of Crazy Lane. It was right here that, last summer the girls had tried to dam the stream hoping to trap and capture the newts that favoured this area. As fast as they built up the muddy barricades however, the steady and relentless flow of the water seemed to work its way around or over them. In the end they had abandoned the job reluctantly, vowing to enlist the aid of Basil and Ronald with a spade or two between them at some later date. As they walked the short distance along the track and into the lower end of Crazy Lane, Hilary and Sally listened with half an ear as Pat chanted a little ditty:

"Adam and Eve and pinch me, went down to the sea to bathe.
Adam and Eve got drownded and who do you think was saved?"

She was trying to entice the two girls into a response, which she would have responded to with gleeful enthusiasm. They however, having heard this age old rhyme countless times before, ignored the plea. Once bitten, twice shy was definitely the best policy here. After a while and for reasons best known to herself, she began to sing another song and this time Hilary and Sally joined in the chorus:

"Dooma looma looma lay, dooma looma looma lay.
Any umbrella's to mend today."

The girls finished their dinner in record time and having promised to clean the eggs the following morning, they ran off down the field to call for Amy. As they passed Paygate cottage, they saw Rosney in the garden and she waved to them. Sally had discovered only recently, that she wore a built up shoe, probably the result of an attack of Polio at some time in her life, which would have stunted the growth in that leg. Ken Monk, Willie's brother who had contracted this disease, some reckoned as a result of bathing in the Brooks, was more severely affected by this nasty illness.

When the girls arrived, slightly breathless at Uplyme, Amy was doing a bit of titivating. They watched as she applied lipstick and then passed a liberally coated powder puff around her cheeks and across her nose with an expertise that Lana Turner would have been proud of. She certainly took a lot more care over her appearance than they did. When she had finished, she smiled into the mirror, the reflective surface highlighting the dimples in her cheeks. "There, that'll do," she said as she turned to face them. "Wait for us in the kitchen will you. I won't be a minute."

There was an interesting tin on the mantle shelf in the kitchen. It was oval in shape and Sally craned her neck to get a better sight of it. The words, 'DE RESZKE MINORS,' was written in bold capitols on its painted surface with, 'Virginia cigarettes' written underneath in smaller letters. There was also a symbol of some kind just below the rim of the lid but this had been partially obliterated by use. It was very old and she reckoned it was probably the receptacle for buttons or some such thing these days. The cigarettes would be long gone, smoked no doubt by someone in the dim and distant past. No one in the family smoked these days as far as she knew. There was also a blue enamel candle stick holder on this shelf, its stem covered in snots of wax. The short blackened wick in the centre of what little remained of its candle, would no doubt be ignited by one of the matches in the box, which stood in a pool of congealed wax in the bowl of the holder. At the other end stood a jar with the words, 'Brands Essence written on its label. It looked as though it had been around for sometime and was most likely, a relic from the time when Mr Powell had been so ill. The only other jar of this rejuvenating substance she had seen was at Wayside, administered to Aunty Sarah by gran, towards the end of their old Aunty's life.

Sally looked up as Mrs Powell came through to the kitchen and passed a large white paper bag to Amy. "Here's a few toffees for you girls to eat while you're at the pictures," she said. "I've been saving up coupons for a while specially to get these for you." The girls grinned and thanked her, their mouths watering in anticipation of this rare treat. They never seemed to be able to save their own sweet ration for occasions like this. "Now mind you don't eat them on the way there. Save them until the main film comes on. Now get along with you or you'll miss the trailers, and as far as I'm concerned, that's usually the best part." As she smiled at them, Sally thought how kind and generous she was It was not just the gift of the sweets that prompted this observation, though this certainly played its part. She was also generous with her time, always prepared to take time off from whatever chore she happened to be doing to tell them a tale or two or listen to accounts of their own experiences. And she was very wise.

Amy popped the toffees into her sling bag along with all the other paraphernalia she felt compelled to carry around with her, tucked a silky scarf around her neck and thus fortified, they set off for Battle. By the time they reached the turning into Marley Lane, they were well into their stride, walking along the grassy footpath in close proximity to one another and chatting non stop. The area around here always reminded Sally of Bangy Smith and his brother and she let her thoughts stray for a few seconds while she thought of them and the other countless tough old men who had toiled in these woods from way back in the dim and distant past.

"We were up here this morning, mum and me, fetching fire wood. There's stacks of it over there," Amy was saying, pointing in the direction of the wood where the rusty old charcoal burners had smoked on and off for a couple of centuries or more. "We stacked our old pram right up to the gunnels with the smaller lengths, me and mum and she pushed that back home while I dragged the longer lengths, and I got them all sawed up before I had me dinner. Starved I was by that time. We've got an old saw bench just like yours up at Sylvian. It's got the same three sets of crosses, or bearers I think they're called and another bit that fits right along on top of them. You can fit any length of wood along it. My dad made it years and years ago before he got ill. I still miss him you know, that's why I'm always going down to the shed, imagining him bending over that old bench of his, making and mending or just looking out of the windows. I know he won't be there of course, but it doesn't stop me looking and hoping. It's not the same without a dad."

In the silence that followed Amy's discourse, Sally thought about but could not imagine life without her own father. She felt a rush of sympathy and admiration for her friend who, in spite of her obvious feeling of loss, still retained that keen sense of humour that she had always possessed. She was just the same on the outside, evidently saving her grieving for private moments. This was the first time she had spoken to them of her father since his recent death.

After a few moments however, she squared her shoulders, smiled around at the other girls then began to entertain them with a few impressions of Popeye the Sailor Man and Olive Oyl, mimicking first one and then the other.

"Oim Popeye the one eyed sailor man. I los' me eye in the mos' ahful battle. Urm ,urm, blow me down, oi as got an idya," she began. The she called out in a high pitched squeaky voice, "Popeye, Popeye, It's liddle Swee' Pea, it'll be killed to death." She paused here for a few seconds while she composed her facial expressions and prepared her voice box for Popeye once again. "Unhand me Bluto you, you that's what you are," she said, her voice even more slurry and indistinct, moving this way and that as she tried to get away from her imaginary assailant. Her audience all began to giggle.

When the laughter, hers and theirs, had subsided she stood up and straightened her skirt. She had one more trick up her sleeve however, and as the other girls began to move away she brought them to a halt with the name 'Poopy Pappy,' the mere mention of which, brought a renewed outburst of laughter from them. Before she had time to imitate this unfortunate old man though, Sally grabbed her arm and propelled her forward, reminding her of the distance between where they were and where they needed to be - Battle Picture House. They would need to half walk and half run now anyway to get there on time. She breathed a sigh of relief. All this laughter was tiring to say the least. Best of all though, Amy was very much one of them again, for the time being anyway. Her grown up manner was skin deep, a mere cover up for the youngster underneath.

They puffed up to the top end of Marley Lane, jogged the last few yards down the road then joined the slow moving queue outside the Picture House. As they stood there, Amy's gaze immediately gravitated towards a poster advertising a film to be released later in the year, starring Jane Wyman and James Stewart. Hilary, Sally and Pat however, were soon deep into a discussion on some of the children's hour programmes they had listened to on Hilary's wireless recently and did not give it more than a cursory glance. At Sylvian they were seldom allowed the luxury of listening to their own programmes on the wireless. The precious accumulator renewed on a weekly basis, only supplied enough juice for grown up, serious programmes like news bulletins and world affairs programmes.

Once they were through the doorway of the picture house and waiting to pay for their tickets at the kiosk, Pat pointed towards an old poster with just a portrait of a little man with soulful eyes and a paint brush moustache on its simply decorated surface. Instantly recognisable as Charlie Chaplin, the figure stood with his hands resting on top of an old walking stick, while his overlarge flat feet stuck out in front of him at an angle of forty five degrees. Sally was struck anew at the ability of this little black clad figure to evoke in his audience, a rare and unique combination of two opposing emotions, pathos on the one hand with a marked sense of the comic on the other. All in this one unassuming little man. She remembered hearing her father and Uncle Alf talking about him, a while ago now. They were saying that he had spent some of his formative years in a workhouse. Whether he used this experience consciously or unconsciously she had no idea, but something of the soul of the man seemed to emanate from the depths of the eyes that looked back at her.

There were more posters advertising forthcoming films and Sally scanned them carefully. There was still a Laurel and Hardy film she wanted to see and was waiting for it to be shown again, if not in the Battle Picture House, then perhaps the Gaiety or the Ritz Cinema in Hastings. In this film the two comedians were furniture removers and the sequence where they tried to get a piano from the bottom of the house to the top floor by a sequence of narrow staircases she had heard was hilarious. She liked these comedians nearly as much as she liked Charlie Chapman - but not quite.

The lights went down soon after they had been ushered into there seats and as they faded, there was an instinctive hush in the audience. It was not long however, before the sound of rustling bags and whispering started, with the occasional giggle as someone in the audience took the micky out of one or other of the adverts on the screen. Once the main film began to roll however, the murmurings ceased once again and the background whirring of the projection machine could be heard above the films sound effects. The film was composed of the usual cast, Tarzan and Jane with a selection of appealing animals, monkeys in particular and the villain. There was always a villain or two. There were sudden intakes of breath as Tarzan propelled himself through the jungle at the end of long, thick strategically placed ropes to perform particularly difficult rescue operations. And even more so when he gave the most remarkable swimming and diving performances, plunging into crystal clear waters from unbelievable heights.

After a while, Amy reached into her handbag, withdrew the bag of toffees and proffered them to one and all. "Only take one," she said in a loud whisper as she handed them around. "We've got to save some for later, while we're walking home. We'll be really hungry by then." As Sally sucked and chewed on her mint flavoured toffee, her thoughts drifted away from Tarzan, his menagerie and super human exploits, to a day long ago now when she and the other girls had been to the Churchyard in Sedlescombe, gathering chestnuts. She remembered how tired she had felt on the homeward journey and how the Horlicks tablets Amy had produced as if by magic from her pocket, had rejuvenated her. She even remembered the songs they had sung, and one in particular struck her memory chords, 'air, air, air I've got non on me noddle, But I don't care a damn as down the road I toddle,' and she smiled as she recited and hummed the whole song to herself. It was the one she most associated with Bangy Smith. It was a pity that Amy had become so grown up lately.

As the lights went up, they rubbed their eyes as they adjusted to the change from crepuscular to the sudden glare of the artificial lighting. They rose from their seats in unison, joining the general melee of chattering, clattering youngsters making for the exit and as they burst out into the fresh air, they all took a deep breath.

"That was good, I enjoyed that," said Hilary as they made their way up the short incline towards Marley Lane. "It's even better to be out in the fresh air again though. It was a bit sweaty in there and so forth." And Sally at least was inclined to agree with her. Pictures were okay but you could not beat being out of doors, especially on a day like this, she reckoned.

"There's a train coming," said Pat excitedly as they walked towards the level crossing. "They're closing the gates look, see." And she pointed ahead, the first as usual to notice any change taking place around them. They hurried towards the crossing and after a while a train puffed slowly past them towards the station. The man on the footplate, dressed from top to toe in the darkest navy blue, smiled and waved to them as the train chugged slowly past. Then they watched as it drew even more slowly, into Battle station.

"That's lucky, you don't see so many steam trains these days, they're mostly these new fangled things," said Hilary as the gates opened and they stepped warily over the crossing. "Trains were especially important during the war, did you know that? Dad, Pop Cotton was talking to mum about it only the other day. They weren't just used for moving troops about and so forth you know, food and coal and people had to be got from place to place as well. They, the drivers and conductors got bombed and shot up in their trains by the Germans time and time again, same as everything and everyone else did and they often worked night and day to get the damaged lines and so forth repaired. Dad said they kept the country moving, or some such thing. In fact he said he would go as far as to say, they were as much a part of the war effort as the Army, Navy and Air-force were. He said something about them being the backbone of the country or some such thing. You don't think about things like that, do you? You just take them for granted most of the time. Even women worked on the railways during the war, mostly as signallers I believe. Some of them still do I expect. Well, who wants a game of 'I spy' then?" she asked after pausing to allow them to digest the content of her report, and it took them a full minute or so to respond to her question.

The game, with its fair share of the obscure versus the ridiculous was side stepped when the common or garden word, 'feet' came up as an 'I spy' object, setting them off on a recitation of nonsense poems. Sally started off with the one that had triggered the poetic diatribe, with the other girls joining in enthusiastically.

"It was the ninety tenth of Julember, the rain was snowing sleet.
A poor man stood in the middle of the road, and his shoes were full of feet."

Then they giggled as they launched themselves off into the next bit of nonsense and the next, and the ditty's continued.

> *"One fine day in the middle of the night, two dead men got up to fight.*
> *Back to back they faced each other, drew their swords and shot each other.*
>
> *There was an old man of Kilbride, who went to a funeral and cried.*
> *When asked who was dead, he just stammered and said, I don't know I just came for the ride.*
>
> *As I was going up stair, I saw a man who wasn't there.*
> *He wasn't there again today, I wish that man would go away."*

"That's enough, my brain's hurting," said Hilary after a while. "Come on let's see if we can catch our shadows." And she proceeded to put on a very convincing display as she ran off, zig-zagging across the pathway apparently trying her hardest to outmanoeuvre her shadow - followed closely by Pat. "It's no good," she called back breathlessly after a short while. "It can read your mind. It's always one step ahead of you no matter which way you go. Even Betty couldn't run fast enough to catch up with it. Fancy a look round the old barn," she asked, turning round and pointing in the direction of the vernacular ruin.

"No, we haven't got time, I'm going out with Ivy Simmons and Joan Jarvis this evening and I've still got to get all my things ready," replied Amy. "Anyway, the old googly moosh'll get us if we go in there, just look at the state of it."

"Don't be daft, there's only bats and things in there apart from bits of old machinery and such like, and they won't hurt you," said Sally. "You'd have been in there like a flash not that long ago. You were always ready for a bit of fun in the old days. Do you remember when we were taking a short cut across old Mad March Hair's garden at Luck's Ness, and you caught your knickers on the barbed wire on the top of his fence? We'd been chestnutting up in the woods I think, or had we been bird nesting? Blowed if I can remember. It might have been that day when you waded out to get those dab chick eggs and got soaking wet. We never did get any did we? That long stick we tied to the end of the spoon just kept twisting and turning all over the place, it was much too flimsy. Anyway, we all thought it was funny, a bit of a laugh, you catching your knickers like that, until we realised you'd cut yourself that is. When I saw the top of your leg bleeding like that, I thought I was going to faint. Barbed wire is lethal. It should never be allowed I don't think." and she shuddered at the memory. I bet you wouldn't do any of those things now though. You're much too lady like," she added as she pranced about, pouting her lips and patting her hair with mock affectation. "Never mind we've had some laughs, haven't we," she said sobering up momentarily and falling back into line with them all.

By the time they got to the end of Marley Lane, they were tired and hungry and conversation between them had become rather sporadic, with food and a bit of a rest, clearly uppermost in their minds. Sally was often surprised and always grateful, that her mum seemed able to anticipate their home coming and always seemed to have a meal if not ready, then very nearly so. Her mum was the best cook in the world, she reckoned, and her mouth watered as she went through a list of her favourite food, trying to second guess what it would be this time. This train of thoughts was interrupted as the sound of singing filtered slowly through from her ears to her brain.

"When Irish eyes are smiling, sure it's like a morn in Spring.
In the lilt of Irish laughter, you can hear the Angels sing."

Amy was singing solo and as Sally listened, the quality of voice of this naturally gifted singer, plus the plaintive words of the song, brought tears to her eyes.

CHAPTER 17

The sound of Mum's voice and the rattle of a cup on its saucer brought Sally slowly out of a deep sleep. "It's half past three," she whispered. "By the time you drink this and get dressed, it won't be far off getting light and we need to be on our way before the dawn chorus starts. Pat's already up and dressed. She got up same time as I did."

Sally shot up in bed, as the recall of the previous evenings plans, suddenly dispelled any lingering drowsiness. In between sipping the hot tea, she rummaged around in the dark for the clothes she had left in readiness the night before. Having located them wedged between mattress and the frame of the bed, she pulled off her nightclothes and shrugged herself into her vest, knickers, frock and cardigan and hurried through to the kitchen. Mum and Pat were all ready and waiting by the scullery door, coats in hand and as Sally joined them, the trio made their way outside and into the stillness of this early Spring morning. As they made their way along the lane, they stopped instinctively to listen as the silvery tones of a solitary blackbird broke softly into the silence of the early morning.

"Now you just listen, they'll all start singing now," whispered mum. "It's like one has to send out the signal before the others can join in the chorus. A bit like a choir really, waiting for the masters opening chord. We won't have to wait long."

Sally stood still in the middle of the lane with her mum and sister and listened with singular concentration as other birds, two's and threes at a time, joined in the chorus. She closed her eyes as individual song patterns gradually merged into low murmurings, rising steadily in volume until the world seemed to be filled with their enchantment. They stood for several minutes listening to this miracle of nature before moving forward together, in silent unison.

The thin light of dawn was just creeping up over the landscape as they approached Paygate corner and from the direction of the cottage roof, rising over and above the sounds of the other song birds, came the melodious tones of another blackbird, singing its little heart out.

A fine layer of mist, still and silent in its early morning formation, hung over the Brooks as they passed by. Further down New Road, they all sniffed appreciatively as from the direction of Marley Lane, drifted the characteristic whiff of smoke from the old charcoal burners.

"This was one of my favourite walks and smells if it comes to that, when we first came to Sylvian," said mum after a long silence. "I used to bring Freda and Betty and then Hazel down here just to look at the charcoal burners and chat to the old boys when they were out in these woods. On the odd occasion when I had a bit of spare time that is. Freda and Betty still remember it. Of course there were hop fields all along here at one time, and not that long ago either. People now have to go all the way to the hop farms in Bodiam and such places to earn a bit of extra money." She paused here for a while and they continued on their journey, now walking up the long straight road towards Whatlington. "This bit of road here always reminds me of when me and your dad used to come down here on that old Harley Davidson motor bike of his," she continued after a while. "Even before we moved down here we used to come and see Aunty Sarah and Granpy, down near Gensing gardens and then at Wayside, and we knew when we got to this stretch of road that we were nearly there. In the early days when Sylvia was a baby, there'd be me with Sylvia on my lap, Cis, young Frank and Alan in that huge side-car. Then your uncle Frank and sometimes Alf would be sitting pillion behind your dad. He, your dad, always dressed the part. He had this reefer jacket that he always wore and a thick cap that he always put on back to front. Where he got those huge leather gauntlet gloves from that he always wore I never did know. He probably made them himself. And the goggles he wore nearly swamped face and had to be seen to be believed.

Anyway, once we were all in or on the thing, he'd kick start the engine and we'd roar away, and I mean roar. You could here us coming a mile off. I was as nervous as a spoonful of jelly when I first got on that motorbike, mostly because it was so noisy I suppose, but I soon got used to it. He was very careful your dad and he never took any risks, especially with Sylvia and the boys on board." She paused here and when she spoke again her voice was low and sad. "How he loved that little girl. He'll never get over her death until his dying day. Nor will I for that matter."

"I'll tell you dainty wee daisy mum," said Pat suddenly, seeking to relieve her mum of such sad thoughts with the first thing that came into her mind. "You can join in if you want to," she added hardly drawing breath before she began her recitation.

"Dainty wee daisy woke with the sun.
Up said the skylark mornings begun
Dainty wee daisy lifted her head.
I am so thirsty skylark she said."

Then she ran ahead of the other two and when she turned around again to face them, her hands, claw like and pseudo menacing were pointed towards them. And she proceeded to give them a recitation of, 'the home of the grizzly, izzly bear, awooooo.

"Is that better?" She asked and just before she turned around and sprinted off again, she called out, "Come on, we've still got a long way to go."

By the time they reached the turning into Stream Lane, it was full on daylight, but the high hedges and a large oak tree that overhung the lane, shadowed the way ahead. All around them a thousand birds continued to trill their territorial recitals, covering the sound of muffled footsteps and the vocal interaction between the three of them with a sweet cacophony of sound. They passed the site of an old Post Mill, then paused for a while when they reached Spilstead Farm House, mum in particular having a keen interest in old buildings. According to Jumbo James, this steep pitched roofed house had been called 'Slaughters' at some time in its history. He reckoned it was based on the name of one of its occupiers sometime in the dim and distant past. Sally however, preferred to think of it as an old slaughter house, like the one down beside the village green, owned by Mr Holmes.

Further along the lane, Sally stopped and peered through a gate and up a pathway leading to Durhamford, an ancient black and white building that looked as though it had stood in and on that ground since Jesus was born. If she remembered rightly, Jumbo James had told them that it had been called both Stream House and also Tanhouse, somewhere in its long and ancient history. The word Durhamford, its original name, he reckoned was derived from the word deer and then hamm, an old name for a water meadow. This impressive old building had housed both single family units and also several families at a time, over the years. Now however, it was occupied by just one family whose identity was unknown to her. She lingered here for a while with mum looking over her shoulder, both inspecting every fine detail on this old house that was available to their eyes from this view-point.

By the time they moved on, Pat was way ahead of them, and by the time they caught up with her she was past Glebe Cottage and almost to the end of the lane. They crossed over the road together and made their way towards the old church, which stood in ancient dignity amongst the tall chestnut and yew trees. From here, they could hear the raucous calls of the rooks in the tall trees further down Church Hill, almost but not quite drowning out the more gentle songs of other birds.

After climbing the stone steps, they stood with their arms resting on the wooden gate and looked at the gravestones. The same yellow and white lichen splodges clothed the grand and the lowly ones alike and were also echoed in the old wooden seat, placed in the churchyard by some benevolent villager eons ago. The early morning light imbued the whole scene with a kind of mellow harmony, as though some higher entity had indeed had a hand in its creation. Without a word being said, Sally knew that uppermost in all their minds, was the recent death and burial of Ann whose little grave was on the outer margins of this churchyard. Somehow, in this tranquil moment, one could sense her little spirit hovering somewhere between the bird song and the few white gauzy wisps of cloud that decorated the early morning sky. Into Sally's mind also, came a memory of the Lady of Pevensey Castle with the aura of grief that set her apart from the rest of the world. Where was she now, she wondered.

After several minutes of silent contemplation, they turned reluctantly away from the church and made their way down the hill, and after a while mum began to speak again.

"There used to be some old cottages along here that for some reason or other have been pulled down," she said. One of them was used as an infants school at one time, run by two elderly ladies. They weren't taken down that long ago, those cottages and you'd probably find brick and stuff from them if you looked around. Highfields over there, would have been built nigh on a hundred years ago I reckon," she added pointing towards a big house, just visible through the old rookery trees. Fred Soan, Albert's uncle used to work up there at one time as a gardener and handy man and I think his wife, C worked there as well, but I don't know if that was in the Thorpe's time or when Mr Pratt had the place.

Mrs Thorpe still lives there as far as I know, but old Mr Thorpe died - last year I think it was. She was his second wife and is quite a bit younger than he was. He was a solicitor and he also did some kind of beneficial work for the Buchanan Hospital, and I understand that's where he first came into contact with her. Mind you his first wife was an invalid and would have been in there from time to time, so he probably knew her from back then. Anyway, she was Matron in the Buchanan for some time and quite a force to be reckoned with by all accounts, very efficient she was. She wouldn't put up with any nonsense and the nurses were a bit in fear and trembling of her. They stood to attention when she was doing her rounds. They knew they'd get a good ticking off from her if they upset her in any way. She'd also praise them if she thought they deserved it though and she didn't have favourites. She was very fair in that way. And as you know, she and old Mr Thorpe always put on party's and things for the local children, so she wasn't that bad."

"I want to be a nurse when I grow up," said Pat. "Or a blacksmith and look after horses, shoe them and that sort of thing. I've watched Mr Taylor doing it so many times, I reckon I could easily do it."

"Don't be daft you can't be a blacksmith, girls aren't blacksmith's, you'll just have to be a nurse," replied Sally decisively. "You could have a horse though and keep it in the field along with the sheep and chickens. I'm sure dad'd let you. Mind you he did mention the cow again the other day, the one he promised us ages ago, but then cows and horses get on alright together I suppose. And he did say that Mr Collins was getting rid of some of his sheep so you wouldn't have to worry about them. Tell you what, I'll have a word with him about it if you want."

By this time they were level with the school, its silent playground still decorated with chalked out hop-scotch pitches and the scuffed remnants of various other games. As they reached the bottom of short hill, Sally glanced towards the small orchard on one of its banks where in late summer, youngsters, she amongst them, clambered over the hedge to scrump the delicious July Pippin apples from its trees. She always picked up the wind falls, which she had discovered were sweeter than those plucked straight from the trees. It was quick and easy to separate the nibbled ones from the sound. The former she discarded, the latter she popped straight up her knicker legs.

Further up the lane and just visible from the road, was Mr Crumps house, where from its large and well stocked garden always came the first new potatoes of the season. Whether this was due to the position of the garden or some secret formula of his, she had no idea. What she did know, was that several other keen gardeners in the village tried in vain every year to topple him from his agrarian pedestal, so far without success.

They stopped walking and talking when they reached the top of the village green, responding instinctively to the unnatural silence of the place. The normal hustle and bustle of the village, usually so alive with activity was hushed. It was so quiet you could almost feel it breathing rhythmically in and out as it slumbered. Then as they looked downwards, the hazy pink glow of the rising sun seemed to accentuate the mellow stonework in the buildings on either side of the green, until it seemed as though the whole village had been caught in some time warp, like a Brigadoon or Sleeping Beauty's palace.

As they moved on and before they had drawn level with the pump, Sally looked over to Ditch's old shop, which was now called the Work Box. There was always a fascinating array of hand made embroideries and other works of skill and patience, in its window. Women often stood with their noses pressed up against the window, their eyes moving from one piece of handicraft to another. She often stood there herself with Pat and Hilary, admiring the works of art, the display of neatly stitched and woven items. The two ladies who owned the shop sold anything and everything connected with sewing and knitting, the shelves in the little shop itself, always neatly stacked and filled to the gunnels with materials to attract the attention of shoppers.

"I wonder if Mrs Bryant's up yet," whispered Pat suddenly as she looked and pointed towards a little cottage beside the green. "She told me once that she's always up as soon as it gets light, summer or winter. She could be out in her back garden I suppose."

"You mean Mrs Gullible don't you?" replied Sally. "That's what everyone calls her. She seems to believe everything anyone tells her and her favourite expression is, 'well I never.' Some of the kids in the village tease her, they tell her all sorts of unlikely things, and then they laugh about it. She was out in her garden the other day when I was walking down through the village with Hilary, and one of the boys told her that he didn't eat lamb. When she said 'why, don't you like it then?' He said 'it's not that, I don't like mint sauce.' And they all fell about laughing. She just stood there looking puzzled, she did. She makes lots of chutterny as she calls it, and sometimes her place really stinks of vinegar. Her tea's awful, worse even than Mrs Moon's. It's grey and looks and tastes like its been strained through one of her old lisle stockings, or so they reckon. I've never tasted it myself or ever wanted to if it comes to that. And she's always, always got her hair done up in those awful pipe cleaner things. Still she's ever so kind and she's always smiling. Like Mrs Carder really, she's always smiling but she's a bit simple minded, isn't she. I don't expect she can help it."

"That's not very kind my girl," replied mum. Then she paused for a moment as she thought about it. "Well I suppose you're right really, Mrs Carder is a simple little soul, though uncomplicated might be a better way to describe her. She's often in her own little world and I sometimes wonder if she's not better off that way. She gets by, she does a bit of gardening and such like and she will pass the time of day with you when she feels like it. She has that strange habit of stroking the back of one hand with the fingers of the other, doesn't she? I suppose she gets a bit of comfort from it. But she's alright she is. She hasn't got it in her to harm a flea, let alone a human being."

"Nor has Bill Holmes, but he does get the hump sometimes," said Sally grinning. "Johnny watsit called there the other day and Bill said, 'do you want a toffee.' And Johnny said, 'no thanks Bill, they get stuck in my teeth.' And Bill replied angrily, 'No, a tup o toffee,' and stalked off back indoors. Poor old Johnny was quite embarrassed. Well, I wasn't there at the time but Johnny told some of the boys and they told us about it. They thought it was quite funny, still do if it comes to that."

Mum remained quiet here. She had demonstrated on more than one occasion, and in no uncertain terms, just how sensitive she was to issues of discrimination for whatever reason. Sally remembered woefully, the ticking off they had received from her when it was brought to her notice that they had been teasing Ellen Brown. She did not raise her voice very often, but had felt the need to do so on this occasion. Sally still got a bit hot under the collar when she remembered it, and did not pursue the subject of Bill Holmes and his affliction any further. None of them meant to be unkind, she was sure of that. It was just that certain things sparked off this bubble of humour, this warped ability to see the funny side of the most unlikely, even dangerous situations. Like the spontaneous fit of giggling, brought on by the spectacle of Mrs Skilton slipping over in the snow and ice outside Wiltons the newsagents back in the winter and struggling to get back on to her feet again. Although common sense warned them that the poor lady might have hurt herself, they had been convulsed with nervous laughter as they had tried half heartedly to help her to stand up. Perhaps when she was a grown up she would be able to control these feelings. She hoped so.

They walked on in silence for a while, each in a little world of private thoughts. The bird song was more sporadic now, and was accompanied by movement as the little creatures went about the business of feeding themselves and their babies. The territorial protection ritual was over and done with - for the time being anyway. There was no movement or delicious aroma emanating from Gregory's bake house, which for six days a week was a hive of activity by this time of day. Sally was grateful for this. She was hungry enough by this time without having to resist the tantalising smell of baking bread, donuts and every cake and pastry imaginable.

As they crossed over the bridge they looked towards Luffs Farm, where a fine spiral of smoke was already rising from the farmhouse chimney-stack. Mr Farrow would almost certainly be in the cow sheds by now in the process of milking the animals, having cleaned their teats with Udsal, taken from a large tin always placed in readiness for this purpose. Yesterday as they passed by the farm, he had been pushing a wheelbarrow around the side of the barn, his tall upright figure balancing the heavy load with ease. As he had walked, the pitch-fork stuck in the top of the load had wobbled to and fro with every step he took. Tony, one of the sons of Jessie Kenward the builder who had provided both the expertise and a lot of the muscle power with the building of Sylvian, also worked on the farm these days. According to Mr Farrow he had taken to the work as though he had been born to it. It seemed he was as much at home on the old Tractor as he was at milking the cows or driving them from one field to the next. Mr Budgen also worked on the farm with his faithful Shire Horses on an ad hoc basis, eschewing the use of the new fangled machines as he called them.

From the back of the farmhouse, a loud quaking and clucking suggested that Mrs Farrow was already out and about feeding her feathered friends, and maybe collecting their eggs. Then she too would join Mr Farrow, helping with the next stage of the milking process. There was no Sunday lay in for either of them or any other farmer or farm worker if it came to that. They passed Farrow's steps with barely a glance towards its concreted slopes, which was most unusual. Pat and Sally were just too tired and hungry by this time to indulge in this pleasing pastime. Uppermost in both their minds, was the anticipation of eggs, bacon and fried bread that mum had promised them for their breakfast. Mum also was anxious to get home for by this time Dora and Jacky would be up and about and dad would be chomping at the bit, waiting to get on with his chores. He was probably standing on the underground tank at this very moment, looking towards Paygate Corner and waiting impatiently for their return.

After breakfast, Pat and Sally collected the milk from Battle Barn, pumped the water from underground to top tank and then prepared themselves for the day ahead. They guessed that by the end of it they would be very tired indeed.

CHAPTER 18

Sally sat with her elbows on the windowsill, looking down the field towards the lane. Yes it was definitely there, she had not been mistaken. There was a clearly defined ridge in this field. It was not straight like the course of an old waterway would have been and which she had assumed it was when she had first noticed it, but moved out in a wide symmetrical curve from the fruit trees down towards the bottom of the field. She could see it very clearly this morning where the sheep had nibbled the grass down until it looked as though it had been cut by dad's old scythe. It was man made, of that she was certain. What puzzled her was the when and by whom. Was it from as far back as the Stone Age, she wondered or as recent as 1066 and the Battle of Hastings. The latter of course, took place just up the road from Blackbrooks and the land for miles around had been affected by it or had changed dramatically in the years following this event. Then again, the Romans did their share of digging and building according to Jumbo James so she could not rule them out. Or it could even be an ancient burial place used by folk from the Stone Age. Now wouldn't that be something. She would have to have a word with her dad when he was in a good mood. Hopefully he would let her and her sisters dig down a foot or two, to find out what, if anything, remained.

Still she had other things on her mind today and as she moved away from the window, she began to plan for the arrival of her cousin, Eileen Troughton. She was due to arrive sometime this afternoon with her parents, Aunty Edie and Uncle George and they would be staying at Sylvian for a whole week. Once she and Pat had done the pumping and collected the milk, they ran down the field to call for Hilary. Ronald would be spending the day with a friend of his but until then, Hilary needed to be there for him. While they waited, they picked up some of Ronald's comics and began to idle through them. Sally grinned to herself as she flicked through the Dandy, and saw Korky the Cat with his very human expression winking up from the page at her. Then the Desperate Dan character with his unbelievably large bristly chin and then the huge pie poised half way towards his mouth caught her eye. And as she read through the inevitable speech bubbles her grin widened, and looking up she saw the same amused expression on her sister's face.

"What's this maple syrup stuff then," she asked, more to herself than to anyone in particular, not expecting nor receiving a reply from her sister who was happily ensconced with the Beano. As she looked over Pat's shoulder she saw a scruffy figure, a huge grin spread right across its puggy face and with the most improbable hair, moving manically from one carefully marked out cell on the page to the next. Dennis the Menace he was called, a character she had not noticed before and definitely one she would be looking out for in the future. Over the page was Lord Snooty, looking every part the toff in his pin stripe trousers and top hat. He however, was really just one of the lads and she blamed his mum for dressing him up in such unsuitable clothes. She leaned forward and picked up a comic she was not familiar with from the neat pile, Puck, it was called and she leafed through its flimsy pages. Then she picked up another called the Rainbow, with a character called Tiger Tim running around all over its pages. She liked the look of him. He had the same kind expression as this Biffo the Bear character. Ronald liked his comics, no doubt about that and he almost certainly did a swap with some of his friends at school, she reckoned. Sometimes when they were here, they would listen to Children's Hour on the wireless and that was a rare treat. At home, the wireless was used strictly for the 'News' and other grown up programme's. Even so, the accumulator, which powered the thing, barely lasted the seven days between the topped up one being delivered and the spent one taken away by the Hornbrooks delivery van.

Later, as the three girls wondered slowly back up the field, they chatted and made plans for the next day or two. There was shopping to do this morning, but that was the only chore. Miss Worm-Leighton or Aunty Nin as they called her was staying at Sylvian for a week or two and always took over the task of preparing vegetables and even a bit of cooking if necessary and if she got the chance. Although short and stout, she moved surprisingly quickly and in spite of her tendency to be a bit bossy, she and mum worked together quite harmoniously. She was the Sister in charge of a large children's Nursery in West London, which during the war in particular, had operated on a twenty four hour basis, while the mothers did their bit for the war effort. If Sally remembered rightly, her first visit here had been in the company of Aunty Lil and Uncle Alf. She also got the impression that Aunty Cis and Aunty Nin had either worked, or were still working together, but she was not absolutely sure of that. What she did know however, was that from her very first visit, she had firmly adopted Sylvian as her second home and their mum as the sister she had never had.

The girls stood on the underground tank early in the afternoon, watching and waiting for the bus from Hastings, which should, if they were right with their calculations, be carrying Eileen and her parents on the last leg of their journey from Buckinghamshire. As they heard it chug towards and then over the brow of the hill, they ran down the field and along the lane, with the kitten following closely at their heels, then watched as Uncle George helped first Aunty Edie and then Eileen off the bus with their luggage. After a brief greeting, Eileen passed her case over to her father, scooped the kitten up in her arms and it was ages before she could be persuaded to put it down again. She was mad on animals, cats in particular and as her mum said, would fill the house with animals of every description if she were given half a chance. Mum was waiting for them by the top gate and Sally knew that the large, cosy covered tea pot would be standing on a tray, filled to the gunnels with boiling water, ready to transfer from pot to tea cups in a jiffy. Then they all trooped through to the kitchen, leaving the luggage by the door in readiness for its transfer to one of the huts, as and when.

Later, as the girls sat chatting on the underground tank they watched as the sun dipped slowly below the horizon, leaving a pink luminous glow in its wake. Then as the light faded, the sky began to change from a light to a darkening blue.

Eileen was more than willing to share with the household chores, and somehow her enthusiasm and free and easy way, communicated itself to the other girls. There was still the shopping to be done, but they had planned to leave the list in the shop while they did a bit of exploring in and around the village, and then collect the shopping on their way home again. That way they would kill two birds with one stone, so to speak.

They walked along the main road to the village, talking non stop and seemed to get there in no time. As they passed the shopping list and the two shopping bags over to Freda and turned to leave, Mr Phillips' head popped up over the counter. "I saw you coming and thought you'd appreciate a bit of sustenance to keep you going on your travels," he said and smiled as he passed a large bag of broken biscuits over the counter. "They're not all broken mind you, there's some goodens in there as well," he said as they took possession of the bag and thanked him.

As soon as they were out of the shop, Hilary opened up the bag and they all fished through the goodies to find their favourite pieces. There were lots of thick oaten bits that were Sally's particulate favourites, and she was soon in possession of a good fistful. As they walked up through the village, munching happily away on their biscuits, they began to extol the virtues of this kind and generous man.

The sound of cackling geese came from the back garden of the Queen's Head as they passed by, reminding Sally of the Battle barn ones that had plagued her and her sisters for so many years. These particular creatures, more like guard dogs than the proverbial 'feathered friends,' were not so much in evidence these days, perhaps having got used to the girl's regular sorties to the farm after all these years. For this she was very grateful. They had given her many anxious moments in the past. Then out of the corner of her eye she caught a movement to her left, and as she turned, she saw Fraggles on his bicycle. He was peddling furiously down the hill, head down and had passed by the pump in a flash. Perhaps they should rename him rocket or arrow even, she thought. He had had his hair cut ages ago and had outgrown his old nick-name of Fraggles anyway. She turned around as she heard a crackly sound as Hilary screwed up the top of the paper bag and popped it, along with the remnants of their snack into the pocket of her dress.

"Right, Brede Lane then it is? Asked Hilary as she wiped a few crumbs from her mouth with the back of her hand. "We can go up Hurst Lane then if you like and down by the church. That won't be too far, will it?"

They started off along the lane at brisk pace, accompanied by but only partially conscious of the bees and other insects buzzing away happily in and out of the hedgerows. They could see some children in the play area at the bottom end of East View Terrace as they passed by, but they were too far away to be identified and they did not have the time to investigate further anyway. It was while they were nearing the top of the slight incline towards the entrance to Hurst Lane, that Sally spotted the massive brown and white bull lumbering towards them. Although firmly attached by its thick ring to the hook on the end of a long pole carried by a young farm worker, she was taking no chances. She summed up the situation in a split second, and was up and over the hedge before the other girls knew what was happening. As she peered tentatively over the hedge, she saw with relief that the creature was being led into the field on the other side of the lane and she breathed a silent sigh of relief. She was not to be persuaded out of her sanctuary however, until the five bar gate into which the bull had been released was firmly closed and locked. There was no way she was going to risk a close encounter with a creature with manic bloodshot eyes and attitude that scared the living daylights out of her. Even Denis Crow with his warped sense of humour and unpredictable tempers, did not induce the same kind of primeval fear in her.

Once they had regrouped and put in their penny's worth on the merits and otherwise of farm animals and bulls in particular, they proceeded along the lane, stopping to admire the big house owned by Sir John and Lady Keeling. The gardens surrounding this house were extensive and the immaculate condition of its shrubberies, lawns, flower and vegetable gardens was due to the effort and expertise of gardeners like Cecil Taylor who had worked there since his demob from the forces after the war. He was up there alongside gardeners like Mr Lawrence in knowledge and application according to dad and men like him were worth their weight in gold. Gardeners he always said were under rated and undervalued, their extensive knowledge and experience, taken for granted.

As they turned a corner, Flora and Hector's bungalow came into view and they could see Hector, in bib and brace overalls, kneeling down beside one of the flower beds in the front garden. He was a slight man, with a round weather beaten face and an unnatural looking hair line. Sally was sure he wore a wig. He stood up as they paused beside his gate ready to pass the time of day with him, then as he began to walk down the path towards them, he called back over his shoulder, "here Flora, here's some of Dolly's girls come to see us." Almost immediately his wife came through the front door wiping her hands on her apron and walked down the pathway towards them. Sally had no idea how her mum had become acquainted with this couple who as far as she could make out, seldom ventured very far from their little bungalow. Perhaps she would find out one of these days.

"What're you girls up to then?" asked Hector, opening the gate and letting them into the garden. "It's a tidy step from your neck o' the woods. Mind you, when you was small, Dolly used to come here with you, mostly pushing you two little ones in that old pram your dad made. Don't suppose you remember that, do you?" Sally, who had no recollection of being wheeled here in that old pram of theirs, just smiled and shook her head. Then after introducing Eileen to the old couple, she began to tell them about their encounter with the Brook Lodge bull, just down the lane from here. Hector grinned from ear to ear before replying. "No need to be affeared of them big old dosy beef uns. Now them little old dairy bulls, they be another matter. They'd toss you from here to kingdom come, soon as look at you. I've walked alongside that old bull, calm as you like but if I see a Jersey or Guernsey up in that lane, I be off indoors quicker'n a fly on an old midden heap. Can we be offerin' you girls a drink while you're here then," he asked before his wife could get in a word in edgeways. "We've got a bit of lemonade in the larder."

They had a similar lean to pantry as the one in Mrs moon's cottage in the lane below Sylvian and in it, an identical perforated zinc faced larder, and it was from here that Flora withdrew a bottle of the resuscitating liquid. As they drank their fill, Hector continued to regale them with tips and tales and bits of gossip. He was a born entertainer, never happier then when he had an attentive audience and he was very adept at embellishing a tale.

"Old Higgins were round her tother day and he's always on about what a good gardener he is. Gardener I tells him, you ain't no gardener. An ingrown toe nail's about all you be capable of growin. Well,' I didn' xactly say that but it were in me mind if you know what I mean. He be one of those folk who knows everything about just about absolutely nothin,' if you get me gist. He didn't stay long, reckoned he had to get back to saw up some wood for his missus or somethin'. Old Pop hasn't been this way fer some time, too busy by half I expect. We usually sees him once or twice a year, don't we mother," he continued not waiting for or expecting a reply from his other half." That's when his brothers be visiting. This be their favourite walk all around here and they don't half step it out. Lean as whippets, the three of 'em. Last time I sees him, I gave him a decent stone fer that scythe of his, reckoned his one got dropped and broke in half or somethin'. You needs a decent stone or your likely cut your hand nearly orf."

Sally wondered if she dare ask him if she could listen to that old recording of Dame Clara Butt again. Once, when they had been caught out in a heavy shower of rain along the lane here, the couple had invited them in and played that record to them while they had waited for it to stop, and it had made an immediate and lasting an impression on her. She would volunteer to wind up the Gramophone, she was used to that, and even if the record did start slowing down a bit after a while, it would not matter. That seemed to accentuate the extraordinary quality of this powerful voice. Time however, was passing and they still had a long way to go. And once they entered the house, there would be all sorts of excuses to keep them there. They were a very hospitable couple. So she passed her empty glass back to Flora instead and began to make her way down the pathway with the other girls, followed by Hector and Flora.

"It be a bit dry the old garden. Could do with a drap 'o rain afore long," Hector was saying. "Look at that old tree over there, it be going rusty." And he pointed towards a silver birch, the bark on its trunk and branches streaked with rusty brown. Sally was a bit puzzled about this. Surely rust was caused by too much rain not too little. But she let it pass. "Be off with you then," he said as they moved back into the lane. "Look out fer thet Trevor. He went along side here early on with his gun under his arm and that dog of his walking alongside. It be pigeons or squaggers they be after I reckon." And he stood beside his gateway and watched as they walked away.

"Look at that butterfly over there," said Sally further down the lane as she pointed towards a creature, flashing its iridescent colours in and out of the lush vegetation.

"It's a dragon fly not a butterfly. There must be water around here somewhere," replied Hilary as they all stopped to admire the appearance and antics of this colourful bug, which was darting in and over the tall grass and bushes. Then it settled on the top of a tall rush like plant only a few yards from where they were standing, and for a few seconds they were able to admire the extraordinary beauty of this little creature. There were some late flowering foxgloves amongst the other vegetation here with just the top most cups of pale mauve remaining to reveal their whereabouts. The lower stems would be covered with fat green seed pods that when ripe would burst to replicate its kind in the surrounding countryside. Nature was quite amazing when you really thought about it, Sally reckoned.

Mrs Graves was the only other person they saw along this lonely lane. With her tall and sprightly figure, she was very much an older version of her daughter, Josie Farrow. And like her daughter, she always took the time to pass the time of day with them. If she had been going to Luffs farm to see her daughter, she would most likely have taken the shorter route via Church Hill, just round the corner from where she lived. Coming this way could only mean one thing. She was out for her constitutional. She was a close neighbour of Mrs Bentham – and her brother Beelzebub, Sally reminded herself. She would keep a wary eye out for him when they walked passed that front gate. She was not up to another confrontation, not just yet anyway.

They paused for a while when they reached the Church, fascinated as always by the memorials to departed souls, ancient and modern. After a while, Sally's eyes were drawn to one side of the churchyard, where a profusion of bright red flowers decorated a rose bush on an ancient looking grave.

"Look over there. Those flowers, aren't they lovely," said Sally pointing across the graveyard. "Reminds me of the poem about roses that I've got in one of my exercise books at home. It goes, 'I wonder I wonder if anyone knows, who lives in the heart of this velvety rose. Now is it a goblin or is it an elf, or is it the queen of the fairies herself.' I expect you know it."

"Yes I know it and it's my favourite, well one of them," replied Pat. "My absolute favourite is the one about the wee elf though," and she proceeded to recite a recently learned piece of poetry.

"Under a toadstool crept a wee elf, out of the rain to shelter himself.
Under the toad stall sound asleep, there lay a dormouse all in a heap.
Alas the wee elf feared to fly away lest he get wet for the next shelter maybe a mile.
So the wee elf smiled a wee smile, tugged to the toad stall tattered in two, holding it round him gaily he flew.
Soon he was safe home as dry as could be, soon woke the dormouse, 'good gracious me.
Where is my toadstool,' loud he lamented.
And that's how umbrellas first were invented."

"That reminds me of another poem, but for the life of me I can't remember the beginning of it," said Hilary. The end bit goes like this though:

I asked him why he was so small and why he didn't grow.
He slightly frowned and with his eye, he looked me through and through.
I'm just as big for me said he, as you are big for you."

After a bit more poetry, prose and general chit chat, they left the Church and began to walk down the hill towards the village. When they got to the top of the village green, they looked towards the Pump around which a group of youngsters were playing. Willie and Roy were there and the girls walked across the grass to pass the time of day with them. They stayed just long enough to arrange to meet up for a game of tracking in Staffords woods the next day and then they were off. The time was getting on now and with the shopping still to be collected from Mr Phillips, they needed to get a move on. They were still chattering as they hurried passed Barrack Cottages but paused when Kit Harris's head popped up over the low hedge and she started talking to them.

"I never seem to get enough time to do a good job out here," she said after commenting on the weather and other customary subjects. "It's best not to interfere too much amongst the flowers and things though I reckon. They have a way of looking after themselves without us lot interfering. Well you can't improve on nature, can you?"

As Mrs Harris's maiden name had been 'Playford,' one of Bangy Smith's family names, Sally reasoned that they were probably related in some way. She hoped so. They both had a slight frame and that same cheeky grin, so to her mind it was so. The poor lady had lost her husband in the Great War, shortly after they were married and had evidently borne her grief with the same stoicism as a lot of other women who found themselves in similar circumstances. She was a Great Aunty to Basil Beeching, and also to Barbara Hind, another friend of theirs at school. Greta Hodger was also a great niece of hers, though a year or two younger than the other two. Robin Ede, the tall handsome gamekeeper at Westfield Place was her nephew and Greta and Barbara's, mothers' were her nieces. All in all, they were a close, supportive, hardworking family and as mum always said, that was what mattered. Arthur Dawson, the linesman and his wife lived next door to Mrs Harris but of those two grown ups there was no sign.

After a short while, they moved on and after collecting the shopping, walked briskly away from the village. On the right hand side, they could see Mr Farrow's herd of milking cows munching away on the grass in the lower meadows, free now from the water, which flooded the area each winter. And it was not long before they could see the tell tale signs of them having been driven from the milking sheds to these lush pastures via the junction of Chapel Hill with the main road. The aroma however, was not really objectionable to them. For one thing they were used to the smell and as dad said, it was only fermented grass after all.

The smell of cooking invaded their nostrils as they walked through the top gate, and became even more enticing as they burst through to the kitchen. Mum, Aunty Edie and Aunty Nin were busily tending pans of simmering vegetables on the top of the range and checking the contents of the oven, side stepping one another as they performed these domestic chores. Aunty Edie, red faced and smiling came across the room and took the shopping bags from them, placing them on to the side table to be sorted as and when one or other of them had the time. All the girls loved her and who could help it. Sally had never known her to raise her voice in anger and any calamity would be met with her usual expression, 'not to worry, it'll all come out in the wash.' Strangely, they were all on their best behaviour when she was around. Not because she frightened them, quite the opposite. They just did not want to hurt her feelings in any way. Although different in many ways from her sister Nell, who was Uncle Fred's wife, they both had sparkly, mischievous eyes.

Aunty Nin hustled them outside while the final preparation for the meal took place, making it clear that they were getting under her feet. They moved towards the underground tank and sat on its hard surface, chatting about this and that, conscious all the time of the delicious aromas emanating from the kitchen to tantalise their empty tummies. When at long last Nin's short stout figure appeared by the door, they did not wait for her to speak. She just stepped aside as they scrambled up from the hard surface of the tank and moved through the doorway, towards the plates of steaming food.

***

As Hilary, Eileen and Sally hurried down the field and along the lane the next afternoon to meet up with Willie and Roy, they were surprised to see not just the two boys, but also a group of ten or so other youngsters assembled in Crazy Lane. Ron Hudson was amongst them, his characteristic laugh, which for some reason had given rise to his old nickname of Wangy, rising over and above the chattering of the other youngsters. Keith Card, a newcomer to the village was also there as were Ronald Elkins and Patty and Basil Winchester.

"Thought you'd never get here," said Roy and grinned as Sally took a deep breath. Before she had time to reply however, he said, "okay, okay, I was only joking. We got here early that's all. This lot, or some of them anyway, heard what you said yesterday and thought they'd come along for a game or two. As there's a lot of us, we thought we'd hide two at a time with me and Willie taking first go if you like and then we'll just work it out from there, okay?"

After pausing for a few seconds to let his words sink in, he and Willie ran off down the track with the others walking at a safe distance behind. Sally watched until they jumped over the stream and into Staffords wood. And then they disappeared into the thick tangle of bracken and out of sight.

Ron Hudson was the next one to jump over the stream and as soon as he reached the other side, set up the usual chant of, "oller if you're far away, whistle if you're near."

One by one they joined him then stopped and listened in silence for the appropriate response. After a while the sound of a muffled shout reached them and they cupped their ears as they tried to calculate direction and distance. The two boys were too good at this game to give themselves away so soon however, so they decided to split into small groups and search in different directions. At first they could see where the bracken had been pushed aside as the two boys had made their hurried entry into the wood, and they all moved off in the same direction. It was not long however, before the bracken closed in around them with any tell tale signs of disturbance having petered out. The three girls moved away from the other youngsters to quarter the wood on their own. They stopped and listened in silence when the tantalisingly covert responses from the oft repeated chant of 'oller if you're far away, whistle if you're near, echoed eerily through the wood. It was Basil and Ronald who finally tracked them down, and after a brief discourse on the why's and wherefores of their success, the two boys took off to do their stint.

After several more games of this sophisticated form of hide and seek, the three girls found themselves for the first time in the role of hiders, rather than seekers and they ran off, not altogether happy with this change of roles.

"I know where we'll go, said Hilary, pausing to wait for the other two to catch up with her. We'll go up by the old climbing tree, near that wild gooseberry bush that's got those really sour berries on it. The bracken's really thick up there," and she moved ahead with the other two close on her heels.

Before they reached their hiding place, they could hear the war cry, followed by voices that seemed to be getting steadily nearer and they dived head first through the thick mass of bracken and lay there, hearts pounding as though a pack of blood hounds were on their trail. After a while the sound of voices faded and they sat up and one by one, placed their forefinger against their lips to denote the need for absolute silence. A few more minutes passed before they deemed it safe, and then one by one they relaxed, giggled softly and then began to talk in whispers.

"It's just as well we didn't let you bring the kitten with you Eileen," whispered Sally. "It would have wriggled out of your arms and got lost for good and all in this bracken and stuff. You'd never believe how quickly it can move. It'd be up a tree or lost in the undergrowth before you could begin to catch it again."

"I know it would, but I still wish we'd brought it with us," replied Eileen. "I'd have held on to it so's it didn't get lost, it always behaves when I've got hold of it. I'm going to ask mum if I can have one when we get back home."

From there, the conversation went from furry animals and a recitation of the Persian cat rhyme, to school activities and even the mention of a pair of reading glasses, bought from Woolworth's for sixpence years ago, that had been shared by gran and granddad Cotton. And every now and again as they chatted, Sally looked up through the tracery of bracken fronds towards the sun as it blinked in and out of the clouds.

So absorbed had they become in their whispered conversations, that they forgot to respond to the calls around them. It was only when they began to giggle when taking turns to recite verses from 'Old Macdonald had a farm,' that their hideaway was discovered. It was Basil and Ronald, deciding to use stealth and their ability to move noiselessly through the wood, who had tracked them down. They were on to them they reckoned, even before they had heard them giggling.

"They're over here," Ronald called out loudly, waving his arms about above the thick canopy of bracken. Then he stuck two fingers between his lips and whistled shrilly in short sharp bursts turning around as he did so. The other youngsters were soon on the scene and very definitely not impressed nor taken in by the girls feeble excuses, and Sally could not blame them. If the boot had been on the other foot, she reasoned, she would have been just as angry as they were. It took several minutes for them all to have their say, and by common consent it was decided that the three girls should be seekers rather than hiders for the rest of the afternoon.

After a while, they tired of the game and made their way down to the stream where they lingered for a while, milling around and dangling their hands in the water. Then Roy suddenly turned and laying flat on his belly, began to scoop the cool water from the side of the stream with one cupped hand, sozzling it noisily up into his wide open mouth. "This water's fast flowing and if it's good enough to grow a bit of cress and a few newts here and there, it's good enough for me to wet my whistle with," he said shaking his hand and wiping it down the side of his trousers as he sat back up again. The other youngsters, deciding their need was as great as his, immediately followed suit, their prone torso's decorating the bank of the stream like animated logs.

After a short discussion, they decided to walk through to Hart's Green and home via Cottage Lane. At first, as they began to make their way slowly along the footpath, they played a noisy, ridiculous game of 'I spy.' Then after a while they drifted off in smaller groups and by the time they reached Hart's Green, the noise levels had gone down and the pace of progress had increased.

As they passed the tall bank on the right hand side of the lane, now overgrown with bushes and lush vegetation, Sally smiled to herself. Back in the spring, she Pat and Hilary had offered to take Aunty Nin to the primrose secret at the top of the bank here, which at that time had been covered in a carpet of green and pale yellow. What they had not taken into consideration was the amount of rain that had fallen overnight, reducing the narrow sloping pathway up into the wooded area, from a secret passage into a muddy slide. They had pulled from the front and pushed from behind as they tried in vain to get the short stout lady up the slippery slope, their giggling eventually reducing them to a state of helplessness. To give her her due however, she had seen the funny side of the whole incident, and as they had tried half heartedly to clean her up afterwards, had smiled saying something about needing a block and tackle to get her up there, whatever that meant. In the end they had to take her the long way round, through the field beside The Lawrence's cottage and into the wood that way. Sally did not envisage her asking to repeat the experience, or if it came to that, even accompanying them on any other outing. She got the impression that Aunty Nin did not trust them entirely and she did not honestly blame her.

As they approached Ashdown Cottage, Greta Hodger ran across the garden and peered curiously through the gateway at them. Her mother, working busily around the vegetable plot, looked up and smiled in their direction. Then she walked over to where her daughter was standing and stood beside her to pass the time of day with them. As she straightened up the bib of her apron, which was slightly askew, Sally mentioned having spoken to her aunty, Mrs Harris the day before. As they chatted, she thought how different the two ladies were from one another, in facial features and even in build. Mrs Hodger was taller and more robust looking than her aunty and the eyes were very different. And yet there were similarities. There were certain expressions and an overall calm demeanour that alerted you to the connection between these two ladies.

The three girls stayed and chatted for a short while before hurrying after the others who were now straggling slowly along the way. They drew level with them just as they were passing a heap of manure stacked near the hedge in the field on the left hand side of the lane, which stank to high Heaven. As they moved instinctively across to the other side of the lane where the tall pine trees grew, Sally remembered what old Hector had called these piles of decomposing manure. Midden heaps he called them. Well that's as may be for ones of a certain size and state of decomposition, she though to herself, but this steaming pile could not be called anything but a dung heap.

Before they divided into two groups at the junction of Chapel Hill and Crazy Lane, they made a loose arrangement to meet up again, and it was left to Willie and Roy to finalise the arrangement. Then the groups headed off in different directions, one towards the village and the other towards Black Brooks.

When they got home, Eileen went in search of the kitten and with it safely tucked under her arm, gathered Pat, Dora and Jacky around her and together they played games of 'I spy,' dominoes and snakes and ladders.

***

The rag rolled sky that greeted them as they left the house to fetch the milk from the farm, suggested rain but not for a day or two, Sally reckoned and should not jeopardise their trip to the seaside. It was warm and that was what really mattered. As she and Eileen hurried across the field, they planned the day ahead, what they should wear and what they would take to eat and drink. Sally had her usual gripe about missing that old yellow top that Hazel had given her and which she had worn and loved for so long, and how it would have been ideal for the beach today. She would have to wear the pale blue one instead with the floral skirt that Hilary had given her. She, Hilary would almost certainly be there by the time they got back and would help prepare the sandwiches and drink, she always did.

Dora and Jacky were sitting up at the table eating their breakfast of boiled eggs and dunkers with obvious relish when they arrived back with the milk. Eileen chuckled when Dora told her that her egg was just right and not slipey, which was one of Dora's favourite words at the moment. Undercooked eggs had always made her heave and had got her into trouble a couple of times with dad who could not stand wasted food or fussy eaters. Mum always made sure these days that boiled eggs were firm but not overcooked, the way they all liked them, and had got it to a fine art. She was good to them was their mum, and the best cook in all the world.

There was standing room only on the bottom deck of the bus, so Pat, Hilary, Eileen and Sally trooped up the stairs to search out seats on the top deck, where they preferred to be anyway. Luckily there were a few at the back of the bus and they made their way along the gangway towards them, rocking from side to side with the movement of the bus. They knew most of the youngsters on board and exchanged a few words here and there before sitting down.

As they drove through Kent Street, someone called out the name Brian Martin, and they all stood up and waved to the lone cyclist, now being overtaken by their slightly faster mode of transport. He cycled everywhere, and often when Hilary and Sally were way out in the countryside, would suddenly draw alongside them as if by magic, staying just long enough to pass the time of day before shooting off again. He had already heard about Peter Sansom's idea of putting in a cycle track at Wayside, and these days it was generally for information on this subject that he sought them out.

They alighted from the bus outside the White Rock Pavilion along with several other youngsters, crossed over the road and made their way onto the beach beside the Pier. They quickly sought out a suitable spot, dropped their bags onto the pebbles and unravelled their towels, spreading them out onto the pebbly ground. It did not take them long to remove their outer garments, exposing their bathing costumes, multi coloured and softly elasticated throughout, which they had donned before leaving home. Sitting on a deck chair to their immediate right, was a lady in a black costume with a book in her hands. What Sally thought was a bit strange about her was the black, red and green turban wound around her head, but then her attention was soon diverted away, towards the movements and activities within their own little group, and before long, was making her way painfully and slowly across the pebbles along with the others.

It took a while for them to get used to the coldness of the water, but once the initial shock had worn off, they were splashing about in the shallow water along with lots of other youngsters some wearing inflated rubber rings around their middles. After a while the cry went up that Biddy the tub man was on his way and as they looked along the beach, they saw a short, stocky figure splashing towards them, a shallow wooden tub under his arm. A ripple of excitement went through the scattered groups of youngsters, who moved instinctively to the edge of the water to give this much loved character, the space and attention he deserved. He had been a regular and popular performer along this stretch of beach between the wars, and luckily the suspension of any beach activities throughout the six long years of this last awful conflict, had not affected his performance nor dimmed his enthusiasm for his craft. His appearances were regular and just as entertaining as ever. They all cheered as his cry rang out, "Look out, look out Biddy's about." Then there was a hush as children and grownups alike prepared themselves to be entertained by this unique performer, who having made his way through the waves, now stood waist deep in water.

He began his act by spinning the barrel around furiously, controlling its dips and wobbles with just a light touch from his strong and expert hands. Then while it was still in motion, he jumped nimbly aboard, continuing to propel the thing around at speed until Sally felt herself go very nearly light headed with dizziness. After a while, he stopped paddling and dangled his hands in the water until his little tub stopped spinning. Then he grinned, jumped to his feet and began to perform a series of acrobatics in and out of the water, stopping every now to control the bucking boat, which was constantly in danger of getting away from him. When he began to dive around and under the barrel, they tried to second guess whether it would be his feet or his grinning face that would appear out of the water first. He stopped every now and again to invite someone, preferably a lady he said, to participate in one of his stunts. On this particular day however, no one was prepared or stupid enough, to gamble their dignity on such a dubious frolic.

All too soon the performance was over, and this excellent swimmer cum showman, who some reckoned was also a lifeboat man, began to take his leave. They watched the stocky figure as it made its way along the beach in the direction of the dilapidated old West Pier, to do yet another performance for yet another fascinated audience. Then they turned their attention back to recently abandoned pursuits and began to dip in and out of the sea, riding the waves until they were tired and hungry. After a while, they made their way back across the beach and sank thankfully down onto the pebbly surface and gave themselves a perfunctory rub down with their towels. Then they delved into their bags for sustenance and sat munching away in silence until the last crumb had been devoured.

The art of changing out of bathing costume into day clothes without exposing oneself was a delicate operation, requiring a bit of ingenuity. The girls overcame this problem by simply taking it in turns to link the towels around each other, forming an enclosure that would shield the dresser very effectively from prying eyes. Once dressed, they sat around chatting and combing their hair. Sally watched as Eileen combed hers, parting it very carefully down the middle then letting it fall down over her ears in loose waves. She quite fancied that style herself. A centre parting would make a change from the one on the side of her head that she had had for as far back as she could remember.

They strode up the beach towards the promenade, the pebbles no problem now that they had donned their sturdy shoes. They were going to see Aunty Mable who lived in Anglesea Terrace, just off London road and after the visit, would walk to Silver Hill and get the bus home from there. As they made their way westward along the lower promenade, Eileen stopped to admire bottle alley, this work of art drawing the same exclamations of surprise and appreciation as it did from most folk. Her attempts to count the various colours and shades in this display, resulted in a bit of a delay as she ran to and fro, making sure she was not double counting. By the time they got to Christ Church, the clock on the Church itself was ringing out the time of day and they hurried past, puffing slightly with effort of climbing this hill at such a brisk pace. They paused for a few seconds when they reached the bottom of Anglesea Terrace, to catch their breath and for Sally at least to psych herself up for the visit. The large, imposing house where their Aunty lived and worked was no different from all the others in the terrace and yet as soon as she walked through the doorway, she knew she would feel uneasy.

***

Number 10 Anglesea Terrace was owned and run as a guesthouse by Mrs Monti who, like their Aunt was a member of a religious faith called 'The Plymouth Brethren.' All the residents were very elderly and mostly infirm, and were taken care of by Aunty Mable and another lady who came in on a daily basis. Apart from their laundry that is, which was dealt with elsewhere. The place was always unnaturally quiet with the sounds and movements of ordinary every day life as Sally understood it, non existent. The residents seemed to sit for most of the time in large armchairs, just dosing, and even when they were awake, their eyes seemed to lack any kind of life or sparkle. Granny Cotton was very old and a bit on the thin side, but she was so different from these wrinkly automatons. She was always on the go, doing a bit here and a bit there and giving Dora and Jacky a hard time when they played their games too noisily around her. And she always insisted - and got, a rice pudding to herself every day. Aunty Mable did her best here, no doubt about that. As mum always said, she was a kindly little soul. Her heart was in the right place. But this was a very strange and unnatural household indeed she reckoned and she did not know quite what could be done about it.

Hilary rang the bell, and the door was opened a few seconds later by Aunty Mable who peered short sightedly at them with her small brown eyes. Then having identified them, she whispered a welcome and ushered them inside. Mouse like in appearance and demeanour, she was so totally different from her parents, Aunty Sarah and Granpy that it had been noticed and commented on by other family members. There had certainly been very little warmth in the relationship between parents and daughter, which Sally thought was a bit sad, and especially so since the old couple had died. This did happen in some families from time to time unfortunately, she had noticed. What made the situation even more sad as far as Sally was concerned, was that her two brothers had been killed in the Great War. Today she was dressed in navy blue with a white apron tied carefully around her middle and on top of her head was a lace edged bonnet. She walked them along the corridor and knocked on one of the large oak doors, which they knew would open up into Mrs Monti's study. Then they entered when permission was given to do so.

"Dolly's children are here," Aunty Mable said as she opened the door. Then she stood to one side as they walked in single file through the doorway and towards the lady seated behind a large Victorian desk. Sally was always tongue tied when faced with this large august figure, an animated version of Mrs Long, the old lady who had occupied one of the cottages near Sylvian many years ago. She had the same putty coloured hands and long finger nails, and even her eyes had that same strange mesmeric stare. She could read your mind, Sally was sure of that.

"I have some surplus sheets and pillow cases, which I have promised to your mother," she said looking directly at Sally who tried but failed to lower her eyes. "They're rather heavy but your Aunt has made them up into three separate parcels so you can take it in turns to carry them. Make sure the children have a drink before they leave Mable," she added then turned back to her clerical duties, effectively dismissing the little group who turned and left the room in silence.

"That place is seriously creepy. I couldn't wait to get out of there," said Hilary, as having taken their leave of the house and its occupants with a sigh of relief, they were walking back down the terrace towards London road. "I wouldn't want your Auntie's job for all the tea in China, would you?" she added, tucking one of the parcels more firmly under her arm. "She must take her religion very seriously that's all I can say. It's just work, work and more work, as far as I can see and she's so weeny, she looks like a puff of wind would blow her away. And she does all that knitting and sewing as well, doesn't she? She dressed some lovely dollies for Dora and Jacky last Christmas if I remember rightly."

"Yes she did, and she's made a lot of things for us older ones as well in the past. She's not so bad," replied Sally. "I really can't make out why she stays there. Perhaps it's something to do with her religion. She used to have quite a bit of money at one time but goodness knows what's happened to it all. Perhaps she's got it hidden under her mattress or something. I was dying to go to the lav while we were in there, but I didn't dare ask," she said changing the subject "But then I was pretty sure I could make it to Silver Hill and that we'd have enough time before the bus came along, so I didn't worry too much. I'm not going on my own though. It's ever so dark and spooky and just like a dungeon down there so one of you'll have to come with me. The others can wait at the top there with these parcels. They're a bit heavy, aren't they," she added as she moved her load from under her arm pit to a more frontal position.

They still had several minutes to wait for the bus even though they had all decided to use the public lavatory, just to be on the safe side. There was a dog, similar in size and colour to Trev's little old terrier running around on the opposite pavement and they watched as it cocked its leg up against a few posts and walls before moving off down one of the side streets. Sally was not sure that it was a good idea for dogs to run around in built up areas like this. It was different out in the countryside where they could run for miles, with only an occasional tractor or farm truck to look out for. Mind you, as she thought this, she remembered the incidences of sheep worrying that occurred from time to time and the distress it caused to sheep and farmers alike. She also remembered Mr Geerings little old terrier that had been shot by Mr Collins all those years ago when it had been seen in a field of sheep. There seemed to be fors and against with pretty well everything in life if you really thought about it, she reckoned. It depended on what your opinion was on any particular subject to start with, but mostly it boiled down to how good you were at arguing your case. A bit like politics really.

They made it to the top deck of the bus where at this time of day, there were plenty of seats for themselves and some to spare on which they deposited their parcels and bags. As they passed Wayside, they could see Granny Sansom pottering around in the front garden. Although they waved, she did not see them but just continued to tend her little patch. Even without that wrap around overall, Sally would have recognised her anywhere. It was the way she moved for one thing, and also those strands of hair that always fell untidily around her face, no matter how carefully she pinned it all back and tried to tame it. The difference between her and the old folk in that home in Anglesea Terrace suddenly struck her. There was still life and movement in their old gran, and even though her eyes were a bit pale and watery these days, there was still a sparkle in them. Sally had been on the receiving end of her wrath from time to time, but even that was preferable to the passive acceptance of those other old folk with their seemingly pointless lives. It was almost as though they were controlled by some invisible wiring system, that they had been programmed to respond exclusively to some remote device that controlled life and limb.

They rang the bell when the bus was just over the brow of the hill, gathered up their belongings and made their way along the aisle. As she was queuing behind the other girls to ascend the stairs, Sally glanced instinctively towards home, where just visible beyond Browns house, and the fields and hedges she could make out the line upon line of pegged out washing moving to and fro in the light breeze. Amongst it she was pretty certain were a couple of flannelette sheets that summer or winter, dad preferred to snuggle into after a hard days work. As far as she could make out, that was his one and only concession to luxury and comfort.

In the evening, once the eating and chores had been taken care of, they sat on the underground tank, and chatted as they watched the sun dipping towards the horizon. So far there was no sign of the rain forecast by the cloud formation earlier in the day and already the western sky was beginning to take on a pinkie, orangey hue. The old saying of 'red sky at night, shepherds delight,' came instinctively to Sally's mind as she looked at the horizontal glow of the early evening sky, and that meant, she reckoned that for the next couple of days at least, they would be able to go about their outdoor pursuits without the need for macs and wellies.

As they sat there mum, Aunty Edie and Aunty Nin wandered out and chatted to the girls for a while before moving away towards the back of the house via the veranda. With Dora and Jacky already in bed, Granny Cotton would no doubt be sitting in the most comfortable armchair in the kitchen, just enjoying a bit of peace and quiet. Dad and Uncle George had already left the house. The girls had watched them walk off down the field towards dad's old work sheds at the bottom where they had disappeared through one of the doorways. Though different in temperament, they were two of a kind when it came to innovation, the make do and mend principle and Sally could imagine them moving around inside, sorting out bits of wood, metal and such like to fashion some kind of vernacular contraption. For some reason, as she continued to look down the field, she though about Betty and the beautifully tailored suit she had worn on her last visit home. As she and her younger sisters had run down the field to meet her, Sally had been struck by the style and quality of the pale blue two piece garment with its long flared skirt and matching top. Her sister had bought the material in a market near where she lived in London, and had fashioned the soft material into this very stylish suit. It was called the New Look this style and was a kind of reaction to the austerity of the war years when material along with just about every other commodity, was in short supply. Even now, with the war just a distant memory, shortages of many things still remained and she was pretty sure that material as well as clothes, was still on ration. She was due home again next weekend, this sister of theirs, and Sally could not wait to see her. She always helped with the chores as well. Just like in the old days.

Then her thoughts moved on to the hop-picking season, which would soon be upon them. She could almost smell the aroma of the wood fires and taste the sweet smoky tea and the cold apple pie. And there was money to be earned as well to pay for their winter clothes. Then she smiled as she recalled the words of the old measurer when it rained and all the women trooped off to the drying sheds to shelter. 'What them women be wanting to go into drying sheds fer. This only be dry rain,' he would say. Life wasn't half bad when you really thought about it, Sally reckoned.

CHAPTER 19

There was trouble brewing in the Holy Land. Reports in the newspaper and over the airwaves were getting more and more serious, with a threat of war in the region now a sobering reality. It seemed that the trickle of Jewish people into Palestine in decades before the start of this awful war, had escalated into a deluge with indigenous peoples being displaced at a rate that could not be sustained. The suggestion of the creation of a Jewish state within Palestine had been met by dire warnings from neighbouring countries, and Sally was becoming increasingly worried that this conflict could escalate into a full-scale war, like the one that had turned the world upside down so recently, and this realisation filled her with horror.

There had been a worsening of the situation within the region long before the furore created by the killing of two British Sergeants by Jewish terrorists in a place called Haifa a few months ago. It seemed that incidents of equal seriousness were now being reported almost daily. She pricked up her ears at the mention of names like the Haganah and Menachem Begin, leader of the Irgun. She was reading reports in the newspapers that frightened the life out of her, even though she barely understood the full significance of the content of many of these reports. Glubb Pasha, who she had first thought must be some Arab prince, she now realised was a British Army Officer commanding the Arab Legion.

When she had asked her father why a Jewish state could not be created in Germany, where many of these people had originated from, he told her that it was not as simple as that. These people, after all the suffering they had endured over the centuries, were now determined to follow the tenet laid down in the Old Testament – as they saw it. As descendants of Abraham, they considered themselves to be God's chosen people with Jerusalem as the capitol of their 'Promised Land'. They were tired of being branded 'Wandering Jews,' and sought once and for all to secure a homeland that was their God-given right. He explained that for centuries these people had been made scapegoats of and ousted from one country after another. Whenever anything went wrong, the Jews got the blame for it. They felt alienated and were now determined to return to the land, which according to their interpretation of the Old Testament, belonged to them.

The trouble as far as he could make out, was that the Jews were not the only 'Tribe' who were descendants of Abraham. Others, it seemed, had the same claim.

Pushing aside these disturbing thoughts, which were not within her remit to solve anyway, she moved to a contemplation of the planned activities of the day ahead.

***

There were goats tethered on the piece of spare ground next to Windy Ridge. They had appeared there as if by magic along with an old tin shack. Pat, Hilary and Sally leaned over the rickety fence that separated them from these fascinating creatures, to examine and assess the length of the ropes that fastened these animals from their collars to the thick posts that had been hammered into the ground. It was not that they did not trust these animals but they were an unknown quantity and they had learned from experience that caution was often the better part of valour. As they stood there, chatting and making their assessment, Sally's eye caught a movement on New Road and in a split second she had sussed out the form and identity of the object and ducked instinctively.

"Watch out, old Beelzebub's coming down the road there," she said excitedly pulling the other girls down beside her. "I haven't seen him for ages. Look he's nearly down to Paygate, we'd best keep quiet."

"He can't see or hear us from here and anyway he doesn't take much notice of us if we don't tease him," said Hilary looking towards the object of Sally's fear and excitement. "I thought for a moment that the old bull had got out and was coming to get us and so forth. Look he's nearly out of sight already," she said, standing up and pulling the other two up beside her. "Now what about these ere goats then. We've got to go across here anyway if we want to get to the twitten, and they don't look very fierce to me. They're all nanny's anyway, there's no billy goat anywhere to be seen. Come on let's go over and stroke them," she said as she straddled the old fence and made her way across the coarse grass with Pat and Sally following her. The animals looked up at their approach but continued to chew, their jaws moving up and down and side to side as they regarded the girls with their strangely disturbing eyes.

"Lets see if we can find them some leaves and things for a change. They like them I know they do," said Pat after a while. "Mrs Pepler's got a goat and it loves them, it's always chewing up the bushes and things in her garden. She told me and dad that when we went to her place once. It's not quite like these goats though. It's white same as these but it's got light brown splodges all over it as well. And it's got floppy ears. It's getting a bit old now though," she added as she moved towards the hedge followed by the other two, where they snapped off several branches, the leaves now a bit sparse with the onset of autumn.

The goats showed immediate interest, coming over to the girls and curling their rubbery lips around this unexpected delicacy. "There, what did I tell you," she said as she abandoned her last twig to a particularly impudent animal. "That's their favourite food I reckon."

"I wonder who they belong to, and whose going to milk them," said Hilary. "I'll have to ask dad when he comes home, he's bound to know. Come on then, race you to the twitten," she added as she took off towards the other side of the rough ground. "Poo, that old sewer doesn't half pong," she said when they reached the other side. And she pointed down to an area where a growth of stinging of nettles, now looking a bit brown around the edges, proliferated in this smelly stew. "Mostly you'd hardly know it was there, but something's stirred it up today. Could be the goats I suppose, looking for a bit of extra grub. Perhaps they don't get stung by the nettles like we do."

As they walked up through the twitten, they saw Mr Geering in his garden and stopped to ask him about the goats. "They belong to Bunny Finch," he told them. "He's leaving them down there until he gets some sheds and things sorted out in his field, and he reckons he's a bit short on grazing there at the moment as well. Knowing him, they'll probably be here until Kingdom come.

Old Cokey Coleman came past here yesterday. He'd walked all the way from Cripps Corner to see them old goats and he kept me talking for nigh on an hour. I very nearly told him that it was a good job he was not a farmer or he'd have a lot of two legged donkeys running around. He wouldn't have taken much notice though even if he'd understood what I was talking about. He was too busy telling me about all the work he gets through and all the antics and things he gets up to as well. Spends a lot of time on his own he does so you've got to make allowances for the old fellow, I suppose. Well, I'd best be getting on then. I'm supposed to be finding a cabbage for Mrs Geering. And I don't want you girls to think I'm an old chatter box like old Cokey, do I?"

The girls grinned at him and then continued on their way, up through the twitten and into Crazy Lane. They were going to see Eileen Lawrence and Sally was carrying some windfall Bramley apples in her old haversack to give to Mrs Lawrence. If they were lucky, there would still be enough blackberries around to gather and take home for a blackberry and apple pie. They had already gathered pounds of the fruit that mum had turned into various concoctions including bramble jelly. It was delicious on home made bread and rice pudding in particular. The woods and hedges around the Lawrence's cottage could always be relied upon to yield a goodly crop of the rich dark fruit for creatures and humans alike.

As they walked along Cottage Lane, chatting about this and that, Sally found her thoughts wandering. Her ability to conduct parallel conversations, one silent and inward, the other an outwardly spoken one, had got her into trouble more than once when the inward one had taken more than its fair share of her concentration. She seemed unable however, to stop this mental process no matter how hard she tried.

At the moment as she talked, she was thinking about her visit to London earlier in the year, when she had stayed with Aunty Lil and Uncle Alf. Celia, newly demobbed from the Forces, had also been home at the time and one memorable day had been spent on a shopping expedition with her cousin and Aunty Lil. Celia was in need of a complete wardrobe of clothes having spent most of the war years and its aftermath in uniform. Sally reckoned they must have visited pretty well every clothes shop in London, seeming to spend hours in each one. She had really thought at the time she would die of boredom. The only thing that kept her sane that day she reckoned, was being able to look through newly replaced windows at the rebuilding that was taking place all around the big City. That there was still a long way to go was undeniable with in places, whole streets needing a complete make over.

She had been offered a visit to Madame Taussauds the next day as a kind of reward but had declined the offer. She would never forget in a million years, her previous experience in that place, with its diabolical chamber of horrors. She'd had nightmares for ages afterwards. Celia was also practising something called shorthand, which was a crucial part of her secretarial duties as far as Sally could make out. When she had picked up the book and idled through its pages, she had been thoroughly confused by its content. It was filled with what looked like some kind of strange and ancient hieroglyphic scribblings, interspersed with words like 'short forms.' Celia must be very clever to understand these squiggly words, she reckoned and so was her aunty for being able to test her daughter on this mysterious language.

Sally had also spent a day with Aunty Cis, who had taken her to a local park where they had fed the ducks and where she had played around for a while on the swings and other amusements. She had felt awkward, a bit like a fish out of water however, never ever having had to rely solely on her own initiative. She had always taken for granted the interaction with siblings and friends, that instinctive sharing of ideas and experiences that had shaped and motivated her behaviour. She had seen her cousin David only briefly before he had left the house having to fulfil some previous arrangement. He was the youngest member of the Johnson family and although a year or two younger than she was, seemed quite mature for his years. He had benefited from having older siblings she reckoned and from his father, who was very knowledgeable. She was fond of her Aunty though who was not averse to playing a game or two of snakes and ladders. Every time her tiddly wink finished up on a snake's head and she had to go back a line or two, she just treated it as a huge joke. She was a good sport, no doubt about that and Sally could understand her own mum's sadness when Aunty Cis and her family had left Sylvian all those years ago.

Sally had seen her Uncle Frank briefly in the evening and she remembered having studied his hands carefully to see if they were any different from other peoples. He was renowned for his freehand drawing of the lines around the Rolls Royce cars and carriages, the finest example of the coordination between hand and eye that you would ever see, according to dad. Sally had felt tongue tied in his company, and was rather in awe of him. And so was her aunty, she reckoned. The old saying, 'he doesn't suffer fools gladly,' always came to mind when she was in his company. They had also called in to see Aunty Nel, but other members of the family had been absent that day, obviously at work. She had seen Uncle Fred, who popped down to Sylvian now on a regular basis, quite recently. She had seen very little of her cousins Freddie and Thelma over the years however, and would have welcomed the chance to have become a little better acquainted with them. Still, there was a possibility that they might all visit Sylvian together in the not too distant future.

Sally had also spent some time with Aunty Nin, who amongst other things had taken her to Derry and Toms and then on to Lyons Corner House for lunch. They had started the meal with clear soup and as she had lifted her knife to cut the roll, which had accompanied it, Aunty Nin had whispered, 'you must not use your knife, you must pull the roll apart with your hands.' It was something to do with etiquette or some such thing she had been told, which sounded quite ridiculous. However she had not looked at a roll in quite the same way since then.

Later in the day, she had been taken to sample a knickerbockerglory and her eyes had nearly popped out of her head as she had contemplated and then sampled this extravagant concoction. She had worked her way down through the tall glass with the elongated spoon, until the last vestiges of melted ice cream and fruit juice had been scooped up and eaten.

The next afternoon, Aunty Nin had taken her to see a Laurel and Hardy film and she had laughed all the way through the performance, perfecting the catch phrase, 'another fine mess you've got me into,' boring all and sundry for ages afterwards, as she tried with little success to mimic the two unique performers. This had been followed by her first sight let alone taste of the largest, juiciest peach in the world. As she had slurped her way through this extraordinary fruit, she could not make up her mind whether she would have chosen this peach with its soft velvety skin or the knicker-bocker glory as the more delectable a treat. When it came down to it however, the best part of all on this visit of hers to London had been meeting Betty from work and spending some evenings with her sister.

The little flat Betty rented from an elderly lady was spick and span with her hand embroidered runners and table cloths adorning every surface. And the whole flat smelled of freshly laundered clothes. They never stopped talking the pair of them and when Sally had to say goodbye on her last evening in London, she had experienced a feeling akin to home-sickness.

Sally suddenly snapped out of these thoughts realising she hadn't been listening to Hilary at all and now gave her full attention to what her friend was saying. Hilary was talking about old Fred and his embarrassment when she and Sally had crept up on him on the footpath beside the allotments in the village. They had overheard him praising George's carrots. 'Them be bigger'n a bulls pizzle,' he had said as he leaned over the fence. Then when he saw them, the realisation of what they had most likely overheard, caused him to apologise.

'That's okay,' Sally had replied automatically not having a clue as to what he was apologising for.

Then George, grinning from ear to ear had replied, e'll likely lock iself in a dark cupboard and lose the key now you've eard im sayin that.' It was a while before they worked out what the two old men had been talking about and when the penny eventually dropped, they fell about laughing.

They saw Mr Lawrence near the greenhouse at the top end of Stafford's huge garden and waved to him. How he managed to keep the place in such good order was a puzzle to many people. It was a combination of method and organisation according to dad, and lots and lots of sheer hard work.

As they walked across the field towards The Lawrence's cottage, they could see Eileen in the garden and after a second or two they realised she was not alone. By the time they identified the other girl with her as being Sylvia Gain, the two girls were nearly up to the gate and were already walking over towards them.

"It's no good looking for blackberries now," said Eileen when they explained one of the reasons for their visit. "They were finished ages ago. We can take a walk round the fields though if you want to. I know where we're likely to find some Hazel nuts. Me and Syl got some the other day and we've put some in a jam jar and dug them in the garden over there," and she pointed to the far end of the vegetable patch. "We got that idea from you lot. We've got a stick in there to show where we've put them and we told dad so's he doesn't dig them up by mistake. I expect I'll have to keep reminding him though, he does get a bit forgetful at times."

They all wandered round to the back of the cottage, past the old well and into the warm kitchen where they deposited the apples with Mrs Lawrence. As they were talking and passing the time of day, Mrs Lawrence quickly prepared and packaged a few sandwiches, which she passed to Eileen who popped them into her coat pocket. After a while they wandered back out again and took off across the field next to Mr Dennis's bungalow and garden.

They eventually came to an area where the hazel trees, clearly having been coppiced at some stage of their growth, were offering up their bountiful harvest. As the girls stooped to gather the golden nuts, Sally noticed that a round hole with a characteristic gnawed edge to it had been made in the side of a fair number of them. There was a dormouse or perhaps several of them in the area, and for some reason she felt a glow of pleasure. She had only ever seen pictures of these little creatures but she had always had a soft spot for them, same as she had for red squirrels.

Other creatures, namely jays and squirrels were also fond of nuts and acorns and stowed them away as a source of food during the lean winter months, she knew that. Some of the ones that had been forgotten about or merely mislaid, would very quickly spring into life, sending up their little growing shoots to become if they were lucky, one of another generation of trees. Some creatures she had heard, nibbled off the little growing tip in some nuts and acorns before they buried them in the ground, whether by design or accident, she had no idea. It was all a bit of a mystery as were so many things in life. For instance, what prompted the trees to decorate their branches with those elongated catkins that hung there in early spring or motivated the pussy willow and other equally interesting and various fruits and flowers to decorate others? And that was just a small part of what happened in Nature. The questions could go on and on, but she was not complaining. After all, you did not have to know all the why's and wherefores of old Mother Nature's creations to appreciate what she had to offer or to gather in the prolific harvests that she provided, thank goodness.

In the distance Sally could see a tractor grinding up the ground, cutting a swathe of brown through the hazy green of a faraway field. Mr Dennis perhaps, preparing the earth for the next crop in his rotation. Like gardeners and mums, farmers worked all hours of the day and night, she'd been told. Well as far as she was concerned, anyone who worked as hard as her mum worked very hard indeed. As she was thinking this, Eileen brought the bag of sandwiches out of her pocket and offered them around. There were neatly cut fish paste and spam sandwiches in the package, and it took Sally a moment or two to make her choice. Both were favourite fillings of hers. She had recently discovered that the initials SPAM stood for Special Pressed American Meat, which was interesting she supposed.

As they stood there in a tight little group, chatting and munching, she idly noticed signs signalling that the year was into its last quarter. They were there in the hedges and woods all around. The colours of the leaves were changing with some already brown and desiccated looking, a few still green, while others were an agreeable shade of red and butter yellow. Before they moved on, they took a few nuts from their pockets, popped them into their mouths and the kernels from the ones they could crack with their teeth, they chewed up greedily.

On the way home, although they could see a few wind dogs overhead, heavy black clouds were already banking up on the horizon with a mixture of birds and leaves circling overhead, aided by the ever increasing wind. No wonder there had been no blackberries to gather from those prickly, stinging nettle infested bushes. The year was certainly showing its age. It was there not only in the subtle colour changes but also in the ever shortening daylight hours and there was that noticeable chill in the air. It would soon be time to don their liberty bodices and prepare for the cold northeast winds that could freeze the balls off a brass monkey.

As they crossed over the road from Crazy Lane and began to walk towards the bottom gate, a strong smell of paraffin assailed their nostrils. It smelled rather like Mrs Floyd's shop up the road except it was a darned sight more powerful. It could only mean one thing. Mr and Mrs Paine had been delivering the stuff. They lived round Brede Lane and carried an enormous tank of paraffin around on the back of an old truck, delivering it to all the outlying areas. Dad purchased a regular supply from them, which was used in the table lamps and also to fuel the various paraffin stoves, both in the house and also occasionally in a shed or the greenhouse. If they had arrived home a little earlier, they could have watched the process of this smelly liquid being transferred from tank to smaller containers and stashed away in the bottom shed, but never mind. They had watched the process many times before and could if push came to shove, have done the job between them.

Another more appetising smell reached their nostrils as they walked towards the scullery door. The aroma of freshly baked bread. They began to feel hungry all over again.

***

When they went to fetch the milk the next morning, Mr Collins was in the kitchen finishing his breakfast. He was going deaf, there was no doubt about it. It was more noticeable than ever this morning. As he chatted to them while they waited for Miss Collins to get the milk, he leaned forward and placed one cupped hand behind his ear, listening intently for the responses to his questions. Now and again, even though they articulated as clearly as they knew how, he would ask them to repeat the words. Uncle Fred reckoned it was because he did not wear a suitable hat to protect his ears from the cold north-east wind that assaulted them and everything else it came into contact with in the winter. Dad however, was of the opinion that it was more to do with having had his ears blasted by standing too close to a field gun in the Great War. Whatever the cause, the result was the same, and the girls reckoned it was better to listen without comment whenever possible. This disability had not interfered with his sense of humour however, and he was telling them a story the authenticity of which, Sally thought was questionable.

"It was this friend of mine see who lives in Robertsbridge," he began. "Well he had one of these visitations or some such thing that some folks get, and was a bit worried so he asked the old Rector roundabouts for a blessing. You know what that old man of God up and told him? He said, you go to the other place don't you, the Chapel. Why don't you ask the Reverend up there to give you a blessing. I can't do that said Jack pulling himself up to his full five feet one inch, he be gettin is hay in. The old Rector was speechless, Jack reckoned. He just walked away without a word. He never did get his blessing as far as I know." The girls just grinned but remained silent, so he continued "Guess what your father said to me the other day when I was complaining about the pigeons coming down to sample my green stuff. He told me that all I'd need to do was to stand around on a freezing cold morning and make a sound like a cabbage. Then when the old pigeons come down, you shoots 'em, he said. Well here's your milk then he said chuckling and rising to his feet. "I've got work to do even if you haven't."

As they walked away, they tried to extract fact from fantasy, but failed. Sally had heard the anecdote about the pigeons before, quoted if she remembered rightly by old Bunny Finch, so that was a bit iffy. Now if Mrs or

Miss Collins, who knew him far better than they did had been there when he was actually talking, the girls would have got some idea of the truth or otherwise of his words from the expressions on their faces. They however had been elsewhere. Sally remembered ruefully what he had told her years ago about her mum having bought her from a raggle taggle Gypsy who had called at the door. 'You looked so bedraggled and forlorn that your mother felt sorry for you,' he had said. She had more than half believed him at the time and the effect of that pronouncement had stayed with her for a very long time. Were these tales they had just heard really based on truth, or were they another figment of his imagination or peculiar sense of humour. Goodness only knew, and did it really matter? After all, they all indulged in a bit of make believe from time to time and after a while you began to be able to differentiate between truth and make believe. Now and again you got it wrong and were reminded in no uncertain terms, that you were gullible, but that was life as they say.

***

It was getting noticeably colder now and the light browns and faded greens of late autumn had metamorphosed into a kind of brindled khaki, with the occasional bit of green holly or ivy poking stubbornly through the leafless blackthorn hedges. The bland colours on Mother Nature's palette now reflected the onset of cold barren winter, with the chance for plant life at least to rest and gather their strength for reproducing, each in its own image, the next generation of fruits, nuts and flowers. For some animals, it would be a constant struggle to find enough food to sustain them through these dark frugal days of winter, while others would curl themselves up, shut their eyes and wait out the days and long nights of winter in a kind of stupor. And the light was different now. It was more silver toned and grey, as opposed to the golden shimmer of a hot summers day.

As Sally lay in bed waiting for sleep to interrupt her thoughts, she pondered on the fast approaching New Year. Nineteen forty eight promised to be a time of change for the better, in more ways than one she reckoned. For a start, the plans for a National Health Service were well on course with free health care for each and everyone, plus a Welfare State, which would provide financial help for all those in need. These promises it seemed were going to be fulfilled in spite of the huge war debt having to be repaid to the USA for services rendered. Her father doubted whether the Socialists would be given enough time by the electorate to fulfil all their ambitious plans, plus the ongoing and extensive rebuilding of the physical body of the country, which would be a shame really. If you started something you at least deserved the chance to finish it, but there you go.

Once again that was life, wasn't it and you had to poke up with what it dished out to you. Still she had other things to think about and look forward to as well. The cow that dad had first spoken about all those years ago, should be grazing the field and providing milk for the family by early Spring. The connection of an electrical supply that had been suggested by various members of the family however, would have to wait. Every time the subject was raised, dad's answer was always the same. 'I'm not having one of those poles, one of those monstrosities across my field.'

He, like the rest of them though would be looking forward to visits from various Aunties and Uncles, who would be here on working holidays. Sally often eves-dropped on their conversations as they sat around the kitchen table or in the garden in the evenings, making further attempts to put the world to rights. There would be other visitors here as well, mostly from London and the surrounding area. And she had been promised a holiday with Anne Saul and her family in Eastbourne during the Easter holidays. One way or another, it looked like there was another busy year ahead for them all.

Just before she drifted off into the land of nod, she heard the eerie sound of a dog fox barking and snuggled even further down under the bedclothes. The very last words that crept into her conscious mind were those of a melancholy poem that she had read recently and that for some reason had made such an impression on her.

When you are old and grey and full of sleep, and nodding by the fire.
Take down this book and slowly read.
And dream of the soft look your eyes had once and of their shadows deep.
How many loved your moments of glad grace. And loved your beauty with love false or true.
But one man loved the Pilgrim soul in you. And loved the sorrows of your changing face.
And bending down beside the glowing bars, murmur a little sadly how love fled.
And paced upon the mountains overhead. And hid his face amid a crowd of stars.